Educational Supervision:

Perspectives, Issues, and Controversies

Educational Supervision:

Perspectives, Issues, and Controversies

✦ ✦ ✦ ✦

Edited by

Jeffrey Glanz
Kean College of New Jersey

Richard F. Neville
University of Maryland Baltimore County

Christopher-Gordon Publishers, Inc.

Credits

Every effort has been made to contact copyright holders for permission to reproduce borrowed material where necessary. We apologize for any oversights and would be happy to rectify them in future printings.

Perspective 1: "How Can We Move Toward a Community Theory of Supervision?" by Thomas J. Sergiovanni is drawn in part from material from *Leadership for the Schoolhouse: How is it Different? Why is it Important,* San Francisco, Jossey-Bass, 1996.

Chritopher-Gordon Publishers, Inc.
480 Washington Street
Norwood, MA 02062

Printed in the United States of America

10 9 8 7 6 5 4 3 2 1   02 01 00 99 98 97

ISBN: 0-926842-57-9

Brief Contents

Part One   Controversial Critical Issues 1

Issue 1.   Should Supervision Be Abolished? 3

Issue 2.   Can We Put back the *S* in ASCD? 25

Issue 3.   Do Teachers Benefit from Supervision? 43

Issue 4.   Is the Estrangement between Curriculum and Supervision Reconcilable? 71

Issue 5.   Can a Supervisor Be a Coach? 91

Issue 6.   Has the Field of Supervision Evolved to a Point That It Should Be Called Something Else? 113

Issue 7.   Is a Collegial Relationship Possible Between Supervisors and Teachers? 135

Issue 8.   Is Staff Development Supervision? 155

Issue 9.   Should There Be National Standards in the Preparation of Supervisors? 175

Issue 10.   Should Educational Supervision Be Influenced by Business Management Practices? 201

Issue 11.   Is Clinical Supervision a Viable Model for Use in the Public Schools? 223

Issue 12.   Will Technology Replace the Role of the Supervisor? 241

Part Two   Perspectives On Critical Issues 261

Perspective 1.   How Can We Move Toward a Community Theory of Supervision? Wrong Theory/Wrong Practice 263

Perspective 2.   Is Supervision More Than the Surveillance of Instruction? 285

Perspective 3.   What is the New Superviosry Role in an Age of Complexity? 299

Perspective 4.   How Does the Law Affect Educational Supervision? 319

Perspective 5.   Why Is Advocacy for Diversity in Appointing Supervisory Leaders a Moral Imperative? 341

Afterword: Closing Reflections 353

Contents

Foreword, Arthur Blumberg xiii

Preface xvii

Introduction: Viewing Issues in Supervision
Holistically and Critically xxi

Part One   Controversial Critical Issues 1

Issue 1.   Should Supervision Be Abolished? 3

YES—Robert J. Starratt, Fordham University 4
NO—Robert J. Alfonso, East Tennessee State University 13

Jerry Starratt, author of *The Drama of Leadership*, wonders why supervision has not already been abolished. He seriously suggests that we abolish supervision because, among other reasons, it diminishes the professional autonomy of teachers. Bob Alfonso, co-author of *Instructional Supervision: A Behavior System*, laments the fact that this question needs addressing in the first place and argues that supervision should be strengthened, thereby creating a link between needs of individuals and requirements of organizations.

Issue 2.   Can We Put back the S in ASCD? 25

YES—Jean McClain Smith and Barbara S. Thomson, The Ohio 26
    State University
NO—Robert J. Krajewski, University of Wisconsin–Lacrosse 32

Smith and Thomson, teacher educators and leaders within the Association for Supervision and Curriculum Development (ASCD), maintain that ASCD has been and remains vitally concerned with instructional supervision. Moreover, they assert, ASCD is the only national organization that has promoted and advanced supervision as a field. International supervision leader and co-author of *Clinical Supervision* (3rd ed.), Bob Krajewski counters by documenting the lack of attention given to the *S* and believes that "if supervision is not an integral part of ASCD, in reality, neither can curriculum be."

Issue 3.   Do Teachers Benefit from Supervision? 43

YES—Lee Goldsberry, University of Southern Maine 44
NO—Duncan Waite, University of Georgia 56

Professor of education Lee Goldsberry, in a lively and provocative discussion, claims that teachers do benefit from supervision qua evaluation, whereas Duncan Waite, author of the recent *Rethinking Instructional Supervision*, contends that the evidence that teachers benefit from supervision is "scant and primarily anecdotal" and that evaluation done under the guise of supervision is only "slightly better than a poke in the eye with a sharp stick!"

*Issue 4.   Is the Estrangement between Curriculum and
    Supervision Reconcilable?* 71

YES—O. L. Davis, Jr., University of Texas at Austin 72
NO—Peter P. Grimmett, Simon Fraser University 79

O. L. Davis, Jr., editor of the *Journal of Curriculum and Supervision*, asserts that a "robust" relationship between curriculum development and supervision is not only desirable and possible but urgent. Peter Grimmett, professor and noted scholar, maintains that a reconciliation between supervision and curriculum is not feasible "as long as schools remain bureaucratized."

Issue 5.   Can a Supervisor Be a Coach? 91

YES—Thomas L. McGreal, University of Illinois at Urbana–Champaign . 92
NO—James F. Nolan, Jr., The Pennsylvania State University 100

Tom McGreal, author of *Successful Teacher Evaluation*, maintains that a supervisor can indeed serve as a coach and that it is "done every day by supervisors who through personal skill, integrity, commitment, and friendship coach teachers in extraordinary ways." Jim Nolan, co-author of *Classroom Management*, claims that "teacher evaluation and teacher supervision are separate functions and can not be carried out simultaneously by the same person in an effective manner."

Issue 6.   Has the Field of Supervision Evolved to a Point That It Should Be Called Something Else? 113

YES—Stephen P. Gordon, Southwest Texas State University 114
NO—Jeffrey Glanz, Kean College of New Jersey 124

Steve Gordon, co-author of *Supervision of Instruction*, argues that the term *supervision* should be allowed to "wither and die" and that *instructional leadership* would be a more appropriate name. Jeff Glanz, co-editor of this text and former teacher and supervisor for the N.Y.C. Board of Education, asserts that the field has not evolved as much as it has been submerged. He argues that it is time to address what supervision means and avoid euphemistic labels for supervision that only conceal its intended purpose.

Issue 7.   Is a Collegial Relationship Possible Between Supervisors and Teachers? 135

YES—Barbara Nelson Pavan, Temple University 136
NO—Ben M. Harris, University of Texas at Austin 144

Barbara Pavan, co-author of *Nongradedness*, states that collegiality is an essential component of good supervisory practice and that it can, should, and must be nurtured and sustained. Ben Harris, noted authority in the field and author of *Supervisory Behavior in Education*, challenges the notion that collegiality is an appropriate or adequate concept on which to build teacher–supervisor relationships. Rather, he asserts, to "abdicate leadership" in "exchange for collegiality could be an educational tragedy."

Issue 8.   Is Staff Development Supervision? 155

YES—Cheryl Granade Sullivan, Educational Consultant 156
NO—Gary A. Griffin, University of Arizona 162

Cheryl Sullivan, noted educational consultant, claims that supervision and staff development have similar purposes. Dr. Sullivan maintains that any attempt to differentiate supervision from staff development is artificial and "somewhat academic." She indicates that "a merger may be better than a split," resulting in a new term: *Super Development*. Gary Griffin, noted scholar and prolific author, argues that staff development and supervision have fundamentally different purposes and effects. Only staff development, asserts Dr. Griffin, can "result in deep and meaningful school change."

Issue 9.   Should There Be National Standards in the Preparation of Supervisors? 175

YES—Gerald R. Firth, University of Georgia 176
NO—Helen M. Hazi, West Virginia University 187

Gerald Firth, established scholar and former ASCD president, puts forth his argument that national standards are "essential for the preparation of professional school supervisors." Dr. Firth presents 10 arguments to support his contention. Helen Hazi, professor and legal scholar specializing in supervision, bases her opposition to national standards on a postmodernist rationale arguing, in part, that is it not "feasible to completely encapsulate a field of knowledge by arbitrarily identifying some standards."

Issue 10.   Should Educational Supervision Be Influenced by Business Management Practices? 201

YES—Francis M. Duffy, Gallaudet University 202
NO—Edward Pajak, University of Georgia 210

Frank Duffy, author of *Designing High Performance Schools*, relies on research on organization development in the business world to frame a case for applying business management practices to schools. He discusses a "new model of educational supervision" that he calls *Knowledge Work Supervision.* Ed Pajak, author of *Approaches to Clinical Supervision,* charges that "ideas from the business world are too often adopted by educators wholesale . . . without careful consideration of the factors that make schools and supervision in schools unique."

Issue 11.   Is Clinical Supervision a Viable Model for Use in the Public Schools? 223

YES—Robert H. Anderson, University of South Florida 224
NO—Noreen B. Garman, University of Pittsburgh 230

Robert Anderson, internationally known author and innovator and currently the TECO Energy Chair in Education at the University of South Florida, argues that clinical supervision "appears to make at least some positive difference in the professional effectiveness of both teachers and supervisors." Although Noreen Garman, professor and prolific scholar, feels somewhat "uncomfortable with the functionalist perspective" taken in this volume, she contributes to the discourse by raising a number of critical issues that question the viability of clinical supervision practice.

Issue 12.   Will Technology Replace the Role of the Supervisor? 241

YES—Saundra J. Tracy, Butler University 242
NO—Joyce E. Killian, Southern Illinois University 250

Saundra Tracy, co-author of *Assisting and Assessing Educational Personnel: The Impact of Clinical Supervision,* argues that technology will in fact replace the role(s) of the supervisor. Technology, according to Tracy, will dramatically alter "teaching and learning as we know it today." Professor Joyce Killian, acknowledging technology's potential to improve supervisory practice, cautions against readily accepting the rhetoric of technology. One-to-one supervision is still most viable, says Killian.

Part Two   Perspectives on Critical Issues 261

Perspective 1.   How Can We Move Toward a Community Theory of Supervision? Wrong Theory/ Wrong Practice? *263*

Thomas J. Sergiovanni, Trinity University, San Antonio

Radford Professor of Education at Trinity University and distinguished scholar, Thomas Sergiovanni argues that a community practice of supervision is possible to the extent to which a community theory of supervision is developed. He explicates this commuity theory of supervision, draws implications for leadership, and explains the role of supervision as pedagogical leadership.

Perspective 2.   Is Supervision More Than the Surveillance of Instruction? *285*

John Smyth, Flinders University of South Australia

Internationally known professor of teacher education and director of the Flinders Institute for the Study of Teaching at the Flinders University of South Australia, John Smyth asserts that supervision is not merely a technical process in which teachers are observed or are even engaged in collaborative conferences utilizing professional strategies or techniques. Rather, supervision, as conceived by Smyth, is a challenging quest to understand the "micro-politics of the classroom and how it is constructed by social, economic, cultural, and political structures originating beyond the classroom." Conceived as such, supervision should be concerned with much more than merely surveilling instruction.

Perspective 3.   What is the New Supervisory Role in an Age of Complexity? *299*

Karolyn J. Snyder, University of South Florida

Internationally recognized scholar and professor and co-author with Robert H. Anderson of *Managing Productive Schools*, Karolyn Snyder examines the work of teachers and supervisors in a postmodern age in which they confront a society characterized by ambiguity and uncertainty. In light of these conditions Snyder calls for the constant attention to the needs of students. She maintains that this is best accomplished by gathering information and studying the "deep patterns within a school or classroom" as a foundation for the new work of supervisors. "Building strong professional learning teams" becomes the school supervisor's central focus.

Perspective 4.   How Does the Law Affect Educational Supervision? *319*

Nicholas Celso, III, Kean College of New Jersey

Attorney and professor of education, Nick Celso offers a comprehensive legal analysis of educational supervision that is often taken for granted by practitioners and professors alike. The law, according to Dr. Celso, is a "potent force" in the professional relationships between supervisors and teachers. Misunderstood and underestimated, legal issues fundamentally influence degrees of trust and collaboration among school personnel.

Perspective 5. *Why Is Advocacy for Diversity in Appointing Supervisory Leaders a Moral Imperative?* 341

Carl D. Glickman and Ronald L. Mells, University of Georgia

Noted author and scholar, Carl Glickman, with his colleague Ron Mells, a former school administrator, affirm that advocating diversity is unquestionably a moral imperative. They extend discussion of this issue by advocating that a "school or district should not simply look diverse (ethnically, culturally, or racially), but should be used to lend perspectives and gain the richest information possible on how to best educate both minority and majority students as well." In this essay, each author presents an experience that has shaped his viewpoint about the importance of achieving diversity in educational settings. They conclude by stating that the very foundation of American democracy is inextricably entwined with the attempt to embrace and achieve diversity.

Afterword: Closing Reflections 353

Contributors 355

Index 367

Foreword

✦ ✦ ✦ ✦ ✦

Though there are exceptions, most of the prominent literature concerning supervision in schools represents a particular author's or set of co-authors' view on the nature of supervision or supervisory practice and how it may be most efficaciously conceived (see, e.g., Alfonso, Firth, & Neville, 1981; Blumburg, 1974; Glickman, Gordon, & Ross-Gordon, 1995; Goldhammer, Anderson, & Krajewski, 1993; Harris, 1963; Sergiovanni & Starratt, 1993). *Educational Supervision: Perspectives, Issues, and Controversies* presents a different story. Its focus is on supervision in the schools as a field of professional practice and not on the practice itself. It is not concerned, for example, with how best a supervisor (under whatever title she or he travels) might use himself or herself in order to help a teacher become better, but with the issues and arguments that give spark and life to the field as a field.

As a way of being somewhat more specific about this last point and thus this book, picture yourself as a fly on the wall at a semiannual meeting of COPIS, the Council of Professors of Instructional Supervision. The meeting is being held on the first weekend in November on the campus of a major university. There are about 45 professors present plus a dozen or so graduate students. You have been on the wall for a full day, watching and listening to both the formal program, which has involved the typical academic pattern of panel discussions and presentations of research findings, and the more informal times of coffee breaks, lunches, and social hours. Here are some of the things you might have seen and heard:

- A panel whose focus was the need of both professors and practitioners to define more clearly what they mean by a "profession" of supervision. This discussion involved questions of whether there are specific and teachable supervisory skills as well as the problem of the desirability and feasibility of establishing standards for graduate programs that purport to educate and train both field supervisors and professors.

- A debate between two professors on whether it is possible and desirable to pattern the practice of educational supervision after the understandings of supervisory practice as it has developed in industrial settings. Differences between the debaters arose over the manner in which the culture of the school as a professional organization makes the supervisory demands in industry incompatible with those in a school setting. The ensuing discussion from the audience focused on the manner in which the ideal of collegiality that is supposed to characterize school changes the way supervision, however defined, may be exercised.

- At some point in the program the question was raised concerning the extent to which—or even if—supervision as it is practiced in the schools has an effect on the quality of teaching in a system. Testimony was given about positive individual case experience, but it was pointed out that the nagging question of system-wide results of the practice of supervision continues to arise. Some concerns were raised about the inherent contradiction that is perceived to exist between the very concept of *super*vision (translated implicitly into "evaluation") and the whole notion of developing cooperative work teams of teachers and administrator-supervisors.

- Numerous discussions occurred during coffee breaks and other informal times during the day. Close observation and listening were required of you, the fly on the wall, to pick up the variety of conversations and arguments that took place. By listening closely, you heard, "Is he really serious with his proposal that supervision as we know it should be abolished?" "No, I think he just wants to provoke us" and "I don't buy into that notion that technology will replace traditional supervision." "Why not? Are you afraid to join the twenty-first century?" and "Do we have any evidence that clinical supervision makes a difference that really is a difference?" And more.

The fly-on-the-wall metaphor is, I think, an appropriate stance for the reader, especially the graduate student reader, to take while studying this book. The table of contents is, from my experience, indicative of the type of discussion that occurs when professors of educational supervision convene their meetings. And so, in one sense, *Educational Supervision: Perspectives, Issues, and Controversies* is an opportunity for graduate students in particular to "crawl inside their professor's head" and learn what it is that concerns him or her in meetings with colleagues. As well, it will be found that there is a good bit of passion involved in the discussions that emerge in the mini-debates that constitute Part One of the book, "Controversial Critical Issues." It could hardly be otherwise when, following the fly-on-the-wall fantasy, the titles of these issues include such questions as "Should Supervision Be Abolished," "Do Teachers Benefit from Supervision," and "Has the Field of Supervision Evolved to the Point That It Should Be Called Something Else."

All is not controversy, however. Part Two of the book is entitled "Perspectives on Critical Issues." Here the reader is asked not to be part of a debate, as it were, but, implicitly, to think through with the author of each chapter the implications of that "perspective's" message about the field and practice of supervision. Perhaps the best way to think about the substance of what is offered in Part Two is to consider it as an invitation to join a conversation about one's work. Not just any conversation, however, but one that asks its participants to ponder what it might mean to take seriously the ideas and proposals raised in each the five chapters that make up this section of the book. Consider these thoughts, for example:

- What would it mean for the field and practice of supervision to think of and try to create schools that more closely resemble a community than a formal organization? If the essential ingredients of the glue that binds a community together are commonly held "centers of values, sentiments, and beliefs," how would creating such a school-community affect the way we organize our schools and thus affect the character of the supervision that is practiced in them?

- What would it mean for the practice of supervision if everything we knew about how and why it is currently conceived was suddenly obliterated from our memories, our text books, and our scholarly and professional journals? What would those of us who practice or study and write about supervision do tomorrow? Would we create some brave new educational world? If we did, what would it look like?

- Suppose we cast aside currently accepted organization theory with its heavy focus or order and control and took the position instead that life, by definition, is always on the brink of disorderliness, even chaos—more unpredictable than predictable. How would we gather our wits, both as individuals and as work groups, to deal with, live with, and welcome that condition of life that might best be described as uncertainty? What would schools look like? And how would we describe the role of the supervisor under a mantle of uncertainty?

- Fittingly, as I started writing this foreword on the birthday of Dr. Martin Luther King, Jr., what can and should be done by school leaders, lay and professional, if they have as one of their primary purposes the development and appointment of ethnically diverse school supervisory leadership? If, that is, they were to consider such a purpose to be a moral imperative of their responsibilities?

So much for a brief overview of what this book is about. The manner in which it is structured by the editors should prove attractive to both students and professors. First, each topic is preceded by a brief summary of its essential argument and by a series of questions that can be used by the reader to guide her or his thinking while reading. Second, at the close of each topic discussed there is both a series of review questions and a series of problems that have arisen in the writing that might serve a research agenda.

Another aspect the book's structure that makes it readily useful, both in and out of the classroom, is that it may be entered at any point. It is not necessary, that is, to attend to Issue 4 before Issue 5, or to Perspective 2 before Perspective 3. Each stands by itself as a separate contribution to thinking about the world of supervision in schools.

Educational Supervision: Perspectives, Issues, and Controversies is an excellent vehicle for students or practicing supervisors or administrators to get some valuable insight into their field that goes beyond their everyday work world.

—Arthur J. Blumberg

References

Alfonso, R. J., Firth, G. H., & Neville, R. F. (1981). *Instructional supervision: A behavior system.* Boston: Allyn & Bacon.

Blumberg, A. (1974). *Supervisors and teachers: A private cold war.* Berkeley, CA: McCutcheon.

Glickman, C. D., Gordon, S. P., & Ross-Gordon, J. M. (1995). *Supervision for instruction: A developmental approach.* Boston: Allyn & Bacon.

Goldhammer, R., Anderson, R. H., & Krajewski, R. J. (1993). *Clinical supervision: Special methods for the supervision of teachers* (3rd ed.). Fort Worth: Harcourt Brace Jovanovich.

Harris, B. M. (1963). *Supervisor behavior in education.* Englewood Cliffs, NJ: Prentice-Hall.

Sergiovanni, T. J., & Starratt, R. J. (1993). *Supervision: A redefinition* (5th ed.). NewYork: McGraw-Hill.

Preface

✦   ✦   ✦   ✦   ✦

This book is about educational supervision, a function that is often misunderstood, underappreciated, and frequently controversial. Whether performed by superintendents, principals, assistant principals, supervisors of special subjects, or teachers, supervision has historically sought to improve the quality of teaching. Although employing varied methods, leaders in educational settings have strived to promote professional growth of teachers, foster curriculum development, and support instruction. Confronting a plethora of problems, educational supervisors have not always been successful.

In an attempt to remain responsive to everchanging circumstances and social realities, the field of educational supervision has attempted to clarify its purposes, establish the boundaries of its responsibility, and define and resolve fundamental issues. Critical issues abound, and the exploration of these issues provides insight, if not "the answers" about the theory and practice of the field. Indeed, the resolution or at least the resolve to address these issues, among others, will affect the future direction of supervision in the schools.

Educational Supervision: Perspectives, Issues, and Controversies is a text for undergraduate and graduate students who are engaged in the study of issues in educational supervision. The book will also serve as an invaluable resource for the field and as a discussion piece used in dialogue with administrators, supervisors, and teachers within a district or school. Whether used as a main or supplementary text in a course on issues in supervision or as a reference work, it is essentially a compendium of informed commentaries on current issues written by some of the most prominent scholars in the field. In a sense, this book represents a "snapshot" of the field, highlighting some of the controversial and timely issues affecting educational supervision.[1]

The first part of the book presents 12 opposing or sharply contrasting viewpoints on critical issues in the field of educational supervision. Although by no means exhaustive, these controversial issues provide a forum for consideration, discussion, and critique of ideas that have dominated discourse in the field for many years. Although not all of these issues can be easily resolved, our goal is to prompt reflection and a continuing "dialectic" about the theory and practice of supervision. These contrasting viewpoints and the challenge of the guiding and follow-up questions may help the reader to consider critical factors that have shaped and continue to shape discourse in this field. Part Two of the book focuses on five statements of "perspective," which by their conceptual and theoretical breadth provide more than a glimpse of the larger context within which supervisory issues are expressed.

The statements included in this volume are, for the most part, original and are published here for the first time. We asked the contributors to present the discussion of these critical issues in an informal, conversational manner. We hope the issues "come alive" for you. We hope that reading these issues will challenge and inform your thinking. Each issue and perspective is introduced by highlighting key points and providing appropriate background information, followed by a postnote that summarizes the positions taken. Relevant references for further analysis and study are provided, as are guiding and discussion questions. You are encouraged to critically analyze these issues, develop your own position, and decide the direction the field should take. We also encourage you to consider other relevant issues that have not been raised in our book. We hope that you will share the issues you identify with us for possible inclusion in future editions of this work.

We would like to acknowledge the encouragement of the Council of Professors of Instructional Supervision (COPIS), who took the time to hear our original proposal at our San Francisco meeting in March, 1995. Special thanks to Drs. Helen Hazi, Ben Harris, and Peter Oliva, who provided valuable insights and suggestions on the development of this effort.

We would also like to thank Susanne Canavan, Executive Vice President of Christopher-Gordon Publishers, for her encouragement and sage guidance in addressing many details associated with the project. And most particularly, we would like to express our appreciation to the contributing scholars and to our students and supervisory colleagues in the public schools.

The format adopted for this volume is inspired, in part, by the format developed by Dushkin Publishers (see, e.g., Noll, 1994).

We dedicate this book to our students of supervision and to our colleagues in the field.

A Brief Note to Instructors

✦ ✦ ✦ ✦ ✦

We are certain that this text can be used in many effective ways in your classroom. The issues and perspectives highlighted are timely and controversial, for the most part, and can stimulate much discussion. We are certain you won't be limited by the suggestions noted below for using our text. Please share with us your ideas about how you used the text with your class. Here are some suggestions[2]:

1. *Journal writing.* Encourage students to reflect and react to issues and perspectives by keeping a running record in a personal journal.
2. *Think-pair-share.* Probably one of the most popular cooperative learning strategies, think-pair-share encourages increased student participation and higher-order thinking skills. Pose high-order questions (issues), allow for wait time (about a minute), and then have students pair with a fellow classmate to share their insights. If you like, a whole-class discussion can ensue to allow volunteers to share their ideas.
3. *Guided peer questioning.* After reading a selection or listening to your lecture, students brainstorm their own questions. Then, in pairs or small groups, they pose their questions to each other and answer each others' questions.
4. *Debates.* Individuals or groups may read given issues or perspectives and conduct class debates, after which discussion can ensue.
5. *Oral group reports.* Assign issues or perspectives and have students plan and conduct oral presentations that not only highlight arguments presented in the text but also encourage students to develop their own reactions based on experiences, research, and so forth.
6. *Minute papers.* Short, on-the-spot writing assignments (taking only about a minute) help students reflect and react to a given issue or perspective. You might, for instance, ask "What was the most convincing point made by this author?" or "What was the most confusing point?"
7. *Term papers.* Students react to an issue or perspective or conduct further research; either task could take the form of a traditional term paper.
8. *Letters.* Students could be encouraged to write the authors sharing experiences or reactions to their ideas. All e-mail correspondence should be sent to jglanz@turbo.kean.edu. Messages will be forwarded to the appropriate author(s).
9. *Internet sharing.* The Internet, the largest telecommunications network in the world, can be creatively used to put readers of the text in touch with other students, practitioners, and professors of supervision. University and private linkages could be established to share views and perspectives (e.g., e-mail). Encouraging

computer-literate students in your class to develop internet applications for class presentations could be a good start. A long-term goal would be to establish a "supervision network" of sorts.

10. *Structured academic controversy.* This strategy involves challenging readers to find avenues of mutual agreement between authors of various issues. Students are asked to discuss ways in which both authors could reach consensus. In other words, if both authors were asked to write a collaborative chapter, how could the issue under discussion be developed?[3]

11. *Creating other issues.* The fact that many important issues were not addressed in this volume gives students the opportunity to develop their own critical questions. Research can be conducted and reports written that can be shared with the class.

The material in the postnotes, the review questions, and "For Further Research" may also be helpful as follow-up assignments. Homework and essay exam questions can be culled from these sections. We realize, of course, that you may not wish to use any of these questions and may prefer to develop your own. We hope this book engages your students in lively discussions and contributes to the reasoned examination of critical issues in supervision.

Endnotes

1. We are indebted to Peter F. Oliva, whose work has seriously addressed a number of important unresolved issues in supervision. This book, in part, is an outgrowth of the 11 critical issues he highlighted in Chapter 2 of his widely acknowledged text (1989).
2. Some of these ideas were culled from Cuseo (1995).
3. This strategy was suggested by Robert Garmston as a possible format for this text.

References

Cuseo, J. (1995, Winter). College writing and cooperative learning: Implications for writing across the curriculum. *Cooperative Learning and College Teaching, 5,* 2–5.

Noll, J. W. (Ed.). (1994). *Taking sides: Clashing views on controversial educational issues* (7th ed.). Guilford, CT: The Dushkin Publishing Group.

Oliva, P. F. (1989). *Supervision for today's schools* (3rd ed.). New York: Longman.

Introduction

Viewing Issues in Supervision Holistically and Critically

✦ ✦ ✦ ✦ ✦

To change our perspective in a conflict is to move from a point of view to a viewing point

—T. F. Crum

In developing this book we've been motivated by our belief in the importance of educational opportunities that promote critical thinking and challenge educators to provide curricula that meet the diverse needs of a pluralistic and multicultural society. Confronted by complex social, political, technological, and moral issues, educational leaders, perhaps more so than ever before, are responsible for educational programs that are both educative and personal in meaning. In this context, we believe that educational supervision is a vital partner in the promotion of educational excellence. Notwithstanding our affirming appraisal of the import of educational supervision, we are cognizant of the many problems that confront supervisors in their efforts to improve curriculum and instruction. Educational supervision may be in crisis, but we may also be at a historic juncture where supervision, as a specialized area of study and practice, can more fully achieve its purpose. By promoting critical inquiry and reclaiming the human dimension of educational leadership, supervision can become a vehicle for educational change and transformation.[1]

In keeping with this vision we present this collaborative volume as one effort to stimulate constructive discourse, which is a precondition to the refinement of supervisory practice. The framework we have chosen, the presentation of divergent ideas about educational supervision, may, to some, seem a bit confrontational, and given the nature of divergent thinking, it is! Nevertheless, we believe the framework, or the format, if you will, is compelling and conducive to much needed conversation in the field. Obviously this volume will not lift educational supervision, as a field of study, from the background to the foreground of educational leadership. Our hope, and the hope of our contributing authors and colleagues, is that it will bring attention to vital areas of concern, reawaken interest, and stimulate discourse.

Perspectives, issues, and controversies: What is the relationship among these three words we have chosen as the subtitle for this book? Definitions of sorts are in order. Perspectives are points of view or frames of reference; issues are particular topics or problems that deserve serious attention; controversies are issues that are in dispute and may or may not be resolved easily. In combination they configure an agenda for discourse about the nature and practice of educational supervision. This book therefore presents a diversity of views about issues in educational supervision that, although they may or may not engender controversy, are significant nonetheless. We challenge readers to consider the varied and exciting ways of viewing issues in the field. Often opinions are developed myopically with only slight consideration of the different ways of constructing knowledge and viewing situations or issues. In order to facilitate a broader perspective for understanding issues and developing viewpoints, we will introduce a framework that forms the basis for many of the guiding and review questions we have written throughout the volume.

A Multidimensional Paradigm

This volume serves as a forum for the exchange of views regarding significant issues affecting educational supervision. Controversy can be the basis for change and improvement. Providing a forum for discourse among scholars not only will give a balanced perspective, but will likely prompt the reexamination of critical issues affecting supervision as a field of study and a professional practice. Such discourse may advance understanding of the issues and associated practices and procedures.

The reader is encouraged to view issues in education and supervision holistically and critically. Viewing issues in multidimensional ways generally precludes the myopia and provincialism that often lead to unidimensional thinking; it engenders clearer insights into critical problems affecting the field and enables more viable solutions to emerge.

To achieve a more global perspective about educational supervision, we need to remain mindful of the relationship among language, thought, and human behavior. A colleague once quoted Voltaire: "There are too many of us present" which evoked an incredulous reply, "But there are too many of us in this room." "I'm sure," said the colleague, "that there are at least six of us. There is what you are, what you think you are, and what I think you are. And there is what I am, what I think I am, and what you think I am." What did this mean? Momentarily stunned, the professor regained his composure and realized an inherent truth that he perhaps knew subconsciously but never articulated. He had taken for granted the multifaceted dimensions of reality. His assumptions erroneously shaped his perceptions and behavior. The professor also realized that the picture he had of himself was due to his unconscious assumptions. What he thinks he is is not him—it is an abstraction, a map of his real self. And what his supervisor thinks he is further complicates the equation.

As educators, we are bound by our perspectives, our unique vantage points. Reality is perceived and understood by our belief systems, which are in turn based on assumptions gleaned from our experiences or semantic environments. Reality is dependent on our thinking patterns, belief systems, and mindsets, or as Sergiovanni calls them, "mindscapes" (Sergiovanni, 1991, p. 41). Our belief systems are intimately connected to the language we use to articulate and communicate meanings (Wittgenstein, 1958), which influence our actions and behaviors. How we think shapes the world in which we live. As Arthur Schopenhauer, the German philosopher, once said, "The world in which a man lives shapes itself chiefly by the way in which he looks at it."

Consider the instructor who begins his course by asking his students to stand and walk over to the window. As they peer through the window he asks them to describe what they see. As they convey their perceptions he records responses on the board. "Is there anything else you see?" "Is what you are seeing representative of what's out there?" "Is what you are describing an accurate assessment of what you've seen?" After a brief, albeit intense, discussion it is apparent that the students had not thoroughly examined their assumptions and perceptions, but a discrepancy between the structure of their verbal maps and the structure of reality itself is readily discernible.

Quoting Nietzsche, the instructor explains that "all seeing is essentially perspective and so is all knowing." The instructor reads them *It Looks Like This* (Webber, 1976) and has them peruse *The True Story of the 3 Little Pigs* (Wolf, 1989). The class discusses the implications of these stories for viewing issues in education from varied perspectives. Students confront the principle that knowledge about something can be advanced by a global or multidimensional perspective. The illustration on the next page may clarify a multiple-perspective approach to the examination of educational issues. To investigate bilingual education, for example, without attending to a variety of reference points will yield an incomplete, if not inaccurate, assessment. Each foundation or perspective sheds light on a particular aspect of the problem. Multiple frames or lenses provide a more complete understanding of the issue (For similar ideas in sociology and organizational theory see, for example, Berger & Luckmann, 1966; Bolman & Deal, 1991).

We are detectives of sorts. We collect an array of data to inform the conclusions that we can justifiably make. To utilize a few points of view may lead to incomplete analyses, if not misevaluations. All of us must be challenged to view issues globally. One of the ways to accomplish this is to pose key questions that challenge us to think on a broad scale. Teaching our students to think critically is perhaps the most important skill we can impart. The benefits of critical thinking are immeasurable:

A Multidimensional Model for Educational Issues

The ability to think critically is important on a personal level too. Teaching our students how to think can promote their sense of personal empowerment and autonomy. In a culture so dominated by the media, it will be increasingly difficult for individuals to think for themselves, to critically analyze and evaluate the social and political messages that pervade their lives, and to know that they are making their own decisions rather than being persuaded to follow the agendas of others. Those who are able to critically analyze issues that affect their personal, social, and political decision-making will feel more in control of their lives. In this respect, teaching our students to think critically will help them become empowered autonomous individuals, which presumably will help them lead more successful and fulfilling lives. (King, 1995)

Knowledge-based and comprehension-type questions form the basis for more higher-order thinking. Thought-provoking questions should include processes such as application, synthesis, compare and contrast, inference, prediction, and evaluation. Presented with a critical issue in supervision (e.g., the role of the supervisor in a site-based managed school), we could ask:

- What is site-based management?
- What are the historical antecedents for site-based management?
- How does site-based management differ from other ways of managing schools?
- What are the implications of site-based management for the role and function of supervision?
- What are the political ramifications for shared decision making in a site-based-managed school?

- How do teachers, students, administrators, parents, and community leaders each view site-based management?
- How do other foundations (e.g., social, economic, cultural, philosophical, etc.) affect site-based-management?
- What does the literature indicate about the efficacy of site-based management in terms of academic and affective outcomes?
- How do we prepare future supervisors to work in site-based managed settings?
- Imagine you are being interviewed for a principalship at a school that will be the district "model" of a site-based-managed school. How do you respond when asked how you would facilitate school-based management? Be as specific as possible. What qualities should the board look for in a principal of a site-based-managed school?
- Interview a teacher, parent, student, and/or supervisor of a site-based-managed school. Describe their experiences, both positive and negative. Visit a site-based-managed school. What are the advantages and disadvantages of site-based management?
- Why would site-based management work or not work in your school/district?
- Brainstorm other insights or ideas that you consider important to the issue.[2]

We need to consider possible answers to these questions in order to thoroughly understand the complex dimensions of the supervisor's role as related to the issue of site-based management. As multidimensional viewpoints or perspectives are considered through reasoned conversation, knowledge may be constructed to inform practice. As readers of the perspectives and controversies presented in this volume you are urged to consider each issue globally and critically using this multidimensional framework.

A final word about how this volume is organized is in order. We have framed issues in the first part of the book using a "pro/con" format. Admittedly, there are other frameworks that might have been used to organize the positions taken in this section. Our decision to use the "yes/no" pattern of deliberation was prompted by our interest in providing a format that would challenge readers to take a position— to actively engage in discussion of these issues rather than merely read statements of position by authorities in the field. We realize that yes/no thinking systems are potentially limiting (de Bono, 1972), as we are aware that "total perspective is an optical illusion" (Durant & Durant, 1968). Yet we assert that by our encouragment of divergent thinking through questioning that doesn't presume a dependence upon one right answer and realizes the complexity among knowledge, truth, and inquiry, the reader may be better prepared to understand critical issues in the field. To this end, Parts One and Two will each be prefaced with key questions that we hope will prompt multiframed thinking.

Multiframed thinking will also be encouraged through guiding and follow-up questions throughout the text. Your capacity to think in different ways at the same time about a specific issue not only will reveal the complex prism through which issues related to supervision can be understood, but will promote critical thinking, a major objective of this volume.

Endnotes

1. Our vision here is inspired, in part, by the recent work of Giroux (1992), Pajak (1993), and Waite (1995).
2. On the importance of brainstorming to encourage critical thinking see Osborn (1965).

References

Berger, P. L., & Luckmann, T. (1966). *The social construction of reality: A treatise on the sociology of knowledge.* New York: Doubleday.

Bolman, L. G., & Deal, T. E. (1991). *Reframing organization.* San Francisco: Jossey-Bass.

de Bono, E. (1972). *Po: Yes and no.* New York: Penguin Books.

Crum, T. F. (1987). *The magic of conflict.* New York: Simon & Schuster.

Durant, W., & Durant, A. (1968). *The lessons of history.* New York: Simon & Schuster.

Giroux, H. A. (1992). Educational leadership and the crisis of democratic government. *Educational Researcher, 21*(4), 4–11.

King, A. (1995, Winter). Guided peer questioning: A cooperative learning approach to critical thinking. *Cooperative Learning and College Teaching, 5*(2), 15–19.

Osborn, A. F. (1965). *Applied imagination.* New York: Charles Scribner's Sons.

Pajak, E. (1993). Change and continuity in supervision and leadership. In G. Cawelti (Ed.), *Challenges and achievements of American education* (pp. 158–186). Alexandria, VA: Association for Supervision and Curriculum Development.

Sergiovanni, T. J. (1991). *The principalship: A reflective practice perspective.* Boston: Allyn & Bacon.

Waite, D. (1995). *Rethinking instructional supervision: Notes on its language and culture.* London: The Falmer Press.

Webber, I. E. (1976). *It looks like this: A point-of-view book.* San Francisco: International Society for General Semantics.

Wittgenstein, L. (1958). *Philosophical investigations.* Oxford: Basil Blackwell.

Wolf, A. (1989). *The true story of the 3 little pigs.* New York: Viking Press.

Part One

Controversial Critical Issues

✦ ✦ ✦ ✦

There are [at least] two sides to every question.

—*Protagoras*

A controversial issue involves a problem about which different individuals and groups urge conflicting *courses of action*.

—Fraser (cited in Stenhouse, 1970)

✦ ✦ ✦

The issues in this first section of the book address critical questions that affect fundamental premises of the theory and practice of educational supervision. Answers to these questions explore the rationale for supervision as a role and function in schools, the viability of organizations that support supervisory practice, the relationships of supervision with other school functions and disciplines, underlying conflicts in roles and responsibilities of supervisors, relationships among school personnel, policy decisions regarding training of prospective supervisors, techniques of supervisory practice, the status of supervision as a professional practice and field of inquiry, and the very future of educational supervision.

- What is the fundamental or specific issue addressed?
- What facts and opinions does the author cite to support her or his view?
- Can you summarize each view concisely?
- How do social, political, economic, cultural, philosophical, historical, legal, and other factors impact on the issue?
- Do you agree or disagree with the author's conclusions? Explain.
- Can you suggest another way of viewing this issue?
- What are some of the ways in which supervision is viewed?

The Issues

Should Supervision Be Abolished?

Can We Put back the *S* in ASCD?

Do Teachers Benefit from Supervision?

Is the Estrangement between Curriculum and Supervision Reconcilable?

Can a Supervisor Be a Coach?

Has the Field of Supervision Evolved to a Point That It Should Be Called Something Else?

Is a Collegial Relationship Possible between Supervisors and Teachers?

Is Staff Development Supervision?

Should There Be National Standards in the Preparation of Supervisors?

Should Educational Supervision Be Influenced by Business Management Practices?

Is Clinical Supervision a Viable Model for Use in the Public Schools?

Will Technology Replace the Role of the Supervisor?

Reference

Stenhouse, L. (1970). Controversial value issues in the classroom. In W. G. Carr (Ed.), *Values and the curriculum* (pp. 103–115). Washington, DC: National Education Association Publications.

Issue 1

Should Supervision Be Abolished?

✦ ✦ ✦ ✦

YES—Robert J. Starratt, Fordham University
NO—Robert J. Alfonso, East Tennessee State University

✦ ✦ ✦

Issue Summary

YES: A distinguished author and professor, Jerry Starratt argues for the abolition of supervision. He poses some hard-hitting questions and offers some provocative suggestions for reconceptualizing roles for supervisors. Dr. Starratt's analysis examines the legitimacy of the basic assumptions underlying the theory and practice of supervision. He challenges us to consider many taken-for-granted notions we have about the practice of supervision in schools.

NO: Bob Alfonso, former vice-president for academic affairs, dean of education, and professor, presents the case for supervision as a "specialized and important function." Dr. Alfonso, relying on organizational theory, argues that "supervision *cannot* be abolished." Affirming his belief in teacher autonomy and professionalism, Alfonso insists that supervision is not "inherently demeaning" to teachers but is an "important instructional support for teachers" as well as an "organizational obligation."

Guiding Questions

1. What role does supervision play in your school?
2. What is the role of the supervisor?
3. How should supervision be conducted?
4. What is effective teaching practice?
5. Does supervision promote effective teaching?
6. What specific supervisory practices are effective?
7. What specific supervisory practices are ineffective?

Should Supervision be Abolished? *Yes*

Robert J. Starratt

In writing this essay,[1] I would like to address policymakers and practicing supervisors as well as professors of supervision. The essay suggests that teacher supervision by building-level or system-level administrators be abolished as a practice in all schools and school systems. To some that may sound outrageous, indefensible, even arbitrary. I am not using that suggestion for shock value. Rather, I am proposing the abolition of supervision for serious consideration.

I want to make clear at the outset what I mean by supervision. I am speaking of supervision, as experienced by most teachers, as evaluation of classroom teaching. Whether that practice follows procedures under the rubric of clinical supervision, human resource development supervision, democratic supervision, classroom effectiveness supervision, or whatever, it does not matter. No matter how sophisticated the procedure, if it involves a supervisor observing a classroom teaching episode, a post-observation conference with the teacher, and a written report that goes onto the teacher's file, then that is the supervision I propose we abolish.

I am not talking simply about abolishing bad supervisory practice: Both "good" and "bad" supervision should be abolished. In the literature and theory of supervision, there are many commendable activities put forth that supervisors should practice: creating trust, building community, creating teamwork, networking teachers, building a culture of professionalism, working with teachers on curriculum development, and helping to shape faculty development programs. All of these proposed activities are praiseworthy. I am speaking, however, of the supervisory practice that occupies 80 to 90 percent of the practice of supervision in a given school, when it is practiced by principals, assistant principals, department chairs, instructional leaders, or district supervisors—namely, when supervision fulfills a bureaucratic function of personnel evaluation, performance evaluation, instructional evaluation, assessment, or whatever other name is given to it.

Arthur Blumberg (1974) calls attention to the "cold war" between teachers and supervisors. This study not only highlights the resentment of teachers toward their supervisors, but also points to the ineffectiveness of most supervisory episodes. In a theme issue of *Impact (the New York State ASCD Journal)*, teacher voices again record their negative experiences of supervision. This same issue attempts to explore the "underside of supervision," those unspoken sources of tension, misunderstanding, and conflict found in cross-gender, cross-cultural, and cross-generational relationships (Starratt, 1984). When these underside issues poison the interaction between supervisor and supervisee, the effort degenerates into a dishonest and sometimes dehumanizing activity (Sergiovanni & Starratt, 1988).

Without going into the more murky underside issues, Bates (1986) and others (Foster, 1986; Starratt, 1990) highlight how bureaucratic procedures become powerful administrative means, sometimes thoughtlessly used, to control teachers. When supervisors notify teachers that they want to initiate a supervisory visit to the teachers' classes, they seem aware of how that notification announces the power relationships between them. This relationship places the teacher in a rather defenseless position to resist such intrusions. The unequal power relationship, even for the best-intentioned supervisors and the most pliable teachers, grants unspoken rights to the supervisor and places the professional judgment of the teacher in a subservient position to that of the supervisor. When the relationship is reinforced in the professional literature by a rationalistic concept of leadership, and by bureaucratic models that foster tighter control through standardization and accountability measures in the name of school reform, then the professional autonomy of the teacher appears further diminished (Blase, 1990; Wise, 1988).

More naturalistic descriptions of school administrators (Morris, 1984) testify to the unpredictable but incessant flow of events that confront administrators in everyday school life, causing them to lurch and stagger through a schedule laden with conflicts, crises, and instant problems, interspersed with meetings, paperwork, insistent telephone messages, and veiled threats from a dissatisfied community. Within such a chaotic schedule, administrators must find time to carry out their supervisory responsibilities. Those administrators who take these responsibilities seriously rarely find the time for in-depth work with a teacher, either because they are too distracted by more pressing problems, because they do not know enough about the subject matter, or because they cannot allow themselves to get that close to teachers.

Beyond these problems from the administrators' side, or perhaps partly because of them, the research on the relationship between supervision and evaluation strategies and advances in student learning is at best inconclusive. Some may interject at this point, "But what about the effective schools research? Does that not show a relationship between the instructional leadership of the principal and increases in student achievement scores?" A closer look at the evidence indicates that those claims require many cautions and reservations (see Issue 3).

Even in her generally supportive review of the literature on effective schools, Susan Rosenholtz (1985) was not able to connect directly principals' monitoring of teachers to changes in teachers' behavior—teachers tended to pick up ideas for changing their teaching from other teachers. Rather, the principal's visits to classes tended to reinforce goal clarity and student motivation. Furthermore, Rosenholtz cautions that the tight coupling of highly specific instructional goals (improved scores on basic reading and math tests) with classroom protocols in inner-city elementary schools might not be possible or appropriate in suburban schools where other instructional goals legitimately compete with basic literacy goals.

In a recent study of reform efforts, some of which specifically include effective school strategies, Murphy (1990) points to modest results, as long as the very narrowly defined and very elementary objectives of learning in language and mathematics are kept in mind. Even Murphy's claims for modest gains, however, do not tie specific teacher behaviors to student outcomes. Student time on the learning task seems to be the major variable contributing to increased scores.

Other research efforts to trace relationships between discrete teacher behaviors and increased student performance have again and again resulted in inconsistent and contradictory findings (Wise, Darling-Hammond, McLaughlin, & Bernstein, 1984). If the research on teachers' effects on student outcomes is inconclusive, then how can supervision, which is supposed to effect improved teaching, be claimed to have an effect on student outcomes?

Perhaps we can back away from claims to benefit student learning and be content with claims that supervision improves teaching. Joyce and Showers (1983) seem to imply that for teachers to gain mastery over a new teaching protocol, considerable training and carefully monitored trial and error efforts are required. That is hardly what teachers experience in a supervisory episode. Stoldowsky (1984) points out the limitations of a supervisory episode: The one class observed may not be representative of all or most classes taught by that teacher; another observer sitting in on the same class may see different phenomena and offer a different interpretation of those events. Where teachers have adopted more formal teaching protocols, as with the Hunter model, it has come about through fairly extensive training, not through a sporadic class observation. To my knowledge there is no research that shows that supervision, as it is generally practiced, results in substantial and sustained changes in teachers' teaching. If one can point to an individual instance where a supervisory episode led to a major change in a teacher's performance, that might be the exception that proves the rule, and more than likely the example would concern a beginning teacher within the first three years of his or her career.

From another sector of the educational community, those concerned with teacher preparation and certification, comes other disturbing news. For over three decades, teacher educators have discussed the notion of teaching competence and competency-based teacher education. At present, the language of competency-based teacher education has disappeared from the literature on teacher preparation. Why so? Could it be that the task of identifying essential competencies and then of preparing teachers to develop them proved too elusive? In any event despite the change in language, I have the impression that most teacher education programs continue to pursue the developing of competencies. They talk about it as: developing teacher effectiveness or teacher responsiveness; or strategic teaching in the content areas; or teaching problem solving and critical thinking.

Teacher education programs and teacher certification criteria assume that teachers can and do learn how and what to teach; in other words, they develop a competency or beginning mastery of the skills of teaching. However, there is by no means agreement on what competence means or how one might teach it to acquire it, even if its definition were universally agreed upon (Noddings, 1974; Short, 1984).

At least four meanings are given to the term competence: (1) a behavior or performance (the most specific and narrow meaning of the term; (2) a knowledge or skill (which implies choosing to use it and knowing why one does what is chosen); (3) a degree of capability deemed sufficient (which implies a judgment by someone other than the teacher concerning the adequacy of the competence being exercised, and also that there are specific measures of the degree of sufficiency expected); (4) a quality of a person or a state of being (which implies a level of mastery of a complex whole, including a multiplicity of skills, knowledge, strategies, dispositions toward children, values, and attitudes (Short, 1984, pp. 169–170).

Yet teacher education programs do not seem to address the ambiguities surrounding what they are supposed to be teaching, nor can they validate that their courses and programs result in teaching protocols that directly affect uniform student learnings (Noddings, 1984). On the other hand, the profession of teaching is little different in this regard from many other professions. The evaluation of professional competence is fraught with difficulties both in terms of evaluation technology and in terms of the field agreeing to an operational definition of competence (McGaghie, 1991). Whether we are talking about three young lawyers, three young doctors, or three young teachers who have graduated from their professional schools with identical records, their common exposure to the same courses, and their achievement of the same grades are no guarantee of any common achievement in professional practice. Their clients would judge them to differ markedly in their professional "competence."

If teacher education programs can be questioned on the grounds of their uncertain understandings of professional competence, if what conceptions of competence do guide their programs are inadequately grounded in compelling research on practice, and if, furthermore, there is little research evidence that any teacher behaviors, skills, or other variables that are factored into the definition of competence universally or uniformly relate to student achievement—then by what logic do supervisors respond to these same questions about competence? Can they presume to know what competence is and how to recognize it and measure its sufficiency in classrooms, and, beyond that, to coach or instruct teachers in the improvement of their competence, when those charged with the preparation of those same teachers cannot or at least have not as yet been able to provide convincing answers?

While all the above arguments might cause one to wonder why the practice of supervision is allowed to survive, the most telling arguments against it are emerging out of recent research on teaching. This research is providing a much more comprehensive picture of classroom teaching as it takes place over time throughout a school year. Teachers are seen as managing an intensely complex, unpredictable, and constantly shifting ecology of minds, emotions, physical stimulations and discomforts, imaginations and fantasy worlds, and multiple interpretations of metaphorical language, all simultaneously in motion and interpenetrating one another (Bowers & Finders, 1991). Teachers are constantly responding to highly nuanced and sometimes quite obvious cues; they make numerous decisions to slow down or speed up the pace, shift to a new example, try out another activity, build on a student's question to a transition to another topic, stop to correct a false impression, pause to let student disagreements continue to be verbalized, summarize the discussion, refer to an earlier lesson, refer to something on the evening news—the possible choices seem and are endless.

Studies of teacher thinking (Clark & Peterson, 1986; Jackson, 1977: Yinger, 1987) and teacher planning (Borko & Niles, 1987; Clark & Yinger, 1979; Housner & Griffey, 1985) reveal the nature of teaching as teachers plan activities that may capture the interest and curiosity of pupils and that will provide a launching pad for improvisations into discussions and inquiries that students prompt by their questions and comments. Teachers create impromptu learning opportunities as the class develops, through the subtle reading of student interest and possibilities in the materials the teacher assembled for this class (Huberman, 1990). They may not be able to say precisely how they do it, but then neither can a sculptor say how he saw the form emerging in an apparently formless block of wood, which led him to shape and reshape the piece as he worked on it.

There is another point only hinted at in the literature (Duke, 1987; Friedman, Jackson, & Boles, 1983; Juska, 1991), and that has to do with the special relationships each teacher establishes with each class. Besides the satisfaction of seeing a student succeed in academics, teachers also invest a lot of their energies and feelings in the personal and social growth of the youngsters they meet in class every day. Sometimes they will say quite simply that it is more important right now for a student to work out some negative feelings than to succeed in the math lesson. Teachers know that students' affective lives influence their ability to learn the academic material.

After the first month or so, the experienced teacher has gotten to know the cast of characters in the class. Most important, the teacher has (or has not) established credibility with the students. Unless youngsters find teachers credible, they will not take the classwork seriously. They have to know, even with the most severe and demanding of teachers, that behind the surface there is real caring and concern for them as individuals. The building of this chemistry of credibility and acceptance involves an unspoken commitment of each to each. "This is my class," teachers will say. "These are my kids." There is a possessiveness about the relationship.

Given the picture of present classroom teaching—its craft nature; the multiple meanings associated with competence; the unpredictability of everyday life in classrooms; within the collectivity of students in the classroom, the layer upon layer of meanings, feelings, symbolic connecting and disconnecting; and the strong affective bond between teacher and class—how could a supervisor come into a classroom and presume to offer advice on how to teach the classroom better, based on one visit? Yet supervisors do this everyday without the slightest hesitation. In most cases, the institutional arrangements provide a seeming legitimacy to this practice, supported by a last-resort argument of the legal authority granted to supervisors.

The assumptions behind supervision tend to be that:

- There are general prescriptions of relatively uniform teaching protocols that will be helpful to teachers (e.g., more time spent on seat work, working through exercises; using more than one stimulus or example to convey the concept; offering positive reinforcement; setting goals clearly on the board so the students know what they are expected to learn during this class).
- Every class will be relatively the same and therefore a visit on this day will be representative of how the teacher always teaches.
- Teaching is involved exclusively with learning the prescribed syllabus of the school.
- One way of teaching is clearly superior to others.
- One way of teaching is best for most or all of the children in the classroom.
- The supervisor has the requisite expertise to tell the teacher all of the above.

Is it any wonder that veteran teachers of 7 or 20 years' experience find the experience of supervision humiliating? Why should they be required to submit to bureaucratic intrusions into the sanctuary of their classes and to the subsequent vacuous conversation called "conferencing," which always begins with the condescending question, "Well, how do you think the class went?" or worse, "Tell me how you felt about that class." Administrators seem to have little or no idea of how angry, frustrated, and exasperated teachers feel about being supervised. When added to other reminders of their powerlessness within the bureaucratic authority structures of school systems, supervision remains a constant source of alienation and anger (Friedman, Jackson, & Boles, 1983; Palonsky 1986). Yet teachers cloak their anger in a passive submission to the ritual. It is no small source of amazement that teacher unions, once they had the negotiating power, did not demand an end to the practice.

If we seriously take account of the evidence presented, we should wonder why we did not abolish supervision earlier. On the other hand, might there be a role for supervisors in some kind of a restructured position? I believe that there are two roles for supervisors after the abolition of supervision. One role is as a teacher evaluator, and the other is as a facilitator of staff development.

As an evaluator, the former supervisor would be in charge of evaluating beginning teachers prior to their receiving tenure. Evaluators would not deal with tenured teachers. As an evaluator for beginning teachers, the former supervisor would have more time to work with a much smaller number of teachers and to follow up on evaluations with basic staff development work. Because of the increased commitment to assisting beginning teachers, school systems would be able to develop a core of young teachers who would stay with the profession because of the increased sense of support and pride in mastering the basics of teaching. Such school systems would also be able to secure more evidence of incompetence of a beginning teacher as a basis of denying tenure. Furthermore, the role of the former supervisor would be clearer as regards both formative and summative evaluation, and in making more professional judgments on matters of tenure. This is not to say that the evaluation of teaching is based on clearer principles than is the supervising of teaching, as was implied in the earlier discussion of teaching competence. Evaluation systems clearly need a substantial overhaul as well. But that is the subject of another paper.

In the second role, as facilitators of staff development, former supervisors would be responsible for setting up support systems and administrative arrangements for the provision of a multitude of staff development activities (see Issue 8). Tenured teachers would be expected to participate in ongoing staff development, but they would choose from a multiplicity of opportunities. The content and variety of staff development programs, as well as whatever monitoring systems the schools might employ, should be chosen by a committee of experienced teachers. The former supervisors would continue to find professional satisfaction in assisting teachers in their professional improvement but now as an administrative colleague rather than as a judge or a supposed universal repository of all wisdom about teaching.

Those principals who never cared about supervision in the first place, who would much prefer policing the corridors, running pep rallies, checking on the upkeep of the physical plant, negotiating school–community difficulties, or counseling youngsters with discipline problems—they would be freer to do the things they are happiest doing. All that would be required of them is that they see that someone evaluates beginning teachers and that someone facilitates teacher development.

My thoughts in this essay are intended to start a discussion. The essay is not intended to belittle practicing supervisors but rather to suggest alternatives to an increasingly untenable bureaucratic role. There may be additional arguments to support this modest proposal, and there may be other ways to restructure supervision. The important point is to take the proposal seriously and either defeat it with compelling evidence and argument to the contrary or do something with it.

If my proposal has merit, then it should raise some questions for those doing research and teaching in educational supervision at the graduate level. Granted that much of the literature and theory on supervision tends to discourage the practice of supervision as it is presented in this essay; nevertheless, I rarely find professors of educational supervision examining the legitimacy of the *basic assumptions* underlying supervision, either in theory or in practice. At best, we as a community of scholars seem continually to be in search of ways to improve a badly flawed practice.

If the practice of supervision is as flawed as I make it out to be, why has there not been more sustained and outspoken criticism of practice from the professorate? Why do we continue our association with ASCD, which increasingly seems to dabble in prepackaged quick fixes for supervisors (see Issue 2)? Why do we not do more research in teaching to discover why the practice of supervision has been such a colossal failure?

These are hard questions, I realize. Is it not time, however, we begin to discuss them?

Endnote

1. This chapter was previously published in *Wingspan, 8*(1), July 1992, pp. 14–19.

References

Bates, R. (1986, April). *The culture of administration, the process of schooling, and the politics of culture.* Paper presented at the annual meeting of the American Educational Research Association, San Francisco, CA.

Blase, J. (1990). Some negative effects of principals' control-oriented and protective political behavior. *American Educational Research Journal, 27,* 727–753.

Blumberg, A. (1974). *Supervisors and teachers: A private cold war.* Berkeley, CA: McCutchan Publishing.

Borko, H., & Niles, J. (1987). Descriptions of teacher planning: Ideas for teachers and researchers. In V. Richardson-Koehler (Ed.), *Educators' handbook* (pp. 67–83). New York: Longman.

Bowers, C.A., & Flinders, D. (1991). *Responsive teaching.* New York: Teachers College Press.

Clark, C., & Peterson, P. (1986). Teachers' thought processes. In M. Wittrock (Ed.), *Handbook of research on teaching* (pp. 255–296). New York: Macmillan.

Clark, C., & Yinger, R. (1979). *Three studies of teacher planning.* East Lansing, MI: Michigan State University Institute for Research on Teaching (Research Series No. 55).

Duke, D. (1987). Understanding what it means to be a teacher. *Educational Leadership, 44*(7), 26–32.

Foster, W. (1986). *Paradigms and promises*. Buffalo, NY: Prometheus Books.

Friedman, S., Jackson, J., & Boles, K. (1983). Teaching: An imperiled profession. In L. S. Shulman & G. S. Sykes (Eds.), *Handbook of teaching and policy* (pp. 261–299). New York: Longman.

Housner, L., & Griffey, D. (1985). Teacher cognition: Differences in planning and interactive decision-making between experienced and inexperienced teachers. *Research Quarterly for Exercise and Sport, 56,* 45–53.

Huberman, M. (1990, April). *The social context of instruction in schools*. Paper presented at the annual meeting of the American Educational Research Association, Boston.

Jackson, P. (1977). The way teachers think. In J. Glidewell (Ed.), *The social context of learning and development* (pp. 19–50). New York: Gardiner Press.

Joyce, B., & Showers, B. (1983). *Power in staff development through research on training*. Alexandria, VA: Association for Supervision and Curriculum Development.

Juska, J. (1991). Observations. *Phi Delta Kappan, 72,* 468–470.

McGaghie, W. (1991). Professional competence evaluation. *Educational Researcher, 20*(1), 3–9.

Morris, V. C. (1984). *Principals in action: The reality of managing schools*. Columbus, OH: Merrill.

Murphy, J. (1990). The educational reform movement of the 1980's: A comprehensive analysis. In J. Murphy (Ed.), *The reform of American education in the 1980's: Perspectives and cases*. Berkeley, CA: McCutchan.

Noddings, N. (1974). Competence theories and the science of education. *Educational Theory, 24,* 356–364.

Noddings, N. (1984). Competence in teaching: A linguistic analysis. In E. Short (Ed.), *Competence: Inquiries into its meaning and acquisition in educational settings* (pp. 17–28). Lanham, MD: University Press of America.

Palonsky, S. (1986). *900 shows a year: A look at teaching form the teacher's side of the desk*. New York: Random House.

Rosenholtz, S. (1985). Effective schools: Interpreting the evidence. *American Journal of Education, 25,* 352–388.

Sergiovanni, T. J., & Starratt, R. J. (1988). *Supervision: Human perspectives* (4th ed.). New York: McGraw-Hill.

Short, E. (1984). Gleanings and possibilities. In E. Short (Ed.), *Competence: Inquiries into its meaning and acquisition in educational settings* (pp. 161–180). Lanham, MD: University Press of America.

Starratt, R. J. (1984). The underside of supervision. *Impact, 19*(1), 5–16.

Starratt, R. J. (1990). *The drama of schooling/The schooling of drama*. London: The Falmer Press.

Stoldowsky, S. (1984). Teacher evaluation: The limits of looking. *Educational Researcher, 13*(9), 11–19.

Wise, A., Darling-Hammond, L., McLaughlin, M., & Bernstein, H. T. (1984). *Teacher evaluation: A study of effective practices*. Santa Monica, CA: Rand Corporation.

Wise, A. (1988). Two conflicting trends in school reform: Legislated learning revisited. *Phi Delta Kappan, 69*(5), 328–333.

Yinger, R. (1987, April). *By the seat of your pants: An inquiry into improvisation and teaching*. Paper presented at the annual meeting of the American Educational Research Association, Washington, DC.

Should Supervision be Abolished? *No*

Robert J. Alfonso

It is a sad commentary that a book dealing with the supervision of instruction finds it necessary to raise the issue of whether supervision should even exist or should be abolished. After 300 years, more or less, from Colonial times to the present, why would anyone now question its need? While we might debate its form, its effectiveness, and whether and how it can be improved, it is difficult to conceive of a school system without the supervision of instruction. Schools have frequently been described as "loosely coupled systems;" without supervision they would quickly become even more so.

Supervision in all organizations—schools included—contributes to effectiveness, to goal attainment. It does so by interpreting and giving meaning to organizational goals; by gaining commitment to what become mutually shared objectives; by assisting people in making their work efficient, effective, and personally rewarding; by building communication networks across organizational levels; and by helping to create an organization that values human beings and recognizes and rewards excellence.

These are common purposes of supervision. Added to these in schools are the special knowledge about and expertise in teaching that supervisors bring to their work and the technical skills that enable them to perform a specialized and important function.

Abolish supervision? And replace it with what? Every formal organization—and many informal ones—provides for some system of supervision uniquely appropriate to the organization and the nature of its work. While it may be argued that instructional supervision has not always been based on a model consistent with the nature of school and the characteristics of the teaching profession, that argument (or condition, if it exists) does not then lead one to the conclusion that supervision should be abandoned.

Can an organization exist without supervision? Probably not, at least not for long. Without it there is no direction, there is no sense of goals or purpose. The result for an organization is atrophy at best and anarchy at worst. The simple fact is that supervision *cannot* be abolished. The nature of organizations is such that some person or persons have to provide direction, reinforcement, assistance, and reward or recognition. Glickman (1985) uses the metaphor of "glue," noting that supervision in schools is the function that draws together discrete elements of instructional effectiveness and provides a link between teacher needs and organizational goals, working toward harmony in their vision of what a school should be. But, as Glickman notes, harmony does not occur by chance, and without a strong, effective, and adequately staffed program of supervision, an effective school is unlikely to result (pp. 4–5).

Supervision in schools continues to struggle to define itself, even though it has been referred to as the "in thing" in American schooling, directly related to research associated with the school effectiveness movement (Sergiovanni & Starratt 1988). It was found that effective schools were characterized by principals and other supervisors who exercised strong instructional leadership. I would assert that virtually all effective organizations have a strong supervisory structure—not heavy-handed, not demeaning, but strong in terms of skills, knowledge, and presence. By presence I refer to ongoing, regular involvement with those they supervise. I find it hard to conceive of an effective organization—an effective school—that does not provide ongoing oversight of its employees. Having said that, I do not support in any sense "bad" supervision, the kind that teachers sometimes find not only useless but insulting. We must not, however, pick out the worst examples of supervision and use them as a basis for asserting that teachers should be unobserved, free to pursue their teaching as they see fit. Teachers already have an enormous amount of autonomy. Few employees in other organizations are so infrequently observed, and teachers have considerable latitude in deciding what to teach and how to teach it. It is normal for healthy adults to desire the maximum amount of autonomy in their lives and work, but it is also in the nature of organizations to exert reasonable authority in order to ensure that goals are achieved. In healthy organizations these needs are recognized and reconciled; effective programs of supervision help bring about this synergy. The "cold war" described by Blumberg (1974) is really a commentary on flawed practice and its failure to link adequately the needs of teachers (as groups and as individuals) with the needs of the organization.

Would abolishing some of the traditional practices of classroom observation and feedback, thereby creating still more autonomy than teachers already have, really result in a more focused, coordinated, and effective school? More likely, the reverse would be true, for carried to an extreme it would result in academic anarchy.

I do not believe that schools are so different from other complex organizations, so unique, that they can conduct their business of teaching and learning without any ongoing oversight responsibility. It is an exercise in wishful thinking to suggest that the work of teachers should be unobserved and unevaluated on a regular basis. What kind of commitment would that be to quality, accountability, and instructional support? Indeed, it would be organizationally irresponsible to say to teachers, "Go ahead, do your work; you've got tenure now. We won't pay much attention to what you do and won't observe and critique your work. In short, you won't have any supervision, and you will not be evaluated anymore." Moreover, teachers *do* desire feedback on their performance. They don't want bad or irrelevant supervision; what they do seek—as do all conscientious employees in any organization—is evidence that their good work is recognized and appreciated. The much maligned "report in the teacher file" may be a report that validates effective performance; this is hardly an insulting or demeaning conclusion to a classroom observation. On the contrary, it is a positive outcome, a reinforcing behavior.

The literature on instructional supervision gives major emphasis to bringing about change in teacher behavior, yet research results do not appear to demonstrate dramatic changes as a result of supervision. Perhaps too much is expected. It is also an assumption open to debate that a classroom observation should always result in a change in teacher behavior. Why? A classroom observation might be one that affirms what a teacher is doing, which provides support. Teachers do not always need to be "changed." That is presumptive arrogance on the part of those who hold such a view. It also appears that remediation is a basic tenet of many advocates of clinical supervision and perhaps accounts also for the gradual demise of what many had seen as a promising means of improving classroom instruction. The legion of very effective and committed teachers need classroom observations that acknowledge and reinforce effective work, not those that merely point out areas where change is needed or that result in bland, unspecific written reports. Glatthorn (1990) also points out that in effective schools supervisors see their role as both monitoring *and* supporting: monitoring to be certain that school policies are being implemented and supporting to help teachers implement those policies effectively.

If supervisory practice (which has been described as primarily classroom observation) is seriously flawed or woefully ineffective, one might study the reasons why rather than attempt to abolish it. For example, does a school system place a high priority on supervision, on providing instructional support for teachers? Are supervisors well prepared for their role? Who does the supervision in a school? How much time is allocated for it? Are supervisory personnel sufficiently experienced and intellectually sound enough to merit the respect of teachers? Are supervisors supervising what they "know," or are they supervising at grade levels or in subject areas where they have limited or no knowledge or experience? Is the function of supervision obsolete, or is it a victim of neglect in our schools and in university preparation programs?

In the essay preceding this one, it is argued that the practice of supervision (described essentially as classroom observation, which includes a pre- and postconference and results in a report placed in a teacher's file) be abolished. It is further argued that this practice should be followed only until a teacher is tenured. From that point on there would be no regular or even occasional observation unless, I presume, a problem occurred that was so serious that it would come to the attention of the school administration. Instead of classroom evaluations, an extensive program of staff development would become a substitute; the record of staff development is not so sterling, however, that one could confidently substitute it for the supervision of instruction.

As important as staff development is, it cannot be a substitute for supervision (see Issue 8). Genuine supervision is always practiced as part of an organization's work system. The essential element in the supervisors' work in all organizations is its direct and continuing involvement with those responsible for the production of goods and services (Alfonso, Firth, & Neville, 1981). If schools do not have supervision that takes place close to teachers, and thus does not enable supervisors to observe and interact with teachers on a regular basis, they do not have supervision. Given, therefore, the classic understanding of supervision, many schools do not have much supervision at all. In the absence of a designated and effective program of instructional supervision, other factors such as culture and organizational history and constraints combine to exert important influence on teacher behavior (Alfonso, 1986).

Pajak (1989) comments on the need for supervisors to emphasize teamwork and cooperation and to be sensitive to anything that might enhance or undermine these conditions. ". . . the construction of images and narratives that give meaning to what goes on in schools is of necessity a collaborative activity that relies on a continuous, open dialogue" (p. 101). Note in particular Pajak's emphasis on collaborative and continuous—characteristics of a close-in, effective system of supervision.

While I am in favor of strong staff development programs, they would likely be more effective when tied to a systematic program of supervisory presence *in* classrooms, observing firsthand what staff development activities might be needed as well as when such activities are having positive results. An effective program of instructional improvement would bring together the processes of evaluation, staff development, and supervision (Alfonso, 1984). Eliminating one of these weakens the link, breaks an important relationship.

As noted, teachers have a high degree of autonomy. That is as it should be: they are professional, well-educated, and possessed of a substantial body of knowledge and skill. Further, the particular nature of teaching requires that teachers be free to exercise independent judgment and free from excessive intrusions, and that they make a multitude of professional decisions during a day, month, or year, all of this within a very complex environment. Teachers are supported in their professional role by the concept of academic freedom, which has greater liveliness in higher education but which also has applicability to schools.

But academic freedom has limits. It does not grant unfettered freedom, license without any restraints. Nor should the granting of tenure suggest that from that point on teaching will always remain at a high or acceptable level and that continuing supervision is not needed. That is not a valid assumption. Changes in organizational goals, curriculum, and the student body, and changes in teachers themselves can all combine in such a way as to render a once effective teacher ineffective. A program of ongoing supervision is absolutely needed to mitigate and respond to such changes. Staff development alone cannot do it. Further, without classroom observation how can it be verified that the efforts of staff development are actually taking root in classrooms?

In order to determine whether new initiatives or approaches to teaching have taken hold and are understood and implemented by teachers, supervisors need the opportunity to observe and interact with teachers in their classrooms. This is not inherently demeaning or insulting to teachers; it is important instructional support for them, and it is an organizational obligation. It is also an example of how supervision and staff development "connect" (see Issue 8).

In making the case for abolishing supervision, six assumptions that underlie prevailing supervision practice are listed. Where these assumptions come from I do not know, but I do not believe they are embraced by most supervisors. Perhaps supervisors' behavior may sometimes contradict my belief, but I do not think that these assumptions represent supervisors' core beliefs. If this is what they actually believe and if these assumptions guide their practice, then I, too, vote to abolish supervision. But I do not think this is the case. Most certainly these assumptions do not represent the thinking of those who teach courses in supervision, and such a set of assumptions is not represented in the history of the Association for Supervision and Curriculum Development (ASCD) literature or in the thinking and scholarship of the Council of Professors of Instructional Supervision (COPIS).

Such a list of assumptions, alongside a discussion of classroom complexity, suggests that teachers are rather sophisticated high fliers, managing an incredibly complex academic theater each day, while supervisors are dullards, simplistic, and petty bureaucrats who haven't the foggiest notion of what teaching is all about. I do not believe this to be the case—not for all supervisors and, I might add, not for all teachers.

I concur with the description of classroom complexity and also with the assertion that no casual visitor can walk in for a brief visit and understand the dynamics of a classroom, an environment in which the supervisor is not a participant, but only an observer with limited ability to grasp the subtleties and special communication that exists in a dynamic and healthy learning setting.

But most supervisors are not so ill-informed or so intellectually arrogant that they presume to understand everything happening in a classroom—the private jokes or why a teacher deals with a student or students in a particular way. Nor are they so dogmatic as to reach a conclusive judgment based on a brief classroom visit. Impressions gained, however, may lead to follow-up. Supervisors, after all, were classroom teachers themselves and are not unmindful of the nuances of the classroom environment, the special chemistry that exists between teachers and students that no casual observer can fully appreciate—or even recognize.

A classroom observation, whether clinical supervision or any other kind, does not make claim to a full understanding of a teacher's skills, strengths, weaknesses, and teaching strategies, or of classroom dynamics, recognizing that even the supervisor's presence may alter circumstances. Can anything be gained by such brief, occasional observations? Of course. Could more be gained by frequent visits and interaction? Of course. And that should be the goal rather than abolishing such activity.

Harris (1975), in discussing the various ways in which evidence is collected about teaching–learning activities, concludes that of all the sources the most reliable and fully descriptive are based on direct observations; the more systematic and objective they are and the better trained the observer, the more useful and rich is the information or evidence obtained. Harris also notes that much attention has been on negative aspects of observations (nonrenewal of contract, for example), but positive uses of observation data, like good news, get little attention.

There is much ineffective supervisory practice, but as Harris notes, good practice is often overlooked. To cite the worst, the most ineffective, the occasionally demeaning supervisory behavior is to construct a straw man, one loosely supported by some research that indicates teachers' negative feelings about some of the supervision they have received. To argue that supervision should not be abolished is not to argue for the continuation of ineffective practice. Surely, however, it is not responsible either to suggest that all or most supervision is ineffective and contributes little or nothing to improving instruction or achieving school goals. It is true that supervision as practiced does not live up to our expectations. The same about school administration, school counselors, school boards, or about schools in general. And about teaching. There is much teaching that is excellent, but schools are also rife with flawed practice.

As important as classroom observation is, viewing supervision as this practice alone is too narrow a definition. Supervision that focuses on one teacher at a time in one classroom at a time is doomed to fail. There are simply not enough supervisors, hours in the day, or weeks in the year for such an approach to succeed, but classroom observation is a valid component of a comprehensive program of supervision and can provide helpful information for teachers about their performance.

Instead of abolishing supervision, including the infrequent observation of classroom teaching, it is interesting to consider what might be the result of strengthening supervision, creating a stronger link with teaching and the instructional program. Schools and teachers just might be more effective if additional supervisory support were provided and if there were regular, ongoing, high-quality interaction between teachers and supervisors. It seems to me that we would stand a better chance of improving goal attainment if we provided more supervisory support for teachers than if we provided less—or none.

Unfortunately, in many school systems there is scarcely enough genuine supervision so that one could even have a basis for judging it as good or bad; we might judge it irrelevant, possibly, because it is not readily available. It is quite possible—even likely—that there are too few supervisors and too little supervision. Rather than abolishing it, we should be seeking to strengthen it both quantitatively and qualitatively.

What has been described as "the reluctant profession" (Mosher & Purpel, 1972) is obviously still reluctant, avoiding responsibility, hesitant to exert its rightful role, uncertain about the degree of its importance and acceptance, and still struggling to define itself in theory, research, and practice. But supervision is not a new thing, either in schools or in other organizations. Its history is as long as the history of organizations, and its history in schools is as long as the history of formal schooling.

Every organization creates a system to help make its work effective and efficient, to be certain that goals are attained. No organization is without supervision—not hospitals, department stores, churches, youth organizations, the military, restaurants, automobile plants, or higher education. Would school boards and parents opt for a school system without supervision and evaluation? Hardly. The suggestion that supervision be abolished cannot be seriously considered. Supervision has been described as an "organizational imperative" (Alfonso, Firth, & Neville, 1981). This need is met in a variety of ways, and the supervision that is most effective is that most consistent with the nature of the organization in which it takes place. It is very possible that despite its long history, educational supervision has not yet reached that state. That should be our goal. Abolish Supervision? No! Improve it? Yes!

References

Alfonso, R. J. (1984). *Integrating supervision evaluation, and staff development: A concept paper.* Paper presented at the annual meeting of the American Educational Research Association, New Orleans, LA.

Alfonso, R. J. (1986). *The unseen supervisor: Organization and culture as determinants of teacher behavior.* Paper presented at the annual meeting of the American Educational Research Association, San Francisco, CA.

Alfonso, R. J., Firth, G. R., & Neville, R. F. (1981). *Instructional supervision: A behavior system.* Boston: Allyn & Bacon.

Blumberg, A. (1974). *Supervisors and teachers: A private cold war.* Berkeley, CA: McCutchan.

Glatthorn, A. A. (1990). *Supervisory leadership: Introduction to instructional supervision.* New York: HarperCollins.

Glickman, C. (1985). *Supervision of instruction: A developmental approach.* Boston: Allyn & Bacon.

Harris, B. (1975). *Supervisory behavior in education.* Englewood Cliffs, NJ: Prentice-Hall.

Mosher, R. L., & Purpel, D. E. (1972). *Supervision: The reluctant profession.* Boston: Houghton Mifflin.

Pajak, E. (1989). The *central office supervisor of curriculum and instruction.* Boston: Allyn & Bacon.

Sergiovanni, T. J., & Starratt, R. J. (1988). *Supervision: Human perspectives* (4th ed.). New York: McGraw-Hill.

Postnote

Should Supervision Be Abolished?

Regardless of your position on this issue, you will likely concur that professors and/or practitioners rarely explore the legitimacy of the basic underlying assumptions of the theory and practice of supervision. An examination of these fundamental premises is essential to better understand the nature and future of supervision in schools. Both authors persuasively present their case and challenge us to assess the efficacy of supervision.

Review Questions for

The Yes Response:

1. What is your reaction to Professor Starratt's definition of supervision? Does it match your own definition?
2. What arguments does Dr. Starratt propose to abolish "good" supervision? Are these arguments convincing? Why or why not?
3. When a supervisor observes you, do you feel that your "professional autonomy" is diminished? Explain.
4. Do you find the experience of being observed humiliating? Explain.
5. Has supervision as defined by Starratt ever benefited you? Explain.
6. When a supervisor asks you during a postconference, "Well, how do you think the class went," do you feel this comment is condescending? Explain.
7. From your own perspective, support the abrogation of supervision. How are your arguments different from those presented in this chapter?
8. What immediate or long-term effects would be evident in the absence of supervision?
9. React to Starratt's recommendations for reconceptualizing the roles for supervisors after the abolition of supervision. Describe ways to reconceptualize supervision that are not discussed.
10. Should tenured teachers be evaluated? Why or why not?

The No Response:

1. Dr. Alfonso observes that it is a "sad commentary that a book dealing with the supervision of instruction finds it necessary to raise the issue of whether supervision should even exist, or should be abolished." Why do you think we have included this issue, "Should Supervision Be Abolished?" in this volume? What major assumptions underlie supervision that warrant this issue being included? Is this issue of concern to you, your school, and/or your district? Explain.

2. Can an organization exist without supervision? How can supervision contribute to organizational effectiveness?

3. Assume that supervision was abolished by district or state mandate in your current school. How is your school different in terms of each of the following: organization, student achievement, teacher evaluation, and instructional improvement?

4. How would Alfonso define supervision? What's your reaction to his definition?

5. Alfonso states that "teachers have an enormous amount of autonomy." Do you as a teacher or do your teachers have "enormous autonomy?" Explain.

6. Alfonso states that schools are not "so different from other organizations" that they need no supervision. Are schools similar to or dissimilar from other organizations such as hospitals and police departments? How are they similar or dissimilar?

7. Should teachers who have tenure be observed? Why or why not?

8. Were you adequately prepared to supervise? What aspects of your university preparation training program were helpful and what areas were neglected?

9. Alfonso alludes to and dismisses as unrealistic Starratt's six assumptions that undergird supervision. Do you agree or disagree with Alfonso? Explain.

For Further Research

1. Before determining whether or not to abolish supervision, consider some basic questions, such as: why do people choose to become supervisors; what do supervisors find most gratifying about their job; what are some difficulties encountered by supervisors; what are some images the public may have of supervisors; and what is an effective supervisor. Prepare to discuss these questions in class.

2. Some who argue for the abrogation of supervision believe that supervision as traditionally conceived is no longer necessary in teacher-empowered schools. Why do you think this is so? What are the legal ramifications of a school with no "supervisors?" Examine the views of Caldwell and Spinks (1988), Murphy (1994), and Wohlstetter and Odden (1992, 1995) in regard to whether or not supervisors are necessary in teacher-empowered schools. Develop arguments (pro/con) highlighting both perspectives.

3. React to the following position: "Supervision has been questioned as a method for monitoring teachers. My guess is that this will continue as teachers are given more responsibility for establishing professional goals and keeping track of their attainment. On the other hand, self-monitoring is not supervision. The latter is difficult to carry out absent clear pedagogical standards, impartial observers, and the inability to link compensation with performance."

4. Dr. Starratt claims that "effective schools" research indicating a positive relationship between instructional leadership and increases in student achievement is flawed. Research a supporter of the "effective schools" research and explain how Starratt's view could be countered.

5. Compare Starratt's discussion of the impact of supervision on teaching with ideas expressed by Goldsberry in Issue 3 and with Smyth's analysis in Perspective 2. In your opinion, does supervision benefit teachers? (See Issue 3.)

6. Starratt argues against a bureaucratic role for supervision. What is the historical and current relationship between supervision and bureaucracy? See, for example, Bolin and Panaritus (1992), Firth & Eiken (1982), and Glanz (1991).

7. Compare Starratt's arguments in this chapter with arguments made in Starratt (1992).

8. How would Dr. Starratt respond to the "collaborative" model for supervision described by Tsui (1995)? Compare Starratt's views with those of Pavan's in Issue 7. Would Starratt agree or disagree with views expressed by Harris in Issue 7? Explain.

9. Describe the "cold war" as referred to by Blumberg (1980). Is the "cold war" still on? Explain.

10. Read Waite's (1995) book, *Rethinking Instructional Supervision,* and explore his understanding of the importance of supervision. What purpose does supervision serve, according to Waite? What is the role of the teacher in supervision, according to Waite? How would Professor Waite react to each of the arguments presented by the authors of this chapter?

11. Interview some teachers about their attitudes toward supervisors. Relate how different teachers describe their experiences with supervision. How do these teachers feel about the issue under discussion in this chapter?

12. Examine Alfonso and Firth's (1990) appraisal of the field of instructional supervision. Has progress been made in terms of the areas they address? What do the authors mean when they call for "a reality-based, pragmatic approach to research in supervision?"

13. According to Starratt, bureaucratic school organization seems antithetical to the interests and needs of teachers as professionals. How does bureaucracy affect teachers and supervisors? What is the impact of the schools' bureaucratic structure on the process and function of supervision? See, for example, Firth and Eiken (1982). How would Starratt react to Firth and Eiken's thesis that "the delivery of supervision to schools is influenced by the type of bureaucratic structure in which such services must operate?" Describe how different organizational theorists conceptualize supervision (e.g., Shafritz & Ott, 1992). What kinds of supervision are most successful in different organizational contexts?

References

Alfonso R. J., & Firth, G. R. (1990). Supervision: Needed research. *Journal of Curriculum and Supervision, 5,* 181–188.

Blumberg, A. (1980). *Supervisors and teachers: A private cold war.* Berkeley, CA: McCutchan.

Bolin, F., & Panaritis, P. (1992). Searching for a common purpose: A perspective on the history of supervision. In C. D. Glickman (Ed.), *Supervision in transition* (pp. 30–43). Alexandria, VA: Association for Supervision and Curriculum Development.

Caldwell, B. J., & Spinks, J. M. (1988). *The self-managing school.* London: The Falmer Press.

Firth, G. R., & Eiken, K. P. (1982). Impact of the schools' bureaucratic structure on supervision. In T. J. Sergiovanni (Ed.), *Supervision of teaching* (pp. 153–169). Washington, DC: Association for Supervision and Curriculum Development.

Glanz, J. (1991). *Bureaucracy and professionalism: The evolution of public school supervision.* New Jersey: Fairleigh Dickinson University Press.

Murphy, J. (1994). *Redefining the principalship in restructured schools. NASSP Bulletin, 78,* 94–99.

Shafritz, J. M., & Ott, J. S. (1992). *Classics of Organization Theory* (3rd ed.). Belmont, CA: Wadsworth Publishing Company.

Starratt, R. J. (1992). After supervision. *Journal of Curriculum and Supervision, 8,* 77–86.

Tsui, A. B. M. (1995). Exploring collaborative supervision in inservice teacher education. *Journal of Curriculum and Supervision, 10,* 346–371.

Waite, D. (1995). *Rethinking instructional supervision: Notes on its language and culture.* London: The Falmer Press.

Wohlstetter, P., & Odden, E. R. (1992). Rethinking school-based management policy and research. *Educational Administration Quarterly, 28,* 529–549.

Wohlstetter, P., & Odden, E. R. (1995). Making school-based management work. *Educational Leadership, 52*(5), 32–36.

Issue 2

Can We Put back the *S* in ASCD?

✦ ✦ ✦ ✦

YES—Jean McClain Smith and Barbara S. Thomson,
The Ohio State University
NO—Robert J. Krajewski, University of Wisconsin-Lacrosse

✦ ✦ ✦

Issue Summary

YES: Drs. Smith and Thomson assert that the Association for Supervision and Curriculum Development (ASCD) has been the premier national and international organization furthering the interests of both curriculum specialists and supervisors; it is described as an international community of educators committed to the development of learning environments in which all learners succeed. The authors contend that ASCD has always addressed the needs and interests of those concerned with supervising instruction. "To argue that ASCD has not attended to supervision," explain the authors, "is patently untrue."

NO: Professor of education and a 1993 ASCD Affiliate Publications Award winner, Bob Krajewski counters the claim that ASCD has adequately attended to the *S*. He provides evidence to support his claim by examining four factors (definition, history, role/practice, and role training) that have in his judgment "relegated supervision to less importance than curriculum in ASCD."

Guiding Questions

1. How can an organization such as ASCD best support individuals who are charged with the supervision of instruction?
2. What evidence is there to support each of the views presented?
3. Are you currently a member of ASCD? If so, why is ASCD membership important?
4. If you were responsible for supervision in your school, would you join ASCD?
5. How does a professional organization make decisions on its program priorities and action initiatives?
6. What has ASCD done to bolster supervision as a process and as a function in schools?
7. Which of the two essays did you find most persuasive? Why?

Can We Put back the *S* in ASCD? *Yes*

Jean McClain Smith and *Barbara S. Thomson*

We don't think the *S* in ASCD has to be "put back" because it has always been an essential component of ASCD! It is a vital organization that has clearly attended to the important relationship between curriculum development and the supervision of instruction. In this essay we will argue that ASCD was formed on the basis of the fact that supervision and curriculum are inextricably entwined, and that it has indeed provided the requisite leadership in the field. As the premier organization in education, ASCD has provided and will continue to provide leadership for those who are concerned with curricular matters *and* those who supervise instruction.

Over the last ten years there has been much discussion in the field that ASCD is neglecting supervision, as evidenced by the number of publications, workshops, and conference programs dealing with curriculum. Critics notice, compare, and actually count the activity in each field (e.g., Bolin & Panaritus, 1992; Glanz, 1995). Despite this alleged neglect of supervision, ASCD has always held that curriculum and supervision are connected in both purpose and function. ASCD has always maintained that both functions necessarily support one another. Although ASCD has a thriving business in curriculum materials, a widely held view is that a superior curriculum is not enough. A dynamic, exemplary, cutting-edge curriculum can have greater influence only when paired with an interactive supervision model. Curriculum is "what" is taught, but it cannot come alive without the skilled delivery of "how." A major problem, admittedly, appears to be the commercialism of curriculum and the lack of an effective instructional delivery system tied to supervision. But to merely count articles and conclude that supervision has been shortchanged is nearsighted and doesn't address how curriculum and supervision might better contribute to instructional excellence in our schools.

ASCD has attempted to address this presumed lack of attention, however, in several ways. One of the primary ways it has supported supervision is through the establishment of networks. ASCD has sponsored numerous networks that help members exchange ideas, share common interests, identify and solve problems, grow professionally, and establish collegial relationships. The Instructional Supervision Network is one of the early networks formed. ASCD policy has always been to assist in any way possible and has not dictated to the membership or to the leadership of the supervision network. There has always been an atmosphere of trust and communication that translates into the freedom of the network to produce articles, conduct research, and offer opinion statements about supervision and related matters. ASCD has always encouraged open criticism and constructive advice.

As leaders in this network for many years, we have never felt that curriculum has been heralded and that supervision has been neglected. To the contrary, the *S* in ASCD is well and doing fine, thank you. Let's analyze how supervision has been supported by ASCD and demonstrate the vitality of the *S* in its name.

The Historical *S*

Supervision and curriculum were once considered separate and disparate functions and roles. Yet a significant advance in educational thought occurred in the 1930s, when educators realized that to improve instruction without attending to both curricular matters and supervision was foolhardy and self-defeating. Although supervisors and curriculum specialists had different organizations (the Department of Supervisors and Directors of Instruction and the Society for Curriculum Study), attempts were made to collaborate as a unified group. In 1936 efforts were begun on a joint project by both organizations that resulted in the publication of *The Changing Curriculum* (1937). Since the book was heralded as a significant contribution to both fields, the wheels were set in motion for a merger. The realization that curriculum and supervision were intimately connected spread throughout the country. For example, Glanz (1992) documents that efforts at collaboration between supervisors and curriculum specialists in school systems increased significantly. Landmark work at collaboration, for example, was undertaken in Denver, Colorado, by Jesse Newlon, superintendent of schools, and A. L. Threlkeld, deputy superintendent (Peltier, 1967).

Despite limited opposition, the merger between the Department of Supervisors and Directors of Instruction and the Society for Curriculum Study to form ASCD took place (Glanz, 1994). Supervision has been part of ASCD since 1946, when the current name was adopted. From the onset, then, supervision and curriculum were enmeshed in purpose and function.

Articles about curriculum *and* supervision appeared with great frequency in the new journal, *Educational Leadership*. Conferences and committees dealt with many issues involving the supervision of instruction. To say otherwise is to negate the fundamental premise underlying ASCD, which was and still is to demonstrate how connected supervision and curriculum really are. Let's relate an instance in which ASCD attended to the *S*.

In 1984, one hundred educators were selected by ASCD to assemble at the annual conference in New York to review supervision and address the *S* in ASCD. Gerald Firth, as president elect, was a catalyst in this attempt to make supervision an exciting area of interest and growth. ASCD selected a wide range of educators representing public and private schools and universities from all the states. Professors and field-based practitioners shared a common vision that reaffirmed the importance of supervision. Follow-up meetings were scheduled for further discussion of the importance of supervision in ASCD.

We challenge the assertion that the *S* has been removed or at least downplayed. Many prominent educators have underscored the importance of equal attention to both curriculum and supervision. "Supervision and curriculum development have always been central concerns of the Association for Supervision and Curriculum Development" (Drummond, 1975). Saylor (1966) president of ASCD at the time, stated that "the national professional organization for supervisors" is ASCD. Similarly, J. Harlon Shores (1967), also an ASCD president, stated that "the Board of Directors and Executive Committee are quite conscious of the *S* in ASCD. There are times when it seems that supervision is neglected with the increased attention being given to curriculum development." But he continued, "Supervision and curriculum development are as intimately related as we thought they should be."

In the intervening years, ASCD has published some excellent books on supervision (e.g., Glickman, 1992). Furthermore, each annual conference has included special sessions devoted to the supervision of instruction. The Instructional Supervision Network has met each year and has attracted a respectable number of concerned and enthusiastic educators to discuss critical issues related to supervision. That ASCD has not attended to supervision is patently untrue. Evidence the fact that, historically, ASCD has attempted to address supervisory concerns through various publications (yearbooks and articles), conferences, and the Instructional Supervision Network. ASCD is the organization through which a forum can be established to address issues vital to practitioners and professors of instructional supervision.

The Power of *S*

The *S* in ASCD has not been neglected but has achieved preeminent status for the importance of its work. ASCD has given voice to countless supervisors all over the country and now around the world. Principally through its journal, *Educational Leadership*, ASCD has demonstrated how significant and vital effective supervisory leadership is. Those concerned with the improvement of instruction have achieved a degree of recognition and stature that is due to an association with ASCD. The power of *S* is clearly reflected in both the numbers of supervisors who are part of ASCD and the quality of work published by the organization.

The power of *S* can be further verified by noting the plethora of innovative practices that have been given voice through ASCD. It has provided a forum to discuss how supervision as a process and function can support such innovative practices as cognitive coaching, site-based management, shared decision making, and professional growth. The *S* clearly remains an influential component in our attempt to improve not only instruction but the entire educational process.

The Proactive *S*

As our schools are faced with many perplexing and challenging social and technological changes, supervisors are more important than ever before. Supervisors or those concerned with supervision take the initiative by confronting needed changes rather than merely reacting to chance events. As such they are "proactive."

Supervision remains vital because it is proactive (Daresh & Playko, 1995). As a "proactive process" it demonstrates its vitality and relevance. Proactive supervisors provide dynamic and effective educational leadership. Such leadership includes involvement in curriculum development, staff development, motivating teachers, evaluating instruction, and encouraging positive change. ASCD is the preeminent organization that encourages and promotes such educational leadership.

The Dynamic *S*

You, the reader, may suspect at this point that we are apologists or public relations specialists for ASCD. Nothing could be further from the truth. We recognize that problems exist, but we truly believe that ASCD is a dynamic organization that has contributed greatly to both curriculum and supervision. Supervision can have its shortcomings, especially if it becomes predictable. The predictable *S* is characterized by a reliance on outmoded, autocratic, and noncollaborative methods of supervision. ASCD has attempted to elevate supervision from its autocratic legacies. It has promoted numerous "dynamic" models of supervision that are visionary and effective.

Think about the prominent leaders in the supervision field. Costa, Garmston, Pajak, Sergiovanni, Smyth, Glickman, and Firth, among many others, have gained recognition through ASCD. Their pioneering work and creative energies have created a new vision for supervision that has taken us away from older, less sophisticated conceptions. Newer leaders, such as Glanz, Waite, Hazi, and others, are also gaining reputations in supervision through an association with ASCD.

The *S* in ASCD must not be static or predictable, but should be dynamic, integrated, and evolving as we move closer to the new century. The *S* is critical as sophisticated scholars and practitioners in supervision seek to enhance change, quality, and commitment to excellence in all facets of schooling.

The Current *S*

Examine the ways ASCD currently supports the *S*. Aside from *Educational Leadership,* The *Journal of Curriculum and Supervision* remains a vital forum for reflecting, informing, and debating supervision practices and related policy issues. Founded over ten years ago it has provided and continues to provide a forum for the exchange of ideas related to supervision. In a recent issue, Edmund Short (1995), former journal editor, reviews the studies that had been published over the 10-year period. He states:

> I believe that the leading work in supervision studies already appears in the *Journal*. Moreover, the *Journal* is the primary publication source of scholarly work in supervision in the North American context. Apart from scattered work that has appeared elsewhere in mixed-topic journals, in occasional supervision yearbooks from ASCD, and in the forthcoming *Handbook of Research on Supervision*, the Journal is virtually the only place that now publishes supervision studies. (p. 102)

What other organization would provide such a scholarly forum for supervision if not ASCD?

Moreover, supervisors all over the country are supported by ASCD state affiliates that publish local journals, hold regional conferences, and initiate dialogue about matters related specifically to supervision. The *S* in ASCD is receiving spirited attention all over the country because of the efforts of the organization.

It seems to us that disenchantment with ASCD doesn't emanate from practitioners as much as it does from some professors of supervision. Still, their apparent dissatisfaction is difficult to comprehend given the fact that COPIS, the Council of Professors of Instructional Supervision, is in fact provided a forum each year at ASCD annual conferences. It is time for practitioners and professors alike to band together within ASCD to address issues of mutual concern. ASCD is currently one of the few international organizations, if not the only one, that provide forums for such dialogue to ensue.

The Visionary *S*

As the editors so passionately state in the preface to this book, educational supervision "can become a vehicle for liberation, improvement, and change." To achieve this we must realize "the possibilities for imaginative and visionary educational leadership." ASCD has provided and will in all likelihood continue to provide that visionary leadership.

Collectively, we can make the *S* an influential component of ASCD by reaffirming the purposes that originally led to its formation. Those concerned with supervision as a process and professional practice need ASCD for the track record, the resource of past knowledge and practices, and the communication resources provided. ASCD needs supervision and supervisors to effectuate a complete curriculum-instruction delivery system.

ASCD will continue to meet the diverse and complex needs of its membership. It provides the forum to deliberate upon critical issues and the vision necessary to pursue excellence in education. To accomplish these goals, the *S* in ASCD will be more important than ever.

References

Bolin, F., & Panaritis, P. (1992). Searching for a common purpose: A perspective on the history of supervision. In C. D. Glickman (Ed.), *Supervision in transition* (pp. 30–43). Alexandria, VA: Association for Supervision and Curriculum Development.

The Changing Curriculum. (1937). Joint Committee on Curriculum. New York: D. Appleton-Century Company.

Daresh, J. C., & Playko, M. A. (1995). *Supervision as a proactive process: Concepts and cases.* Project Heights, IL: Waveland Press.

Drummond, H. D. (1975). Foreword. In R. R. Leeper (Ed.), *Role of supervisor and curriculum director in a climate of change* (pp. v-viii). Washington, DC: Association for Supervision and Curriculum Development.

Glanz, J. (1992). Curriculum development and supervision: Antecedents for collaboration and future possibilities. *Journal of Curriculum and Supervision, 7,* 226–244.

Glanz, J. (1994, Spring). The merger of the department of supervisors and the society for curriculum study: Effects on supervision. *Instructional Supervision Network Newsletter, 5,* 2–3.

Glanz, J. (1995). Exploring supervision history: An Invitation and agenda. *Journal of Curriculum and Supervision, 10,* 95–113.

Glickman, C. D. (Ed.). (1992). *Supervision in transition.* Alexandria, VA: Association for Supervision and Curriculum Development.

Peltier, G. L. (1967). Teacher participation in curriculum revision: An historical case study. *History of Education Quarterly, 8,* 209–219.

Saylor, G. (1966). Foreword. In L. M. Berman & M. L. Usery (Eds.), *Personalized supervision: Sources and insights.* Washington, DC: Association for Supervision and Curriculum Development.

Shores, J. H. (1967). Foreword. In R. P. Wahle (Ed.), *Toward professional maturity of supervisors and curriculum workers.* Washington, D C: Association for Supervision and Curriculum Development.

Short, E. C. (1995). A review of studies in the first 10 volumes of the *Journal of Curriculum and Supervision. Journal of Curriculum and Supervision, 11,* 87–105.

Can We Put back the *S* in ASCD? *No*

Robert J. Krajewski

Where did it go? What happened to the *S* in ASCD (Association for Supervision and Curriculum Development)? Although an integral part of the title, supervision is the area most frequently overlooked and forgotten. Curriculum, on the other hand, is openly discussed, changed, understood, and used. Can the *S* be given in its rightful importance in the title "ASCD?" A more accurate question might be "Was *S* ever an equal in there?" I believe the answer is no, and I believe my rationale is, unfortunately, accurate and compelling.

When Muriel Crosby (1969) surveyed the 1960–68 issues of ASCD's *Educational Leadership*, she discovered that less than seven articles per year were supervision related. Her findings were not dissimilar from those of (then) ASCD editor Bob Leeper (1970), who noted that between 1943 and 1970 supervision and professionalization themes in ASCD booklets and yearbooks and in monthly and yearly themes of *Educational Leadership* were respectively only 30 percent and 41 percent of the total. Also, Comfort, Bowen, and Gansneder (1974) reported that in the 1971–73 issues of *Harvard Educational Review,* and the 1972–73 issues of *Educational Leadership, NASSP Bulletin, Phi Delta Kappan*, and *Today's Education,* curriculum articles outnumbered supervision articles by a 7-to-1 ratio.

Since one of my areas of expertise is supervision, such findings and frustrations led me to write an article for *Educational Leadership* titled "Putting the *S* Back in ASCD" (Krajewski, 1976). Frankly, because of the article's controversial and sensitive nature, I was surprised that Bob Leeper would print it, but he did. In the article I presented a quantitative examination of the 1971–75 annual conference themes and sessions, the analyses of which were that (1) supervision was not mentioned in the themes, and (2) the average ratio for sessions was at least 4 to 1 favoring curriculum over supervision. Among my recommendations and conclusions were:

- There is imminent danger if this trend continues.
- Teachers need instructional support to implement new curricular changes.
- ASCD should offer services that allow supervisory leadership to surface.
- ASCD should provide concomitant development of supervision and curriculum programs.
- Dynamic input from ASCD membership is needed to champion supervision.

Whether there was any cause–effect relationship is not clear, but for several years afterward the emphasis on supervision began to increase in ASCD, both in annual conference offerings and in print.

Most notable print offerings were ASCD's 1980 *Clinical Supervision: A State of the Art Review*, and their 1982 yearbook, *Supervision of Teaching*. Other professional literature became available as well. Clinical supervision, for example, was the theme of special issues of the *Journal of Research and Development in Education*, *Contemporary Education*, and a Phi Delta Kappa *Fastback*, all published in the 1970s. Except for the usual complement of supervision texts, however, the emphasis was short-lived. Although no recent studies have been conducted, it would probably be safe to say that supervision lags behind curriculum in ASCD as well as in other educational organizations' areas of emphasis.

Why is that? Why does supervision not enjoy a status similar to that of curriculum? To answer that question, many factors must be considered. I'll address four: definition, history, role/practice, and role training

Definition

Curriculum is based on a philosophical foundation from which we develop (and assess) instructional goals that meet needs of preparing students for life. Curriculum is a concrete entity, generally comprising accepted facts, and usually designed by and taught by teachers. Teachers deal with curriculum every day, all day. They are provided updated texts (prepared by teachers for professional text companies) and continually updated supporting materials (usually prepared for commercial companies by teachers or former teachers), supplies, and assistance from their school district with which to teach the curriculum. Generally, curriculum committees composed mostly of teachers have ownership in the selection of all these materials and thus ownership of the curriculum itself. Teacher training programs include ample foundation in subject matter they intend to teach, and curriculum supervisors and administrators are promoted from teacher ranks. In addition, parents, school board members, and community school supporters all have been to school and have an understanding of curriculum.

Curriculum is dynamic and is continually updated because trends in society demand it. Communication advances now provide instant access to news information throughout the globe. Present-day wars, for example, are brought into our homes via television. Internet and other programs allow students to communicate with people directly on their home computers. In many schools, the media center, computer laboratories, or even computers in the classroom provide students Internet access as well. Curriculum enhancement is amazing. In a geography class or foreign language class, for example, a student can obtain items like an instant printout of current information on a city, area, or country of choice, including pictures. Want to know how to get from one part of London to another by the tube? The Internet is interactive, and when you ask you can receive an instant picture of the subway routes with detailed directions of how to get from A to B. The information supplied is specific as to the color of line you should take, where you must transfer (if applicable), and how long it will take to get there. Press a print button and it is in your hands—in color if you have a color printer.

Supervision is based on an administrative foundation that focuses on improving curriculum delivery. Less concrete than curriculum, supervision focuses on changing teacher behavior to improve students' learning process and products. In contrast to curriculum, teachers are not involved in supervision every day. Historically their supervision involvement has been as recipient (or object/target) rather than as designer. Teacher ownership is practically nonexistent. Supervision is generally designed and implemented by administrators and/or supervisors who might purchase supervision texts (prepared by university professors who at one time probably taught in K–12 schools) but are provided few supervision materials and/or assistance from their school district. Although supervisors and administrators are promoted from teacher ranks, their professional training programs contain little supervision knowledge or skill content and are almost devoid of skill acquisition. In addition, parents, school board members, and community school supporters have little understanding of supervision. Those who do, view it from a business framework. Their training and practice, while including the people–people dimension, generally reflect working with a standard and regulated input to produce a specific product. In schools the input is the individual student, and each student has a unique composition of ability, cognitive and physical skills, emotions, attitude, and so forth. From these unique inputs, teachers are expected to produce—and supervisors and administrators are supposed to hold them accountable for—a somewhat consistent product with specific knowledge and skills.

Let's take a closer look at supervision definitions. Over the years many practitioners and so-called experts have attempted, without success, to arrive at an agreeable, workable, comprehensible, nonthreatening definition. Some define supervision as a component of administration, some as a component of teaching. Some definitions exclude the supervisor from the classroom environment, while others say supervision necessitates face-to-face interaction with teachers. Each supervision proponent or guru has developed his or her own philosophy of supervision, perhaps with a following of believers, but none of the philosophies have gained an overall acceptance and understanding by a majority. So we are inundated with terms such as *supervision, collegial supervision, developmental supervision, clinical supervision, instructional supervision, differentiated supervision, peer supervision, cognitive coaching,* and others—each with its own definition. This confusion is enough to discourage and perhaps frighten even the best teacher! Moreover, many teachers view some of the terms as a thinly disguised evaluation process, something done to them, not with them.

Ideally, because it deals with people and behavior rather than facts, supervision should be dynamic; yet it does not compare to curriculum in terms of its contemporaneousness and breadth. Supervision responds more slowly to trends, and its content is less likely to change. Improvement of instruction is its stable goal, and teachers are the stable instrument of instruction with which supervisors work.

The Council of Professors of Instructional Supervision (COPIS), which has met semi-annually since its inception in the mid-1970s and whose more than 50 members are some of the brightest in the field, frequently engage in discussion regarding defining "supervision." To this day COPIS members are unable to agree on a definition. Moreover, some COPIS members amazingly—or, more appropriately in my estimation, sadly—assume that supervision begins only with interactions with on-the-job teachers. They will not acknowledge that efforts of supervising professors in the field working with student teachers or interns can be classified as supervision.

Maybe we are barking up the wrong tree. Let's forget about definitions and work together for the common good of student success and excellent teaching skills. Supervision must not be an evaluation tool. It should be a joint effort of teacher and supervisor working together to make the curriculum come alive for students, to make learning exciting and beneficial. Maybe the definition will evolve after we get back on the job.

History

In this country's first elementary schools, the curriculum consisted of reading, writing, and religion. The Latin Grammar School, which trained ministers, specialized in ancient languages and literature and generally was aristrocratic. With the advent of the academy in the mid eighteenth century, schools' curriculum broadened from the classics to more modern subjects, stressing practical application of knowledge in sciences and arts. Today's curriculum has evolved from those early efforts to reflect a combination of tradition and current needs. While at times controversial, curriculum deals primarily with knowledge and the skills to apply the knowledge.

Supervision has its roots in religion and administration. In the colonial period inspection by community selectmen and clergy ensured that no teachers were hired who were unsound in faith or scandalous in their lives. Supervision's first official appearance was in 1709, when in Boston layman committees inspected and approved teachers, courses of study, and classroom techniques. Three fundamental approaches prevailed: authority and autocratic rule, emphasis on inspection/weeding out of weak teachers, and conformity to standards prescribed by the committees. From that period through the Civil War, inspection of school and classroom for the sake of control emphasized rules and standards. Until the first quarter of the twentieth century, state and local superintendents visited classes; then principals and special supervisors assumed that responsibility. Today supervision remains the responsibility of principals and supervisors, supplemented with some examples of teacher peer coaching.

In 1929 the National Conference on Educational Method, organized in 1921 for those interested in improving conditions in learning, changed its name to the Department of Supervisors and Directors of Instruction (DSDI). The department (an affiliate of NEA) defined supervision as teacher growth in wholesome emotional and mental development, socioeconomic understanding and adjustment, and professional competence. Its yearbooks were published from 1928 to 1943. The Society for Curriculum Study (SCS), organized in 1929, emphasized progressive curriculum revision via developing courses of study. When DSDI and SCS merged in 1943, DSDI had 1996 members and SCS had 713. In 1946 they officially chose Association for Supervision and Curriculum Development as their name. In its 1974 information booklet ASCD defined itself as a professional education organization, composed of leading educators and interested citizens, that promotes the overall improvement of education through the development of programs and practices that facilitate the wholesome growth of all individuals involved in educational endeavors. It is the one professional association interested in a balanced curriculum for all children and youth.

Although supervision has evolved from controlling behavior to changing it, it cannot escape controversy because history continues to associate it primarily with the human condition. Therefore, by its nature, purpose, and frequency of use, it is much more difficult to deal with than curriculum. Furthermore, it is less subject to change than curriculum. Probably for those several reasons, through definition and practice ASCD has always afforded curriculum more emphasis than it has supervision.

Role/Practice

The role of a curriculum director/supervisor can be varied, depending on a district's size and its organizational complexity. Influences on the curriculum include school personnel, school district administration and board, parent and lay expectations, state regulations and federal expectations, and societal idiosyncrasies. Curriculum development and coordination processes consist of "what," "who," and "how." The what components include budget, school philosophy/mission/goals, objectives/content sequence and revision requirement decisions, text selection, and the like. The who components should include faculty, students, principal, parents, community members, business/Chamber of Commerce, central office personnel, school board, and articulated curriculum committees. The how is the essence of the curriculum director's role. It is the manner or process of configuring the interaction of the what and who—that is, who participates in what capacity and in what areas of curriculum development and coordination. While the how can become cumbersome and stressful for the curriculum director/supervisor, it is generally less so than for the supervisor. To a degree, the trends issue presented earlier provides the curriculum director more concrete information with which to work, and generally more resources, too. What school, for example, does not have computers? Some states already have mandated that each school will have Internet access, and many schools already have it. Our President says that by 2000, every school will have access to the Internet.

We saw earlier that the supervisor role has evolved from controlling teacher behavior to changing and supporting behavior to improve instruction. Yet in too many districts today the supervisor role remains varied and ambiguous, and too inclusive. The supervisor's title may be listed as advisor, coordinator, department head, instructional specialist, curriculum coordinator, or the like. Both title and responsibilities may be confusing to the supervisor and the teachers he or she supervises. Most supervisor roles have administrative, curricular, and instructional components that are not mutually exclusive. Few supervisors work solely on instructional improvement; those that do usually have responsibility for too many teachers and thus become frustrated because they feel the quality of their improvement efforts suffers. Too, most supervisors are in staff rather than line positions, as principals are. Some teachers view supervisors as visitors to the school rather than as colleagues.

In many schools the supervisor is the principal or assistant principal(s). While the literature, research, principal professional associations, and accreditation agencies all suggest that principals spend up to half their time working on instructional improvement, reality and research say that that seldom occurs and, furthermore, probably won't occur.

Another major factor, unfortunately, is that the practice of supervision has become synonymous with the word *evaluation*. Confusion crops up among supervisors, principals, supervisees, and those who train supervisors and principals, which tends quickly to cloud the real issues and reasons for supervision. The evaluation cloud can cause intimidation, caution, and uncertainty between supervisor and supervisee (see Issue 5). This does not promote successful supervisory practices.

Role Training

In their training programs, prospective teachers generally receive appropriate and adequate subject matter and curriculum knowledge. University training and degree programs designed for curriculum directors also provide a solid foundation of curriculum content and processes to prepare one for the role. Content, for example, might include curriculum theory, trends/issues, curriculum development/

design, and curriculum evaluation. Process might include curriculum assessment skills, generic planning skills, and organizational/leadership skills. For most curriculum directors role training continues on the job. Arriving daily are new curriculum materials, visual assistance packages, communication products, and computer equipment. Decisions regarding curriculum update have much input from both within and outside the school. Accompanying these pressures is some sort of resource increase, albeit many might consider the increase as never enough.

In an ideal training program for supervisors, the content would include courses in foundational supervision, instructional analysis, curriculum trends, and leadership and organizational skills. There are few institutions, however, that offer pure training and/or degree programs in supervision. Instead, the programs provide a smattering of classes that often don't incorporate successful approaches to supervision that help strengthen and improve teaching techniques through teamwork efforts. Seldom, for example, are courses in analysis of instruction offered. Micro-teaching, if offered, is usually placed in teacher training programs and almost never in supervision training programs. Also, in many cases supervision training is subsumed under principal or superintendent training programs, which face continual scrutiny and directives from state, professional, and federal accreditation agencies. Local, state, and federal political pressures, moreover, are becoming major determiners of such programs as schools continue to face legal considerations and actions from every direction. As a result, there is no training consistency and no longevity in training; whatever preparation supervisors receive comes across as a simple Band-Aid approach. Thus, training at the university level in the areas of supervision does not address necessary and sufficient skills for instructional improvement, especially in analysis of instruction. The training problem lingers, and it continues to interfere with quality supervisory techniques.

Conclusion

Why has this happened? Why have such factors as definition, history, role/practice, and role training relegated supervision to less importance than curriculum in ASCD? Is ASCD aware of this condition? The research presented in this article suggests yes. Does ASCD view this condition as a problem? Perhaps, but the history of the organization from its inception in 1943 clearly indicates that curriculum has always received more attention than supervision. Can ASCD address the problem? I believe it can. Again, history shows that it can if enough members ask it to do so. Will ASCD address the problem? Probably not, because the organization has steadily grown under the present emphasis of curriculum over supervision. ASCD is a successful professional education organization comprising teachers, parents, principals, supervisors, curriculum directors, board members, and some college professors. It is now a very large global organization with affiliates in every state and some countries abroad. These affiliates afford some attention to supervision, but the demands of curriculum, an ever-changing area of prime emphasis, occupy most of their attention. And curriculum emphasis provides ASCD with needed revenue via the various print and visual media members purchase. Although many supervision proponents may not approve, the slogan "If it ain't broke, don't fix it" may be the deciding factor.

In summation, I believe that for the reasons presented herein, the *S* in ASCD will never hold the significance that curriculum does: Curriculum is better defined and is dynamic and ever-changing, while supervision is primarily a process dealing with changing human performance. Further, ASCD history and success patterns suggest that curriculum will continue to receive primary emphasis within the organization, for schools need continual assistance to help them change the curriculum. Also, curricular roles are better defined than those in supervision and training programs because supervisors do not provide trainees with necessary and sufficient skills to effect instructional improvement. In addition, supervision is threatening because of its kinship with evaluation, and it is in many cases performed by principals.

Nevertheless, I strongly believe that in the long run, if supervision is not an integral part of ASCD, in reality neither can curriculum be. Without good supervision techniques, there is not the proper base for teachers to implement the curriculum processes. In retrospect, the recommendations I made two decades ago are as valid today as they were then. I would like to see them implemented in ASCD. Our schools would benefit substantially.

Endnotes

1. Comfort, R. E., Bowen, L. S., & Gansneder, B. M. (1974). Who's writing about what in education's major journals? *Educational Leadership, 31*(8), 666.
2. Crosby, M. (1969, March). *The new supervisor: Caring, coping, becoming.* Paper presented at the annual meeting of the Association for Supervision and Curriculum Development, Washington, DC.
3. Krajewski, R. J. (1976). Putting the "S" back in ASCD. *Educational Leadership, 33*(5). 373–376.
4. Leeper, R. R. (1970). To use an option. *Educational Leadership, 28*(1), 4.

References

Comfort, R. E., Bowen, L. S., & Gansneder, B. M. (1974). Who's writing about what in education's major journals? *Educational Leadership, 31*(8), 666.

Crosby, M. (1969, March). *The new supervisor: Caring, coping, becoming.* Paper presented at the annual meeting of the Association for Supervision and Curriculum Development, Washington, DC.

Krajewski, R. J. (1976). Putting the "S" back in ASCD. *Educational Leadership, 33*(5), 373–376.

Leeper, R. R. (1970). To use an option. *Educational Leadership, 28*(1), 4.

Postnote

Can We Put back the *S* in ASCD?

The Association for Supervision and Curriculum Development has been in the forefront of educational discourse for over fifty years. Although goals and belief systems have changed over the years, ASCD has always tried to provide a forum for the consideration of significant educational concerns, including confrontation of controversial issues. Notwithstanding ASCD's commitment to broad social concerns and specific curricular activities, some observers maintain that the interests and needs of those concerned with supervision have been neglected. They argue that the field of supervision needs an organization that will actively promote discourse about it.

Review Questions for

The Yes Response:

1. If Drs. Smith and Thomson had a chance to respond to Dr. Krajewski's arguments, how do you think they would counter his claims? What would Krajewski say about their arguments favoring ASCD?
2. According to the authors, what role do the Instructional Supervision Network and the *Journal of Curriculum and Supervision* play in promoting the *S* in ASCD?
3. Why is the "predictable *S*" considered such a problem for the theory and practice of supervision? Is supervision in your school "predictable" or "dynamic?" Explain.
4. Compare your vision for supervision with the author's vision.
5. What would happen if the *S* were taken out of ASCD?
6. Summarize in your own words Smith and Thomson's reasons for supporting ASCD.

The No Response:

1. Why does Professor Krajewski declare that the *S* never had an equal place in ASCD?
2. React to the evidence the author provides to demonstrate that the *S* in ASCD has been shortchanged.
3. Explain how each factor that Krajewski presents illustrates why supervision does "not enjoy a status similar to that of curriculum."
4. How do you react to the author's definition of supervision?
5. How has supervision as evaluation affected you as a teacher?
6. What specific recommendations would Krajewski make to ASCD for reinvigorating the *S?*

For Further Research

1. Research the origins of ASCD. What factors contributed to the merger between the supervisory group (the Department of Supervisors and Directors of Instruction) and the curriculum group (the Society for Curriculum Study)? Present a historical overview, including primary and secondary sources. You might want to consult Van Til (1986).

2. ASCD has recently set forth a strategic plan that establishes six goals to be realized by the year 2001. What is ASCD's strategic plan and to what extent do the goals match your own school district's objectives? How do these ASCD goals relate to Goals 2000? Which goals, in your opinion, have the greatest chance of being fulfilled? the least chance? Why?

3. COPIS has long lamented the lack of attention to the *S* in ASCD. Examine the origins of COPIS and examine the extent to which this organization has helped bolster supervision as a field and professional practice. Anderson (1987) has written a short history of COPIS. From reading Anderson's work, can you discern some dissatisfaction some COPIS members might have had with ASCD? Contact a COPIS member (almost any author of this textbook) and find out how you, as a graduate student, might become involved in the organization.

4. ASCD is not the only organization that provides a forum for practitioners and professors of supervision. What other organizations attend to concerns of those who supervise instruction? How do their goals differ from ASCD's?

5. Write a letter to the ASCD executive director attempting to convince him to reinstate the *S* in ASCD? How might he respond?

6. Check ASCD on the Internet and determine whether there is more discussion of curriculum or of supervision. Explore ASCD on the World Wide Web.

7. Invite an ASCD official perhaps from your state affliate to discuss the benefits of ASCD membership.

8. Do a content anaysis of Leeper (1969) and Bruce and Grimsley (1987). Do a content analysis of *Educational Leadership*, ASCD's most popular journal, since 1987. What kinds of articles have been published about supervision? How has the literature changed over the years? Has ASCD attended to the *S*?

9. What other evidence can you cull that indicates that curriculum has indeed dominated discourse in ASCD? See, for example, Short (1995).

10. Conduct a search of the following references and determine the number of citations for "supervision," "curriculum," and "administration:" *ERIC, Education Index,* and *RIE.* Discuss your findings.

11. Read Oliva (in press) for his perspective of the relationship between supervision and curriculum. What might Oliva say about the issue under discussion in this chapter?
12. The two major publications sponsored and published by ASCD are *Educational Leadership* and The *Journal of Curriculum and Supervision,* which began publishing in 1985. Describe the nature and goals of each journal. How have the journals changed over the years? How much attention is paid to supervision compared to curriculum? Who are the prominent authorities in the supervision field and how have their ideas shaped discourse in the field? Do both publications serve the interests of both curriculum and supervision? Explain. What other journals publish articles about supervision?

References

Anderson, R. H. (1987). *COPIS: A brief history.* Unpublished manuscript. (Write to the editors for a copy.)

Bruce, R. E., & Grimsley, E. E. (1987). *Readings in educational supervision.* Alexandria, VA: Association for Supervision and Curriculum Development.

Leeper, R. R. (Ed.). (1969). *Supervision: Emerging profession.* Washington, DC: Association for Supervision and Curriculum Development.

Oliva, P. F. (in press). Supervision and curriculum development. In G. R. Firth & E. Pajak (Eds.), *Handbook of research on school supervision.* New York: Macmillan.

Short, E. C. (1995). A review of studies in the first 10 volumes of the *Journal of Curriculum and Supervision. Journal of Curriculum and Supervision, 11,* 87–105.

Van Til, W. (Ed.). (1986). *ASCD in retrospect.* Washington, DC: Association for Supervision and Curriculum Development.

Issue 3

Do Teachers Benefit from Supervision?

✦ ✦ ✦ ✦

YES—Lee Goldsberry, University of Southern Maine
NO—Duncan Waite, University of Georgia

✦ ✦ ✦

Issue Summary

YES: Professor of education Lee Goldsberry strongly disagrees with Professor Waite's assertion that supervision, designed to help teachers improve teaching, "should be deliberately disconnected from the formal evaluation" of teaching. Dr. Goldsberry asserts that formal personnel evaluation as part of a supervisory program is not only beneficial but essential to ensure accountability and the further development of teacher competence. Hence, teachers do benefit from supervision qua evaluation.

NO: Duncan Waite, author of *Rethinking Instructional Supervision* (1995), cannot support supervisory practice that is in any way aligned with evaluation. Teachers do not benefit, argues Dr. Waite, when evaluation, no matter how well conducted, is part of a supervisory program. In his words, "Evaluation done under the guise of supervision is then only slightly better than a poke in the eye with a sharp stick!"

Guiding Questions

1. What is the fundamental difference between the arguments presented by both authors?
2. How does each author define supervision?
3. How does each author view the practice of supervision?
4. According to both authors, what does effective supervisory practice look like?
5. According to Professor Waite, what significance is there to the premise that supervisors benefit from supervision themselves?
6. Have you benefited from supervision qua evaluation?

Do Teachers Benefit from Supervision? *Yes*

Lee Goldsberry

Remember the learners. When we consider benefits of any aspect of schooling, we should remember the learners served by our school. Do learners benefit from skilled teaching? Certainly. Because skilled teaching considers both the learning needs and the readiness of the individual learner, each youngster may reap different benefits, but when one starts with an assumption of good teaching practice, it seems silly to argue that learners do not benefit at all. Of course, this implies not that each teaching episode is helpful to each learner, but simply that, overall, learners benefit from good teaching. So, too, does it seem silly to suggest that teachers, as learners themselves, do not benefit from supervision when it is well done. Good supervision, like any form of good teaching, suggests clarity of purpose, skilled communication, and techniques matched to the sensitivities and concerns of the individual learner. When we disregard all the foolish and sometimes harmful things that have gone on in the name of supervision in schools and consider only the skilled practice of supervision by caring educators, supervision provides the teacher with information regarding personal teaching practices and with a knowledgeable and skilled colleague with whom to discuss teaching strategies and their effects for learners (both individual and collectively). What caring teacher would not find such supervision helpful?

Surely, Professor Waite, who both writes the opposing perspective on this issue and teaches supervision, will not argue that he believes that teachers do not benefit from supervision when it is done properly. He may point out that supervision often is *not done well.* Sadly, this is true. He and I would surely agree that bad supervision, like bad teaching, has no place in schools. No controversy there. He may also point out that we do not have an adequate research base to prove that teachers everywhere benefit from supervision. Again, this is true. Although there is ample evidence to suggest that *some teachers* have indeed benefitted from supervision,[1] there is no evidence that *good supervision* is widely practiced. So, again, we agree that teachers have benefitted from supervision, but there is no evidence that such benefits are widespread. Where is the controversy here?

The only issue regarding teachers' benefits from supervision on which I know Professor Waite's view is opposed to mine concerns the coupling of supervision with formal personnel evaluation in schools. Professor Waite has been known to assert that the supervision designed to help teachers improve their teaching should be deliberately disconnected from the formal evaluation of that teaching. I strongly disagree. Why do I think formal personnel evaluation must be a part of school supervision? The short answer is for accountability. Accountability is a rightful function of all supervision, and the only reason an organization needs to evaluate performance. When done properly, *thorough evaluation of job performance also contributes considerably to refinement of practice.* Needed accountability and deliberate facilitation of meaningful improvement of one's professional understandings and practices combine to justify formal personnel evaluation as a necessary part of school supervision. The straightforward syllogism is simply this:

- A thorough and just evaluation of one's job performance is necessary for adequately assessing the virtues and shortcomings of one's practices.
- Assessing the virtues and shortcomings of one's practices is necessary both for reasoned enhancement of that performance and for assuring others that the performance meets established standards.
- Therefore, a thorough and just evaluation of one's job performance is necessary both for reasoned enhancement of that performance and for assuring others that the performance meets established standards.

This argument seems so clear that it almost seems a waste of the reader's time to elaborate. But, since it is the foundation for all that follows, bear with me while I devote a paragraph to each statement.

The first premise simply observes that before one can reasonably speak of things done well or poorly, a thorough examination of those things is necessary. The commonplace folly of judging performance on the basis on inadequate information may be a typical characteristic of political decision-making in our society, but that does not make it wise or prudent. Note that this statement does not specify *who* is doing this assessment, only that *someone* needs to do it. To refute this premise is to argue that one can justly judge the qualities of one's performance without a process of careful observation and deliberation. That seems the equivalent of judging the qualities of a book by the glossy pictures on its jacket.

The second premise states that judging the quality of one's job performance is necessary both for a reasonable effort at improving that performance and for an accurate appraisal of how that performance matches established goals or criteria. When one wants to improve a clock's performance, it makes a difference if the clock is stopped, losing an hour a day, or gaining two seconds a week. Even if we simply want to decide if a new clock is needed, we must consider the performance against our goals and criteria. Again, the premise does not indicate *who* judges the performance, only that fair appraisal and reasoned improvement are both dependent on a just identification of the virtues and shortcomings of the performance. To refute this premise suggests that one can improve the draft of a book, or weigh its relative merits as literature, without first reasonably identifying where its qualities excel and where they fall short of excellence.

The conclusion is simply that a thorough and just evaluation is prerequisite both for fair judgment about performance and for reasoned improvement of that performance. Before the reader nods off to dreams less obvious, I will move on to more provocative assertions regarding "formal personnel evaluation." To refute this syllogism, I believe one would have to advocate an editor making suggestions or determining the fate of a manuscript without going to the trouble of thoroughly reviewing it.

What's that you say? Did you suggest that some manuscripts are so bad that one can reject them after the first two pages? (I do hope that this is not one of those.) Good point, reader. Some performances are so far from our standards that we can *fairly* determine the blown criteria or misserved goals early in our assessment. Two observations stem from your insightful point. First, we must *identify* the shortcomings that are so apparent in the first two pages to conclude *reasonably* that the manuscript is unacceptable. Second, even when we fairly judge the introduction to be wonderful, we must reserve judgment on the total manuscript until we have read it. In short, we can conclude that the beginning is *so bad* that no matter where it goes from there it will remain unacceptable; but we cannot conclude that the beginning is *so good* that no matter where it goes from there it will remain good literature. One point here, then, is that an evaluation can be thorough enough to identify a single strength or a single weakness without being thorough enough to identify every strength or every weakness. Another point is that some weaknesses can be so severe as to determine inadequate performance regardless of accompanying strengths. Precisely for this reason, no strength can be powerful enough to compensate for potential weaknesses not yet observed. Hence, *assuming competent performance,* any evaluation must be thorough to be useful. (To the supervisor who may suggest that I have been "bird-walking" I must point out that the reader raised the question that brought us here, but I will take responsibility for getting us back to the plan, having highlighted and reinforced the reader's excellent point.)

As you have probably anticipated from the introduction (Thank you for deciding my shortcomings were not so severe as to justify putting the book down.), the importance of meaningful evaluation is *not* the issue here. Although I do not know as I write this the basis for Professor Waite's position that formal personnel evaluation should not be a part of school supervision, I strongly believe that he will agree that some form of careful evaluation of teaching performance is absolutely necessary for reasonable efforts to improve or judge that performance. The foundation of a fair assessment of a learner's performance before trying to determine an individualized learning plan for that learner is well established in both the theory and the practice of teaching. What might be at issue then?

The Issues

Well, there may be a semantic disagreement as to the meaning of "evaluation." What does the word mean to you? What do teachers think when they hear the word? Might some people associate it with a ritualistic annual inspection that is neither helpful nor pleasant? Could it be that the performance of those who do the formal personnel evaluations should be evaluated to determine if their own contributions are helpful? Sure. So, our first possible issue is in the meaning of "evaluation," or, more precisely, "formal personnel evaluation." If it is to be defined by the abuses done in its name, perhaps we need a new name.

A second possible issue involves the question of *who judges*. What does it say to a "professional teacher" when the system has someone else judge her or his performance? Does it really reflect a lack of respect for the teaching professional when a supervisor or principal is expected to inspect daily teaching practice? Teachers are, and must be, decision-makers. Bringing in someone to second guess these decisions can be annoying and disrespectful. Such supervision suggests that teachers are not autonomous, and it treats these professional adults as children. Is this an issue?

The kind of careful evaluation suggested in the introduction to this essay is great on paper, but get real. Who has the time to do this "ivory tower" approach to supervision? Do you know how many teachers are assigned to a school supervisor? Do you know how many other duties are assigned to a school supervisor? Do you know how many meetings, how many discipline problems, how much bureaucratic paperwork, how many telephone calls or e-mail messages, how much scheduling or workshop planning a supervisor has to do? The textbook kind of supervision with its preobservation conferences and its cycles of supervision is just as fanciful in today's schools as a computer for every kid is (see Issue 11). Maybe the real issue is the difference between pie-in-the-sky "professor-think" and the real world.

In summary then, these are the three potential issues that I have identified above: (1) "evaluation" (or "supervision," for that matter) may be the wrong term for what we need; (2) don't do it for them (or to them)—teachers should self-evaluate; and (3) schools do not have the resources in terms of personnel or time to do the kind of thorough evaluation advocated in the introduction. My responses to these are: (1) a nonissue; (2) a "distraction;" and (3) "true, so what?" (Is it getting less obvious?) Perhaps I should elaborate each point a bit—exposing the thorough and fair reasoning behind each (smile).

A Non-Issue

"Tis but thy name that is my enemy . . . . O, be some other name!"[2] Perhaps we should call evaluation "authentic assessment," and supervision "professional collaboration." Would things then be better? We used to call staff development "inservice teacher education" or just "inservice." Has the practice become more helpful by the change of names? I have heard that Ralph Tyler abandoned the term "evaluation" in favor of "assessment" when he became dismayed by the meanings people attached to the term "evaluation." If this hearsay is true, then I admire his preference for maintaining the meaning if not the term. Whatever we call it, the process of evaluation or authentic assessment should be defined by a set of steps that allows one to appraise performance thoroughly and justly. Changing the name seems unlikely to either redress the wrongs or ensure better practice in the future (see Issue 6). But, if you think calling it something else will contribute to better practice, please do so and then authentically assess how the practice is better at serving the goal.

Perhaps a better plan would be to distinguish between "good" evaluation or supervision and poor practice. When an annual visit from a supervisor that produces the same kind of superficial report that the preceding several annual visits produced is called "evaluation," it is the equivalent of saying that a teacher speaking in a monotone to a group of inattentive and bored kids is "teaching." Both terms are maligned by associating them with such negative, if common, stereotypes. Juliet's observations again seem apt: "It is too rash, too unadvis'd, too sudden; Too like the lightning, which doth cease to be ere one can say 'It lightens.'" Simply put, whatever the malpractice in the past may have been, careful and deliberate appraisal of teaching performance is necessary both for reasonable judgments about teaching improvement and for reasonable judgments about personnel decisions.

Just as our evaluations of students' work cannot be perfect, so our best practice of assessing teaching will be flawed. Just as by making our evaluations of students' work known to them and providing them with explanations as to the specific aspects of their work that are successful and those that are not, so we enable them either to adjust the performance or to argue the assessment. So, too, by providing teachers with grounded, honest, and explicit appraisals of their work, we enable them to consider both our conclusions and our reasoning. Do we believe that our young learners are better able to consider thoughtful appraisals of their work than their teachers are?

The more familiar segment of the initial quotation says: "That which we call a rose by any other name would smell as sweet." Whatever the flower or the process is called it will retain elements that make it distinct. In the case of the rose it may be the smell; in the case of just evaluation or assessment it is a disciplined inquiry into the teaching performance and its consequences for the learners being served. What we call it is not an issue of importance as long as its rigor allows for establishing fair connections between teaching practices and their effects, positive and negative, on learners. Perhaps a good purpose can be served by calling this thorough assessment of teaching practice something other than "teacher evaluation." What we call this process is a non-issue in the sense that devoting time and energy to semantic debate is a luxury we cannot afford. Call it what you will, but make it just and real in our schools.

A Distraction

Do you think I am being foolhardy to call the important question of who does the evaluation a distraction? Maybe so, but hear me out. Please reserve judgment until I am better able to explain my perspective and meaning. Does that seem reasonable to you? Good, because that is exactly the point. John Dewey (1938) and, more recently, Lee Shulman (1988) cautioned us about making "either-or's" or dichotomous choices when the sane thing to do is both. For example, would you rather breathe or eat? Well, the sane answer is "Both. I will not choose to do only one of them." Another example is, would you rather self-evaluate your own performance or have someone whose opinion you respect evaluate it? Why choose? Self-evaluation is surely desirable. Is that less true for careful evaluation from a respected colleague? The distraction is not the suggestion that a good teacher will, and should, evaluate her or his own performance; the distraction is the implication that one must choose between self-evaluation and external evaluation. Good self-evaluation seeks and considers external evaluation. Thus, to do self-evaluation thoroughly, one seeks, not avoids, careful and fair evaluation from respected others to get access to a different perspective.

Must this external evaluation come from a "supervisor," from one who is organizationally a superior? Of course not. Good teachers draw—from students, from parents, from colleagues, and from just about every imaginable resource—ideas that pertain to their own self-evaluation. The suggestion that there are sources of valuable feedback other than a supervisor is yet another distraction. The better question for the issue at hand is: *Is there any reason that a supervisor's evaluation should be provided?* Of course. On any occasion when the teacher's competence is in question, the school organization owes both the teacher and the school's constituency the deliberate and careful assessment of that competence. Does this suggest that procedures should vary for a teacher who is known to be outstanding from those used for teachers whose competence is in question? Certainly. But how do we know teachers to be outstanding? Do we simply trust that every person who has attained the license to teach possesses the skills and dispositions to teach well? To do so is the equivalent of trusting every police officer to be beyond corruption; it is often true and surely desirable, but also untrue often enough to make blind trust foolhardy. Strip away the public posturing, and good teachers will candidly admit that some teachers are not good, just as honest cops will acknowledge that some cops are not. Just as a good police force requires a good internal affairs department or a good chief to guard against corruption, so, too, does a school system require officers or a leader to guard against poor teaching. Formal personnel evaluation exists, in part, to assure everyone that abuses done in the name of teaching will be detected and corrected. The question should not focus on whether or not a school system should have formal personnel evaluation as part of its supervisory program, but rather how the formal personnel evaluation can complement rather than undermine the supervisory mission to improve teaching. If Professor Waite will join me in advocating that sound and just evaluation of teaching performance is necessary both for reasoned improvement and for accountability, perhaps we can agree to work together to explore how the disciplined collection of such information and judgment can guide teachers' self-evaluations and better serve the mission to improve the learning environment for students.

To ask how multiple sources of information can contribute to a teacher's self-evaluation is a useful question. To suggest that sources other than an organizational supervisor can be beneficial for improving teaching is helpful, if obvious. To imply that these alternative sources of information can *replace* a supervisor's evaluation in all cases is a distraction. To be precise, we are distracted from cases, however rare, in which the teacher's competence is in question and a fair and informed judgment is required. In these cases we need, and the teacher deserves, a fair process carefully designed to determine if that teacher is well serving students. Whether or not this process is implemented by someone called "supervisor" is not important. What is important both morally and legally is that this process is rigorous enough to be both thorough and impartial. A teacher's unsubstantiated self-evaluation will not serve this purpose. Let's call this deliberate process "formal teacher evaluation." (If you object to the name, please review the previous section and suggest a better one—as long as the process smells as sweet.)

"Formal teacher evaluation," then, is an established organizational process designed to assess teaching performance in a manner rigorous and fair enough to determine the teacher's competence or lack of it. Can this process include other teachers' assessments or elements of portfolio assessment or a teacher's grounded self-evaluation? Certainly. But however the data are collected, at some point they must be judged for their congruence to established standards of teaching performance.[3] This juncture of judging assembled evidence is the crux of formal teacher evaluation. To suggest that it may be annoying or disrespectful to a teacher to ask her or him to submit to (even welcome) the prospect of an impartial and thorough external assessment of her or his teaching practice is itself disrespectful. Teachers are not autonomous; they must work within the mores of the society and within the boundaries of good teaching practice. *Any human being who believes her or his work should not be subject to some impartial assessment of goodness should not be working with young people.* To portray a teacher as a fragile creature who cannot consider and respond to external criticism without being cowed is disrespectful to the teacher.

So What?

Who has the time to do this ivory tower approach to formal teacher evaluation? This is a genuine concern. Often those charged with supervisory responsibilities have too many teachers to supervise, and too many other responsibilities, to devote much time to supervision. The rigor and thoroughness of formal teacher evaluation practices advocated in this chapter require knowledgeable observers as well as time. Who is prepared to do this demanding service? Thus, it is acknowledged that formal teacher evaluation requires well prepared educators who have the time to observe teaching practice more than occasionally. Indeed, to do the kind of thoughtful evaluation advocated here, one needs to do several observations and carefully consider other sources of relevant information (such as student work, appraisals from current and former students, teacher planning materials, and other artifacts that help illuminate student learning and attitudes toward that learning). Who has time for that in today's schools? Perhaps no one.

If the issue is that schools at present do not have adequate resources to do formal teacher evaluation well, then the only pragmatic conclusion may be that formal teacher evaluation should not be a part of supervision. If we stipulate that we cannot do the job properly, it is difficult to argue that we should do it anyway. Nevertheless, I will so argue. I am reminded of a primary grade teacher whom I greatly respect telling me of a class of youngsters that challenged her greatly. It seems that almost half of the children had been categorized as needing some form of special attention. Several were identified as having behavioral problems. Behavior management needs for this particular class consumed more time than any other class she had experienced. Although she had long used individualized learning objectives with learners who needed them, more learners in this particular class required individual attention from her to make progress toward their learning goals. In short, she found herself devoting so much time to management and to individualized work that she simply could not do all the small-group, hands-on activities that had been so successful for her in the past. She felt she hadn't gotten to know the kids who demanded less individual time than others. She felt frustrated that she could not do the job she expected herself to do.

So it often is with formal teacher evaluation. There are so many other important things to do that many times our practices do not match our intent. I guess when we get a class of learners whose needs seem greater than the time available, we have to do the best we can for each child in that class, knowing that some days we will fall short of our goals. So, too, when we observe that the demands of supervision are often too great for our resources, we may have to struggle to do the best we can. The only option is to say that if we cannot do it properly, we will not do it at all. The temptation can be strong to suggest that it is better to do nothing than to do something less than proper. Please resist this temptation. While the children in my friend's class may not have gotten as much as those in previous or subsequent classes, they certainly did get some help, some valuable learnings, and witnessed a caring and talented teacher who worked very hard on their behalf. Doing some good is sometimes the best we can do. So, if we accept the premise that there are inadequate resources to do formal teacher evaluation as well as we would like, then we must accept some concessions and do the job as well as the resources allow. But please hesitate to accept the premise, as well.

Until an organization attempts to develop a meaningful and useful teacher evaluation program, one cannot fairly assess whether the resources can be made available or not. It is often convenient to hold up expensive "straw man" proposals and to assert that they cost too much. Some progressive middle schools have found ways to provide daily common planning time for teams of teachers. This is no small feat. When a school tackles a "what-can-we-do-to-make-what-we-want-happen" problem, the results are often much more successful than when thought is focused on identifying all the reasons that we cannot do the job. Before we consider any school reform too costly, we should carefully identify what it takes to do the job well and then examine how we can create those resources. When it comes to formal teacher evaluation, these steps are too rarely taken.

To be sure, resources in schools are scarce. So what? Does that mean that we should abandon the meaningful and, I believe, necessary work of designing and implementing purposeful programs of teacher evaluation? No. Perhaps it means that we will have to scale down our hopes to a manageable level. Perhaps it means that we will have to engage in a careful and creative planning process at the local level. But it does not suggest that we should abandon our ideals.

The Final Words

Good teachers view anything that helps them better serve their students as beneficial. When it is done ably and supervision helps teachers improve their service to learners, several studies cited earlier (and Professor Waite, himself) report that teachers appreciate the help. I have suggested that formal teacher evaluation, done well, is a necessary and desirable part of supervision. Before anything can be improved, it must first be evaluated to determine its good and bad parts. Such evaluation can be done in many ways, but must be done for the kind of progressive professional development we want for our teachers.

Self-evaluation by teachers is highly desirable, even necessary, for continued professional development. Good and thorough self-evaluation includes seeking the perceptions of other knowledgeable folks. To serve their dual mission of ensuring competent performance and promoting professional renewal, formal teacher evaluation procedures must be deliberately designed to evoke and abet teacher self-evaluation. This is not a silly "either/or" forced choice where we must choose between fostering self-evaluation and providing thorough and just external evaluation. Both must be included in programs of formal teacher evaluation. Why give either one up?

The way we show respect for professional decision-making is *not* by blindly assuming all decisions made by a professional are magically the best ones. When faced with complex decisions of professional practice, the wise practitioner seeks and welcomes other, often discrepant, perspectives. The way one shows respect for a professional decision-maker is by exploring and verifying the basis of the decision in terms of professional knowledge. Good teachers are not threatened by systems of formal teacher evaluation that are thorough and just. They welcome, and sometimes crave, them.

The cynic will say that formal teacher evaluation systems are neither thorough nor just. Often, they are not. Sadly, often our criminal justice system is neither thorough nor just, either. Human systems, like human creatures, have failings. This does not suggest that we can do without them, but rather that we need to be diligent and conscientious in creating and maintaining them. And, yes, those who evaluate performance should be scrupulous about having their own performance evaluated as well. Good teaching and good supervision both require good amounts of introspection and adaptation to changing learners and times. When we seek to deliberately provide systematic help for this process, we seek a system of evaluation.

Another suggestion that is sometimes heard is that we really need *two* teacher evaluation systems—one for development and one for accountability. According to this notion different people should assess teaching practice for the purpose of helping teachers refine than those who assess their performance for personnel decisions. Assuming, just for fun, that schools were provided the resources in terms of talented folks and time to establish such parallel programs, why would the good insights of the personnel evaluator *not* be used to refine practice? Or, more to the point, why would the good insights of the development facilitator not be used for personnel decisions? The folks who argue that the two functions should be separate imply that the answer to both questions is intimidation. The assumption is that teachers will be too fearful of the personnel decision to "open up" to the person doing it. What does this assumption say of the "professionalism" of teachers?

No one advocates for the superficial and inept practices that have often gone on in the name of formal teacher evaluation, just as no one advocates for the oppressive and thought-stifling practices that have sometimes gone on in the name of classroom teaching. Each image is a harmful caricature that has enough basis in truth to be hurtful to those educators who work diligently each day to be helpful to children's learning. We should work as diligently to combat these harmful images by honoring the caring and intellectually disciplined inquiry that also has characterized life in many classrooms and schools. Indeed, it is in the spirit of this honoring of disciplined inquiry with compassion that I ask that formal teacher evaluation be a regular and meaningful part of each school and of each classroom. The disposition to seek and value information that will help us improve ourselves and our contributions to our communities is the ideal cornerstone for our system of education—and for our system of formal teacher evaluation.

Remember the learners, Professor Waite, for it is ultimately their learning ends that are being served. Good teachers care about how learners are served and are also eager learners themselves. Good supervision is a form of good cooperative learning. Evaluation of teaching performance is best done as a model of the careful, collaborative inquiry that benefits all learners by giving them access to the observations and informed judgments of a respected colleague. When this thoughtful inquiry is done well, surely both teachers and the learners they serve will benefit. Don't you agree?

Endnotes

1. Although the generalizability of any study of supervision may be seriously questioned, many studies report teacher benefits from supervision. Among them are Elgarten (1991), Fenton et al. (1989), Grimmett and Crehan (1990), Herbert and Tankersley (1993), Nolan, Hawkes, and Francis (1993), Pavan (1985), and Russell and Spafford (1986).
2. This and following quotations in this segment are from the balcony scene in *Romeo and Juliet*.
3. It is beyond the scope of this modest essay to suggest how such standards should be established. To be sure, the teacher evaluation process will be greatly influenced by the quality of the standards themselves. Standards can be too precise, limiting teaching practice too narrowly; standards can be too broad, limiting nothing. Finding the right balance is a difficult, and probably ongoing, challenge. But it is, and has been, necessary in order to prevent young learners from being abused by inept or cruel folks who somehow manage to become teachers.

References

Dewey, J. (1938) *Experience and education*. New York: Collier.

Elgarten, G. H. (1991). Testing a new supervisory process for improving instruction. *Journal of Curriculum and Supervision, 6*,118–129.

Fenton, R., Stofflet, F., Straugh, T., & DuRant, M. (1989). *The effects of three models of teacher supervision: Cooperative, supervisor controlled and minimal.* Paper presented at the meeting of the American Educational Research Association, San Francisco.

Grimmett, P. P., & Crehan, P. E. (1990). Barry: A case study of teacher reflection in clinical supervision. *Journal of Curriculum and Supervision, 5*, 214–235.

Herbert, J. M., & Tankersley, M. (1993). More and less effective ways to intervene with classroom teachers. *Journal of Curriculum and Supervision, 9*, 24–40.

Nolan, J., Hawkes, B., & Francis, P. (1993). Case studies: Windows onto clinical supervision. *Educational Leadership, 51*(2), 52–56.

Pavan, B. N. (1985). *Clinical supervision: Research in schools utilizing comparative measures.* Paper presented at the meeting of the American Educational Research Association, Chicago.

Russell, T. L., & Spafford, C. (1986). *Teachers as reflective practitioners in peer clinical supervision.* Paper presented at meeting of the American Educational Research Association, San Francisco.

Shulman, L. (1988). The dangers of dichotomous thinking in education. In P. P. Grimmett & G. L. Erickson (Eds.), *Reflection in teacher education* (pp. 31–38). New York: Teachers College Press.

Do Teachers Benefit from Supervision? *No*

Duncan Waite

Supervision has been touted as the preeminent force for instructional improvement, curriculum development, and staff development. Though I sincerely believe this, I tend to blur or trouble the distinctions between these and other supervisory domains (see Waite, 1994). I suggest to my graduate classes in supervision that some programs and processes—action research and organizational development, as examples—serve all these ends and more. In fact, I wouldn't be writing and teaching about supervision if I weren't an advocate.[1] However, my belief in supervision is sometimes a matter of faith: I believe that supervision, done well, is appreciated by teachers, though there is little evidence to support the claim that it is of benefit, at least as we've historically thought of benefits.[2]

Do teachers benefit from supervision? I would *hope* so. But the answer to this question is much more complex than it may seem at first. As I said above, I believe that teachers appreciate supervision when it is done well. But how many teachers ever get to experience such supervision? Very few, I'd guess. Most, unfortunately, are exposed to supervision done poorly, if at all (see Holland, Veal, Clift, & Johnson, 1991; Waite, 1995). And what passes for supervision in many schools and districts is usually just another form of evaluation. In Georgia, where I live and work, the state mandated an evaluation program based upon Hunter's principles of effective teaching (see Waite, 1994 for further explanation).[3] In the minds of many teachers and administrators this evaluation program *is* supervision. Indeed, the most formidable barrier my supervision students face in carrying out their class assignments is the sour taste left in teachers' mouths from having been observed by their principal or other administrator for their annual evaluations.[4]

The first task my students must accomplish is to convince their colleague(s) that their visit is anything *but* what teachers have had done to them in the past. In fact, and here I warn my students, once teachers get wind of what my students are doing in classrooms, they will beat a path to my students doors to volunteer to be observed! Then my students' biggest headache becomes responding to all the requests that come their way, and they're just learning! It could hardly be said that these students are doing supervision well, though certainly their hearts are in the right place and they deserve to be applauded for their efforts.

So far I've really skirted the question, do teachers benefit from supervision, by answe1ring that they do appreciate it, if done well. I would challenge my colleague, Professor Lee Goldsberry, to answer the question, and I hereby place the burden of proof squarely upon his shoulders. The evidence to support the contention that teachers do benefit from supervision is scant and primarily anecdotal.

Goldsberry will suggest that teachers benefit from supervision qua evaluation.[5] I heartily disagree. I admit that they benefit to the degree that if they receive satisfactory evaluations they are permitted to retain their jobs; but that is as much benefit as they can hope to derive from evaluation, done well or poorly.[6] Evaluation done under the guise of supervision is then only slightly better than a poke in the eye with a sharp stick!

Evaluation benefits the organization, not the individual. The organization may need to know which of its employees are performing up to par and which are not. Is the teacher the beneficiary of evaluation? No! The supervisor who performs the task of evaluation is paying homage to the organization, the bureaucracy, and not the teacher (see Perspective 2). Would teachers elect to be evaluated if given a choice? What do you think? As a teacher, I have better ways to use my time than trying to figure out what my evaluator is looking for and then trying to provide it. Her values and the values she champions when she evaluates me are likely not to be my values and may even run counter to the interests of those I serve, the students.

How are we measuring teachers when we evaluate them? Sergiovanni (1992) and Eisner (1991) have reminded us that what is measurable is what gets valued by most organizations. Can teachers be measured, assessed, and evaluated on how much they love children and make them feel that they belong? These questions deeply bother one of my practitioner colleagues:

> Why does the state of Georgia still use the GTOI [the Georgia Teacher Observation Instrument] as a means of teacher evaluation? I do know that the GTOI is based on effective teaching methods and lessons; however, something gets lost in the recording of that data. It eliminates any notion that becoming an effective teacher is a developmental process and gives the impression that you either "have it" or you don't. To receive any evaluation lower than "S" [satisfactory] is tantamount to making an "F" in school, and I think receiving an "S" isn't good enough for me!
>
> In that one observation a year, with no prior notice or collegial planning, the principal walks into the classroom with that clipboard to observe. No matter how well I planned, my knees go weak. I have learned to keep a "canned" lesson on hand to use. After all, it's my one chance to show him my teaching ability. (Margaret S. Wilson, personal communication, February 1, 1995)

And this from an exceptional experienced teacher! Imagine the effect on someone less secure.

States, bureaucracies, and organizations exert their power over individuals especially through surveillance (Giddens, 1990) and sanction. Foucault (1979) wrote of this as the bureaucratic (i.e., state) tendency to discipline and punish. Some design properties of modern institutions were made with these functions in mind.[7] For instance, Foucault wrote of the panopticon, that innovation of prison design that permitted a solitary guard to observe numerous prisoners without being seen.[8] Evaluation, no matter how well intended, no matter how well carried out, does violence to teachers!

At the heart of the issue is how teachers are to be treated—how they are to be thought of and the relationships that ensue from that. Are teachers simply disposable units, automatons? And is that how we would like supervisors to treat them? If a teacher is "broken," are we to throw him or her away and find a replacement? Or do we as supervisors and supervision theorists have a responsibility, a duty, and a philosophy that requires, insists, that we *value* teachers as human beings first and foremost? Do we value the people with whom we work or are we willing to say, "I value you only if you fit the organizational norms. If not, I m willing to discard you, to treat you like rubbish and toss you on the trash heap?" The effective teaching paradigm does not value people and their diversity; it seeks standardization, not fulfillment of human potential (teachers' and students').[9]

Again we are faced with the question of whose knowledge, whose ends, are being served through evaluation. Is it the teacher's? Doubtful. Here is the real crux of the matter: To whom does the supervisor owe her or his first loyalty? To the teacher as an individual? Or to the organization? Another complicating question is how one defines an organization. Does an organization have an identity and a structure apart from, superior to, those who inhabit it? As a dyed-in-the-wool interactionist (see Waite, 1995), I believe that organizations have no life, no spirit and soul, absent those who populate them—who interact and, in so doing, accomplish or achieve an organization.[10] Simply put, organizations are made up of individuals. There is no organization without them. You cannot have a school without teachers, students, administrators, supervisors, secretaries, paraprofessionals, and such.

And so, in answer to my first question above, I believe supervisors owe their first allegiance to teachers and their students, not to some vague entity called the school or the district. However, some will attempt to deceive others into thinking there is a larger entity to which they owe their allegiance. This is usually done for political purposes (e.g., to more easily control populations). Demagogues and ideologues do as much when they attempt to get people to do that which they disdain in service of God and country, for example.

Organizations, especially undemocratic ones, rely upon such deception; they rely on masses of people so duped that they will lay down their lives or set aside their ideals for a "greater" cause.

Similarly, Glickman, Gordon, and Ross-Gordon (1995, p. 41) write of "a cause beyond oneself" in defining supervision:

> Effective schools do not happen by accident: Supervision is the force that shapes the organization into a productive unit.
>
> Clearly, one characteristic of successful schools is that each teacher has "a cause beyond oneself." (p. 42)

Note the language used here. Still solidly lodged in the effective schools mindset, the authors use "force," "shape," and "productive unit," along with "organization," in the same sentence to define supervision. I take exception to these authors' definition and characterization of supervision. This definition—and evaluation is hereby implicated as well—smacks too much of "efficiency."[11]

We all know that given certain conditions, liberties and rights can be sacrificed. Americans, it has been suggested, would surrender certain rights if violence in America could be counteracted, for example. But who is to say that teachers must give up their rights, their ideals, their time-proven pedagogies, to teach effectively or for their school to become an "effective" school?

While I would not advocate a laissez-faire approach to organizational development, I certainly want to trouble the notion that teachers must set aside their cherished, hard-won beliefs simply because the supervisor, administrator, or even the majority of teachers in a building believe one approach is best for children and that one approach must be practiced by all the teachers in that school.[12] This happens in schools when they are guided by the dictatorship of the majority or an autocratic leader with a plan (Fullan, 1992). Am I not a good teacher if I don't practice Hunter's model of "effective" teaching? Am I not a good teacher if I don't practice whole language or whatever current trend happens to have captured the popular teacher imagination? Add evaluation to the mix, and leverage other than rational persuasion is in force. There is danger here. The threat is real and it is felt by millions of teachers daily.

It might be another matter entirely if other teachers evaluated a fellow teacher—if the information were submitted, for example, to a committee of teachers who would then decide whether to retain their colleague or not. Then again, it might not. In this case, for example, in peer supervision (read peer evaluation), aren't the teachers then only acting in place of the administrator *(in loco bureaucratis),* doing his dirty work? Spying on fellow teachers and passing sentence? On what grounds are these teachers passing judgment? Who develops the evaluation instrument and whose ends are served? The teacher's? Again, it is doubtful.

You might ask what we are to do about the teacher who clearly isn't making it. My answer would depend, of course, on whether you have the good of the teacher or the good of the organization in mind. If you are more concerned about the organization, sack the teacher! Sack 'em all! If you have the well-being of the teacher in mind, work with her or him or reorganize the work! Stop blaming the victim. Find something the person can do where his or her skills and abilities can be of use. Find somewhere he or she can go and be appreciated and find fulfillment, and not be a detriment to children. Our efforts and energies should really be directed toward screening applicants (i.e., at the front end) and before—in preservice education, in teacher assignment and placement—and not on elaborate systems of surveillance and dismissal.

Do teachers benefit from supervision? Not if evaluation is part of it! Do teachers benefit from supervision if evaluation is not involved?

As a believer in supervision I am willing to grant the point for argument's sake. Teachers do benefit from supervision. The point I would like to make is that teachers are neither the only nor the primary beneficiaries of it. The question then becomes, who benefits? And my answer is supervisors themselves! Just as peer tutors benefit from tutoring, so too, do supervisors benefit through supervising.

No one would argue with the notion that students of supervision learn it by doing it. Estabrooke (1995), Goldsberry's student, says as much when she writes:

> I felt my knowledge was inadequate for the task [of supervision] . . . now, I realize that the remaining questions [I had] could not have been answered by more reading, but only through learning from supervising itself. (p. 11)

My own students generally concur:

> During the internship I was able to have several opportunities to practice my observation skills. Just like the teacher, I learn best when I am constructing my own knowledge about the specific techniques. Active learning is necessary to my growth. This [supervision] process provided me the opportunity to learn in ways that will strengthen my style. . . . I reminded each teacher that I was practicing my skill. Every time I entered a classroom I was the one taking the risk. (Anne Marie Keskonis, personal communication, June 8, 1995)

So students of supervision learn by doing. Is it such a stretch to suggest that supervisors, too, learn supervision on the job? Do we expect our graduates and those who have not had the benefit of our instruction to be fully prepared upon assuming a supervisory position? Hardly.

As I have suggested elsewhere (Waite, 1994), there is precious little staff development for supervisors. There needs to be much more. Currently, just as was the case with teachers in the not-too-distant past, supervisors are left to their own devices—the sink-or-swim model of staff development—when it comes to their own professional development.

Supervisors, aside from the education *some* get in graduate programs, get most of their education on the job. As you might imagine, there are distinct advantages and disadvantages to this. The advantages are that the learning is immediate, contextually derived, and immediately applicable. The major disadvantages are, the incestuous nature, for lack of a better term, of the knowledge gained and the very real possibility that taken-for-granted beliefs about ways of doing things are reinforced and never questioned. In short, supervisors trained on the job lack exposure to external sources of innovative ideas.

I've also suggested elsewhere (Waite, 1992) that teachers can easily perform the tasks of supervisors if given the opportunity, especially as these opportunities include freedom of movement and connection to the information pipelines (grapevines, networks, and what have you). One advantage supervisors have over teachers is their freedom of movement. With that freedom of movement comes access to all sorts of information, and information is power.

Supervisors observe in classrooms. Out and about, they have the opportunity to observe in hallways, in the front office, and in the backwaters of the school. They may even be permitted to freely leave the school or travel from school to school, which teachers are not permitted to do. Supervisors are privy to incredible amounts of information. Some use this information to further their own ends, parsing it out in a Machiavellian style to influence or even manipulate others. Some may use the information gained for organizational purposes. And some seek to benefit the teachers, collectively and individually, through the information they gain.

Supervisors soon log hundreds, if not thousands, of hours of classroom observation. Most learn quickly what good teaching looks like and pick up ideas from innovative practitioners. If they are well intentioned, they pass this information on. This role is an important one; let it not be underestimated. As my colleague, Bill Wraga, pointed out: "I learned more about teaching when I became a supervisor than I ever knew as a teacher" (personal communication, April 5, 1995).

That supervisors themselves benefit from participating in supervision, and that they recognize the benefits, is reflected in my supervision students' writing:

> One of the unfortunate things that happens when you be-
> come a supervisor is that you are no longer in the classroom,
> teaching and learning new techniques. Sharing these confer-
> ences with teacher[s] helps me to keep abreast [of] new ideas
> and strategies that teachers are using. *It is the best kind of
> learning that any administrator can have* in order to assess and
> improve instruction in their school. It helps for me to talk to
> teachers and pass along what I learn to other teachers who
> may be experiencing similar problems or to match teachers
> to work together. (Ginny Smiley, personal communication,
> July 27, 1995; emphasis added)

As purveyors of novel ideas and best practices, supervisors more than
anyone mitigate one of the most intractable barriers to reform, teacher
isolation (whether self- or system-imposed). Though supervisors can,
if they're so inclined, become the gossip mongers of their school or
system.

Also, status accrues to the person who assumes a supervisory
position. This status has several roots (one being that discussed
above—knowledge or information gained). The halo effect is evident as well in the way certain teachers and others respond to
supervisors (i.e., because some see something in certain individuals
and thus promote them, others begin to see something special about
them, too—whether it is true or not).

Not the least of the benefits supervisors derive from supervision
is that they get out of the trenches! Teaching is difficult and demanding work (not that supervision/administration is easy, just different),
and the teacher-cum-supervisor steps out of that routine. The possibilities for growth in a new position are endless.

Supervisors, if they comport themselves as caring professionals,
have an opportunity to enlist allies, friends, and compatriots. Being
in the middle, supervisors can curry the favor of people above and
below them (if we may speak hierarchically). An excellent teacher in
a backwater school may remain unknown to most of the teachers and
other professionals in the same school, certainly across the district.
Supervisors are seen out and about, and people recognize them. They
have visibility. [13] A critical analysis might claim that supervisors benefit from teachers' labor, that they earn their stripes on the teachers'
backs, so to speak. Such an analysis might go so far as to suggest that
supervisors exploit teachers or at least are incriminated in their ex-
ploitation. After all, isn't one connotation of the term *supervision,* to
oversee, as in *overseer?*

Supervisors, most days, leave work believing they have helped
someone, have been of service, except, of course, on those days when
their time is taken up with teacher evaluation and paperwork. There
is little evidence to the contrary (i.e., that they have harmed teachers
and students), and what little evidence there is can be easily dis-

missed, denied, or attributed to the system (i.e., "I'm just following orders.") or to teachers' efforts or lack of effort. Whether individually, through clinical supervision, or collectively, through staff and instructional development, supervisors can affect teachers. Usually, this leads to increased good feelings toward the supervisor and the supervisor's sense of accomplishment.

Do teachers benefit from supervision? Not in the traditional sense of the term *benefit* (as in the effective schools paradigm). That is, it would be nearly impossible to prove that, as a result of a supervisor's attentions, a teacher was more "effective" when assessed by measures acceptable within the effective schools paradigm. Most of the benefits derived from supervision, and I would admit there are some, are outside that paradigm. This is one reason why, when monies dry up, staff development is the first area to be cut. Staff development, curriculum development, instructional improvement (the more accepted domains of supervision) are ephemeral, elusive areas and are difficult for cost-conscious administrators to comprehend, value, and fund. The other areas within which supervisors work—group development, organizational development, and action research—are much more difficult to justify to those same cost-conscious administrators; yet are nonetheless extremely important. These areas are simply not seen as fundamentally important by those still firmly entrenched within the effective schools paradigm.

I believe that teachers benefit from being able to dialogue with other knowledgeable and caring professionals, be they teachers, supervisors, or an administrator involved in supervision. Is this supervision? I won't get into that here. That said, however, how often and under what circumstances do teachers engage in such meaningful dialogue, especially as concerns teaching and learning? Supervisors, because of their unique role, are afforded the luxury of so engaging teachers. In such circumstances, everybody benefits.

Endnotes

1. Though much of what is written here may be seen as critical, still I maintain a deep and abiding belief in supervision as a process and in supervisors as professionals. I do not wish to paint all supervisors with the same broad (and critical) brush. I would hope that supervisors and others charged with supervision will examine their beliefs and actions in light of what is written here, and judge themselves accordingly—reflecting upon and perhaps changing their practice. Still, if the shoe fits . . .

2. Here I am thinking in such vacuous terms as teacher effectiveness. For example, does supervision improve a teacher's effectiveness? Or is that a now-defunct and discredited mindset? Beyond that, does supervision have an impact on student learning? As important as these questions are, space considerations and my charge from the editors of this volume preclude me from discussing them at length here.

3. The Georgia Teacher Evaluation Program (GTEP) has only recently been scrapped. In its place, each district must come up with a teacher assessment

plan. Though I am optimistic, I suspect that many district-developed teacher assessment plans and programs will be of little improvement over the state GTEP evaluation.

4. One of my greatest hurdles as a professor of supervision is to wean students from an evaluation mindset when observing teachers.

5. To many of us, evaluation must be divorced from supervision. Unfortunately, precious few administrators are afforded that luxury. Usually, the same person performs both tasks. The question then becomes, can the two processes be separated in the minds of the evaluator and the person being evaluated? This is difficult at best (Acheson & Gall, 1992).

6. Sadly, in this day and age, what with budgetary austerity, downsizing, "reorganization," and the like, even positive evaluations are no guarantee of job security for teachers.

7. Relevant here is Darling-Hammond's (1994) assertion that in the United States the state invests tremendous resources in inservice teacher supervision (i.e., surveillance) precisely because it slights preservice preparation and an investment in teacher professionalism. Perspectives (i.e., paradigms) of professionalism inform these issues.

8. In discussing the panopticon, Giddens (1991, p. 371) notes how "the architectural design of prisons directly influenced the design of other types of organizations. . . . Carceral organizations . . . remain in a minority among modern organizations in general. People either spend only part of the day or week 'on the site' in most organizations or they are 'inmates' continuously for only short periods of time. Being in school or being at work occupies only a proportion of the individual's time. . . . Yet there are evident similarities between carceral and noncarceral organizations, and Foucault is right to point out that the study of the former can help illuminate the latter, as well as vice versa."

  McKinney and Garrison (1994) apply the concept of the panopticon to educational administration: "Unlike earlier times when society merely controlled the body by crude force, the modern world controls the mind. Once we internalize constant surveillance so that we monitor ourselves, we affirm the final horror of self-enslavement" (p. 78). Later, these authors relate how "[as] . . . Foucault tells us, the examination [or evaluation] turns each person into a 'case' within which his individuality may be described, measured, compared with others, and judged. The case also provides a means whereby the individual is to be trained, corrected, classified, normalized, excluded, and so forth" (p. 79).

9. The interested reader may wish to consult Nel Noddings (1984) and George Noblit (1993) on caring, a phenomenon closely akin to how I'm using *value* and *valuing* here. Thanks to Susan Walker for helping clarify this point for me.

10. Having written this, I must confess that I am in the process of rethinking my position, moderating it slightly, or at least reconciling the radical interactionist position with that advocated by Anthony Giddens (1984) and put forward in his text, *The Constitution of Society*. Giddens and others (e.g., Shilling, 1992) advocate a theory Giddens terms "structuration," wherein structures are produced through repeated interactions and thus are somewhat impervious to individuals' attempts to reconstitute those structures, organizations, and such. Still, I am beginning from a radical interactionist stance and am in the process of coming to moderate, however slightly, that position. I am not there yet, as the above indicates.

  Still, a poststructuralist perspective on organizations is more akin to the radical interactionist position I have claimed as my own. For instance, Maxcy (1995) notes that "The architectonic universe we have constructed through the medium of organizational theory is both self-serving and idealized, with the consequence that it forms a type of modernist language game with variables and vectored forces known only to players. The experiences of living human beings are reduced to elliptical semantic structures. . . . Within this [postmodern-poststructuralist] view there is no sanctity of perspective and no mental mirroring of a single and unitary organized world of the school. *The nature of the organization—its chaos and its order—is seen to emerge from transactions between knowers and the known, with knowns shifting and changing relative to human purposes and values*" (emphasis added).

11. Don't teachers have morals and employ moral purposes in teaching and in choosing to become teachers? Don't teachers teach because they believe in certain ideals beyond themselves? Hargreaves (1995, p. 16) notes that "of course, teachers should have moral purposes and talk about their purposes. But common missions that require complete consensus [and/or submission], such as 'educate all children to their full potential,' may become bland and vacuous because they must appease or appeal to so many different interests. At the same time, mission statements can become too fixed to enable sufficient responsiveness to changes in policy mandates, personnel, or student populations. Not that we should dispense with missions and visions altogether, merely that missions will work better if they are temporary and approximate, and do not require complete consensus."

12. We have all been "Hunterized" enough to cringe at that suggestion!

13. This, despite what Pajak (1989) has written about supervisors' "behind-the scenes" tasks and accomplishments. I am not contradicting him here, simply examining another aspect of the supervisory position.

References

Acheson, K. A., & Gall, M. D. (1992). *Techniques in the clinical supervision of teachers: Preservice and inservice applications* (3rd ed.). White Plains, NY: Longman.

Darling-Hammond, L. (1994, November). *The current status of teaching and teacher development in the United States.* Background paper for the National Commission on Teaching and America's Future.

Eisner, E. W. (1991). What really counts in schools? *Educational Leadership, 48*(5), 10–17.

Estabrooke, M. (1995, April). *Purposes into practice: Learning supervision by supervising.* Paper presented at the annual meeting of the American Educational Research Association, San Francisco.

Foucault, M. (1979). *Discipline and punish: The birth of the prison.* New York: Random House.

Fullan, M. (1992). Visions that blind. *Educational Leadership, 49*(5), 19–20.

Giddens, A. (1984). *The constitution of society.* Berkeley: The University of California Press.

Giddens, A. (1990). *The consequences of modernity.* Stanford, CA: Stanford University Press.

Giddens, A. (1991). *Introduction to sociology.* New York: W. W. Norton & Company.

Glickman, C. D., Gordon, S., & Ross-Gordon, J. (1995). *Supervision of instruction: A developmental approach* (3rd ed.). Boston: Allyn & Bacon.

Hargreaves, A. (1995). Renewal in the age of paradox. *Educational Leadership, 52*(7), 14–19.

Holland, P. E., Veal, M. L., Clift, R., & Johnson, M. (1991, April). *A structural analysis of supervision.* Paper presented at the annual meeting of the American Educational Research Association, Chicago.

Maxcy, S. J. (1995). *Democracy, chaos, and the new school order*. Thousand Oaks, CA: Corwin Press.

McKinney, J. R., & Garrison, J. W. (1994). Postmodernism and educational leadership: The new and improved panopticon. In S. J. Maxcy (Ed.), *Postmodern school leadership: Meeting the crisis in educational administration* (pp. 71–83). Westport, CT: Praeger.

Noblit, G. W. (1993). Power and caring. *American Educational Research Journal, 30*, 23–38.

Noddings, N. (1984). *Caring: A feminine approach to ethics and moral education.* Berkeley: University of California Press.

Pajak, E. (1989). *The central office supervisor of curriculum and instruction: Setting the stage for success.* Boston: Allyn & Bacon.

Sergiovanni, T. J. (1992). Why we should seek substitutes for leadership. *Educational Leadership, 49*(5), 41–45.

Shilling, C. (1992). Reconceptualising structure and agency in the sociology of education: Structuration theory and schooling. *British Journal of Sociology of Education, 13*, 69–87.

Waite, D. (1992). Supervision from a situational perspective. *Teaching and Teacher Education, 8*, 319–332.

Waite, D. (1994). Understanding supervision: An exploration of aspiring supervisors' definitions. *Journal of Curriculum and Supervision, 10*, 60–76.

Waite, D. (1995). *Rethinking instructional supervision: Notes on its language and culture.* London: The Falmer Press.

Postnote

Do Teachers Benefit from Supervision?

This lively exchange between Professors Goldsberry and Waite goes to the heart of the nature of supervision and the supervisor's responsibilities. Is supervision evaluation? What does supervision have to do with curriculum development, staff development, and teacher evaluation? What is supervision? How is supervision practiced in your school? Is supervision a voluntary activity, or is it superimposed by fiat? These questions challenge us to reconsider the very purposes of supervision in schools.

Review Questions for

The Yes Response:

1. How does supervision qua evaluation contribute to the "refinement of practice?"
2. What does the word *"evaluation"* mean to you? Do you agree with Goldsberry's definition? Explain.
3. When you have been observed as a teacher, have you felt annoyed and disrespected? Explain.
4. Do you concur with Goldsberry that calling the "assessment of teaching practice" something other than "teacher evaluation" is really a "non-issue?"
5. Do you believe that tenured teachers, for instance, should not be subjected "to some impartial assessment of goodness?" Explain.
6. How do you think Waite would respond to Goldsberry's thesis?

The No Response:

1. From your experience, why don't teachers benefit from "supervision qua evaluation"?
2. How do you react to Waite's assertion that, in effect, evaluation does "violence to teachers"?
3. Waite categorizes himself as a "radical interactionist" in terms of conceiving organizations as lifeless. Yet he wavers in this position. What is your view? Does an organization have an identity and structure apart from the individuals who inhabit it? Explain.
4. Waite maintains that supervisors themselves benefit from evaluation. Does this assertion support or refute his thesis that teachers do not benefit from supervision? Explain.
5. How do you think Goldsberry would respond to Waite's thesis?

For Further Research

1. Anderson (1989) raised thought-provoking questions about the effect of supervision on teacher behavior. Read his article and ascertain the degree to which the field has addressed his questions since the publication of the article. In your opinion, does supervision affect teacher behavior? Explain. Have you been affected by supervisors in positive ways? If so, describe and explain how you, as a supervisor, might influence teachers and instruction in positive ways.

2. The question of whether or not teachers benefit from supervision is an intractable one. Examine the views of the following authors about the benefits of supervision: Blair (1991), Costa and Guditus (1984), Daresh and Playko (1995), Duffy (1984), Levine et al. (1987), and Tanner and Tanner (1987). Summarize, categorize, and react to their views.

3. Consult Nolan (1993). How might supervision "facilitate change in teacher thinking and behavior?"

4. How is Blumberg and Amidon's (1965) early study about non-directive and non-authoritarian supervisory techniques instructive in elucidating this issue? With whom would Blumberg and Amidon agree, Waite or Goldsberry? Explain.

5. Acheson and Gall (1987) maintain that supervision can be effective and can have a positive impact on teacher growth. Explore the reasons and evidence they cite to back up such claims. How does supervision result in improved teaching in the classroom?

6. Interview at least four supervisors and four teachers to ascertain their views and attitudes about the benefits of supervision. How does each respondent define supervision? What specific benefits have they articulated?

7. From your experience, what supervisory activities and strategies seem to positively affect pupil learning?

8. A recent study concluded that "the formal observation process provides some degree of effectiveness in improving [a] school's instructional program." Consult Gordon, Meadows, and Dyal (1995) and explain how the authors in this chapter would react to their findings.

9. Blase and Kirby (1992) indicate that supervisors can influence teachers in a number of positive, meaningful, and powerful ways. Read their study and consider how principals, for example, may influence teachers positively. What evidence, if any, do Blase and Kirby bring to demonstrate effective principals' influence on learning? How would Waite and Goldsberry respond to Blase and Kirby's thesis?

10. Recently, Nevo (1994) posed the question "How can teachers benefit from teacher evaluation?" Describe the ways teachers

benefit from evaluation according to Nevo. How would Waite react to Nevo's thesis? Also consult Withers (1994).

References

Acheson, K. A., & Gall, M. D. (1987). *Techniques in the clinical supervision of teachers* (2nd ed.). New York: Longman.

Anderson, R. H. (1989). Unanswered questions about the effect of supervision on teacher behavior. *Journal of Curriculum and Supervision, 4,* 291–297.

Blair, B. G. (1991). Does "supervise" mean "slanderize"? Planning for effective supervision. *Theory into Practice, 30,* 102–108.

Blase, J., & Kirby, P. C. (1992). *Bringing out the best in teachers: What effective principals do.* Newbury Park: CA: Corwin Press.

Blumberg, A., & Amidon, E. (1965). Teacher perceptions of supervisor-teacher interaction. *Administrator's Notebook, 14,* 1–8.

Costa, A., & Guditus, C. (1984). Do districtwide supervisors make a difference? *Educational Leadership, 41*(5), 84–85.

Daresh, J. C., & Playko, M. A. (1995). *Supervision as a proactive process.* Prospect Heights, IL: Wavelend Press.

Duffy, F. M. (1984). *The case of "open secrets:" Increasing the effectiveness of instructional supervision.* (ERIC report).

Gordon, B. G., Meadows, R. B., & Dyal, A. B. (1995). School principals' perceptions: The use of formal observation of classroom teaching to improve instruction. *Education, 116*(1), 9–15.

Levine, J. et al. (1987). Rural teachers' perceptions of the effectiveness of various supervisory practices. *Research in Rural Education, 4,* 77–82.

Nevo, D. (1994). How can teachers benefit from teacher evaluation? *Journal of Personnel Evaluation in Education, 8,* 109–117.

Nolan, J. (1993). Five conditions that facilitate change in teacher thinking and behavior. *Educational Leadership, 51*(2), 52–56.

Tanner, D., & Tanner, L. N. (1987). *Supervision in education: Problems and practices.* New York: Macmillan.

Withers, G. (1994). Getting value from teacher evaluation. *Journal of Personnel Evaluation in Education, 8,* 185–194.

Issue 4

Is the Estrangement between Curriculum and Supervision Reconcilable?

✦ ✦ ✦ ✦

YES—O. L. Davis, Jr., University of Texas at Austin
NO—Peter P. Grimmett, Simon Fraser University

✦ ✦ ✦

Issue Summary

YES: O. L. Davis, Jr., editor of the *Journal of Curriculum and Supervision*, presents historical evidence that both curriculum and supervision originally had similar purposes, yet underwent significant changes that may have contributed to the "perceived" estrangement. Professor Davis questions the efficacy of any proposal that attempts to differentiate supervision from curriculum development or vice versa. He ends optimistically by viewing recent developments such as "provisions for teacher action research" as unique opportunities for collaboration.

NO: Peter Grimmett, co-editor of *Teacher Development and the Struggle for Authenticity* (1994), maintains that "the estrangement between curriculum and supervision is evident in educational policies, professional role definitions, divisions of labor, and working relationships in schools." His outlook for a reconciliation remains bleak "as long as schools remain bureaucratized organizations . . . "

Guiding Questions

1. How does curriculum discourse influence supervision?
2. How does supervision influence curriculum?
3. In what way(s) is supervision integral to curriculum development?
4. How do supervision and curriculum differ in theory and practice?
5. What are ways in which curriculum theory has helped you in supervising curriculum?
6. How might clarifying the relationship between curriculum and supervision aid principals? professors? the field?

Is the Estrangement between Curriculum and Supervision Reconcilable? *Yes*

O. L. Davis, Jr.

Estrangement takes many forms. It signals alienation and disaffection. It identifies a turning away and the keeping of distance. Estrangement has to do with feelings of people. Ideas and practices can thus be estranged only as individuals who hold ideas and engage in practices are estranged. The asserted estrangement between supervision and curriculum, consequently, likely represents an alienation between some individuals in the supervision and curriculum fields— people who believe that they hold different perceptions about the proper nature of educational practice.

In the present situation, perception certainly reveals a dimension of reality. A number of individuals in both the supervision and curriculum fields appear to understand that the once strong professional bonds with one another have frayed, but have not altogether parted. Estranged, but not separated; estranged with a difference: an implicit desire to return to a more commonly shared sense of educational practice. Can this estrangement be healed?

Yes is an expression of caution, hardly a prediction of a bull market of hope. On the other hand, *yes* reveals optimism in uncertain times. My personal affirmation draws its strength from my considered reflection about the shared and disparate history of supervision and curriculum development and my enlarging sense of the practical.

Management and Method: Foci for Supervision and Curriculum Development

Supervision in American schools grew rapidly in the fertile soil of bureaucratic centralization during the early years of this century (Glanz, 1991). Increasing administrative oversight of schools recognized a prominent *function* of supervision: assurance that teachers offered consistent programs and teaching in school systems. Earlier, a single individual, notably a superintendent, performed this function. However, as systems became larger—city, county, and state—and the superintendency incorporated additional functions, concern for efficiency required that other individuals perform the continuing supervisory function. These newly created supervisors focused their attention on the adequacy of teaching, that is, teachers methods.

This supervisory emphasis, certainly following World War I, recognized two related phenomena. One, most teachers, particularly elementary school teachers, possessed minimal qualifications. Two, the new educational science offered the surety of "method" as a means of standardizing or reducing (that is, controlling) the variations in teaching observable in individual schools or systems. This attention to method reflected concern for general good teaching, "general methods" (e.g., the project method), as well as for "special methods" (e.g., penmanship, primary grades). Supervisors quickly became agents who "checked on" how teachers taught, who "helped" teachers whose methods needed adjustment or correction, and who recommended that teachers be dismissed or continued. Supervisors had much to do; they worked diligently. Subsequently, many supervisors were assigned additional tasks.

Early in this century, most curriculum decisions in local school systems were limited to the establishment of a sequence of studies and the adoption of textbooks. The superintendent or individual school principals made most of these decisions. By World War I, however, a number of city school superintendents recognized the importance of forming committees of teachers and administrators to discuss options and suggest plans for the local curriculum, both throughout the system and for particular courses and grade levels. This curriculum work developed as an additional means of local management or supervision of instruction.

Local school curriculum making became both a growth industry and an emblem of "modern" or "progressive" educational administration by the mid-1930s (e.g., Davis, 1993, 1995). Some kinds of involvement of teachers became a routine practice. Also important, many superintendents assigned the function of curriculum making as a new duty of staff supervisors. In only a few systems (e.g., Denver) was the function of curriculum improvement assigned to specially designated individuals.

Both of these modern functions, supervision and curriculum improvement, were characterized early on by technical considerations, that is, concerns about method. For supervision, checklists and observational procedures entered classrooms with the supervisors. Variations on techniques changed, but supervision continued to be concerned with dimensions of how teachers taught (i.e., their methods). Curriculum improvement, at least that best known through the writings of its major popularizers, required a method or a set of procedures that began with the identification of objectives. In most situations, furthermore, the curriculum "made" was intended to be used uniformly throughout the system; it was a management tool.

Supervision and curriculum making, therefore, were dual functions frequently the responsibility of school supervisors. Both functions stressed management and method. By the mid-1930s, however, and continuing through the early post–World War II era, at least two developments signaled the prospects for substantial changes in the practice of supervision and curriculum improvement.

Democratization, Change, and Teacher Autonomy: Uneven Progress, Detours, and Roadblocks

Attention primarily to management and method in both these school improvement functions emphasized authority and control. Perhaps more important, conventional practice of supervision and curriculum making all too often failed to change either teaching or the nature of the offerings. Even with the methodical use of the new management tools, many teachers simply did not change either their practice or their understandings about their practice.

Significantly, recognition of defects in standard practices of asserted authority and attempted control prompted revisions in ideas and procedures of both supervision and curriculum improvement. The new ideas were based on a more adequate understanding of social change and teacher autonomy as well as the conviction that authoritarian leadership was inconsistent with a democratic society and its schools. Without question, these revisions failed to replace conventional practices and much of their legitimation. On the other hand, they tasted the reality of success in many school systems across the nation and enjoyed rhetorical assent if not actual adoption in practice.

Altered ideas about the processes of curriculum improvement characterized one prominent change. "Curriculum making," both as a rhetorical label and as a system of methods, was reconceptualized as "curriculum development." In this new view, preparation and distribution of a curriculum guide or syllabus were no longer adequate procedures or outcomes. These documents recognizably neither controlled enough nor guided sufficiently. On the other hand, curriculum development was the school function and social process that encouraged through study and deliberation the continual development of teachers ideas about both the substantive content to be taught and improved teaching practices. The function of curriculum development required leadership, but that leadership need not be hierarchical; it often was situational. On the other hand, the function easily could be ill-attended or ignored without adequate personnel (i.e., (an) individual(s) with designated responsibility), administrative support, and resources (e.g., Caswell, 1950; Caswell & Campbell, 1935; Miel, 1946).

In order that curriculum development could be maintained as a visible and continuing local enterprise, many supervisors were designated as "curriculum consultants" or "specialists" with at least implicitly altered roles. These individuals often recognized that teacher participation in curriculum development enterprises many times yielded observable changes not only in what teachers taught but in how they taught. For the most part, they exchanged concern for "evaluation" with concern for "assistance." The functions of supervision and curriculum development in many districts thus became all but indistinct in practice.

Curriculum development in the early post-war years remained largely a system-wide function, although much of its lively reputation deservedly was based on endeavors situated in particular schools. Action research conducted by teachers, individuals, and collaboratives became one popularized basis for the collection and analysis of data upon which conclusions might be transformed into alterations to curriculum and teaching in particular classrooms (e.g., Foshay, 1994).

Subtle changes added fresh dimensions to much of this accepted practice. Certainly by mid-century, most teachers in American schools were better prepared than their predecessors; within a few years, almost all teachers held at least one university degree. Coincidentally, the previously centralized roles of the supervisor or curriculum coordinator eroded. Slowly but consistently, the role of the school principal assumed the functions of supervision and curriculum development. The principal also became recognized as the campus leader of much "staff development," long embedded in both other functions. The fulfillment of these functions in the principalship appears flawed in much practice, but their supportive rhetoric and justification appear to have become institutionalized. In a number of contemporary schools, the functions are performed by campus leadership teams, departmental chairs, and/or groups of teachers. In other schools, leadership encourages and fosters autonomous teacher development. Only a few scattered districts and states presently maintain positions called "supervisor."

The functions of supervision and curriculum development nevertheless persist and commonly are linked closely in practice, even if not explicitly distinguishable. Certainly, roles have changed and, likely, will continue to change. The relationship between authority (or order) and autonomy and democratic participation always produces tension. From practice, new forms of participation and leadership may be expected. Some of these forms will be accepted into routine practice; others will be opposed vigorously, ignored passively, and/or rejected.

Estrangement of Individuals with Ideas: Some Present Problems and Perils

Separation of the functions of supervision and curriculum development seems as wrongheaded now as it ever has been. Particularly deplorable and surely politically unacceptable would be the assignment of these related functions to distinct professional roles. Contemporary public concern favors decreases in expenditures for administrative and nonteaching roles. This sentiment argues forcibly against separation of supervision and curriculum development. Conceptually, moreover, the proposed separation harbors no credible assets. The two functions are related in serious, mindful practice. Needed is nurture of their relationships such that teachers gain increased personal autonomy and responsible accountability, and that their offerings to pupils become more robust and viable.

A particularly unfortunate problem is that some individuals in both the supervision and curriculum development fields presently emphasize differences between these two functions and/or the distinctiveness of one or the other. These individuals are estranged. The larger educational enterprise, in fact, is diverted if not imperiled by the renewed rhetorical claims for special, differentiated, and distinctive (even limited) roles rather than for the understanding, expansion, and relationship of these necessary functions. In large part, most of the individuals concerned are university based and their tempests distract both mindful scholarship and their appropriate relationship with practice. Consequences of this marginalization surely will be as severe as they seem to be unanticipated.

Most university professors who offer courses in supervision do not intend to prepare individuals for supervisory positions in schools. As noted earlier, few such roles exist. Rather, these courses and practica emphasize the *function* of supervision and the purposes and forms taken by that function, in hierarchical organizations and by teachers as individual practitioners or as members of improvement teams. To stress the *role* of supervisor under such circumstances casts supervision itself as moribund. On the other hand, a number of leadership roles to which supervision courses contribute (e.g., superintendent, assistant principal, department chair) can and will exercise real, practical leadership in instructional matters.

The situation seems even more problematic with regard to university professors whose courses have to do with curriculum concerns. Until just past mid-century, curriculum professors regularly worked with school faculties on curriculum matters. They consulted; they conducted studies. They also taught teachers and aspiring school leaders about the social processes and substance of local school curriculum improvement. During the national curriculum project era, these professors were all but bypassed, but many contributed impressively to local efforts to increase teacher understanding and use of the new programs.

During those turbulent times, some university curriculum scholars responded by asserting a new conceptualization. No longer would they function as "workers" within curriculum practice in schools. They claimed a role as theorists about, as well as critics and analysts of, practice. Indeed, some of them deliberately distanced themselves from curriculum practice and began to call themselves "curricularists." Subsequently, many university curriculum courses focused diminished attention on the realities of curriculum practice (e.g., reform and/or improvement). They emphasized instead sociological and philosophic critiques of real or proposed school curriculum decisions. These scholars further asserted legitimacy for their new field of "curriculum studies" as foundational to all educational study and practice. Without question, these individuals understood their *role* as critics and consequently are estranged from practical curriculum workers, some of their own university colleagues, and almost all school practitioners.

A strange reemphasis on an outdated concern for roles, therefore, appears to be a reasonable, long-term threat to continued, fruitful relationships of supervision and curriculum development. Related, if not reconciled in practice, their estrangement appears in the ideas, sentiments, and advocacies of a number of university professors. Such a tired and unseemly situation surely can not long endure. The improvement of curriculum and instruction practice requires focus on practice itself. Attention to practice, on the other hand, is not merely doing anything or something. Certainly, that attention cannot begin or stop with sharp-edged criticism. Concern for improved practice must be thoughtful and deliberative and be set within the domain and community of practice (Reid, 1992).

Beyond Estrangement to Robust Relationship

Curriculum development and supervision as functions of the local school enterprise appear to have received fresh currency. They may be recognized in recent developments in some schools of provisions for teacher action research; for teacher development opportunities through collegial observation, analysis, and discussion; for campus leadership teams; and, as a specific example, for authentic teacher involvement in the relationship of proposed national curriculum standards to local situations. Across the detours of years and the excesses of inflamed rhetoric, the limited number of reports and analyses of these activities reveal a striking similarity to the practices that illuminated earlier conceptions of the robust relationship of supervision and curriculum development in local schools. The pursuit of improved American education could not be served better.

References

Caswell, H. L., & Campbell, D. S. (1935). *Curriculum development* New York: American Book Company.

Caswell, H. L. (1950). *Curriculum development in the public schools.* New York: Teachers College Press.

Davis, O. L., Jr. (1993, April). *Prelude to professional identity and organization: American public school curriculum workers and their annual meetings, 1927–1929.* Proceedings of the Annual Meeting of the Society for the Study of Curriculum History, College Station, TX: The Society (n.d.), 29–36.

Davis, O. L., Jr. (1995, April). *Nationwide cooperation to revise local curricula: American superintendents and their 1920s commission on the curriculum.* Paper presented at the Society for the Study of Curriculum History, San Francisco.

Foshay, A. W. (1994). Action research: An early history in the United States. *Journal of Curriculum and Supervision 9,* 317–325.

Glanz, J. (1991). *Bureaucracy and professionalism: The evolution of public school supervision.* Rutherford, NJ: Fairleigh Dickinson University Press.

Miel, A. (1946). *Changing the curriculum—A social process.* New York: Apple-Century Crofts.

Reid, W. A. (1992). *The pursuit of curriculum: Schooling and the public interest.* Norwood, NJ: Ablex.

Is the Estrangement between Curriculum and Supervision Reconcilable? *No*

Peter. P. Grimmett

From my point of view, the estrangement between curriculum and supervision is evident in educational policies, professional role definitions, divisions of labor, and working relationships in schools, because supervision has become too closely associated with administration.[1] Supervisors are typically prepared by studying administrative behavior rather than curriculum.

The Study of Administrative Behavior

When supervisors study administrative behavior, they learn that the function of administration is to translate policy into the organizational conditions necessary to enable teaching to proceed. These organizational conditions range from resources that are financial, technical, material, and human to settings in which people work and cultures are created. Resources are secured and managed; settings are expressions of experiences and aspirations. Within these settings, administrators have more formal authority than teachers in that they have greater spans of control, greater access to resources, and more opportunities to exercise power over others. Administrators are expected to exercise their authority to use or create organizational conditions to enable teaching to proceed. This is the justification for their organizational authority.

With this administrative task (of translating policy to enable teaching to proceed), however, comes the expectation that teaching is an expression of that policy. Therefore, implicit within the professional task of policy translation is the administrator's responsibility to evaluate the teaching, and, if need be, to enable correction—that is, to supervise. A vast body of literature has been amassed to explain the nature of the professional practice of administrators and the complex, broad character of the conditions in which administrators work, and, in particular, of the nature of the exercise of authority in the form of supervision. Representative of this body of research literature is the *Handbook of Research on Educational Administration* (1988). The major ideas contained in this volume are captured by titles and phrases such as *leadership* and *leader behavior, power* and *influence, bureaucracy, worker motivation, job satisfaction, organizational climate, decision-making, school effects, resource allocation, evaluation, collective bargaining, educational law, policy analysis,* and *policy management.* Concepts such as these constitute the quintessential features of textbooks used as teaching tools in preparation programs for administrators. One such textbook is Hoy and Miskel's (1987) *Educational Administration: Theory, Research, and Practice*. Conspicuously absent in this textbook, which is typical of others used in administrator preparation, is any reference to curriculum. In the *Handbook of Research on Educational Administration*, only in 5 of 747 pages are issues of curriculum addressed.

Administrative theory thus fails to grasp the nature of the supervisory relationship between administrators and teachers. The function of the former is to provide the necessary conditions for the work of the latter, but administrative theory does not deal with the substance of the actual work of teachers. *Administrators are therefore educated in a theoretical context that neglects the essence of teaching, the curriculum.* Because of this lacuna, administrative theorists have not understood what administrators actually do when providing organizational conditions supportive of teaching. This situation gives rise to an apparent estrangement between what administrator preparation programs advocate and what actually occurs in schools. *The estrangement is between the epistemology of educational administration and the real world of the teachers' curriculum.*

The Study of Curriculum

The field of curriculum studies is the study of the nature of the curriculum: how it is conceived from educational policy and from text;[2] how it is designed and implemented;[3] how it is evaluated; how teachers work collectively and individually to change their curriculum; how teachers work with children, adolescents, and young adults; how teachers work with parents, publishers, and others to negotiate learning. It is the task of curriculum theorists to understand and attempt to explain the curriculum, which is the essence of the teaching enterprise.

Over a century ago, a publicly funded school system was established for students to learn a curriculum of value. Because of society's evolving expectations, first of mass educational opportunity, then of equal educational opportunity for all, and then the current emphasis on relevant and quality opportunity for all, the school system has developed into an increasingly complex organizational structure requiring extensive and comprehensive administration. The complexity of school organization notwithstanding, the focus of the enterprise and the primary factor in determining the degrees of equality, relevance, and quality of the educational opportunities afforded our young people is the curriculum. *Therefore, if educational administrators are to translate school policies to enable teachers to do their work and to supervise them in the performance of their work, then they must have an understanding of what teachers do—they must understand the nature of the curriculum.* This would require them to study curriculum theory, in which all of this is addressed and examined. But, in my view, they do not.

The World of Practice

The estrangement between curriculum and educational administration in administrator preparation programs invidiously socializes supervisors to create a further estrangement in schools. Administrators tend to focus on the organizational conditions with which they are comfortable. They attend, for example, to the orderly and efficient procurement and distribution of textual materials, the appointment of teachers, and the setting of budgets. They focus on the character and interdependence of the organizational conditions but not on how those conditions affect the nature of the curriculum. They respond to parents' lobbies, for example, by inviting the latter to shape schooling policy, but they do not determine how such lobbies affect the ways in which teachers construct the curriculum.

From their perspective, teachers do not expect administrators to act any differently, and they become annoyed or puzzled if, under the rubric of instructional supervision, administrators monitor their curriculum too directly. As professionals, teachers are eager to protect their curricular niches and, as Raelin (1986) puts it, effectively dig in, become entrenched, and protect their curriculum and their autonomy when administrators come too close. Such actions by teachers invidiously reinforce the beliefs and practices of administrators who are living the estrangement. Supervision thus ends up focusing its energies on the organizational conditions for teaching and *not on the curriculum enacted in teaching*. This, then, is the breach that fosters the estrangement.

This estrangement is exacerbated by the issue of appropriate standards for the evaluation of teaching. Administrators tend to value criteria that derive from the organizational conditions for teaching rather than those that emerge from the curriculum. Teachers typically expect to be judged by the quality of the cognitive and affective engagement between themselves and their students rather than on their adherence to the structures, rules, and procedures of the school's bureaucracy. For teachers, the source of the evaluation criteria lies in the curriculum. For administrators, the curriculum does not figure easily or neatly as an organizational condition and is therefore frequently dismissed. The dire consequence of this could be a turbulent form of estrangement between administrators and teachers that flares up in the course of supervision, resulting in the kind of tension that Blumberg (1984) has aptly characterized as "a private cold war." In the end, teachers conclude that supervision is perfunctory, fatuous, and irrelevant. Supervisors conclude that their actions do not enable teaching to proceed in better ways than before.

There is a level of estrangement sufficient to produce not only solitudes but also outright enmity between supervisors and teachers. Neither hostility nor war can be tolerated. Neither enables teachers to do their work better. Neither is what administrators want. In the world of supervisory practice, both professional groups want change and improvement, not to mention fullfilling work conditions and the satisfaction of mutual understanding and appreciation. The problem is one of how to reduce the estrangement between curriculum and supervision. One possibility is to make the study of the curriculum a central focus in the preparation of administrators. Another is to abolish supervision altogether and focus instead on teachers helping teachers around matters of curriculum (see Issue 1).

Making Curriculum Studies Central to Administrator Preparation

Making curriculum studies a central focus in administrator preparation programs has an initial attraction and plausibility, but, like clinical supervision (see Issue 11)—a previous attempt to bring curriculum and supervision together—I believe it will not succeed.

Clinical supervision was originally conceived at the Harvard-Newton summer school. The Harvard-Newton summer school constituted a radical attempt at restructuring the integration of curriculum knowledge and teaching practice. This experiment of the late 1950s and early 1960s was created to induct beginning Master's degree students into professional education. The newly admitted elementary interns began their studies by teaching in a Newton elementary school that housed a morning summer program for elementary students. These interns were assigned in groups of four to a supervising master teacher, and each team of five became responsible for one classroom. In the morning, the five teachers took turns teaching the elementary students; in the afternoon, the supervising master teacher conducted a group evaluation of the morning's teaching experience and led a planning session to prepare for teaching the class the following morning. Along with this intensive teaching experience, the interns took courses in curriculum and methodology (Emlaw, Mosher, Sprinthall, & Whiteley, 1963).

This approach was subsequently adopted at the inservice level as a means of fostering teacher development through discussion, observation, and analysis of teaching ". . . in the clinic of the classroom" (Wilhelms in Cogan, 1973, p. ix), hence the nomenclature "clinical." The emphasis was on "colleagueship" (Cogan, 1973, p. 63) between teacher and clinical supervisor, bound together in a "relationship that teaches" (Goldhammer, 1969, p. 365) by the common purpose of enhancing student learning. Certain adaptations evolved at the inservice level. The supervisor is typically not a master teacher but an administrator; the process is usually conducted in dyads rather than in groups; and the concurrent provision of educational content by an external source rarely occurs. Nevertheless, the original proponents of clinical supervision in schools (Cogan, 1973; Goldhammer,

1969; Mosher & Purpel, 1972) were very optimistic that administrators could involve themselves in curriculum matters to produce positive effects on student learning. However, research suggests considerable divergence in how participants view supervision activities. Where teachers relate experiencing high anxiety (McGee & Eaker, 1977; Withall & Wood, 1979) and at best tolerating administrator observations, supervisors themselves hold the contrasting view that their interventions effect improvement in classroom performance (Blumberg, 1984). This finding is hardly surprising, given that the major texts on supervision (e.g., Alfonso, Firth, & Neville, 1975; Cogan, 1973; Glickman, 1990; Goldhammer, Anderson, & Krajewski, 1980; and Sergiovanni & Starratt, 1993) are predicated on the assumption that supervisors can and do make a difference. The early research conducted on supervision (e.g., Coffey, 1967; Reavis, 1977; Skrak, 1973; Zonca, 1972)—most of which was doctoral dissertations—confirmed this premise. Moreover, the voluminous research on school effectiveness (e.g., Brookover, Beady, Flood, Schweizer, & Wisenbaker, 1979; Leithwood & Montgomery, 1982; Purkey & Smith, 1983) tended to suggest that principals typically use supervision as one way of carrying out the instructional leadership role that was found to have such a strong impact on the school's educational program.

Three decades after clinical supervision was first adopted in inservice teacher education, the claim that it can foster teacher development through collegial conditions remains a moot one (see Issue 7). Smyth (1988) argues that clinical supervision has, over the last twenty years or more, essentially lost its collaborative emphasis and been harnessed into a sophisticated mechanism of teacher inspection and surveillance, thereby rendering teachers unable to gain control over their classroom world and work (see Perspective 2). Hargreaves (1994) maintains that supervision (including the clinical approach) is incompatible with healthy collegial relations because it consists of hierarchical relations embedded in bureaucratically driven systems. In his view, clinical supervision amounts to a form of contrived collegiality and rarely, if ever, fosters the conditions associated with interdependent collegiality (see Issue 11). The experiment with a form of supervision that was steeped in curriculum matters failed, then, because administrators, by dint of their preparation and job socialization, were incapable of transforming supervision into a form of inquiry-oriented action research designed to sustain a rich conversation about pedagogical choices in classroom practice. And my contention is that, even if this experiment had been conducted with administrators who had studied curriculum as a central focus in their preparation program, it would still have failed because the orientation of administrators is toward organizational conditions and bureaucracy rather than pedagogy and learning.

Abolishing Supervision

The alternative is to abolish supervision (see Issue 1). Starratt (1992) has argued that supervision should be abolished both as a term and as a practice. The 1992 ASCD Yearbook on supervision (to which, with Olaf Rostad and Blake Ford (1992), I contributed a chapter) essentially suggested that the term "supervision" had outlived its usefulness (see Issue 6). Supervision, with its connotation of hierarchical intervention and imposition, was deemed antithetical to the professional world of "committed, intelligent, resourceful, and dignified people who can discuss, debate, and make informed decisions to reform and sustain meaningful education" (Glickman, 1992, p. 2). Instead, it was regarded as synonymous with instructional leadership and the possibility of "seeing every talented educator (regardless of role) as an instructional leader and supervisor of instruction" (p. 3). With this in place, "the old [hierarchical] order [of supervision] will have crumbled" (p. 3), as is apparently happening in postmodern society.

The research on teacher development (e.g., Fullan & Hargreaves, 1992; Grimmett & Neufeld, 1994; Hargreaves & Fullan, 1991; Lieberman 1995; Little, 1982, 1990) confirms this trend. This body of research suggests that teachers develop more through collegial interaction than through hierarchical intervention. Many studies (e.g., Anderson, Evertson, & Brophy, 1979; Evertson et al., 1982; Good & Grouws, 1979; Sparks, 1983) report that bringing teachers together on their own, in small groups, to study curricular-pedagogical knowledge of teaching has a definite impact on their classroom instructional performance. But to abolish supervision is to have a divorce, not a reconciliation. Consequently, I believe that the uneasy tension that exists between curriculum and supervision (what we are here calling estrangement) will continue as long as schools remain bureaucratized organizations with formally appointed, nonteaching administrators who are given ultimate responsibility for the viability and effectiveness of the educational program.

Endnotes

1. Many of the ideas used in this argument were first generated with my colleague, Dianne Common, when she was Dean of Professional Faculties at Lakehead University. She has since been Head of the Department of Curriculum and Instruction at Pennsylvania State University and is currently Academic Vice-President at the University of Regina. See Common and Grimmett (1992).

2. The idea of text is used in an all encompassing way to include curriculum guidelines, textbooks, instructional aides—those material forms by which the content of the curriculum is circumscribed.

3. Implementation includes all aspects of the instructional dimension (or pedagogy) and the management aspect of teaching.

References

Alfonso, R. J., Firth, G. R., & Neville, R. F. (1975). *Instructional supervision: A behavior system.* Boston: Allyn & Bacon.

Anderson, L., Evertson, C., & Brophy, J. (1979). An experimental study of effective teaching in first-grade reading groups. *Elementary School Journal, 79,* 193–223.

Boyan, N. J. (Ed.). (1988). *Handbook of research on educational administration.* New York: Longman

Blumberg, A. (1984). *Supervisors and teachers: A private cold war* (3rd ed.). Berkeley, CA: McCutchan.

Brookover, W., Beady, C., Flood, P., Schweizer, J., & Wisenbaker, J. (1979). *School social systems and student achievement: Schools can make a difference.* New York: Praeger.

Coffey, W. C. (1967). Change in teachers' verbal classroom behavior resulting from an in-service program in science education. Unpublished doctoral dissertation, University of California at Berkeley. *Dissertation Abstracts International, 1968, 28,* 4506-A.

Cogan, M. (1973). *Clinical supervision.* Boston: Houghton Mifflin.

Common, D. L., & Grimmett, P. P. (1992). Beyond the war of the worlds: A consideration of the estrangement between curriculum and supervision. *Journal of Curriculum and Supervision, 7*(3), 209–225.

Emlaw, R., Mosher, R., Sprinthall, N. A., & Whiteley, J. M. (l963). Teacher effectiveness: A method for prediction and evaluation. *National Elementary Principal, 43*(2), 38–49.

Evertson, C., Emmer, E., Sanford, J., & Clements, B. (1983). Improving classroom management: An experiment in elementary classrooms. *Elementary School Journal, 84,* 173–188.

Fullan, M., & Hargreaves, A. (Eds.). (1992). *Teacher development and educational change.* London: The Falmer Press.

Glickman, C. D. (1990). *Supervision of instruction: A developmental approach* (2nd ed.). Boston: Allyn & Bacon.

Glickman, C. D. (1992). Introduction: Postmodernism and supervision. In C. D. Glickman (Ed.), *Supervision in transition: The 1992 yearbook of the association for Supervision and Curriculum Development* (pp. 1–3). Alexandria, VA: Association for Supervision and Curriculum Development.

Goldhammer, R. (1969). *Clinical supervision: Special methods for the supervision of teachers.* New York: Holt, Rinehart & Winston.

Goldhammer, R., Anderson, R. H., & Krajewski, R. J. (1980). *Clinical supervision: Special methods for the supervision of teachers* (2nd ed.). New York: Holt, Rinehart & Winston.

Good, T. L., & Grouws, D. (1979). The Missouri mathematics effectiveness project: An experimental study in fourth-grade classrooms. *Journal of Educational Psychology, 71,* 355–362.

Grimmett, P. P., & Neufeld, J. (Eds.). (1994). *Teacher development and the struggle for authenticity: Professional growth and restructuring in the context of change.* New York: Teachers College Press.

Grimmett, P. P., Rostad, O., & Ford, B. (1992). The transformation of supervision. In C. D. Glickman (Ed.), *Supervision in transition: The 1992 yearbook of the association for Supervision and Curriculum Development* (pp. 185-202). Alexandria, VA.: Association for Supervision and Curriculum Development.

Hargreaves, A. (1994). *Changing teachers, changing times: Teachers' work and culture in the postmodern age.* London: Cassell.

Hargreaves, A., & Fullan, M. (Eds.) (1991). *Understanding teacher development.* London: Cassell; New York: Teachers College Press.

Hoy, W. K., & Miskel, C. G. (1987). *Educational administration: Theory, research, and practice.* New York: Random House.

Leithwood, K. A., & Montgomery, D. J. (1982). The role of the elementary school principal in program improvement. *Review of Educational Research, 52*(3), 309–339.

Lieberman, A. (1995). *The work of restructuring schools: Building from the ground up.* New York: Teachers College Press.

Little, J. W. (1982). Norms of collegiality and experimentation: Workplace conditions of school success. *American Educational Research Journal, 19,* 325–440.

Little, J. W. (1990). Conditions of professional development in secondary schools. In M. W. McLaughlin, J. E. Talbert, & N. Bascia (Eds.), *The contexts of teaching in secondary schools: Teachers' realities* (pp. 187–223). New York: Teachers College Press.

McGee, J. C., & Eaker, R. (1977). Clinical supervision and teacher anxiety: A collegial approach to the problem. *Contemporary Education, 49,* 24–28.

Mosher, R. L., & Purpel, D. (1972). *Supervision: The reluctant profession.* Boston: Houghton Mifflin.

Purkey, S. C., & Smith, M. S. (1983). Effective schools: A review. *Elementary School Journal, 83*(4), 427–452.

Raelin, J. A. (1986). *The clash of cultures: Managers and professionals.* Boston: Harvard Business School Press.

Reavis, C. (1977). A test of the clinical supervision model. *Journal of Educational Research, 70,* 311–315.

Sergiovanni, T. J., & Starratt, R. J. (1993). *Supervision: A redefinition* (5th ed.). New York: McGraw-Hill.

Skrak, N. D. (1973). The application of immediate secondary reinforcement to classroom teaching observations in clinical supervision. Unpublished doctoral dissertation, University of Pittsburgh. *Dissertation Abstracts International, 34,* 1140A.

Smyth, J. (1988). A "critical" perspective for clinical supervision. *Journal of Curriculum and Supervision, 3*(2), 136–156.

Sparks, G. M. (1983). *Inservice education: Training activities, teacher attitude, and behavior change.* Unpublished doctoral dissertation, Stanford University.

Starratt, R. J. (1992). A modest proposal: Abolish supervision. *Wingspan, 8*(1), 14–19.

Withall, J., & Wood, F. H. (1979). Taking the threat out of classroom observation and feedback. *Journal of Teacher Education, 20*(1), 55–58.

Zonca, P. H. (1972). A case study exploring the effects on an intern teacher of the condition of openness in a clinical supervisory relationship. Unpublished doctoral dissertation, University of Pittsburgh. *Dissertation Abstracts International, 33,* 658A.

Postnote

Is the Estrangement between Curriculum and Supervision Reconcilable?

The estrangement between curriculum and supervision is evident not only in the division of labor, policies, roles, and relationships within schools, but also in our fundamental thinking and theorizing about the two functions. Edmund C. Short, former editor of the *Journal of Curriculum and Supervision*, initially raised this issue by publishing three articles on the topic in 1992. Authors of these articles acknowledged this estrangement between curriculum and supervision and indicated a number of ways this estrangement was evident in practice. Many educators realize the important interrelationships between the two processes and remain hopeful that these two estranged partners can reunite. Yet, given current organizational realities, haphazard efforts at school reform, and continued bifurcation in higher education, professional societies, and certification requirements, many question the feasibility of reconciling differences between curriculum and supervision. Not restoring this partnership may have deleterious consequences for instructional improvement.

Review Questions for

The Yes Response:

1. What evidence does Professor Davis cite to support his contention that the estrangement between the two functions can be reconciled? Is his argument convincing? Why or why not?
2. According to Davis, both functions stressed "management and method" in their early development. What are the consequences of this shared history for current practice of supervision and curriculum?
3. Davis states that "supervision and curriculum . . . development persist and commonly are linked closely in practice." Does his observation ring true in your experience? Can/should supervision and curriculum function as a unit?
4. Davis contends that certain individuals in both fields "emphasize the differences between these two functions." Who are these individuals and how might they react to his claims?
5. Can supervision theorists and "curricularists" divorce themselves from practice? Explain and react to Davis' comments about the attempt by some to "deliberately" distance themselves from practice.
6. How would teacher involvement in action research contribute to a "robust relationship" between curriculum and supervision?

The No Response:

1. What evidence does Professor Grimmett cite to support his contention that the estrangement between the two processes cannot be reconciled? Is his argument convincing? Why or why not?

2. Why must administrators "understand the nature of the curriculum?" How will such an understanding contribute to a reconciliation between supervision and curriculum?

3. Do you agree that supervision is "perfunctory, fatuous, and irrelevant?" Explain.

4. React to Grimmett's assertion that one way to reduce the estrangement is to "abolish supervision altogether and focus instead on teachers helping teachers around matters of curriculum?"

5. Why has clinical supervision not succeeded in bringing curriculum and supervision together?

6. How does bureaucracy contribute to the estrangement between curriculum and supervision?

For Further Research

1. ASCD has long maintained that supervision and curriculum development are inextricably entwined. Examine the nature of this interaction between curriculum and supervision in the following texts: ASCD (1965); Oliva (1993); and Tanner and Tanner (1987).

2. The relationship between supervision and curriculum was explored in an ASCD yearbook a number of years ago. Pohland and Cross (1982) document the apparent disparateness between the two functions, but indicate avenues for interaction. Review their findings and comment upon the degree to which their insights have born fruit.

3. Read Oliva's (in press) discussion of supervision and curriculum development. What position would Oliva assume on the issue of estrangement? How do Daresh and Playko (1995), Glickman, Gordon, and Ross-Gordon (1995), and Harris (1985) react to this issue?

4. As noted in the postnote summary above, the estrangement issue was initially addressed in the *Journal of Curriculum and Supervision* (1992). Consult Common and Grimmett (1992), Glanz (1992), and Consulting Editors (1992) for their views on this issue. Compare and contrast their views with those of the authors of this chapter.

5. Survey curriculum specialists and supervisors in your district about their views on this issue. Compare results with fellow classmates. Is there a common thread among responses? What might explain these findings?

6. Prepare a position statement on this issue. Present the most compelling evidence you can to support your view. Debate the issue with a classmate and then collaborate to develop perhaps a common view.

7. Survey the literature on school-based management (SBM). Is there much discussion among SBM committee members about efforts to foster cooperation among curriculum and supervision personnel? If so, describe these efforts. How has the teacher empowerment trend over the past 10 years contributed to some reconciliation between supervision and curriculum? What are future prospects?

References

ASCD. (1965). *Role of supervisor and curriculum director in a climate of change.* E. R. Leeper (Ed.). Washington, DC: Association for Supervision and Curriculum Development.

Common, D. L., & Grimmett, P. P. (1992). Beyond the war of the worlds: A consideration of the estrangement between curriculum and supervision. *Journal of Curriculum and Supervision, 7,* 209–225.

Consulting Editors. (1992). Estrangement between curriculum and supervision. *Journal of Curriculum and Supervision, 7,* 245–249.

Daresh, J. C., & Playko, M. A. (1995). *Supervision as a proactive process: Concepts and cases.* Prospect Heights, IL: Waveland Press.

Glanz, J. (1992). Curriculum development and supervision: Antecedents for collaboration and future possibilities. *Journal of Curriculum and Supervision 7,* 226–244.

Glickman, C. D., Gordon, S. P., & Ross-Gordon, J. M. (1995). *Supervision of instruction: A developmental approach.* Boston: Allyn & Bacon.

Harris, B. M. (1985). *Supervisory behavior in education* (3rd ed.). Englewood Cliffs, NJ: Prentice-Hall.

Journal of Curriculum and Supervision, 7 (1992).

Oliva, P. F. (1993). *Supervision for today's schools* (3rd ed.). White plains, NY: Longman.

Oliva, P. F. (in press). Supervision and curriculum development. In G. R. Firth & E. Pajak (Eds.), *Handbook of research on school supervision.* New York: Macmillan.

Pohland, P., & Cross, J. (1982). Impact of the curriculum on supervision. In T. J. Sergiovanni (Ed.), *Supervision of teaching* (pp. 133–152). Alexandria, VA: Association for Supervision and Curriculum Development.

Tanner, D., & Tanner, L. N. (1987). *Supervision in education: Problems and practices.* New York: Macmillan.

Issue 5

Can a Supervisor Be a Coach?

✦ ✦ ✦ ✦

YES—Thomas L. McGreal, University of Illinois at
Urbana–Champaign

NO—James F. Nolan, Jr., Pennsylvania State University

✦ ✦ ✦

Issue Summary

YES: Thomas McGreal, co-author of the forthcoming *Personnel Administration for School Improvement* and currently a professor at the University of Illinois at Urbana-Champaign, maintains emphatically that a supervisor can serve as a coach. He begins his essay by presenting three perspectives/definitions of coaching that serve to confirm his position that an "administrator/supervisor can act as a coach." Dr. McGreal reviews "three conditions that appear to be necessary for effective coaching." He ends his response on an optimistic note, stressing "the importance of establishing a context driven by new views of teacher evaluation."

NO: James Nolan, Jr., former associate editor of the *Journal of Curriculum and Supervision* and currently a professor at Penn State University, argues that although both teacher supervision and teacher evaluation are "essential functions," they are incompatible when performed by a single individual. As such, a supervisor or someone responsible for evaluating a teacher cannot serve as a coach—that is, as a promoter of teacher growth and as a collaborator with the teacher. Professor Nolan explains seven ways in which "evaluation and supervision differ significantly from each other." "These differences are fundamental, not trivial, and they demand that the two functions be separated." Dr. Nolan ends his essay by presenting some ways to separate evaluation from supervision.

Guiding Questions

1. Is the aim of supervision to assist or assess teaching?
2. In what way is supervision integral to the process of evaluation?
3. What conditions are necessary for an effective coaching relationship between a teacher and supervisor?
4. What aspects of McGreal's and Nolans' thinking make sense to you? Do you have trouble accepting any of their arguments? If so, which ones?
5. Which of the two essays do you find most persuasive? Why?

Can a Supervisor be a coach? *Yes*

Thomas L. McGreal

This question reflects a fundamental supervision issue that has generated considerable discussion. It could just as easily have been written around the compatibility of formative and summative evaluation or around the relationship between supervision and evaluation. All of these issues exist because of the realities of the school settings in which most supervision occurs. Approximately 90 percent of all "supervision" done in the United States is conducted by line administrators operating within the parameters established by the local evaluation system (Thurston, McGreal, & Kiser, in press). It is this fact that prompts the question under discussion. Since most supervision occurs as a result of the required contacts within the evaluation system (all tenured teachers will be evaluated at least once every two years, with evaluation being equated to observation), the critical issue becomes whether coaching as it is most commonly defined can occur within the power/authority relationships fostered by traditional evaluation systems. Regardless of the inevitability of administrators having to wear multiple hats in their supervisory roles, I do firmly believe that a supervisor can serve as a coach.

It is commonly thought that a "yes, but" response really means "no." This is not the case here. I definitely mean yes, a supervisor can be a coach. But . . . there are unquestionably certain definitional and contextual issues that can significantly influence a supervisor's ability to act as a coach.

First, the definitional issue. A real problem in dealing with the coaching metaphor is that the term has a range of meanings depending on the contexts or conditions surrounding the coaching function. There are a number of different layers of coaching that have gained visibility in the literature and in practice. Each type or view of coaching influences the ability and the likelihood of a supervisor acting as a coach.

One of the first uses of the coaching metaphor originated within a staff development training model advocated by Joyce and Showers (1983). In this model, coaching and peer coaching are used almost synonymously and generally are seen as activities embedded in a staff development model. Joyce and Showers believed that in order to transfer newly learned skills or knowledge to consistent and appropriate application in real classrooms, certain specific fundamentals must be learned and practiced. These fundamentals are related to (1) understanding the theoretical basis of the new skill, (2) observing experts using the skill, (3) practicing the skill with specific feedback, and (4) being coached through the application process. Five specific coaching behaviors were identified that increase the likelihood of a successful experience. The five behaviors are (1) providing a collegial atmosphere,

(2) giving technical feedback, (3) analyzing application attempts, (4) assisting with the adapation of the new skill or concept to the specific context of the teacher's classroom, and (5) facilitating frequent opportunities for practice.

The peers generally referred to in the discussion of this form of coaching are the participants within the staff development experience. Consequently, supervisors/administrators who are actively participating in the staff development activity would be peers with the teachers who are also involved. With this sort of definition, a supervisor could clearly serve as a coach because the coaching process is located within a specific staff development activity and is most likely separated from any kind of evaluation procedure. The Joyce and Showers view of coaching focuses heavily on helping teachers acquire individual teaching skills or expand their repertoire of teaching models and do it within a staff development training experience. Certainly, this is a legitimate definition of a coach, but this form of coaching is not at the heart of the issue under discussion here.

More recent conversations about coaches and coaching are driven by the concept of cognitive coaching as developed by Costa and Garmston (1994).

> Think of the term *coaching,* and you may envision an athletic coach, but we have quite a different metaphor. To us, coaching is a conveyance, like a stagecoach. "To coach means to convey a valued colleague from where he or she is to where he or she wants to be" (Evered & Selman, 1989). Skillful cognitive coaches apply specific strategies to enhance another person's perceptions, decisions, and intellectual functions. Changing these inner thought processes is prerequisite to improving overt behaviors that, in turn, enhance student learning. (p. 2)

At its most basic level, cognitive coaching is a set of nonjudgmental practices built around a planning conference, a lesson observation, and a reflective conference. As such, it is a process that uses the fundamental clinical supervision cycle as the structure for conveying the teacher from one point (or one set of inner thought processes) to another. The framework presumed by cognitive coaching is that teaching is a professional act and that coaches assist teachers in becoming more resourceful, informed, and skillful professionals. Coaches do not attempt to change behaviors. Behaviors change as a result of new perceptions and refined thought processes gained by the teacher through the coaching experience (Costa & Garmston, 1994).

This model emphasizes three goals: trust, learning, and autonomy. Trust is seen as fundamental to learning and autonomy. Because of its importance, trust must be nurtured by the supervisor during each interaction with the teacher. Costa and Garmston believe that trust is built over time and that supervisors encourage trust through demonstrations of their own competence, consistency, personal availability, and confidentiality.

Learning is described as a rearranging and restructuring of teacher thinking that is facilitated by the supervisor during conferences and contacts by encouraging the teacher to imagine, describe, and prepare for a lesson in specific detail. Costa and Garmston assume that teaching involves a series of decisions made before, during, and after instruction. This view leads to the focus of coaching as helping teachers learn to make better decisions.

Autonomy is defined as the teacher's ability and inclination to monitor his or her behavior and actions and to make consciously deliberate decisions about teaching (Pajak, 1993). As a result of supervisory interactions over time, the teacher should eventually become self-supervisory. Thus, the goal of cognitive coaching is to lead teachers to autonomously apply self-analysis and voluntarily change their behaviors and strategies to improve their performance in the classroom.

Can a supervisor act as a cognitive coach? Costa and Garmston are very clear about the answer to this question. It is their feeling and their experience that anyone in the educational setting can become a cognitive coach. In fact, they chose to use a principal–teacher relationship as the model for illustrating the concept throughout their book on cognitive coaching (Costa & Garmston, 1994).

A related, but somewhat different view of coaching has emerged from what is being called "new views" of supervision (Pajak, 1993) or a new paradigm for supervision (Gordon, 1992). These new perspectives of supervision are generally grouped under a "reflective practice" heading (Pajak, 1993). The impetus for viewing supervision from a reflective practice perspective came partly as a response to the dissatisfaction with the technical rationality view of supervision (Smyth, 1984) that characterized much of the use of clinical supervision during the seventies and eighties. In this view, supervision is a process for monitoring teachers' use of theory and research in practice and for helping teachers to change their behavior so that they use theory and research more effectively and efficiently (Nolan & Huber, 1989). This was often seen as part of the deliberate attempt to control and regulate pedagogy and behavior through systems of prescription and evaluation (Smyth, 1984). Much of this happened within the framework of research-based teacher evaluation systems that were developed during the first wave of reform initiatives in the eighties.

These evaluation systems were driven by technical views of teaching that were promoted by proponents of the teacher effectiveness research and the learning-theory-based Madeline Hunter model. Administrators were asked to focus their actions in supervision and evaluation toward promoting these particular views of teaching and to use evaluative sanctions (low ratings, incomplete checkoffs, critical written commentary, lack of recognition within reward systems) if the desired behaviors were not displayed. The assuming of these overtly administrative behaviors within traditional clinical supervision practices offered strong support for the contention that administrators/ supervisors could not perform formative and summative evaluation functions and thus could never legitimately serve as coaches.

Just as the technical-behavioristic view of teaching drove the "old" supervision models, the reflective practice models are shaped by a view of teaching and learning as a complex process much more aligned with the constructivist beliefs about classrooms that are at the heart of current school reform initiatives. This can be seen in Schön's (1988) description of "reflective teaching," which he characterizes as listening carefully and responding appropriately to students in order to help them comprehend something with which they are experiencing difficulty. Reflective teaching also involves assisting students to discover and build on knowledge that they already possess and helping them to integrate their existing knowledge with the knowledge learned in school (Pajak, 1993). This leads to a perspective on supervision in which changing teacher behaviors is not the primary goal.

The major task of the supervisor from the perspective of reflective practice is to assist teachers in engaging in reflective thinking about their own practice. Thus, as described by Nolan and Huber (1989), "the aims of supervision become (1) engaging the teacher in the process of reflective behavior while (2) fostering critical inquiry into the process of teaching and learning, thereby (3) increasing the teacher's understanding of teaching practice and (4) broadening and deepening the repertoire of images and metaphors the teacher can use to deal with problems" (p. 128). Thus, all activities that support, guide, or encourage reflective teaching may be considered instructional supervision. In order to help teachers to become more reflective, Schön (1988) suggests that supervisors should assume the stance of a coach. The supervisor as coach can facilitate increased teacher reflection about teaching practice through advice, through critique, through description, through demonstration, or through questions. As Pajak (1993) describes it:

> A reflective supervisor tries to help, encourage, and provoke the teacher into reflecting on events in the classroom. The teacher's reflection is supported by the supervisor's own reflection-in-action on the process of supervision. The supervisor models reflection, in other words, by analyzing what he or she sees, how it is interpreted, how it might be tested, and what actions might follow from that interpretation. (p. 288)

As with cognitive coaching, much of this form of supervision occurs within the traditional clinical supervision preobservation conference, observation, and postobservation reflective conference. Also, as Costa and Garmston (1994) have proclaimed, Schön (1988) indicates that coaching for reflective teaching may be carried out by administrators and teachers.

So, to this point I have reviewed what could be considered the three most commonly used perspectives/definitions of the coaching metaphor used in supervision settings. These are (1) coaching as used within staff development training models, (2) coaching driven by current work in cognitive coaching, and (3) coaching as a part of a new supervision paradigm that encourages reflective practice. In all three perspectives, the definition and description of coaching, as presented by the developer or a major proponent, supports the contention that an administrator/supervisor can act as a coach.

I am not so naive as to believe that if the literature supports the concept that a supervisor can act as a coach it will happen easily. In reviewing the coaching literature there appears to be universal agreement that a strong trusting relationship needs to exist between the two parties, and that it will best be accomplished in a setting that is characterized by a visible collegial culture. The presence of these two conditions can result in a strong enough personal relationship to overcome the organizational and philosophic impediments that can significantly hinder a supportive relationship between a supervisor and a teacher. Nolan, Hawkes, and Francis (1993), in reviewing a number of case studies of clinical supervision experiences, found that despite a variety of roles held by the supervisors (including line administrative positions), they were all able to develop trusting and collegial relationships. It seemed clear that the qualities of the relationship between the supervisor and the teacher were more important to the success of the supervision or coaching experience than the roles of the participants or the constraints within the organization.

Unfortunately, the quality of supervisor–teacher relationships is not always strong enough to prevent internal procedures and practices from intruding on the level of trust that is necessary for successful coaching to occur. Glickman (1987), while supporting the contention that supervisors can act as coaches, found three conditions that appear to be necessary for effective coaching. The three were that (1) a trusting relationship has been established between the administrator and the teacher, (2) the teacher knows for certain which of the two functions is being performed, coaching or evaluation, and (3) the administrator's behaviors are scrupulously consistent with each of the functions.

In most cases, the major culprit in breaking down levels of trust between teachers and administrators, and in establishing procedural requirements that prevent the separation of coaching and evaluation functions, is the local teacher evaluation system. It is not hard to see that my "yes, but" response to the question is to a large degree prompted by my feeling that traditional evaluation practices must be reshaped if supervisor as coach is to become common practice. It might be asked why it should become common practice when it is likely that the kind of relationship that can best support effective coaching can be better established between peers. It is my feeling that if coaching is a process that can help improve classroom teaching, then we have to provide conditions that will support administrators maintaining a significant role in coaching.

Considering that the conversation about the value and usefulness of peer coaching has been going on for a number of years, it is hard to find any significant increase in its use within schools. The working lives of teachers and the increasing demands on their time, especially as teachers are being asked to rethink many of their traditional classroom practices, has made it virtually impossible to find the time or the energy required to carry out a coaching activity. This has been particularly true in middle, junior, and senior high school settings, where there are only a handful of functioning peer coaching programs anywhere in the country. Continuing time and resource problems make it unlikely that there will be any significant increase in the amount of peer involvement in coaching. So, if it is going to happen, and the evidence appears to be good that it should, then our current supervision and evaluation practices must be designed to allow and encourage more collegial and trusting relationships to be formed between teachers and administrators.

Quietly and steadily there is a next generation of teacher evaluation systems taking shape. The purpose of these systems, in most cases, is to philosophically and structurally align teacher evaluation and professional development by shifting the emphasis from summative to formative evaluation. At the heart of the evaluation redesign is the use of new understandings about what students know and need to be able to do to be successful, about how adult professionals grow and develop, and about the importance of restructuring the roles, relationships, and responsibilities within schools in order to support teaching and learning (Thurston, McGreal, & Kiser, in press).

The result of the application of these new understandings is the rethinking of many of the traditional forms of evaluation and development. Classrooms that are increasingly characterized by collaborative learning activities, increased levels of student involvement, longer instructional periods, teaching teams, de-tracked classrooms, inclusive instruction, and integrated curriculums no longer fit evaluation practices that were built for frontal and explicit instruction teaching. Collaborative decision-making models in which leadership teams are actively involved in the work of the school and in which administrators and teachers act more like partners than adversaries make evaluation systems based on power relationships completely inappropriate.

Recognizing these new complexities in teaching and in school relationships, a growing number of schools are redesigning their evaluation procedures so that they are less event centered (individual observations) and more focused on long-term activities that produce individual and team reflection. In this sense, the new systems are responding to the new paradigm of supervision for increased reflective practice. The difference seems to be in a lessening reliance on classroom observation as the primary source of data for conversation and reflection. Observation becomes just one of a number of alternatives that are available for teachers and administrators to use. These alternatives include such activities as artifact collections, action research, student descriptions of life and work in classrooms, portfolio development, journal writing, cognitive coaching involvement, and videotaping. Most of these new systems are adapting traditional goal-setting evaluation models (McGreal, 1983) to include the development of individual professional development plans for tenured, experienced teachers. These plans reflect the teacher's interests, level of development, training, experience, and context. In order to better reflect new realities in schools, many districts are allowing and even encouraging teams of teachers to work together with the administrator to establish team plans. The responsible administrator (principal, assistant principal, department head, team leader) meets with each individual or team and assists in the development of a plan. Once the plan is agreed upon, it becomes *"the teaching teams"* plan—not the individual's or team's with the administrator being responsible for monitoring and evaluating its completion; it belongs to both parties. The administrator becomes coach, partner, facilitator, and resource provider, not evaluator. In order to support and encourage more complex plans, teachers are offered one-, two-, or three-year time frames to develop them.

In order to satisfy Glickman's (1987) condition of separating the tasks of coaching and evaluating, these new systems do not require any summative activity at all. Final write-ups and concluding conferences are confined to progress reports, descriptions, reflections, and next steps. They are jointly written by the teacher(s) and the administrator; they serve as documentation of the experience and are placed in the teacher's file. At the completion of the established time frame for a plan, the cycle begins again. There is no downtime in these systems. All teachers are involved in working on a professional development plan either as individuals or on a team at all times.

Accountability concerns for tenured teachers in these new systems are addressed through the daily interactions and experiences of the supervisor and the teacher. When problems occur, experienced teachers may be moved into an assistance track where more specific direction and support can be provided. This allows supervisors to separate their evaluative responsibilities from their work as coaches and facilitators in the professional growth track. In addition to the professional growth track and the assistance track, a third track exists for probationary teachers. The beginning teacher evaluation track is characterized by the use of multiple data sources, journals, mandatory staff development, and active mentor programs.

There are obviously adaptations of this type of system being used, but the three-track model, with its emphasis on formative, collaborative, and collegial processes, is the next generation of teacher evaluation. Training programs that focus on cognitive coaching, on supervision for reflective practice, on peer coaching, and on collegial supervision and evaluation fit these new models. Administrators and teachers who are involved in these training programs can go back to their schools and use their new supervisory skills within a system that supports and encourages their use. Schools that have developed these new systems report increased levels of trust, more focus on teaching-and learning, and higher levels of teacher conversation and reflection (McGreal, 1995).

This has been a long way around to a "yes" response. Looking at the question in a straightforward way, of course a supervisor can act as a coach. It is done every day by supervisors who, through personal skill, integrity, commitment, and friendship, coach teachers in extraordinary ways. *But . . .* since this is often the exception rather than the rule, the importance of establishing a context driven by new views of teacher evaluation that allow and encourage trust to develop, and that support the separation of the evaluation function from coaching, cannot be overlooked. It is the development of these new evaluation contexts that will eventually allow me to remove the "but" from this answer.

References

Costa, A., & Garmston, R. (1994). *Cognitive coaching: A foundation for renaissance schools.* Norwood, MA: Christopher-Gordon Publishers.

Evered, R., & Selman, J. (1989). Coaching and the art of management. *Organizational Dynamics, 18,* 16–32.

Glickman, C. (1987). Presentation at a National Curriculum Study, Institute for the Association for Supervision and Curriculum Development, Scottsdale, AZ.

Gordon, S. (1992). Paradigms, transitions, and the new supervision. *Journal of Curriculum and Supervision, 8*(1), 62–76.

Joyce, B., & Showers, B. (1983). The coaching of teaching. *Educational Leadership, 40*(1), 4–8, 10.

McGreal, T. (1983). *Successful teacher evaluation.* Alexandria, VA: Association for Supervision and Curriculum Development.

McGreal, T. (1995). *The impact of new evaluation processes on teacher involvement and teacher reflection.* A report to the Illinois Association for Supervision and Curriculum Development. Champaign, IL: The University of Illinois.

Nolan, J., Hawkes, B., & Francis, P. (1993). Case studies: Windows onto clinical supervision. *Educational Leadership, 40,* 52–56.

Nolan, J., & Huber, T. (1989). Nurturing the reflective practitioner through instructional supervision: A review of the literature. *Journal of Curriculum and Supervision, 4*(2), 126–145.

Pajak, E. (1993). *Approaches to clinical supervision: Alternatives for improving instruction.* Norwood, MA: Christopher-Gordon Publishers.

Schön, D. (1988). Coaching reflective teaching. In P. Grimmett & G. Erickson (Eds.), *Reflection in teacher education.* New York: Teachers College Press.

Smyth, W. J. (1984). Toward a "critical consciousness" in the instructional supervision of experienced teachers. *Curriculum Inquiry, 14,* 429–439.

Thurston, P., McGreal, T., & Kiser, M. (in press). *Personnel administration for school improvement: A legal, organizational, and policy perspective.* New York: Longman.

Can a Supervisor Be a Coach? *No*

James F. Nolan, Jr.

One of the maladies that plague the field of supervision is a lack of agreement among practitioners and scholars concerning common definitions for important terms. Therefore, I feel compelled to restate the title of this chapter so as to make clear the position I am defending.[1] As I see it, the question asks whether the same individual can simultaneously carry out the roles of teacher evaluator and teacher supervisor or coach. As I define it, teacher evaluation is an organizational function designed to make comprehensive judgments concerning teacher performance and competence for the purpose of personnel decisions such as tenure and continuing employment. This is a state-mandated function carried out only by those who are properly certified by the state. Typically, the superintendent of schools is officially responsible for teacher evaluation and chooses to delegate this responsibility to individuals within the school district who are properly certificated, that is administrators and supervisors.

In my view, teacher supervision is an organizational function concerned with promoting teacher growth and leading to improvement in teaching performance and greater student learning. It is a function that can be carried out by multiple individuals who find themselves in multiple roles within the school system—teachers, administrators, supervisors, and the like. As I see it, teacher coaching is a form of supervision whether it is conducted by fellow teachers or by supervisors and administrators. Coaching refers to the process of working collaboratively with the teacher in the classroom context to improve the teacher's performance and student learning through a process of data collection and conferencing. You can find a more expanded definition of coaching in an earlier article I co-authored with Keith Hillkirk (Nolan & Hillkirk, 1991). I am going to use the labels *evaluation* and *supervision* to denote the two functions throughout the rest of the essay. In other words, the essence of the question "Can a supervisor be a coach?" centers on the compatibility of the functions of supervision and evaluation.

The question of whether teacher supervision and teacher evaluation are compatible roles for the same individual has plagued both practice and scholarship for many decades (see Bolin & Panaritis, 1992; Glanz, 1990). Individuals who have developed models of teacher supervision are divided on the issue. Some (Hunter and Acheson and Gall) see no inherent conflict between the two roles; others (Cogan, Glickman, Smyth) believe that the roles should be separated, while still others (such as Blumberg) suggest that the two would best be separated but that it is possible to carry out both simultaneously (Pajak, 1993). The world of practice is equally if not more confused than the world of scholarship. Some school districts define teacher supervision and evaluation as the same function both in policy and in practice. Many districts make a distinction between teacher supervision and evaluation in policy, but end up practicing what McGreal (1983) called "common law evaluation"—that is, using the exact same procedures for both functions with the result that teachers end up perceiving the entire process as evaluative. Many of these districts attempt to soften the threat of evaluation by couching evaluation in a language of growth and improvement, but this euphemistic strategy often ends up creating mass confusion and excessive entanglements between supervision and evaluation (Hazi, 1994). Finally, there are some districts, growing in number over the last decade, that have managed to separate the two functions in both policy and practice.

My intent in this chapter is to argue that teacher evaluation and teacher supervision are separate functions and cannot be carried out simultaneously by the same person in an effective manner. I will argue this point by demonstrating the basic incompatibility of the two functions on seven different dimensions and by showing how the two functions can be separated even in a district with limited financial resources. So, can a supervisor be a coach? My answer is no.

Basic Incompatibility of Teacher Evaluation and Supervision

Teacher evaluation and supervision are incompatible functions in at least seven different dimensions: (1) their basic purpose; (2) the rationale for their existence; (3) their scope; (4) the inherent nature of the relationship; (5) observation procedures; (6) the role of expertise; and (7) the teacher's perspective on the entire process.

Basic Purpose

The purpose of teacher evaluation is to make judgments concerning the overall quality of the teacher's performance and his or her competence in carrying out assigned duties. The process results in some form of summative rating (e.g., 78/80 or a qualitative judgment such as outstanding, satisfactory, or unsatisfactory). Developing either a numerical or qualitative rating demands that the evaluator have in mind some explicit or, at worst, implicit model or standard of competent or excellent performance against which the performance of the teacher can be compared. Absent some such explicit criterion of performance and observational data, it is impossible to make and justify a numerical or qualitative rating. In short, the basic purpose of teacher evaluation is to ascertain whether or not all teachers meet at least a minimum standard of competent performance as judged by an evaluator with appropriate expertise.

The purpose of supervision, on the other hand, is to promote individual teacher growth beyond the current level of performance. This involves making sense of the complex world of the classroom and helping the teacher become aware of his or her behavior and its consequences for learners. As opposed to being driven by some externally adopted model of teacher performance, the supervisory process is driven by the teacher's platform of beliefs about teaching and learning. It is not important in supervision to make a global pronouncement of teacher proficiency. The task is to start where the teacher is and reach beyond that. In short, the purpose of supervision is to strengthen the teacher's current level of performance in ways that are consistent with the his or her educational platform.

Rationale

The rationale for the existence of teacher evaluation derives from the legitimate right of the state to protect children from harm through incompetent, immoral, or unprofessional teacher behavior. This right is operationalized through a process of inspection delegated to the local school district by the state. Thus, teacher evaluation is a legalistic and bureaucratic process, which must be carefully articulated to ensure that the rights of the state and its children are protected and to ensure that the teacher's rights to due process are not violated. Teacher tenure laws further delineate the teacher's due process rights and shift the burden of proof in a dismissal hearing. The assumption implicit in the process of teacher evaluation is that teachers are motivated to improve their teaching performance by extrinsic motivators such as a rating process that carries the threat of an unsatisfactory rating and subsequent dismissal. (see Perspective 4)

The rationale for supervision/coaching, in contrast, derives from the complex nature of the teaching environment itself. Classroom environments are marked by simultaneity and multidimensionality, requiring teachers to make a multitude of important decisions on a daily basis (Doyle, 1986). The task of promoting cognitive, affective, and psychomotor growth for 25 or more students simultaneously is amazingly complex. No other professional works with so many clients at the same time. As a result of the complexity of this work environment, teachers benefit tremendously from having a skilled colleague who can act as another set of eyes and ears to capture classroom events and then help the teacher to make sense of what is happening in the classroom and what impact it is having on individual learners. Supervision is not intended as a legalistic or bureaucratic process; it is a professional, community-building activity that recognizes that teachers are spurred by internal motivators such as a desire to improve their own professional competence and a desire to maximize student learning.

Scope

Teacher evaluation is very broad in scope. It must examine not only the teacher's classroom performance but also his or her contribution to the school as an organization. In fact, many teachers who are dismissed through the evaluation process are dismissed not for poor classroom performance but rather for issues and behaviors that are connected to minimal contractual obligations and extra-classroom behavior. In terms of classroom teaching, effective evaluation demands that the teacher be observed for the entire spectrum of classes. For elementary teachers, this means observing language arts, math, science, social studies, and so forth. For secondary teachers, this means observing the entire spectrum of courses and students the teacher is assigned. Additionally, effective evaluation demands seeing the teacher over time rather than only once or twice. Unless the evaluator takes the time to develop a comprehensive view of teacher performance, it is not possible to make or defend a global judgment of effectiveness such as that demanded by most state teacher evaluation systems.

Unlike evaluation, supervision can narrow its focus considerably. Since improvement in performance rather than global judgments of competence is the goal, the supervision process can be focused on one class or one type of teaching situation over time. In fact, case studies in clinical supervision indicate that a specified focus in the same environment over time is a critical dimension of improving teacher performance (Nolan, Hawkes, & Francis, 1993).

Nature of the Relationship

The evaluator's role is to make a professional judgment concerning the teacher's overall performance and competence. As stated earlier, one of his or her major responsibilities is to protect the interest of the state and its children and for that reason only properly certificated personnel can carry out the process of teacher evaluation. Although the evaluator may know and like the teacher in question, it is imperative that he or she maintain a certain degree of distance in order to make a fair assessment of the teacher's performance. It is also imperative that the roles remain distinct. The evaluator is always the evaluator, and the evaluatee is always the evaluatee. The roles can never be merged or blended. It seems that the most appropriate stance for the evaluator is as what Garman (1982) calls a "neutral observer," and that the highest level of collaboration one can hope for is that of "working-acceptance involvement." It is also extremely difficult to establish an atmosphere of trust in this relationship, since the evaluator has all the power and the teacher has all the vulnerability. Additionally, the teacher has no choice about whether to participate in the process or not; it is a state-mandated activity. As Blumberg and Jonas (1987) have pointed out, it is very unlikely in this type of relationship that the teacher will grant the evaluator access to his or her deepest hopes, fears, and beliefs about the teaching and learning process.

In supervision distance is a barrier, and rigid adherence to organizational roles hinders rather than facilitates the process. In the process of supervision, both partners agree to and attempt to work together as colleagues. Sometimes the teacher takes the lead in the process, and sometimes the supervisor takes the lead. It is only by watching the process of supervision develop over time that we realize that leadership is shared and roles are blended and exchanged freely. When the process unfolds as it should, it is possible to reach what Garman (1982) describes as organic reciprocity, in which goals, leadership, expertise, respect, and trust are shared mutually among the participants. In contrast to evaluation, where the evaluator is all powerful and the teacher is vulnerable, forced participant, supervision is a voluntary relationship with mutual vulnerability and shared power.

Observation Procedures

The process of teacher evaluation is standardized and instrument driven; that is, it is driven by the externally developed model of effective teaching performance that is used to judge the teacher's performance and competence. The evaluator who observes the teacher for the purposes of evaluation is handed the task of making a global judgment about the teacher's performance. This requires that data collection take a more global focus, attempting to look at the teaching–learning environment in its entirety rather than at one or a few selected aspects of the teacher's behavior. Failure to maintain this global focus over time risks capturing an incomplete picture of the teacher's behavior, resulting in an unfair evaluation. Additionally, the evaluator's role is to make judgments concerning the teacher's behavior. Observations and inferences may be used to support the judgments made and to help the teacher to recognize the validity of the judgments, but the outcome of the observation is still a set of judgments that are communicated to the teacher. Finally and perhaps most important, the process of observation must be the same for all teachers. In keeping with due process rights and contractual agreements, all teachers in the same job category must be observed with the same instrument and in the same way. Issues of fairness across teachers as well as issues of validity and reliability take precedence over individual teacher needs in the arena of evaluation.

Teacher supervision, by contrast, can be differentiated, individualized, and teacher driven. Teachers can be observed with different frequencies, for different purposes, with different types of data-gathering and conferencing techniques. A wide variety of data sources, including paper and pencil observations, students products, teacher artifacts, interviews, surveys, and the like, can and should be used in the process of teacher supervision (Nolan & Francis, 1992). The focus for observation is typically very narrow, converging on some selected aspect(s) of teacher and/or student behavior. In addition, this narrow focus is typically captured during several observations over time in an attempt to document improved teacher or student performance. This also allows the teacher and supervisor to capture what Garman (1990) has called the "unfolding lesson." Finally, the observer's role is not to make judgments and communicate those to the teacher but rather to collect observational and inferential types of data that can be used to enable the teacher to make better judgments, about his or her own teaching performance and its impact on learners. The supervisor may help the teacher in making these judgments, but does not make the judgments for him or her. As a result, one of the outcomes of the supervision process should be the development of a teacher who is more self-directed and a better decision maker.

The Role of Expertise

In the process of teacher evaluation, the evaluator must possess special expertise. In fact, only those who are properly certificated are allowed to carry out the evaluation process. Throughout the process, the evaluator maintains the role of expert, since it is his or her responsibility to make a fair assessment of the teacher's performance and competence using the established instrument and criteria. The teacher may be asked for his or her opinion, but if this opinion conflicts with that of the evaluator, the evaluator's must prevail. Therefore, expertise for making judgments concerning teacher performance and competence resides solely in the evaluator. Further evidence for one-sided expertise is provided by the fact that teachers are often presented with a written text that describes and judges their performance before any opportunity has occurred for the teacher and evaluator to discuss what has been observed. This places a heavy burden on the evaluator, who must possess pedagogical as well as content expertise in order to make a fair, informed, comprehensive assessment of teacher performance and competence. If the evaluator does not possess content expertise, it is imperative that other, properly certificated experts in the content area be brought into the process.

By contrast, teacher supervision relies on shared expertise. The supervisor brings expertise in supervision (data collecting, inquiry, conferencing), pedagogy, and perhaps content, while the teacher contributes expertise in pedagogy, content, and perhaps supervision, as well as intimate knowledge of his or her students and the history of that particular classroom context. If any of these areas of expertise are missing or untapped, it is extremely difficult to make sense of the teaching–learning environment. Because each of the partners recognizes the expertise of the other and its importance, leadership and power are shared. When disagreements about the meaning of classroom events occur, they are resolved through dialogue and further hypothesis testing, data collection, and interpretation. Neither partner seeks or accepts the role of resident expert.

Teacher Perspective

Teachers see the process of evaluation as a situation in which they are supposed to put their best foot forward for the benefit of the evaluator. It is a "hit me with your best shot" approach. The evaluator plays the role of drama critic, while the teacher is playwright, actor, producer, and director. Because of the negative consequences that can result from poor performance during an observation for evaluation purposes, teachers take few risks. They do not put on plays that are likely to fold; they are much more likely to put on old favorites that have received rave reviews in the past. Showcase lessons that are repeated in whole or in part year after year are not unheard of in the realm of teacher evaluation.

Supervision should be an opportunity for risk taking and experimentation. Often supervision is used to enable teachers to try out new behaviors and techniques in a safe, supportive environment. Joyce and Showers (1987) have demonstrated the importance of supportive, nonevaluative coaching in helping teachers transfer new teaching models to the classroom. Since supervision is aimed at growth over time, experimentation and risk taking are a sine qua non of the process.

Summary

Both teacher evaluation and teacher supervision are essential functions. As Sergiovanni and Starratt (1993) suggest, evaluation establishes an individual teacher's right to enjoy continuing membership in a given school community, while supervision helps that teacher exercise his or her responsibility to promote continuing growth in that particular community and in the profession of teaching as a whole. Though both functions are important, evaluation and supervision differ significantly in terms of their basic purpose, the rationale for their existence, the nature of the relationship between the participants, the scope of the process, the observation procedures employed, the role of expertise, and the teacher's perspective on the process. These differences are fundamental, not trivial, and they demand that the two functions be separated. It is not possible for the same individual to carry out both effectively *at the same time*. As a result of our failure to separate teacher evaluation from teacher supervision, we do a very poor job of both in most schools.

One of the reasons for our failure to separate evaluation from supervision in the past is that school districts were not able to identify how to separate them given the minimal resources typically devoted to them. I believe that it is possible to separate the two and have seen several districts in Pennsylvania do an excellent job of this. Let's turn our attention to precisely how the two can be separated.

Separating Evaluation from Supervision

There are two basic ways to separate evaluation from supervision: by people or by time and procedures. The most obvious way is by people. Using this model, administrators carry out the process of teacher evaluation while teachers and/or other specialists such as content supervisors carry out the process of supervision. The two processes remain completely separate. What happens in the supervision process is confidential, with all data and notes kept by the two participants. In many districts that use this type of arrangement, supervision becomes peer coaching carried out by teachers who have been given the opportunity through staff development to gain the knowledge and skills necessary to engage in effective coaching. This method of separating evaluation from supervision makes the clearer distinction between the two. It is also the model that requires the most resources. Either supervisory personnel must be employed to engage in supervision or teachers must be provided with staff development and some release time to carry out peer coaching. For those districts that can make the required commitment of resources, peer coaching appears to offer substantial benefits. Those that do not have enough resources can consider the other alternative.

A second alternative is to separate the processes by time and procedures. When this model is used, teachers are typically placed on a cycle of supervision and evaluation. Typically, nontenured teachers and those who are new to the district are placed in an evaluative mode until they successfully complete the probationary period. Once that period has passed and tenure has been granted, teachers are typically in an evaluative mode once every three years. During the other two years, they are in a supervisory mode. During the evaluative year of the cycle, the teacher is evaluated by an administrator using the standardized evaluation process. Activities during the supervisory years vary. Some individuals may engage in self-directed staff development, others may engage in goal setting and supervision with the principal, while still others may engage in peer coaching or goal setting with a peer or peers.

If the principal engages in supervision with the teacher during the supervision years of the cycle, the procedures differ substantially from the evaluation procedures used during the evaluation year. For example, observations for the purpose of evaluation are unannounced; driven by the teacher evaluation instrument; standardized across teachers in terms of frequency, focus, and duration; global in nature; and used to communicate observer judgments concerning the effectiveness of the teacher's performance. By contrast, observations for the purpose of supervision are preceded by a preconference, in which the teacher selects a focus for the observation; individualized for each teacher in terms of frequency and duration; focused on a few aspects of teaching and learning as selected by the teacher; and used to collect data that the teacher can use to make judgments about how to improve his or her teaching behavior and its consequences for learners.

During the supervisory years of the cycle, the teacher is not observed for the purposes of evaluation. He or she (having already passed through the probationary period) is presumed to be teaching at a level of satisfactory or better unless some evidence to the contrary surfaces. If such evidence does surface, the teacher is immediately moved into an intensive evaluative mode rather than a supervisory mode.

In both of these models a strong commitment is made to both teacher evaluation and teacher supervision. Teachers are required to complete a rigorous period of intense evaluation before they are granted full membership in the community and before a district commitment to their long term growth is made. Once this probationary period has passed, the district makes a long term commitment to provide the resources necessary to carry out both teacher evaluation and teacher supervision separately and effectively.

Endnote

1. I wish to express my appreciation to Dr. Linda Hoover, Shippensburg University, for her feedback and helpful comments on an earlier version of the manuscript.

References

Blumberg, A., & Jonas, S. (1987). Permitting access: The teacher's control over supervision. *Educational Leadership, 44*(8), 58–63.

Bolin, F., & Panaritis, P. (1992). Searching for a common purpose: A perspective on the history of supervision. In C. Glickman (Ed.), *Supervision in transition* (pp. 30–43). Alexandria, VA: Association for Supervision and Curriculum Development.

Doyle, W. (1986). Classroom organization and management. In M. Wittrock (Ed.), *Handbook of research on teaching* (3rd ed.) (pp. 392–431). New York: Macmillan.

Garman, N. (1982). The clinical approach to supervision. In T. J. Sergiovanni (Ed.), *Supervision of teaching* (pp. 35–52). Alexandria, VA: Association for Supervision and Curriculum Development.

Garman, N. (1990). Theories embedded in the events of clinical supervision: A hermeneutic approach. *Journal of Curriculum and Supervision, 5,* 201–213.

Glanz, J. (1990). Beyond bureaucracy: Notes on the professionalization of public school supervision in the early 20th century. *Journal of Curriculum and Supervision, 5,* 150–170.

Hazi, H. (1994). The teacher evaluation-supervision dilemma: A case of entanglements and irreconcilable differences. *Journal of Curriculum and Supervision, 9,* 195–216.

Joyce, B., & Showers, B. (1987). *Improving student achievement through staff development.* New York: Longman.

McGreal, T. (1983). *Successful teacher evaluation.* Alexandria, VA: Association for Supervision and Curriculum Development.

Nolan, J., & Francis, P. (1992). Changing perspectives in curriculum and instruction. In C. Glickman (Ed.), *Supervision in transition* (pp. 44–60). Alexandria, VA.: Association for Supervision and Curriculum Development.

Nolan. J., Hawkes, B., & Francis, P. (1993). Case studies: Windows onto clinical supervision. *Educational Leadership, 51*(2), 52–56.

Nolan, J., & Hillkirk, K. (1991). The effects of reflective coaching for veteran teachers. *Journal of Curriculum and Supervision, 7,* 62–76.

Pajak. E. (1993). *Approaches to clinical supervision: Alternatives for improving instruction.* Norwood, MA.: Christopher-Gordon Publishers.

Sergiovanni, T. J., & Starratt, R. J. (1993). *Supervision: A redefinition* (5th ed.). New York: McGraw-Hill.

Postnote

Can a Supervisor Be a Coach?

The improvement–evaluation dilemma in supervision is widely acknowledged. Some educators advocate a complete separation of the two functions. Others disagree that a divorce between the improvement and evaluative functions of supervision is inevitable and necessary. These educators maintain that the two functions are essentially compatible. Others assert that evaluation and improvement can coexist only when teachers and supervisors work collaboratively. Trust, collegiality, and genuine collaboration are considered necessary ingredients for meaningful supervisory relationships. Still others maintain that improvement and evaluation are not easily separated in practice. They say that collegial supervisory relationships may be just as judgmental as hierarchical supervisory relationships. Some argue that quite often evaluation and supervision are considered legally synonymous, so that a separation may be impossible. What do you think? Can a supervisor, responsible for evaluation, maintain a coaching relationship with a teacher?

Review Questions for

The Yes Response:

1. Professor McGreal provides three perspectives/definitions of coaching. Describe differences and similarities of each view of coaching. How do these three views support McGreal's contention that a supervisor can serve as a coach?
2. Compare and contrast Hunter's technical-rational view of supervision with Costa and Garmston's cognitive coaching model. You might want to also refer to Pajak (1993).
3. Have you ever developed a "strong trusting relationship" with a teacher or a supervisor? Describe. Is your experience the norm or the exception to most supervisor–teacher relationships? Explain.
4. How can "current supervision and evaluation practices" be redesigned to foster "more collegial and trusting relationships" between teachers and supervisors?
5. React to McGreal's description of a "three-track model" of teacher evaluation. Can such a model succeed in your school/district?

The No Response:

1. Professor Nolan notes that some school districts "have managed to separate the two functions (evaluation and supervision) in both policy and practice." Do you or does someone you know work in a district where this is the case? If so, describe. If not, what would supervision look like if, in fact, the two functions were separated? Is it practically feasible to actually separate evaluation from supervision?

2. Nolan argues that teacher evaluation and teacher supervision are separate functions. He outlines "seven dimensions" that demonstrate their incompatibility. What is your reaction to Nolan's basic argument? Is there indeed a distinction between supervision and evaluation in purpose and rationale? What about the other dimensions?

3. The author suggests some ways that evaluation and supervision can be separated. Review these basic ways and indicate which way would work best in your school/district. Are there other possible ways to separate the two functions? Describe.

4. Does Nolan's argument persuade you? Can a supervisor serve as a coach? Provide examples.

For Further Research

1. Consult Glanz (1994), in which an attempt at separating evaluation from supervision is described. Could the conditions described in that article be replicated in your school? Why or why not?

2. Compare Nolan's definition of coaching in this chapter with "a more expanded definition of coaching in an earlier article." See Nolan and Hillkirk (1991).

3. Explore the various models of clinical supervision that Pajak (1993) reviews. How would each theorist described address the question, "Can a supervisor be a coach?"

4. Compare Garman's (1982) position on the evaluation/supervision issue with Nolan's stance.

5. Read the recent *NASSP Practitioner* newsletter (1995) that includes a provocative discussion of the role of supervision. The newsletter discusses four schools that have innovative supervisory practices. Discuss each school and the role supervision plays. How similar or dissimilar are these schools from your own? The newsletter concludes with seven intriguing "lessons learned from practice." What is your reaction to these "lessons" and how might Nolan and McGreal respond?

6. How would the following authorities view the issue discussed in this chapter? Cangelosi (1991), Klein (1984), Mosher and Purpel (1972), Oliva (1993), Scriven (1967), Sergiovanni and Starratt (1993), and Wiles and Bondi (1991).

7. Supervision is practiced in noneducational fields, such as counseling and religious studies. Describe how other professionals deal with the evaluation–supervision dilemma. Consult, for example, Pohly (1993) and Williams (1995).

8. Find and describe accounts in which supervisors, principals, and the like, have successfully removed evaluation from supervision. See, for example, Rooney (1993).

9. Conduct a literature review of the *Journal of Personnel Evaluation in Education* and summarize articles and viewpoints about the issue addressed in this chapter.

10. How would Costa and Garmston (1993) address the question, "Can an administrator truly play both roles of evaluator and coach?" (*Hint:* see p. 15 in their text for a start). According to Costa and Garmston, who can serve as a coach and what is supervision? According to Costa and Garmston, how can one build trust, facilitate mutual learning, and enhance growth toward holonomy?

11. Interview or survey teachers and supervisors you know about the issue addressed in this chapter. Report their views and contrast them with your own and those of the authors in this chapter.

12. A number of articles address the issue presented in this chapter. Fewer pieces provide examples in which schools/districts have attempted to reconcile the inherent conflict between evaluation and supervision. Read the following articles and describe attempts to reconcile this dilemma and assess the degree to which these ideas can work in your school/district. See Bryant and Currin (1995), Glanz (1996), Greene (1992), and Poole (1994).

13. Compare and contrast the following views, which reflect the different positions referred to in the postnote summary: Acheson and Gall (1987), Black (1993), Blumberg and Jonas (1987), Brandt (1985), Cangelosi (1991), Costa and Kallick (1993), Garmston (1993), Glatthorn and Newberg (1984), Hazi (1994), Hunter (1988), Isenberg (1990), Pajak (1990), Poole (1994), Popham (1988), Rooney (1993), and Struyk and McCoy (1993).

14. Examine views of Gitlin and Smyth (1989) and Smyth (1991) regarding the views presented in this chapter.

References

Acheson, K., & Gall, M. (1987). *Techniques in the clinical supervision of teachers: Preservice and inservice applications.* New York: Longman.

Black, S. (1993). How teachers are reshaping evaluation procedures. *Educational Leadership, 51,* 38–39.

Blumberg, A., & Jonas, R. S. (1987). The teacher's control over supervision. *Educational Leadership, 44,* 58–62.

Brandt, R. (1985). On teaching and supervising: A conversation with Madeline Hunter. *Educational Leadership, 42,* 61–66.

Bryant, M., & Currin, D. (1995). Views of teacher evaluation from novice and expert evaluators. *Journal of Curriculum and Supervision, 10,* 250–261.

Cangelosi, J. S. (1991). *Evaluating classroom instruction.* New York: Longman.

Costa, A. L., & Garmston, R. J. (1993). *Cognitive coaching: A foundation for renaissance schools.* Norwood, MA: Christopher-Gordon Publishers.

Costa, A. L., & Kallick, B. (1993). Through the lens of a critical friend. *Educational Leadership, 51,* 49—51.

Garman N. B. (1982). The clinical approach to supervision. In T. J. Sergiovanni (Ed.), *Supervision of teaching* (pp. 35–52). Alexandria, VA: Association for Supervision and Curriculum Development.

Garmston, R. (1993). Reflections on cognitive coaching. *Educational Leadership, 51,* 57–61.

Gitlin, A., & Smyth, J. (1989). *Teacher evaluation: Educative alternatives.* New York: Falmer Press.

Glanz, J. (1994) Dilemmas of assistant principals in their supervisory role: Reflections of an assistant principal. *Journal of School Leadership, 4,* 577–593.

Glanz, J. (1996). Improvement versus evaluation as an intractable problem in school supervision: Is a reconciliation possible? *Record in Educational Leadership.*

Glatthorn, A. A., & Newberg, N. A. (1984). A team approach to instructional leadership. *Educational Leadership, 41,* 60–63.

Greene, M. L. (1992). Teacher Supervision as professional development: Does it work? *Journal of Curriculum and Supervision, 7,* 131–148.

Hazi, H. M. (1994). The teacher evaluation-supervision dilemma: A case of entanglements and irreconcilable differences. *Journal of Curriculum and Supervision, 9,* 195–216.

Hunter, M. (1988). Effecting a reconciliation between supervision and evaluation—a reply to Popham. *Journal of Personnel Evaluation in Education, 1,* 275–279.

Isenberg, A. P. (1990). Evaluating teachers—some questions and some considerations. *NASSP Bulletin,* 16–18.

Klein, K. (1984). *Evaluation of teaching: The formative process.* Bloomington, IN: Phi Delta Kappa.

Mosher, R. L., & Purpel, D. E. (1972). *Supervision: The reluctant profession.* New York: Houghton Mifflin.

NASSP Practitioner. (1995). The supervisory continuum: A developmental approach. Volume 22(1).

Nolan, J. F., & Hillkirk, K. (1991). The effects of a reflective coaching project for veteran teachers. *Journal of Curriculum and Supervision, 7,* 62–76.

Oliva, P. F. (1993). *Supervision for today's schools* (3rd ed.). White plains, NY: Longman.

Pajak, E. (1990). Dimensions of supervision. *Educational Leadership, 48,* 78–81.

Pajak, E. (1993). *Approaches to clinical supervision: Alternatives for improving instruction.* Norwood, MA: Christopher-Gordon Publishers.

Pohly, K. (1993). *Transforming the rough places: The ministry of supervision.* Dayton, OH: Whaleprints.

Poole, W. (1994). Removing the "super" from supervision. *Journal of Curriculum and Supervision, 9,* 284–309.

Popham, W. J. (1988). The dysfunctional marriage between formative and summative teacher evaluation. *Journal of Personnel Evaluation in Education, 1,* 269–273.

Rooney, J. (1993). Teacher evaluation: No more "super" vision. *Educational Leadership, 51,* 438–442.

Scriven M. (1967). The methodology of evaluation. In R. E. Stake (Ed.), *Curriculum evaluation.* American Educational Research Association Monograph Series on Evaluation. Chicago: Rand McNally.

Sergiovanni, T. J., & Starratt, R. J. (1993). *Supervision: A Redefinition* (5th ed.). New York: McGraw-Hill.

Smyth, J. (1991). *Teachers as collaborative learners: Challenging dominant forms of supervision.* Philadelphia: Open University Press.

Struyk, L. R., & McCoy, L. H. (1993). Pre-service teachers' use of videotape for self-evaluation. *Clearing House, 67,* 31–34.

Wiles, J., & Bondi, J. (1991). *Supervision: A guide to practice* (3rd ed.). New York: Merrill/Macmillan.

Williams, A. (1995). *Visual and active supervision: Roles, focus, technique.* New York: W.W. Norton & Company.

Issue 6

Has the Field of Supervision Evolved to a Point That It Should Be Called Something Else?

✦ ✦ ✦ ✦

YES—Stephen P. Gordon, Southwest Texas State University
NO—Jeffrey Glanz, Kean College of New Jersey

✦ ✦ ✦

Issue Summary

YES: Steve Gordon,* co-author of the popular supervision text *Supervision of Instruction: A Developmental Approach*, calls for a "radical shift from control supervision to collegial supervision." Dr. Gordon substitutes the term "instructional leadership" for "supervision" and claims supervision has indeed evolved to a point that it should be called something else. A change in name, according to the author, would expedite the reforms necessary for developing essential collegial relationships with teachers.

NO: Jeff Glanz, co-editor of this volume and author of *Bureaucracy and Professionalism*, asserts that although supervision may no longer be fashionable or "pedagogically correct," its primary aim is still to assist teachers and as such be a potent force, if utilized properly, for improving instruction. Efforts to disavow its usefulness or simply call it something else for political (pedagogical) expedience is misguided and ahistorical.

Guiding Questions

1. What assumptions do the authors make about current theory and practice of supervision?
2. How does each author characterize the field of supervision?
3. How does each author define supervision?
4. What specific evidence does each author cite to support his position?
5. According to Professor Gordon, why would "instructional leadership" more accurately describe what supervisors do in schools?
6. According to Professor Glanz, what factors have contributed to supervision remaining incognito?
7. According to each author, what are the prospects for the future of instructional supervision?

*This issue was first framed by Professor Gordon, who upon our request consented to have it included in this book. Our thanks to Steve.

Has the Field of Supervision Evolved to a Point That It Should Be Called Something Else? *Yes*

Stephen P. Gordon

A few years ago, in an article in *The Journal of Curriculum and Supervision* (Gordon, 1992), I discussed the shifting paradigm in supervision, away from the "old supervision" toward the "new supervision." I argued that characteristics of the new supervision were teacher empowerment, integration of supervisory functions, diversity of types of supervisory assistance, continuous collegial support, professional inquiry, and organic rather than mechanical change efforts. Jo Roberts Blaze has captured the spirit of the new supervision in the following description:

> Leadership is shared with teachers, and it is cast in coaching, reflection, collegial investigation, study teams, explorations into the uncertain, and problem solving. It is position-free supervision wherein leaders, teachers, and learners are all one; wherein the underlying spirit is one of expansion, not traditional supervision. Alternatives, not directives or criticism, are the focus, and the community of learners perform professional—indeed, moral—service to students. (cited in Gordon, 1995)

The dictionary definitions of *supervise* (to "watch over," "direct," "oversee," "superintend") are negative mirror images of Blaze's eloquent description. Similarly, despite a reduction in the numbers of supervisors in the corporate sector (due to a combination of technology, downsizing, employee empowerment, and collaborative teams), the corporate concept of supervision, where it still exists, remains one of control. In the book *Stepping up to Supervisor*, for example, Haynes (1991) describes generally agreed-upon duties of supervisors as follows:

1. Assign and distribute work
2. Monitor and control performance
3. Review and evaluate performance
4. Train and develop employees
5. Lead your group
6. Communicate
7. Handle administrative duties (pp. 3–4)

This corporate definition of supervision, like the standard dictionary definitions, clearly reflects a control paradigm. Even Haynes' sixth duty, communication, takes on a decidedly controlling tone when he explains that "a supervisor must communicate to get the job done.

Let your people know what is to be done as well as policies and decisions that affect them" (p. 4). Avila (cited in Gordon, 1995) is correct, then, when she argues that the generally accepted meaning of the word *supervision* is incompatible with "models of empowered professional teachers working alone or with others . . . to enhance instructional effectiveness through inquiry, reflection, sharing, analysis, and generation of alternatives." But what about the term *instructional supervision*? Within our own field, have not those of us who practice, study, and teach supervision changed the meaning of supervision to one more consistent with the nurturance, collegiality, reflective inquiry, and empowerment necessary for professional growth? The answer is yes and no.

Throughout the century there has been a division among scholars concerning whether supervision should be controlling or collegial in nature. An example of control theory is the following quote from an address made by Coffman in 1917:

> The four duties—the laying out and prescribing of materials of instruction, the thinking of teachers and teaching in terms of efficiency levels, the use of standardized tests and scales, and the improvement of the teaching act through criticism of instruction—constitute the scope of supervision. (cited in Barr & Burton, 1926, p. 2)

A second example of control supervision is provided in the 1930 yearbook *The Superintendent Surveys Supervision* (Department of Superintendence,1930), which lists the functions of supervision as inspection, research, training, and guidance. Popham's (1971) *Criterion Referenced Supervision,* Lucio and McNeil's (1979) "Practical Intelligence," and Hunter's (1980, 1984, 1986) version of clinical supervision are more recent examples of control theory. Hunter's (1984) still-popular model, for instance, calls for teachers to be trained in a now complete "science of teaching which is generalizable to all goals in all content" (p. 170), and for that science to be "implemented in classrooms with accountability for its infusion into the program being systematically monitored" (p. 191). Additionally, Hunter (1980) states that "[supervisory] conferences designed to improve instruction must be both diagnostic and prescriptive" (p. 408). These examples are segments in an unbroken line of supervision theories focused on the control of teacher behavior, and their terminology is entirely consistent with the dictionary and corporate definitions of supervision.

From early in the century there has also existed a long line of theories that call for collegial, enabling forms of supervision. This line includes democratic supervision, cooperative supervision, clinical supervision, human resources supervision, developmental supervision, and transformational supervision, among others. Although these theories vary in many respects, they share a set of common principles that contrasts sharply with the control theories of supervision. These principles include the following:

1. A collegial rather than a hierarchical relationship between teachers and formally designated supervisors.
2. Supervision as the province of teachers as well as formally designated supervisors.
3. A focus on teacher growth rather than teacher compliance
4. Facilitation of teachers' collaborating with each other in instructional improvement efforts.
5. Teacher involvement in ongoing reflective inquiry.

If all of this sounds a great deal like the descriptions by Avila, Blaze, and myself, that is because these historical models share many of the same principles that we espouse. At least in terms of the scholarly literature, the "new" supervision is not new at all! It has been discussed in the literature and available to practitioners all along.

For most of the century, then, we have had two families of supervision theories present within the literature, one mirroring the dictionary and corporate definition, the other meaning something quite different. Calling supervision *supervision* has not been a problem for either scholarly camp. After all, both groups knew what *they* meant by supervision, and although they strongly disagreed with the other camp's concept, they understood what the other group meant when they used the term.

Problems with terminology—and my primary argument for calling supervision something different—lie not in scholarly definitions but in conventional practitioners' experiences with and conceptions of supervision. While all of the collegial models mentioned above have been used in professional practice, none of them have ever been used effectively in more than a small percentage of schools. Misinterpretation, misapplication, and co-optation by control supervision have been the typical fate of collegial supervision models. An obvious example is clinical supervision. While functioning as intended by Cogan and Goldhammer in a very small number of schools, it has been stripped of its underlying principles and co-opted by teacher evaluation systems in a very large number of schools.

It is not collegial but control supervision that has historically dominated supervisory practice in the United States. From lay committees conducting school inspections in the eighteenth and nineteenth centuries, to the first professional supervisors demonstrating and monitoring teaching in the early part of the twentieth century, to the 1960s efforts to install "teacher-proof" curricula, right up to the neoscientific management of the 1990s, instructional supervision in the predominant majority of schools has focused on inspection and control of teachers (Gordon, 1992). The "evolution" that has taken place in conventional practice has been toward *new forms of control,* not toward collegiality, empowerment, and transformation.

In the present, control supervision still dominates professional practice. Three activities take place in most schools that practitioners tend to identify as supervision. First and foremost is teacher evaluation, which is a distasteful activity for most evaluators and teachers. The infrequency of classroom evaluations and the lack of connection to professional improvement efforts have meant that traditional teacher evaluation has had almost no effect on teachers' instructional behaviors once the evaluation has been completed. Efforts to tie teacher evaluation to certification for beginning teachers or career ladders have resulted in tremendous expense as well as a great deal of anxiety, stress, competition, and anger on the part of teachers, but they have not brought about long-term changes in teachers instructional behaviors.

The second activity considered to be supervision in conventional practice is monitoring of and assistance with classroom implementation of an instructional model in which the teacher has been recently trained. The most common example in recent years is the Hunter model, but there is an ever-increasing number of packaged programs that belong in this category. School districts may hire outside consultants at considerable expense to train entire faculties in the use of the model, and they expect teachers to return the investment by using the model in the classroom. Rather than clinical supervision or peer coaching, assistance usually takes the form of providing teachers with instructional materials or of troubleshooting during faculty meetings or informal discussions. Classroom monitoring usually occurs during informal walk-throughs or "hallway observations." The exception to this is the Hunter model. In many districts, Hunter's "essential elements" have become the basis of the district's evaluation instrument. In these districts, then, the packaged program and teacher evaluation forms of supervision are combined.

A third form of conventional supervision occurs in states with high-stakes standardized achievement tests. In many schools within these states teachers are expected to teach to the test. In fact, the school's entire curriculum and instructional program may be aligned with the state test. In such schools, supervision, like teaching, is focused on the improvement of test results. In a sense, the test becomes the ultimate "supervisor." This type of supervision may be the most pervasive and controlling, with individual lessons directly related to specific test objectives and formats.

It makes no difference to most teachers that individuals like myself and many of the other authors in this text do not consider any of the three practices described above to be authentic supervision. In conventional schools, supervision *is* what teachers *experience* it to be. It is no wonder, then, that many teachers have extremely negative views of and feelings toward supervision. When my supervision students have asked teachers to make word associations with the term "instructional supervision," not all associations have been negative, but the following responses have been all too common:

Control	Directive
Step-by-step	Irrelevant
Lack of creativity	Waste of time
Lack of free choice	Restricting
Evaluation	Rules
Negative	Dog and pony show
Nonexistent	Big brother
Jumping through hoops	Intimidating
Boring	Constantly under watch
Paperwork	Anxiety
Bureaucrat	Boss
Monitoring instruction	Stress
Guidelines for testing	Need for detailed lesson plans
Authority	Administrative micromanagement
Unrealistic	Yuck!

Although such responses are depressing, they seem to me to be perfectly appropriate in light of what passes for supervision in most schools.

Your reaction to all of this may be that we need to change the practice of supervision, not its name. My argument is that while the primary goal should be a radical shift from control supervision to collegial supervision, changing the name of what we now call supervision, or at least of what is referred to here as collegial supervision, will increase the chance of that transition taking place. As Vygotsky points out, the sense of a word within a particular context is far more powerful than its dictionary *meaning*. The sense of a word "is the sum of all the psychological events aroused in our consciousness by the word" (Vygotsky, 1962). Considering the negative psychological events that the word *supervision* arouses in teachers in many schools, it seems that using that word as the banner under which we attempt to introduce collegiality and empowerment invites confusion at best and suspicion and resistance at worst.

A personal experience illustrates this point. Based on their study of peer supervision, two students of mine decided to start a peer supervision program at a school where they both taught. They got the principal's permission, recruited a dozen potential participants, and invited me to present an overview of clinical and peer *supervision* to the interested teachers. A few days after my presentation, the program coordinators and I discussed the teachers' reactions to the overview I had provided. The teachers were excited about observing each other, collecting and analyzing observation data based on their own instructional concerns, and conferring with each other on instructional improvement efforts. What they were decidedly unenthusiastic about was calling the program peer supervision. They thought the term was hierarchical, antithetical to the principles of collegiality and reflective inquiry I had discussed during the presentation, and demeaning to them as professionals (interestingly, they were just as opposed to calling the program peer coaching, which they also viewed as a hierarchical term). The teachers had all agreed to participate in the program, but they wished to call it "peer observation and interaction," a title to which I readily agreed. This program became quite successful without any additional reference to the term *peer supervision*. Teachers collected a variety of data on each other's teaching, learned new teaching strategies from each other, and collaborated on instructional improvement efforts. By the end of the first year of the program they reported that as a result of their participation they gained new perspectives on students and teaching, reflected more on their instruction, broke out of established patterns of teaching, and engaged in more professional dialogue with other teachers.

Across the nation a growing number of efforts by teachers, administrators, and supervisors, without using the label *instructional supervision*, are relying on the principles of collegial supervision listed above as well as the knowledge, interpersonal skills, technical skills, and tasks typically associated with collegial supervision to improve teaching and learning. Typical examples of these efforts, which still account for only a small fraction of supervisory practice, include the following:

- Administrators and supervisors coordinating a program in which teachers who are experts in technology assist other teachers in developing their instructional expertise and technology through group sessions and one-to-one assistance.
- Principals and teachers using Deming's PDSA (plan, do, study, act) cycle to bring about schoolwide instructional improvement while teachers and students make use of the same model to improve teaching and learning in individual classrooms.
- Parents, trained in classroom observation skills, using observation systems collaboratively developed with teachers to observe student classroom behaviors, then collaboratively interpreting the observation data during postconferences with teachers.
- Teachers participating in action research for instructional improvement individually or with principals, other teachers, parents, or students.
- Collegial groups meeting on a regular basis to share in successes, problems, solutions, theory, research, and dialogue about teaching and learning.
- Experienced mentors, trained in instructional leadership skills, providing technical and emotional support to beginning teachers.
- Teams of teachers designing, teaching, and evaluating interdisciplinary units of instruction, and sharing the units and results with other teachers.

- Teachers designing self-assessment systems including such data as student feedback, videotaped lessons, and student performance, then formulating and implementing data-based self-improvement plans aimed at improving teaching and learning in their classrooms.
- Teachers engaging in reflective writing focused on students, teaching, and learning, including writing in personal journals, case writing, reporting action research results, and biography.

I have participated in or examined programs using each of the above frameworks, and despite the fact that in each case participants were engaged in the professional relationships and activities that I teach about in my university supervision classes, at no time did the teachers participating refer to what was going on as "supervision." Just as well. With all of the historical and psychological baggage that accompanies the word *supervision* in conventional practice, the term becomes an unnecessary barrier to those who attempt to introduce teachers to collegial models of supervision like those described above. Attempts to modify the word rather than replace it—for example, Glickman's *Super-Vision* or my own use of the term *new supervision*—are, in retrospect, likely to have little effect on teachers' perceptions of the term. This is because the new meaning that we offer cannot overpower the sense of the word that teachers have acquired through their experience with conventional supervision. Let us turn our attention, then, to a new term for what is, at least to conventional practitioners, a new supervision.

The term I propose, *instructional leadership,* does not represent a radical change in terminology. There are already some graduate programs that have changed the name of their "supervision" courses to "instructional leadership" courses. Let me say up front that I am not particularly enamored with the word *instruction*. Its dictionary definition is every bit as hierarchical as *supervision's*. However, practitioners do not view *instruction* in the same negative sense that they view *supervision*. To most supervisors and teachers I interact with, *instruction* is merely another word for teaching. Keeping the word *instructional* would help to maintain a link with the historical literature on instructional supervision. However, the real power of the suggested term comes only when the two words, *instructional* and leadership, are considered together.

Unlike *supervision, instructional leadership* is congruent with the five principles of collegial supervision listed earlier. First, regarding the principle of collegiality, although the new term by itself obviously will not produce a more collegial relationship between teachers and principals (who in conventional practice provide most of whatever supervision teachers receive), it does do away with an etymology suggesting the superiority of one of the parties. It reduces, while admittedly not removing, the psychological barrier between teachers and principals attempting to develop symmetrical relationships within the instructional arena.

Second, concerning the principle of supervision as the province of all, given teachers' sense of conventional supervision, most of them have no more desire to provide than to receive supervision. To teachers, instructional leadership has a more positive connotation than supervision. They are already instructional leaders within their own classrooms. Most teachers can describe instructional leadership roles they have assumed beyond their classroom. The concept of instructional leadership offers a wider range of interests and activities than does the conventional conception of supervision.

Third, regarding the principle of teacher growth, "leadership" opens up all types of possibilities. Effective leaders, teachers know, help them to grow. When they have been effective leaders in their classrooms, they have helped students to grow. Preparing for and providing leadership beyond the classroom, provided the leadership is voluntary and within an area of the teacher's interest, is a powerful avenue for teacher development. Contrast this with conventional supervision, which involves inspection and control, and to many teachers restricts rather than fosters professional growth.

Fourth, concerning the principle of teacher collaboration, since the primary form of supervision in most conventional schools is teacher evaluation, for teachers in these schools supervision and teacher collaboration don't mix. In fact, in districts that have tied teacher evaluation to career ladders, supervision is associated with competition, not collaboration. On the other hand, the concept of teacher collaboration for the improvement of teaching and learning has in my experience been one that teachers have been willing to embrace, so long as they are provided sufficient time and administrative support for their collaborative efforts.

Finally, regarding the principle of reflective inquiry, the evaluation systems, forced adoptions of packaged instructional programs, and high-stakes testing associated with conventional supervision mean that efforts to encourage reflective inquiry in the name of supervision are bound to meet with more than a little teacher skepticism. Analyzing teaching and leadership experiences, exploring new ways of improving instruction, and engaging in reflective dialogue with other professionals seems far more congruent with the term *instructional leadership* than with the conventional conception of supervision.

I am not arguing here that changing "instructional supervision" to "instructional leadership" would be a *primary* cause of collegiality replacing control. If collegiality finally prevails in school practice, it will be because of three primary factors. First, PK–12 education has for the last several years come under increasing public pressure to improve the teaching and learning that goes on in our schools. Second, time after time during those same years the control paradigm in general and control supervision in particular have failed to produce the desired improvements. And third, in a variety of school settings, through a variety of frameworks, and under different labels, instructional leadership following the collegial principles outlined above is *working*. The growing documentation on the success of such leadership is becoming increasingly difficult to ignore during this period of educational crisis.

If adopting the term *instructional leadership* will not by itself cause a transition to a collegial paradigm, it can make that transition a smoother one by helping principals and teachers to differentiate collegial improvement efforts from teacher evaluation and school accountability, and to unite under a common banner in pursuit of improved teaching and learning. It will also allow scholars and practitioners who are committed to a collegial approach to instructional leadership to escape an Alice-in-Wonderland professional existence in which they are constantly forced to explain to others that supervision is really quite the opposite of what the rest of the world considers it to be. These reasons seem to me to be sufficient to warrant a change of name.

One argument against changing the name of supervision is that the rich body of research and theory in the supervision literature would be lost. In response to this argument, I point to what used to be called inservice education. In the 1970s and 1980s "inservice education" evolved into "staff development." As the term *staff development* became dominant, some educators maintained that staff development was something completely separate from inservice education. Others used the two terms interchangeably, but tended to refer to the former far more frequently than the latter. Most considered inservice education to be a rather limited subset of staff development. Eventually, however, scholars who had written books, articles, and research reports on "inservice education" began to write about "staff development" instead. Practitioners who had been called inservice education coordinators became staff development coordinators. The fact that the field became known as staff development did not mean that the best of the research and theoretical writing on inservice education was lost (admittedly, there was not a great deal of it). It was still easily located in databases and was referred to as historical information in the new staff development literature. Currently, "staff development" seems to be evolving toward either "professional development" or "teacher development," depending on which author you read. Again, while literature on professional development or teacher development conceptualizes the field differently than earlier literature on staff development or inservice education, the best of the old literature is still reviewed in and accessed through the comprehensive works on professional or teacher development. In like manner, future literature on "instructional leadership" would discuss and build on the best of the supervision literature.

The title of this chapter asks if the field of supervision has evolved to a point that it should be called something else. My answer to this question is a qualified yes. That still small (at least in practice) but now finally growing branch of supervision referred to here as collegial supervision—the branch that will continue to grow and flourish and that is the best hope for improving teaching and learning in our schools—should change its name. *Instructional leadership* would be appropriate. That branch of supervision that has always been focused on surveillance and control—the branch that is still dominant in practice but that seems finally doomed to wither and die because of its repeated failures in a time of educational crisis—should be allowed to live out its remaining years under the name of *supervision,* the word that has become inextricably interwoven with conventional practice.

References

Barr, A. S., & Burton, W. H. (1926). *The supervision of instruction.* New York: Appleton & Company.

Department of Superintendence (1930). *Eighth yearbook: The superintendent surveys supervision.* Washington, DC: National Educational Association.

Gordon, S. P. (1992). Paradigms, transitions, and the new supervision. *Journal of Curriculum and Supervision, 8,* 62–76.

Gordon, S. P. (Ed.). (1995, April), *Newsletter of the Instructional Supervision Special Interest Group of the American Educational Research Association.*

Haynes, M. E. (1991). *Stepping up to supervision* (rev. ed.). Menlo Park, CA: Crisp Publications.

Hunter, M. (1980). Six types of supervisory conferences. *Educational Leadership, 37,* 408–412.

Hunter, M. (1984). Knowing, teaching, and supervising. In P. L. Hosford (Ed.), *Using what we know about teaching.* Alexandria, VA: Association for Supervision and Curriculum Development.

Hunter, M. (1986). Let's eliminate the preobservation conference. *Educational Leadership, 43*(6), 69–70.

Lucio, W. H., & McNeil, J. D. (1979). *Supervision: A synthesis of thought and action* (3rd ed.). New York: McGraw-Hill.

Popham, J. (1971). *Criterion referenced supervision.* Los Angeles: VIMCET Associates.

Vygotsky, L. S. (1962). *Thought and action.* Cambridge, MA: The MIT Press.

Has the Field of Supervision Evolved to a Point That It Should Be Called Something Else? *No*

Jeffrey Glanz

A couple of years ago I was delivering a paper before the Council of Professors of Instructional Supervision (COPIS) in Chicago in which I argued for greater attention to historical investigation of supervision (Glanz, 1994; Glanz, 1995). In concluding my talk, I cautioned the audience that my statements of criticism and concern about the state of supervision as a professional practice and field of study should not be construed as an abandonment of supervision. To the contrary, I affirmed my commitment to supervision as a viable and necessary function in schools. After my presentation a discussion ensued in which my colleague Carl Glickman politely yet forcefully stated that while my plea for continued investigation of supervision was intriguing it was superfluous in the sense that "we don't call it supervision anymore."

Echoing the theme of an ASCD yearbook that he edited and affirming Sergiovanni's (1992) hope that a day will come when "supervision will no longer be needed," Glickman (1992) asserted that the word *supervision* was "becoming obsolete" and that *instructional leadership* was a more apt term. I gather that Glickman and some other scholars profess that either supervision has evolved to a point that we must call it something else or that it is simply defunct. "We now call it 'instructional leadership,' " they say, "we don't call it supervision anymore."[1]

I don't think Glickman, Gordon, Sergiovanni, or Starratt (1992) are disingenuous by purposely eschewing the word *supervision,* but I do think the penchant for substitute language in general is symptomatic of a more widespread trend to speak in euphemisms—sometimes referred to as jargon or educationese. Jerry Pulley (1994), a professor of supervision at the University of Texas-Pan American, in an article entitled "Doublespeak and Euphemisms in Education," maintains that our propensity for political correctness, or what Lasley (1993) calls "pedagogical correctness" in this context, has beclouded our perspective so much that our language has become confused and self-contradictory at best and "grossly deceptive" and evasive at worst.

Given the complex technological and social realities of schooling today, many of us would agree that supervision as a function in schools faces an onerous task of improving instruction and promoting learning. Beleaguered by some fundamental problems, such as unpopular acceptance and given its rather authoritarian legacy (Glanz, in press), it seems to me unfortunate and misguided to burden the field by further exacerbating its identity crisis by denying or not acknowledging its basic purpose and significance. To confront and ameliorate the field's deficits (as for an individual undergoing counseling therapy) we must at least acknowledge our past, however dismal we think it may be. We need to be somewhat clear on the meaning we ascribe to the term *supervision*. Language is important; it is not just a game of semantics. Language defines reality and how we interpret new meanings (Brown, 1958). To say it is "not supervision" offers little solace and doesn't provide much direction for practitioners in the field. Let's call supervision what it is and deal with it. Changing terminologies may be, in Pulley's (1994) words, "euphemistically correct," but it doesn't deal substantively with the underlying issues that beg for consideration and resolution. As Pohly (1993) argues ". . . some people suggest abandoning the term and substituting something more palatable, but that is a false solution because it fails to deal with the condition that produces the resistance" (p. 2).

No, the field of supervision has not evolved to a point that it should be called something else. My contention is that supervision should be called what it is—engaging teachers, face to face, in an effort to improve instruction with information, techniques, and skills that are likely to have beneficial effects on student learning. Yes, supervision can be facilitative and collegial, and supervisors (call them mentors, lead teachers, or persons with formal supervisory responsibilities) can act as coaches and reflective practitioners. Yet at times supervision may rely on expert knowledge and supervisors may employ more directive measures. But regardless of which approach is used it is still supervision. To refuse or deny this crucial point is misguided and ahistorical.

Supervision has not evolved to a point that it should be called something else. My case is based on an examination of why proposals and theories of supervision, historically, have masqueraded under a miscellaneous array of names and approaches. Understanding this historical anomaly will explain why I think the field of supervision should resurface or emerge from the depths of obscurity to actualize its role and function in schools and not succumb to "pedagogical correctness." I will also assert, albeit briefly, that attempts to define supervision in ways that obfuscate its intended purpose are misguided because of the mistaken notion that teachers do not want supervision.

Supervision as Traveling Incognito

Earliest recorded instances of the word *supervision* established the process as entailing "general management, direction, control, and oversight" (Grumet, 1979; Gwynn, 1961; *Oxford English Dictionary*, 1989). Payne (1875), author of the first published textbook on supervision, stated emphatically that teachers must be "held responsible" for work performed in the classroom and that the supervisor, as expert, would "oversee" and ensure "harmony and efficiency." Methods in supervision prior to 1920 were impressionistic and inspectional (Glanz, 1991). The raison d'être of supervision was to eradicate inefficiency and incompetence among the teaching force. Various elaborate rating forms were developed to accomplish this major objective (Boyce, 1915). Improvement of instruction was less important than purging the schools of the inept. Supervision as a role and function in schools was more concerned with evaluative measures that were bureaucratic and inspectional. Supervision of this sort attracted vociferous criticism from teachers and others (Glanz, 1990). Representative of this opposition are comments made by Sallie Hill (1918), a teacher speaking before the Department of Classroom Teachers, decrying supervisory methods of rating. Hill charged:

> There is no democracy in our schools. . . . Here let me say that I do not want to give the impression that we are sensitive. No person who has remained a teacher for ten years can be sensitive. She is either dead or has gone into some other business. . . . There are too many supervisors with big salaries and undue rating powers. (p. 506)

The movement to turn supervisory theory and practice to more democratic and improvement foci, while at the same time minimizing the evaluative function, occurred in the 1920s as a direct result of growing opposition to autocratic supervisory methods. Consequently, supervisors tried to change their image as "snoopervisors" by adopting alternate supervision methods. The following poem, quoted in part, indicates the desired change of focus to more democratic methods in supervision:

> With keenly peering eyes and snooping nose,
> From room to room the Snoopervisor goes.
> He notes each slip, each fault with lofty frown,
> And on his rating card he writes it down;
> His duty done, when he has brought to light,
> The things the teachers do that are not right. . . .
>
> The supervisor enters quietly,
> "What do you need? How can I help today?
> John, let me show you. Mary, try this way."
> He aims to help, encourage and suggest,
> That teachers, pupils all may do their best.
>
> (*Anonymous,* 1929)

Influenced in large measure by John Dewey's (1929) theories of democratic and scientific thinking as well as by Hosic's (1920) ideas of democratic supervision, supervisors attempted to apply scientific methods and cooperative problem-solving approaches to educational problems (Pajak, 1993). More fundamentally, however, the rhetoric of democratic supervision now focused on making supervision more palatable and acceptable among teachers. Despite the advancement of a democratic theory of supervision, the stigma of supervision as an autocratic and inspectional function was not easily lifted. Criticism against supervisory practice in schools continued unabated (Rousmaniere, 1992).

Other models and conceptions of supervision emerged in the decades to follow. Leadership, clinical, developmental, and transformational models, among others, had a common bond in that they emerged as a reaction to bureaucracy in education and were influenced by the human relations (democratic) movement beginning in the early twentieth century (Glanz, in press). Democracy in supervision implied a "deep concern for human relationships" and practices that encouraged and respected the dignity of the teacher (Spears, 1953). Each of the models attempted to support this view of supervision, albeit in very different ways. In doing so, a view was proposed to counter the ill effects of supervision's bureaucratic legacy.

Scholars of late have indicated the need to abandon vestiges of authoritarian conceptions of supervision. To be sure, however, efforts to eliminate the stigma of the "supervisor" and of "supervision" are not new. As early as the third decade of the twentieth century, Reeder (1930) affirmed that supervision as inspection was being intensely criticized by teachers and that a *change in title* might reduce potential conflict. Barr, Burton, and Brueckner (1947) suggested that the term *supervisor* might be replaced by *consultant* or *adviser*. In the fifties, titles such as "director" or "coordinator" were common. Less common, although prevalent, were "helping teacher," and "resource person" (Spears, 1953). In the sixties and seventies, "change agents" were in vogue. Wilhelms (1973) acknowledged the tendency for many educators to eschew the word *supervisor*.

Efforts to reconstruct supervision as a role and function have been as much an attempt to avoid the field's autocratic heritage as it has been to find its niche in schools. Attempts to downplay the field's legacy of evaluative and inspectional practices and to accentuate its improvement function have led to confusion of purpose and direction. Put simply, the field of supervision has never come to grips with its legacy. Beset by a lack of consensus in defining its purpose, a low approval rating, and a host of other seemingly intractable problems, supervision has remained vulnerable to a plethora of proposals and theories. We who are concerned about supervision have never adequately addressed the fundamental and underlying problems of the field. Consequently, supervision as a role and function has traveled incognito.

It was in fact Harold Spears, an assistant superintendent in San Francisco and author of a widely used textbook of supervision in the fifties, who first expressed a concern that the field was traveling incognito. Spears (1953) stated:

> Thirty or forty years ago, when supervision was first settling down in the organizational scheme of things as a service to the classroom teacher, a supervisor was a supervisor. Today, when supervision is attaching itself to almost anything that has to do with furthering learning, a supervisor masquerades under a miscellaneous array of titles. Supervision today often travels incognito. (p. 84)

Vulnerable, ill-defined, and unwilling to stake a claim to its intended purpose, the field of supervision has tried to conceal itself, and so problems have intensified. The fact that supervision has been traveling incognito has had significant consequences for it as a field of study and as a professional practice (Hazi & Glanz, 1996).

Supervision has been referred to in various ways (e.g., "glue"), but I think a more appropriate and accurate metaphor might be "tofu." Although I hope to elaborate on this metaphor in more detail in the future, suffice it to say that because we have not addressed or resolved several critical issues, supervision has become "anything and everything" and as such is very much like tofu, a food that assumes the distinctive characteristics or flavors of its host dish. In spite of its identity crisis, the field of supervision hasn't evolved into something else; it has just been submerged. It's time that the field come to grips with what it is all about.

Teachers Want Supervision

Teachers, in my view, want one-to-one help. They want feedback from, for example, an assistant principal who observes a lesson and conducts a post observation conference during which insights and suggestions for improvement are offered. In this scenario, both supervisor and supervisee can be co-inquirers. Often recommendations for improvement are not dictated but rather emerge amidst a reflective, inductive dialogue between teacher and supervisor. The supervisor facilitates and guides the teacher to understand the complexities of classroom interaction. Although supervision can sometimes be threatening, particularly for preservice teachers and nontenured faculty, it offers an opportunity to obtain valuable information about teaching and learning.

Teachers want supervision of this sort. They want supervision that is well informed, practical, and helpful, regardless of who offers it (see, for example, Blumberg & Jonas, 1987; Brandt, 1985; Glanz, 1996; Whistler, 1984). Some of those who advocate abandonment of *supervision* as a term aren't cognizant or accepting of this premise. Supervision shouldn't be called something else. To do so, to be "pedagogically correct" by eschewing the label, not only potentially limits viable options for improving instruction but does little if anything to explain what supervisory practices may in fact contribute to our efforts at school renewal. Whether called cognitive coaching, instructional leadership, critical inquiry, or evaluation, if it is about working face to face with classroom teachers to refine teaching practice (Nolan, 1995), then it is still supervision to me.

Conclusion

Some view the evolution of the practice of instructional supervision as a progression from crude, unsophisticated approaches to more refined techniques and methodologies. Cognitive coaching, for example, is considered a refinement of earlier clinical approaches that only emphasized behavioral changes. For others supervision, as traditionally conceived and practiced, is defunct. For still others, current proposals and theories of supervision are merely masquerading under a miscellaneous array of names and approaches in order to renounce the field's bureaucratic heritage. Supervision, as a function, may no longer be fashionable or "pedagogically correct," but regardless of what it is called, it is still supervision. Its primary aim is still to assist teachers in improving instruction. As long as this remains of vital importance, the field of supervision can emerge as a potent force for promoting excellence in schools.

Endnote

1. It is interesting to note that a prominent journal in the field formerly called the *Record in Educational Administration and Supervision* recently changed its name to the *Record in Educational Leadership*.

References

Anonymous. (1929). The snoopervisor, the whoopervisor, and the supervisor. *Playground and Recreation, XXIII*, 558.

Barr, A. S., Burton, W. H., & Brueckner, L. J. (1947). *Supervision: Democratic leadership for the improvement of learning* (2nd ed.). New York: Appleton-Century.

Blumberg, A., & Jonas, R. S. (1987). The teacher's control over supervision. *Educational Leadership, 44*(8), 58–62.

Boyce, A. C. (1915). Methods for measuring teachers' efficiency. *Fourteenth Yearbook of the National Society for the Study of Education, Part II* (pp. 9–81). Chicago: The University of Chicago Press.

Brandt, R. (1985). On teaching and supervising: A conversation with Madeline Hunter. *Educational Leadership, 42*(5), 61–66.

Brown, R. (1958). *Words and things*. Illinois: The Free Press.

Dewey, J. (1929). *The sources of a science of education*. New York: Liveright.

Glanz, J. (1990). Beyond bureaucracy: Notes on the professionalization of public school supervision in the early twentieth century. *Journal of Curriculum and Supervision, 5*, 150–170.

Glanz, J. (1991). *Bureaucracy and professionalism: The evolution of public school supervision*. Cranbury, NJ: Fairleigh Dickinson University Press.

Glanz, J. (1994). *History of educational supervision: Proposals and prospects.* Paper presented at the meeting of the Council of Professors of Instructional Supervision (COPIS), Chicago, Illinois.

Glanz, J. (1995). Exploring supervision history: An Invitation and agenda. *Journal of Curriculum and Supervision, 10,* 95–113.

Glanz, J. (1996). Improvement versus evaluation as an intractable problem in school supervision: Is a reconciliation possible? *Record in Educational Leadership.*

Glanz, J. (in press). Histories, antecedents, and legacies: Constructing a history of school supervision. In G. R. Firth & E. Pajak (Eds.), *Handbook of research on school supervision.* New York: Macmillan.

Glickman, C. D. (1992). Introduction: Postmodernism and supervision. In C. D. Glickman (Ed.), *Supervision in transition* (pp. 30–43). Alexandria, VA: Association for Supervision and Curriculum Development.

Grumet, M. (1979). Supervision and situation: A methodology of self-report for teacher education. *Journal of Curriculum Theorizing, 1,* 191–257.

Gwynn, J. M. (1961). *Theory and practice of supervision.* New York: Dodd Mead & Co.

Hazi, H. M., & Glanz, J. (1996). *Supervision travelling incognito: Its roots, its evolution, its future.* Unpublished manuscript.

Hill, S. (1918). Defects of supervision and constructive suggestions thereon. *National Educational Association Proceedings, 56,* 347–350.

Hosic, J. F. (1920). The democratization of supervision. *School and Society, 11,* 331–336.

Lasley, T. J. (1993). Rx for pedagogical correctness: Professional correctness. *Clearing House, 67,* 77–79.

Nolan, J. F. (1995, April). Time for a name change? A response. *Instructional Supervision AERA/SIG Newsletter, 15,* 4.

Oxford English Dictionary. (1989). Oxford: Clarendon Press.

Pajak, E. (1993). *Approaches to clinical supervision: Alternatives for improving instruction.* Norwood, MA: Christopher-Gordon Publishers.

Payne, W. H. (1875). *Chapters in school supervision.* New York: Van Antwerp Bragg and Company

Pohly, K. (1993). *Transforming the rough places: The ministry of supervision.* Dayton, OH: Whaleprints.

Pulley, J. L. (1994). Doublespeak and euphemisms in education. *The Clearing House, 67,* 271–273.

Reeder, W. G. (1930). *The fundamentals of public school administration.* New York: Macmillan.

Rousmaniere, K. (1992). *City teachers: Teaching in New York City schools in the 1920s.* Unpublished doctoral dissertation, Columbia University.

Sergiovanni, T. J. (1992). Moral authority and the regeneration of supervision. In C. D. Glickman (Ed.), *Supervision in transition* (pp. 30–43). Alexandria, VA: Association for Supervision and Curriculum Development.

Spears, H. (1953). *Improving the supervision of instruction.* Englewood Cliffs, NJ: Prentice-Hall.

Starratt, R. J. (1992). After supervision. *Journal of Curriculum and Supervision, 8,* 77–86.

Whistler, N. L. (1984). How teachers view their supervision. *Catalyst for Change, 14,* 26–29.

Wilhelms, F. T. (1973). *Supervision in a new key.* Washington, DC: Association for Supervision and Curriculum Development.

Postnote

Has the Field of Supervision Evolved to a Point That It Should Be Called Something Else?

Both views taken together represent the complexity of dimensions involved in understanding how the field of supervision has evolved. The rise and evolution of supervision as a function and a role have perhaps not been studied sufficiently. Clearly, however, the field has been shaped and influenced by a plethora of educational and non-educational factors. The history of supervision is a history of the interaction of broad social and intellectual movements within American society. The evolution of supervision and how current trends and forces continue to shape discourse in the field warrant analysis.

Review Questions for

The Yes Response:

1. Describe what Dr. Gordon refers to as the "spirit of the new supervision"? Have you experienced this "spirit" in your school/district?
2. How would Madeline Hunter respond to the author's assertion that her model of supervision is fundamentally based on control theory?
3. How would Professor Harris in Issue 7 respond to Gordon's clarion call in favor of collegial supervision?
4. The author says that collegial supervision has been coopted by control supervision. From your experience, is this true? Explain.
5. Do you agree with Gordon's observation that "control theory still dominates professional practice"? If so, explain how.
6. The author describes three forms of conventional supervision. Which form most closely resembles your school/district?
7. Gordon lists a number of responses that some people have made in relation to the term *supervision*. Which terms best describe your reaction to supervision. Explain by providing examples.
8. React to the author's claim that the term *supervision* is unnecessary.
9. How would Glanz respond to the arguments presented by this author?

The No Response:

1. Why do you think Carl Glickman objects to the word "supervision"? You might want to consult the ASCD yearbook edited by Glickman (1992).
2. What recommendation does Glanz make to deal with the field's authoritarian legacy? How do you react to his recommendation?

3. What does it mean to be "pedagogically correct?" Can you provide some examples? Explain.

4. According to Glanz, why hasn't the field evolved to a point that it should be called something else?

5. How does Glanz define supervision? How does his definition compare to yours? To Gordon's?

6. What precipitated a change away from evaluative supervision in the 1920s, and what relevance might this have today?

7. According to Glanz, what brought about the emergence of various models of supervision over the last 30 years? How are models of supervision today influenced by the factors Glanz highlights?

8. What does it mean that supervision has traveled "incognito?" Do you agree or disagree? Explain and give examples.

9. Why has Glanz metaphorically referred to supervision as "tofu"? What is your reaction to supervision as tofu? What are possible implications for the field if one accepts this metaphor?

10. In your estimation, do teachers want supervision? What supervisory practices would teachers welcome, if any?

11. How would Gordon respond to the arguments presented by this author?

For Further Research

1. Gordon notes that the word *instruction* has hierarchical connotations. What is the etymology of the word, and how might the term *instructional leadership* fare in your school/district?

2. Compare Glanz's discussion of the origins of supervision with Sergiovanni's (see Perspective 1). Research the origins of educational supervision.

3. Develop a list of other arguments each author could have made to present or strengthen his position.

4. Design a questionnaire and conduct a survey of teachers in a school other than your own about reactions to supervision. Tabulate and present your findings. Conduct a literature review of similar studies and present findings.

5. Interview a few supervisors to ascertain their reactions to the issue under discussion. Present your findings.

6. Select three references from each essay in this chapter and write an annotated bibliography (total of six references) describing, in part, the author's view of supervision.

7. Consult *Instructional Supervision AERA/SIG Newsletter, 15,* and review the responses to the question: "Has the field traditionally known as instructional supervision evolved to a point where it should be called something else?" (pp. 4-5). Which response most closely resembles your own? Write your own response.

8. What is the future of supervision? Examine Anderson's (1982) remarks. Have his hopes for supervision been realized? Compare Kanawati and Glickman's (in press) views about the future of supervision with your own view.

9. Why has the field of supervision had difficulty in defining itself? Review five ways in which different authorities in the field have defined supervision. See, for example, Bolin (1987) and Krey and Burke (1989).

10. Compare Gordon's (1992) views with the views presented in this chapter. Have his hope and vision for a "new supervision" been realized?

References

Anderson, R. H. (1982). Creating a future for supervision. In T. J. Sergiovanni (Ed.), *Supervision of teaching* (pp. 153–169). Washington, DC: Association for Supervision and Curriculum Development.

Bolin, F. S. (1987). On defining supervision. *Journal of Curriculum and Supervision, 2,* 368–380.

Glickman, C. D. (Ed.). (1992). *Supervision in transition.* Alexandria, VA: Association for Supervision and Curriculum Development.

Gordon, S. P. (1992). Paradigms, transitions, and the new supervision. *Journal of Curriculum and Supervision, 8,* 62–76.

Kanawati, D. G., & Glickman, C. D. (in press). Future directions of supervision. In G. R. Firth & E. Pajak (Eds.), *Handbook of research on school supervision.* New York: Macmillan.

Krey, R. D., & Burke, P. J. (1989). *A design for instructional supervision.* Springfield, IL: Charles C. Thomas.

Issue 7

Is a Collegial Relationship Possible between Supervisors and Teachers?

✦ ✦ ✦ ✦

YES—Barbara Nelson Pavan, Temple University
NO—Ben M. Harris, University of Texas at Austin

✦ ✦ ✦

Issue Summary

YES: Barbara Pavan, professor of educational administration at Temple University, affirms that a collegial relationship between teachers and supervisors is not only possible but essential for the growth of teachers, students, and supervisors. Dr. Pavan underscores her theme by emphasizing at the outset of her essay that "Unless supervisors develop a collegial relationship with teachers, they are basically ineffective as they seek to improve the instructional program for children." She describes how supervision can contribute to the development of collegial relationships in schools.

NO: Ben Harris, M. K. Hage Centennial Professor Emeritus at the University of Texas at Austin, believes that collegiality is a "misguided paradigm for defining teacher–supervisor relationships." In his essay, Harris argues that collegiality is inappropriate "to the mission, purposes, and organizational contexts of public elementary and secondary schools." In its stead, Harris advocates "collaborative teamwork" relationships that "go beyond the daily concerns of individual classroom teachers."

Guiding Questions

1. What does collegiality mean to you?
2. What factors impede collegial relationships between teachers and supervisors?
3. Is fostering one-to-one collegial relationships necessary? Why or why not?
4. What aspects of Pavan's arguments would Harris agree with? disagree with?
5. What aspects of Harris's arguments would Pavan agree with? disagree with?
6. What aspects of Pavans' and Harris' thinking make most sense to you? Did you have trouble accepting any of their arguments? If so, which ones?

Is a Collegial Relationship Possible between Supervisors and Teachers? *Yes*

Barbara Nelson Pavan

Unless supervisors develop a collegial relationship with teachers, they are basically ineffective as they seek to improve the instructional program for children. The assumption that professionals such as teachers will respond to bureaucratic, hierarchical orders once they are behind the classroom door should by now be laid to rest. Monitoring teachers' performance by direct supervision ("snoopervision") has probably had the effect of teachers even more stubbornly resisting ideas that might be useful to them, merely because of the method by which those ideas have been delivered. The phrase, "teachers as professionals," has been mouthed all too often by those who then treat teachers as workers with a minimal education, a lack of ideas, and no interest in their students' welfare. Our schools are filled with so much talent in the form of intelligent, competent, and knowledgeable teachers that is underutilized because of our continued reliance on the bureaucratic organizational model rather than on restructuring into a learning community model.

It is not only possible for teachers and supervisors to have a collegial relationship, it is essential for the improvement of schools. Too many of these relationships have not been collegial, yet most supervision textbooks indicate not only how such interactions may be fostered but that they should be fostered.

An analysis of effective schools research indicates that productive school culture requires four process variables to sustain itself: (1) collaborative planning and collegial relationships; (2) building a sense of community through appropriate use of ceremony, symbols, and rules; (3) sharing clear goals and high expectations; and (4) maintaining order and discipline (Purkey & Smith, 1983). Without faculty-supervisory-administrative collegial relationships, this nurturing culture is nonexistent for either students or teachers.

What Are Supervisors Supposed to Do?

What are the actual functions of supervision? Ben Harris (1985, p. 18) has presented us with a classic list of professional supervisory competencies:

1. Developing curriculum
2. Providing materials
3. Providing staff for instruction
4. Organizing for instruction

5. Relating special pupil services
6. Arranging for inservice education
7. Developing public relations
8. Providing facilities for instruction
9. Evaluating instruction

An overlap between supervisory tasks and administrative tasks is noted when the list of principal tasks that follows is compared to the list given above. Some of the differences result from the number of categories or the terminology used. Principalship textbooks typically include a list of administrative tasks comprising:

1. Instruction and curriculum
2. Pupil personnel
3. Community and school relations
4. Staff personnel
5. Community relations
6. Financial and facility management

Many supervisory functions have been assigned to building principals as districts have eliminated supervisors to cut costs. Often all supervisory functions except teacher evaluation have been neglected. Teachers are the ones most affected by the manner in which these tasks are implemented and therefore should be involved in decisions about them.

An extensive effort by the Association for Supervision and Curriculum Development (ASCD) led by Pajak (1990) identifies the following 12 dimensions of supervision, listed in order of importance:

1. *Communication*: ensuring open and clear communication among individuals and groups throughout the organization.
2. *Staff development*: developing and facilitating meaningful opportunities for professional growth.
3. *Instructional program*: supporting and coordinating efforts to improve the instructional program.
4. *Planning and change*: initiating and implementing collaboratively developed strategies for continuous improvement.
5. *Motivating and organizing*: helping people to develop a shared vision and achieve collective aims.
6. *Observation and conferencing*: providing feedback to teachers based on classroom observation.
7. *Curriculum*: coordinating and integrating the process of curriculum development and implementation.
8. *Problem solving and decision making*: using a variety of strategies to clarify and analyze problems and to make decisions.

9. *Service to teachers*: providing materials, resources, and assistance to support teaching and learning.
10. *Personal development*: recognizing and reflecting upon one's personal and professional beliefs, abilities, and actions.
11. *Community relations*: establishing and maintaining open and productive relations between the school and its community.
12. *Research and program evaluation*: encouraging experimentation and assessing outcomes.

Reflecting the current writings in the field of supervision, the language used to describe these 12 dimensions is notably different from the language used by Harris and principalship textbooks, with phrases such as "open and clear communication," "facilitating," "supporting," "collaboratively developed," "helping people to develop a shared vision," "providing feedback," "integrating," "using a variety of strategies to clarify and analyze problems and to make decisions," "assistance to support teaching and learning," and "encouraging experimentation." The picture that comes to mind is that of a supervisor who involves all teachers in the instructional life of the school, one who has the group process skills to ensure that the talents of all staff are utilized and that each teacher is involved in improving the instructional program for the benefit of the particular students in this school in his or her own way. This picture, derived from the language of Pajak's 12 dimensions, is one that underscores those conditions and circumstances essential to the development of professional relationships. The supervision textbook by Glickman, Gordon, and Ross-Gordon (1995) clearly advocates this approach.

The prime purpose for having people in the role of supervisor is to increase the learning of children by improving what actually happens in classrooms. While the development of curriculum is crucial, that is probably more efficiently accomplished in other places than in the individual school; but the selection of curriculum, materials, and learning activities for instruction to fit the needs of particular students and teachers should be determined at the school level. Thus, the major reason for having supervisors is to observe the instructional process for each and every teacher or teacher team and to assist teachers to improve learning by analyzing the teaching–learning process and providing information on teaching alternatives and the skills to enable teachers to change their instructional strategies. This is more likely to be accomplished by engaging teachers in reflection not only on their individual teaching practices but on the total school environment and its impact on the children. An inquiry, problem-solving climate that nurtures questioning and risk taking will foster this reflection.

As one measure of the development and legitimization of collegial supervision it should be noted that 3 of the 13 chapters in the 1982 ASCD Yearbook, *Supervision of Teaching*, mention collegiality, including Alfonso and Goldsberry's (1982) "Colleagueship in Supervision," which notes ways that the organization might promote such a relationship. Ten years later nearly every yearbook chapter in *Supervision in Transition* advocates collegiality, with Sergiovanni (1992) ending his final chapter with "Valuing Collegiality," which he notes is "the existence of a set of norms and values that defines the faculty as a community of like-minded people who are bonded to work together in a common commitment . . . obligated to work together for the common good. The source for such collegiality rests in professional and moral authority . . . Under such circumstances, external supervision will no longer be needed."

School-Based Management and Collegiality

Teacher empowerment means different things to different groups and individuals. Empowered teachers make decisions about the school as a group, with the decisions based on what is best for the children rather than themselves. Teacher empowerment may mean giving up some individual autonomy for the benefit of the school program. In other words, with empowerment comes responsibility for students' learning. Instead of efforts spent assigning blame to those either within or outside the school, supervisors and teachers must work together to facilitate learning of all the students.

In a truly teacher-empowered or school-based-management school, staff (parents may also be included) have control over all resources including personnel and financial. The supervisor or administrator becomes a member of the group. An enlightened staff studies, debates, and decides the staff roles needed and which individuals should fill them. Utilization of the building and selection of materials are also the prerogative of the staff. Additionally, they should decide on what staff development is needed and how the staff will be supervised and evaluated. All this must be done within the funds allocated by the school district and within district, state, and federal guidelines. The expertise of the staff or their ability to see the need for and willingness to seek expertise when needed, will determine the quality of the school program.

Collegiality and a democratic learning community are notions that have run through the writing on administration and supervision for most of this century (since Dewey and Counts). These concepts are used so frequently, and yet so little evidence is seen of them in practice that it is easy to become dismayed. There is a role for the supervisor in providing expertise in group processes: research knowledge about specific issues the school is studying, and the rationale for certain practices; to indicate inconsistencies in the discussion by questioning and probing; and to illuminate the ramifications of decisions that are being considered. Still, the final decision must be made by the consensus of the involved faculty, not the supervisor or administrator.

How Might a Collegial Relationship Be Fostered?

Cogan (1973, p. 68) defined "clinical supervision as colleagueship . . . the teacher and clinical supervisor work together as associates and equals [they have different, not similar, competencies] . . . bound together by a common purpose . . . the improvement of student's learning through the improvement of the teacher's instruction . . . [which] does not diminish the autonomy and independence the teacher should have." The collegial relationship "ceases to exist when either assumes an ascendant role or is accorded an ascendant role by the other."

Supervisors need to use their communication and change agent skills to develop a supportive environment where teachers know that they can trust supervisors to work with them to improve instruction for the students in their school. This is accomplished by spending time in classrooms and talking with teachers about what is happening in their classrooms with their students. A trusting relationship is developed when supervisors do not claim to know "the one right way" to handle a particular situation, but will explore with teachers a variety of possible options. In other words, the supervisor and teacher(s) reflect upon the issue presented by the teacher(s) and engage in a dialogue about teaching and learning.

Clinical supervision developed during the 1960s from the interactions of Morris Cogan, Robert Goldhammer, Robert Anderson, and others at the Harvard Graduate School of Education as they sought to develop student teachers, graduate students, and master classroom teachers. The collegial relationship between the supervised and the supervisor was to support teachers as they reflected on their teaching. I have expanded and updated this model to help supervisors to improve their practice (Pavan, 1993). Costa and Garmston (1994) also base their cognitive coaching on clinical supervision. (For excellent descriptions of all but the Pavan model, see Pajak, 1993.)

Even though there has been no conclusive research to demonstrate that the time spent on teacher evaluations has any effect on the improvement of instruction, every supervision, personnel, or principalship textbook notes teacher evaluation as an important aspect of these jobs. The practice of supervision is all too frequently limited to evaluation or rating of teaching, the ritualistic completion of a district form. Probably this experience suggests to teachers that those officially charged with the function of supervision are not to be approached with instructional issues, and therefore teachers report that they go to other teachers for instructional assistance. Peer coaching would not only build on this past practice but acknowledge the expertise that teachers have.

I have proposed an Instructional Improvement through Inquiry (III) model (Pavan, 1993) to facilitate the development of a collegial teacher–supervisory relationship. This model is also useful for developing collaborative peer coaching. The steps of the process look like a clinical supervisory cycle:

- *Plan*—proposed lesson is reviewed by the teacher and the observer(s), and a specific focus for observation is jointly determined.
- *Observe*—observer collects objective data in the classroom related to the purpose previously determined.
- *Analyze*—observer reviews collected data looking for patterns in relation to the plan, pedagogical theory, and research.
- *Feedback*—all collected data and analyses are shared with the teacher so lesson dynamics are understood, followed by joint analysis to determine future plans.
- *Reflect*—there is individual or joint examination of all elements of the cycle, especially analysis of the supervisors's role.

Even more important than the steps in the III process are the concepts or assumptions that govern the process. This is a collaborative approach in which teacher and observer work together using inquiry and hypothesis testing as a vehicle and both are responsible for instructional improvement. In order to facilitate this work, the supervisor must be knowledgeable in clinical supervision, learning theory, instructional methodology, effective teaching practices, communication, and organizational change, in addition to data collection, analysis of teaching, and conferencing skills. Judgment or evaluation of individuals is not the goal of III, but professional growth of both teacher and supervisor is assumed to be a precursor of instructional improvement, which then leads to increased student learning.

Training is needed for educators to learn to work together in different and more productive ways. It is common knowledge that new practices in education are rarely accompanied by sufficient (or even minimal) staff development. To gain the expertise needed both supervisors and teachers need training and the opportunity to practice their new skills. Additionally, top-level administrators must demonstrate that the school environment fosters professional development. Also, time needs to be provided for this to happen. A 3- to 5-year plan should be instituted that not only documents training time but emphasizes the development of a supportive school climate.

Professionals at the school care about and respect each other by assuming a long-term commitment to collegial interaction and the development of a learning community for both students and faculty. The "rationale that examined professional behavior is more likely to be useful—for everyone—than unexamined behavior" (Goldhammer, 1969, p. 71) or Schön's (1983) conception of "reflective practitioner" which are understood to indicate that seeking together to solve problems or to grow as professionals is more productive than finding individuals to blame.

A Personal Example

The Franklin School in Lexington, Massachusetts, was a team teaching school with nongraded multi-age teams before my arrival as principal. From the beginning I sought to have all involved faculty make decisions about the school using a consensus process. We had many lively meetings as we struggled to decide (some issues even went to the next meeting), yet we could formulate a plan that everyone was willing to try. While I made daily walk-around visits to all classrooms, I started the clinical supervision process as a way to discuss teaching with each teacher. Since I was new and this was not past practice, teachers were apprehensive at first. However, within the first year teachers were coming to me saying, "Ellen told me that you really helped her to organize the learning areas in her room. Would you work with me?" and "I'm going to try this out and I need you to see what happens." With few exceptions the teachers were able and willing to talk with me honestly because I shared information and thoughts in an open manner with them. I was the sole teacher evaluator. At an early faculty meeting I said that I was required to fill out an evaluation form for each teacher once a year. However, I said I would evaluate the present performance of the teacher, saying nothing about past problems that had been resolved, because documentation of growth provides the most useful record. Never have I seen or worked with a more dedicated, enthusiastic, or hard working group of teachers.

Five essential elements together contribute to this ethos of collegiality that energize the faculty at the Franklin School:

1. A team teaching structure with daily planning time for each team.
2. Teachers on each team having shared responsibility for the learning of all the students on their team.
3. An adult learning community where issues are researched and options discussed until consensus is reached.
4. Openness of the principal by listening to different views and sharing information.
5. Decision making by each team for team issues and by the entire faculty for school-wide issues.

Yes, a collegial relationship between teachers and supervisors (even between teacher and principals) is not only possible but essential for the growth and development of students, teachers, supervisors, and principals.

References

Alfonso, R. J., & Goldsberry, L. (1982). Colleagueship in supervision. In T. J. Sergiovanni (Ed.), *Supervision of teaching* (pp.90–107). Alexandria, VA: Association for Supervision and Curriculum Development.

Cogan, M. L. (1973). *Clinical supervision.* Boston: Houghton Mifflin.

Costa, A. L., & Garmston, R. L. (1994). *Cognitive coaching: A foundation for renaissance schools.* Norwood, MA: Christopher-Gordon Publishers.

Glickman, C. D., Gordon, G. S., & Ross-Gordon, J. M. (1995). *Supervision of instruction: A developmental approach.* Boston: Allyn & Bacon.

Goldhammer, R. (1969). *Clinical supervision: Special methods for the supervision of teachers.* New York: Holt, Rinehart & Winston.

Harris, B. (1985). *Supervisory behavior in education.* Englewood Cliffs, NJ: Prentice-Hall.

Pajak, E. (1990). Dimensions of supervision. *Educational Leadership, 48*(1), 78–81.

Pajak, E. (1993). *Approaches to clinical supervision: Alternatives for improving instruction.* Norwood, MA: Christopher-Gordon Publishers.

Pavan, B. N. (1993). Examining clinical supervision practice. In R. H. Anderson & K. J. Snyder (Eds.), *Clinical supervision: Coaching for higher performance* (pp.135–167). Lancaster, PA: Technomic.

Purkey, S. C., & Smith, M. S. (1983). Effective schools: A review. *Elementary School Journal, 83*(4), 427–452.

Schön, D. A. (1983). *The reflective practitioner: How professionals think in action.* New York: Basic Books.

Sergiovanni, T. J. (1992). Moral authority and the regeneration of supervision. In C. D. Glickman (Ed.), *Supervision in transition* (pp. 203–214). Alexandria, VA: Association for Supervision and Curriculum Development.

Is a Collegial Relationship Possible Between Supervisors and Teachers? *No*

Ben M. Harris

Overview

This issue as stated needs some revising, since, I suppose, any kind of relationship is "possible" under some circumstances. But the essence of this issue concerns appropriateness, effectiveness, and feasibility of collegial relationships between supervisors and classroom teachers. In arguing against such a relationship in many if not all instances, I shall stress two major factors and add a brief description of relationships more promising than collegial ones.

The main factors arguing against the development of collegial relationships among teachers and supervisors can be briefly identified as follows:

1. Collegiality, as a set of concepts and practices with an ancient heritage of church and university traditions, is simply an inappropriate, even dangerous, paradigm for schools in modern democratic society.
2. Practical realities involving the urgent and differentiated roles, responsibilities, and priorities of teachers and supervisors are serious deterrents to collegiality becoming the genuine basis for effective professional relationships.
3. Alternative relationships are necessary to accomplish the mutual professional goals of teachers and supervisors. These alternatives call for collaborative and team relationships that are at odds with many underlying assumptions and traditions of collegiality.

Definitional Perspectives

Webster's 3rd International (Gove, 1986) provides a starting point for a position on collegial relationships. The terms *collegial, collegialism, colleagues,* and *collegium* are each instructive about the ancient heritage of the concept and related institutional traditions. *Collegial* is defined as "(1) . . . of or relating to a college or university. (2) . . . of or relating to a collegium or group of colleges" (p. 445). *Collegialism* is defined as ". . . a theory of church policy that defines the church as a society of voluntary members, independent of the state, self-governing and with authority vested in the members" (p. 445). More operational insights are provided in the definitions of the terms *colleague* and *collegium.* A *colleague* is "an associate or co-worker typically in a profession or civil or ecclesiastical office and often of similar rank or state" (p. 444). *Collegium* is defined as ". . . an association of individuals of the same class or rank formed to promote their common interest in some business or enterprise; (2) An executive body with each member having approximately equal power and authority" (p. 445).

In essence, these terms imply a very special relationship between and among individuals—voluntary, independent of authority, self-governing, of similar rank and class, holding common interest, and having equal power and authority.

Misguided Paradigm

This is a misguided paradigm for defining teacher–supervisor relationships because its origins, current university applications, and underlying concepts are not appropriate to the mission, purposes, and organizational contexts of public elementary and secondary schools.

The Mission of Schools

Schooling calls for serving the students and the related needs of the society above the interests of individual practitioners. Defined collegial relationships imply individual autonomy for the teacher, isolations from the influences of society, and a set of well-defined precepts justifying the exercise of unmediated authority. Such a relationship, stressing a closed system with authority and autonomy heavily concentrated in the hands of either teacher or supervisor, is inconsistent with the interests of clients—students, parents, community, and the larger society.

Purposes of Schools

Schools in modern society are highly specialized and unique. They involve learning objectives that are as critical to the optimum growth and development of children and youth as are food, shelter, affection, and disease prevention. Yet each individual student, family, and community is highly differentiated from others; hence, the teacher at the vortex of relationships with individual students must also be assisted and guided in being responsible to the clients being served. The supervisor, by contrast, is among those agents of the school who must represent and mediate in behalf of those clients beyond the scope of the individual teacher. Anson (1994), in his introduction to a volume on "personalizing education" suggests a way of thinking beyond outmoded collegial relationships: ". . . We are beginning to understand that all actors in the education arena must be free to bring their own perception and experience into education. This freeing up of individuals will ensure the kind of creativity and energy demanded . . ." (p. 5).

The emphasis on all actors is in direct conflict with the emphasis on autonomy, equality of authority, sameness of rank, and self-governance. It also clearly reflects the need to rethink how society can be well served, including the great diversity of children's needs. What is not required is resort to insular and simplistic notions of scholarly academic freedom or autonomy.

Organizational Context

Teachers and supervisor pursue common goals within organizations that are changing and becoming more diverse. However, schools are still not likely to become voluntary associations without linkages to government, community, and family. Furthermore, the notions implicit in an essentially collegial relationship, with teachers and supervisor making independent or negotiated decisions about curriculum, materials, schedules, teaching methods, etc., ignores much of what is known about effective schooling: ". . . effective and collaborative schools . . . do not go it alone, but are actively part of a wider network in which external and internal influences . . . are equally important" (Fullan, 1994, p. 13).

In a still broader context if schools are to responsibly sustain and enhance community life in a democratic society, then democratic participation in all phases of the instructional program is required. ". . . The possibility [exists] for professional educators and citizens to work together in creating more democratic schools that serve the common good of the whole community" (Apple & Beane, 1995, p. 8). Heckman, Confer, and Peacock (1995) emphasize, from the experiences of a school restructuring project, that ". . . educational advancement is achieved and interconnections between school and community are best developed when all local learning resources work collectively as the axis for change" (p. 188).

Practical Considerations

Collegiality as a way of conceptualizing supervision in relation to the individual teacher is full of serious problems in common daily operations as well as problems of educational improvement and reform. If a superordinate goal shared by teachers, supervisors, students, parents, and the larger society can be clearly identified, it surely must be that of improving learning opportunities for all students. At the heart of any such goal-related activity is supervision of instruction. But this involves systematic efforts to improve curriculum, materials, teaching, support services, assessments, and leadership for instruction.

Collegial relationships combined with the teacher-centered realities of school life offer little promise of ensuring either minimum standards of educational quality or the reforms and restructuring urgently needed in a rapidly changing society.

Maintaining Quality Standards

Maintaining minimum standards of quality requires supervisory leadership to ensure selection of the best qualified teachers for the most appropriate assignments. Furthermore, novice teachers need mentoring and intensive continuing training in many aspects of classroom instruction beyond what is offered in preservice programs. The existing quality of teaching practice in nearly all schools and districts is less than uniformly high, even among experienced teachers. Unless attention is given to continuing teaching skill development, many teachers will be denied opportunities to become truly competent even by current standards.

Many well recognized teaching practices (Gage, 1985) are simply not a part of the repertoire of large segments of the teaching profession. Hence, the implementation of any given curriculum varies widely among teachers with common assignments. Variations that represent creativity and added value are always desirable, but much variation can be clearly observed as more uninspired than creative.

Ensuring that all children have access to teaching that promotes significant learning at current standards of good practice is not a collegial responsibility. Each teacher will hopefully do his or her best. But supervision is responsible to ensure that every teachers' best efforts are good enough and to initiate supervisory interventions that are needed, securing the students' right to meaningful learning.

Dramatic Improvements

When more dramatic improvements in teaching and learning are at stake, collegial relationships are even less practical. Teachers are busy, even overworked, captives of the classroom. The individual teacher's view of the school and of the world of schooling is largely that of a single classroom and often a single subject and grade level as well. Managing that classroom well and dedicating time, energy, and professional skill to ensuring learning for every student, every day until a new class arrives on the scene is a very demanding responsibility. It is high priority in the lives of good teachers and should be, because that teacher–student interface is the heart and soul of quality education.

However, supervisors are not engaged in that demanding routine as are classroom teachers. They are not colleagues in this sense at all. Supervisors are onlookers as experienced teachers, and they bring to the school and its teachers one or more unique perspectives and special professional skills. These supervisory perspectives derive from observing and analyzing many teachers at work, from knowing the broad scope and sequence of the curriculum, from responding to pressures from both within and outside the school, from seeing students' achievements as they progress through the system and across subject areas. Rarely can a classroom teacher have the same perspective on teaching and learning as that of a professional instructional supervisor. They work in different worlds in some ways.

Supervisors' special professional skills distinguish them from the teacher, just as the demands of the classroom distinguish the latter from the former. Supervisors who are professionally competent are curriculum design and development specialists, media specialists, training and staff development specialists, and experts in teaching methods and instructional evaluation. No supervisor is likely to be expert in all these specialties, of course. These are, however, the unique professional resources that supervisors bring to the tasks of restructuring schooling. Where teachers possess such expertise they, too, should be given opportunities to make such contributions along with supervisors (Conley & Levinson, 1993). However, the responsibility for providing technical leadership for improving whole schools and whole educational programs in ways that move beyond current levels of common practice and learning outcomes must be heavily vested in a team of supervisory personnel. Such leadership, like good teaching, is very demanding and requires full-time professional attention.

Collegiality, with its emphasis on power sharing, autonomy, and individualistic prerogatives, is poorly suited to facing the complexities of restructuring whole systems. Few informed educators or scholars would argue for reform and restructuring based on top-down political and bureaucratic mandates (Fullan, 1994). Neither is it practical to seek dramatic and urgently needed improvements in the very nature of schooling on the basis of one-teacher or one-school faculty at a time (Hess & Easton, 1992). Individual teachers will surely be critically important partners in any major effort at school improvement, but systemic changes occur in the cross-current of social, cultural, and technical movements that need professional orchestration. Many fine accomplished musicians do not make a symphony orchestra. It takes composers, directors, arrangers, and managers, too.

Collaborative Teaming Alternative

The traditional emphasis of collegiality on individual autonomy, power sharing, and commonality of interests leaves much to be desired in developing teacher–supervisor relationships for maintenance as well as for change. What is required is a much more fundamental view of these relationships when mission, purpose, and organizational contexts are seen as much more dynamic and multifaceted. As important as the dyadic relationships between two professionals may be, the systemic realities call for defining relationships in ways that embrace the large community of interests and influences on teaching and learning.

At the broadest level, relationships must be defined in fundamental human terms. When more narrowly defined, the complexities of ensuring quality education for all students still requires a framework embracing the differentiated roles, responsibilities, interests, and priorities of many stakeholders.

Charles L. Black, Jr. (1995), in arguing for the practical side of the humanities, notes: ". . . The Great Society will never rise above its source, which is appreciation for the thoughts and feelings of others . . . having continual regard to the feelings and thoughts, the judgments, the desires, of all its members" (p. 6).

A collaborative, teamwork relationship is needed to even begin to operationalize professional leadership reflecting such humanistic ideals. A set of characteristics of collaboration and teamwork in instructional supervision has been formulated and analyzed (Harris & Ovando, 1992). Central to such relationships are mutual respect, tolerance for differences, commitment to consensus building, and courageous expressions of differences. These characteristic features of teacher–supervisor relationships are equally applicable to a large array of stakeholders. But unique to the organizational context of schooling are relationships that emphasize differentiation of responsibilities and teaming as essential features. Overriding all of these characteristics is one that is perhaps most widely neglected—respect for the wisdom of the profession: its theory, research, and collective experience.

A profession is not a loosely connected cluster of well-meaning, hard-working individuals doing their own thing. ". . . But there is a body of practice more clearly recognized, like any fine art in its rarity than in its commonness. Every change effort should stand multiple tests and one of those tests must be the wisdom of best practices" (Harris, 1985, p. 44).

Summary

Collegiality is neither an appropriate nor adequate concept on which to build teacher–supervisor relationships. The long traditions of collegiality in church and academic institutions have given emphasis to notions of power sharing, individual and collective autonomy, and closed systems that are not consistent with the current realities or needs of schools in a democratic society. Practical problems with a collegial view of supervision relate to the mission and purpose of elementary and secondary schools. Our orientation of service to society and individual students should not be superseded by putting teacher, supervisor, or bureaucratic interests above those of clients.

The urgent and persistent needs for dramatic changes in the structure and quality of schooling in our society give special emphasis to teamwork, and the unique skills of supervisors. As specialists in curriculum, staff development, teaching methods, and instructional evaluation, supervisors must assume leadership responsibilities with visions of teaching and learning that go beyond the daily concerns of individual classroom teachers. To abdicate leadership for instructional change in exchange for collegiality could be an educational tragedy.

References

Anson, R. J. (1994). Personalizing systemic reform. In R. J. Anson (Ed.), *Systemic reform: Perspective on personalizing education* (pp. 1–6). Washington, DC: Office of Educational Research and Improvement.

Apple, M. W., & Beane, J. A. (1995). Lessons from democratic schools. In M. W. Apple & J. A. Beane, (Eds.), *Democratic schools* (pp. 101–105). Alexandria, VA: Association for Supervision and Curriculum Development.

Black, C. L., Jr. (1995). The human imagination and the great society. *Texas Journal of Ideas, History and Culture, 18*(1), 4–15.

Conley, S., & Levinson, R. (1993). Teacher work design and job satisfaction. *Educational Administration Quarterly, 29,* 453–478.

Fullan, M. G. (1994). Coordinating top-down and bottom-up strategies for educational reform. In R. J. Anson (Ed.), *Systemic reform: Perspectives on personalizing education* (pp. 7–23). Washington, DC: Office of Educational Research and Improvement.

Gage, N. L. (1985). *Hard gains in the soft sciences: The case of pedagogy.* Bloomington, IN: Phi Delta Kappa.

Gove, P. B. (Ed.), (1986). *Webster's third international dictionary of the English language.* Springfield, MA: Merriam-Webster, Inc.

Harris, B. M. (1985). *Supervisory behavior in education* (3rd ed.). Englewood Cliffs, NJ: Prentice-Hall.

Harris, B. M. & Ovando, M. N. (1992). Collaborative supervision and the developmental evaluation of teaching. *SANNY's Journal, 23*(1) 12–18.

Heckman, P. E., Confer, C. B., & Peacock, J. (1995). Democracy in a multicultural school and community. In J. Oakes & K. Quartz (Eds.), *Creating new educational communities* (pp. 187-201). Chicago: University of Chicago Press.

Hess, G. A., & Easton, J. Q. (1992). Who's making decisions: Monitoring authority shifts in Chicago school reform. In G. A. Hess (Ed.), *Empowering teachers and parents: School restructuring through the eyes of anthropologists* (pp. 157–176). Westport, CT: Bergin and Garvey.

Postnote

Is a Collegial Relationship Possible between Supervisors and Teachers?

Given the hierarchical nature that characterizes most schools, fostering collegiality between supervisors and teachers has been problematic. Some argue that the adoption of a factory-like model that turns schools into bureaucracies is ill-suited to meet the diverse needs of students, parents, and teachers in schools. Schools in a democratic society, it is maintained, need to renew their commitment to the ideals that encourage teachers and students to accept their social and political responsibilities. Collegiality, with its emphasis on power sharing and active participation, is seen by many as critical. Supervision as such becomes collegial and interactive rather than didactic and evaluative. Yet as we have seen in this chapter, consensus on this topic is elusive for a variety of not-so-obvious reasons.

Review Questions for

The Yes Response:

1. Pavan, quoting Harris (1985), lists nine supervisory competencies. Prioritize the list of functions presented by noting which is most/least important to you as a supervisor.
2. Dr. Pavan differentiates between supervisory and administrative tasks. Can you as a supervisor differentiate between these tasks on the job? Explain. What special problems may develop as you tend to either administrative or supervisory duties?
3. Explain how Pajak's 12 dimensions, as discussed by Pavan, differ "from the language used by Harris and principalship textbooks."
4. Describe Pavan's Inquiry (III) model and how this model might be implemented in your school/district.
5. Pavan provides an example of how colleagueship was established at the Franklin school. Would this be possible in your school? Why or why not?

The No Response:

1. Dr. Harris identifies three main factors that impede the development of collegial relationships among teachers and supervisors. What assumptions underlie these factors, and to what extent do these factors persuade or dissuade you?
2. What is your reaction to Harris' definition of collegiality? Describe in detail any collegial relationships you have had with teachers or supervisors in your school or district.
3. Why does Harris argue that colleagueship "is a misguided paradigm for defining teacher–supervisor relationships, and what evidence does he cite to support his assertion?

4. What is your reaction to Harris' main thesis that questions the value and efficacy of "collegial relationships?"
5. What is your reaction to Harris' metaphor that musicians in an orchestra need "composers, directors, arrangers, and managers?"
6. What are the implications of Harris' thesis for schools as organizations and for teacher–supervisor relationships?
7. The author is in favor of "collaborative teamwork" in schools, but questions the viability of "collegial relationships." In your estimation, what is the difference between the two terms?

For Further Research

1. Compare Pavan's "learning community model" with Sergiovanni's description of learning organizations in Perspective 1. What are some differences and similarities?
2. Compare Alfonso and Goldsberry's (1982) discussion of colleagueship with Pavan's description in this chapter. Would Harris agree or disagree with Alfonso and Goldsberry's thesis?
3. Consult the literature on teacher empowerment and colleagueship. Conduct an ERIC search, for example. Is there a difference between empowerment and colleagueship? Explain.
4. Identify a site-based-managed school and describe how collegiality is achieved and maintained. What problems do site-based schools typically encounter in regard to achieving a degree of collegiality? Explain.
5. Pavan (1993) has "expanded and updated" the clinical supervision model "to assist supervisors in improving their practice." Describe Pavan's efforts. Would such a system work in your school/district?
6. Describe Costa and Garmston's (1994) view of "collegiality." Describe their model of cognitive coaching and how you might employ their ideas in your school/district.
7. Pavan claims that "there has been no conclusive research to demonstrate that the time spent on teacher evaluation has any effect on the improvement of instruction." Is this true according to your experience? Explain.
8. Read Candoli's (1995) book *Site-Based Management: How to Make it Work in Your School* and describe how shared decision making may influence the nature and practice of supervision. How is collegiality achieved?
9. The *Journal of School Leadership* published by Technomic has addressed issues of collegiality and site-based management to a great extent. Conduct a literature review and summarize two different perspectives about the nature of collegiality in schools and the role supervision plays in site-based-managed schools.
10. Joseph Murray, Professor and Chair of the Department of Educational Leadership at Vanderbilt University, has written extensively on issues related to school improvement and the role that

educational leaders play in that process. Survey some of his work and explain how he might define supervision and its impact on the school organization. How does he address the issues discussed in this chapter?

11. Conduct a comparative analysis of how the following authors view the issue of collegiality in supervision: Alfonso, Firth, and Neville (1975), Barth (1990), Blase and Blase (1994), Blase and Kirby (1992), Grimmett and Crehan (1991), Lieberman and Miller (1984), and Rosenholtz (1989). How might each author encourage collegiality? How would Harris respond to their ideas?

12. Sergiovanni (1992) considers collegiality a "professional virtue." Describe the two dimensions of collegiality as discussed by Sergiovanni. What is Sergiovanni's conception of colleagueship and how might it be achieved in schools? Can his ideas be implemented in your school/district? Why or why not? How are collegiality and school culture connected? How is collegiality linked to better teaching and to more effective schools? What are the consequences for teachers' performance and school outcomes when collegiality is absent? What is the connection between collegiality and leadership?

13. Read Munro's (1991) thoughtful article, "Supervision: What's Imposition Got to Do with It?" How would Munro address the issue discussed in this chapter? Also read McBride and Skau's (1995) article and explain how trust and collegiality can be nurtured and sustained.

References

Alfonso R. J., Firth, G. R., & Neville, R. F. (1975). *Instructional supervision: A behavior system*. Boston: Allyn & Bacon.

Alfonso, R. J., & Goldsberry, L. (1982). Colleagueship in supervision. In T. J. Sergiovanni (Ed.), *Supervision of teaching* (pp. 90-107). Washington, DC: Association for Supervision and Curriculum Development.

Barth, R. (1990). *Improving schools from within*. San Francisco: Jossey-Bass.

Blase, J., & Blase, J. R. (1994). *Empowering teachers: What successful principals do*. Thousand Oaks, CA: Corwin Press.

Blase, J., & Kirby, P. C. (1992). *Bringing out the best in teachers: What effective principals do*. Newbury Park, CA: Corwin Press.

Candoli C. (1995). *Site-based management: How to make it work in your school*. Lancaster, PA: Technomic.

Costa, A., & Garmston, R. (1994). *Cognitive coaching: Approaching renaissance schools*. Norwood, MA: Christopher-Gordon Publishers.

Grimmett, P. P., & Crehan, E. P. (1991). The nature of collegiality in teacher development. In M. Fullan & A. Hargreaves (Eds.), *Teacher development and educational change*. Philadelphia: The Falmer Press.

Harris, B. M. (1985). *Supervisory behavior in education* (3rd ed.). Englewood Cliffs, NJ: Prentice-Hall.

Lieberman, A., & Miller, L. (1984). *Teachers, their world and their work*. Alexandria, VA: Association for Supervision and Curriculum Development.

McBride, M., & Skau, K. G. (1995). Trust, empowerment, and reflection: Essentials of supervision. *Journal of Curriculum and Supervision, 10,* 262–277.

Munro, P. M. (1991). Supervision: What's imposition got to do with it? *Journal of Curriculum and Supervision, 7,* 77–89.

Pavan, B. (1993). Examining clinical supervision practice. In R. H. Anderson & K. J. Snyder (Eds.), *Clinical supervision: Coaching for higher performance.* Lancaster, PA: Technomic.

Rosenholtz, S. J. (1989). *Teachers' workplace: The social organization of schools.* White Plains, NY: Longman.

Sergiovanni, T. J. (1992). *Moral leadership: Getting to the heart of school improvement.* San Francisco: Jossey-Bass.

Issue 8

Is Staff Development Supervision?

✦ ✦ ✦ ✦

YES—Cheryl Granade Sullivan, Educational Consultant
NO—Gary A. Griffin, University of Arizona

✦ ✦ ✦

Issue Summary

YES: Cheryl Sullivan, author of *Clinical Supervision: A State of the Art Review,* says that current efforts in staff development emerged from earlier democratic methods in supervision. Staff development is supervision, argues Dr. Sullivan, to the extent that both aim to ultimately promote teacher development and pupil achievement. As she concludes, "Continuous learning is, and can be, facilitated by the continuity—as opposed to fragmentation—of opportunity in staff development and supervisory endeavors."

NO: Professor and head of the Department of Teaching and Teacher Education at the University of Arizona, Gary Griffin sees "staff development as something *other than* supervision . . . I do not see staff development as subsumed under or within supervision." Professor Griffin frames his argument by guiding the reader through a "personal journey" that reveals the evolution of his ideas and beliefs about supervision. He then shares some "lessons" he has learned about school improvement which underlie how he thinks staff development can and should occur.

Guiding Questions

1. Do you prefer to be called a staff developer or a supervisor? Why? What is the difference?
2. How are staff development and supervision related?
3. What assumption about supervision and staff development does each author make?
4. What is the fundamental point of contention between the authors?
5. Does the term *super development* accurately reflect the purposes of both supervision and staff development?
6. As you read Griffin's conception of staff development, reflect on whether you have experienced staff development in similar ways.
7. What aspects of Sullivans' and Griffins' thinking make sense to you?

Is Staff Development Supervision? *Yes*

Cheryl Granade Sullivan

Myrna Lehman, an ESOL teacher, and Carol Montesinos, a seventh grade teacher, are recognized by their school system as expert teachers (Sullivan, et al. 1995). Recently they assessed a program in which they had participated. Their comments included the following:

CAROL: I have improved in the craft of teaching. And I know why and how I am a competent teacher.

MYRNA: I have more confidence in my personal and professional lives. I speak up for what I believe in at school. I can promote my ideas so that others listen to me.

These reflections were echoed by band teacher Jim Littlefield and secondary social studies teacher Barbara Atchley, who added that they had also been reenergized by new ideas and sharing with colleagues.

Are these descriptions and behaviors the result of staff development? Or are they outcomes of supervision? The answer to each question is yes. The activities that led to these comments could—and did—occur under areas labeled supervision or staff development. The dichotomy sometimes made between supervision and staff development is a false one, commonalties can be found in the purposes of both. Further, there are similarities and overlap in delivery systems. The purpose of this essay is to explore the ways in which supervision and staff development are alike.

Purposes

What goals should supervision strive toward? What should staff development accomplish? Who should be served?

Supervision as a field within education has been fraught with ambiguity. Key questions have included "Who should supervise?" and "For what purposes?" To these queries, there have been no consistent responses. Answers have changed with changing American concepts of what constitutes schooling, how adults and children are viewed, and even what societal mores indicate about the treatment of human beings.

Throughout early periods in American schooling, supervision included a variety of procedures but usually maintained one goal: inspection of teachers (Sullivan, 1980). Generally, a group of laymen took on the task of ensuring teachers' conformity to standards prescribed by a lay committee. Some referred to this approach as "snoopervision." In the twentieth century, shifts in orientation caused supervisory theory to become more democratic, cooperative, and creative (Burnham, 1976).

While the term *supervisor* may still carry denotations and connotations suggesting rank, the purpose or function as it has come to be envisioned is not hierarchical. Rather, service is often a major focus. Glickman (1985) speaks of "direct assistance." Oliva (1984) actually defines supervision as ". . . a means of offering to teachers specialized help in improving instruction" (p. 9).

Though this change in orientation is espoused by most who study and design supervisory practice, there remain differences in definition. Discussions have focused on whether supervision is a role or a function. Debates have centered on the relationship of curriculum development and supervision (see Issue 4). Best practice has been envisioned as scientific (McNeil, 1982) and also as artistic (Eisner, 1982). The Council of Professors of Instructional Supervision (COPIS) meets twice each year to discuss, describe, and define supervision, yet problems of definition still abound.

In a field in which there are diverse voices and controversies— leading in some sense to the publication of this volume—there is remarkable consistency about the purposes of supervision. The expression of these goals frequently takes the form of "improvement of instruction" and "teacher development." Goldsberry (1984) is one who links these topics of teacher effectiveness to school effectiveness. The expected outcome is student, teacher, school, and system success. In fact, the mission statement of the Association for Supervision and Curriculum Development (ASCD) concludes with the words ". . . for the success of all learners" (ASCD, 1995, p. 90).

Such purposes and outcomes are related to the goals set by the National Staff Development Council (NSDC), the only national organization dedicated solely to staff development. Key ideas from the NSDC mission statement (Sparks, 1995) include:

- Ensuring success for all students
- Improving schools
- Advancing individual and organizational development

The road to these staff development goals in many ways parallels the history of supervision. The field of professional development of teachers, like the field of supervision, suffers from confusion and, as described by Lieberman and Miller (1992) ". . . continues to be obvious on one hand and elusive on the other" (p. 1045).

Just as supervision was done *to* teachers, so staff development has a record of operating from a deficit orientation. The view was that something was wrong with teachers and/or teaching, and inservice was provided to "fix" the problem. Often, transfer of information was stressed over any concerns about teaching techniques or learning styles.

Thus, teachers were told content to ensure that curriculum would be clear and correct. Increased awareness about the role of the teacher and school improvement has caused shifts in the desired outcomes and delivery systems of staff development. Hence, the current NSDC mission statement. In stated purpose, the fields of supervision and staff development coincide.

Delivery Systems

If current goals are similar, what about ways of accomplishing those outcomes?

As a designated field, supervision is an older recognized entity than staff development. Texts as early as the 1920s (e.g., Burton, 1922) listed the improvement of inservice as one of the duties of supervision, and in a later, more comprehensive description, Harris (1975) specified that arranging for inservice education was one of the ten supervisory tasks. Until the late 1960s, staff development was, by definition, included in supervision. Beginning in 1969, staff development emerged as its own field of endeavor. Brandt (1994) is clear: "Over time, staff development has become an established professional function" (p. 2). Dillon-Peterson (1994), noting that staff development is now widespread, observes ". . . near total inclusion in all sizes of school districts today" (p. 3).

Previously, both supervision and staff development have had top-down approaches: supervision in the form of "snoopervision," staff development in the form of viewing teachers as deficient. These approaches no longer represent effective practice. Increasingly, the calls from the fields of supervision and staff development are for teacher-focused, teacher-initiated efforts that are school based. Effective practice occurs over time with opportunities for feedback and adjustments. Supervision correctly practiced is not just a few random classroom visits from someone with an impressive title. Staff development is not just an event.

Further, effective practice demands moving away from compartmentalization and the assigning of supervisory and staff development functions to singular, designated roles. Comprehensive, cooperative approaches are called for, as Wood and Thompson (1993) clearly state:

> The roles of superintendents, central office administrators, curriculum specialists and supervisors are also changing significantly. If district administrators are to lead and support in a decentralized system, they must become as deeply engaged in staff development as teachers, principals, and others. (p. 54)

Field-based responses to the needs of students, teachers, and schools include clinical supervision, peer coaching, developmental supervision, and site-based study groups. These examples have in common (1) a concern for meeting teachers where they are, (2) teacher participation in goal setting, and (3) growth and commitment to a long-term effort.

Griffin (1991), in writing about staff development, includes assumptions that teachers can and should design what they need for growth. These premises are consistent with supervisory behavior. The *Handbook of Educational Supervision* (Marks, Stoops, & King-Stoops, 1985) states as a basic principle that supervision is a cooperative team-type service; such as clinical supervision, which by definition is collegial in nature (see Issue 7). Its processes can be carried out by a variety of role incumbents, but are always initiated by teachers setting goals for their own improvement.

Clearly, there are shared approaches in the doing as well in the purposes of supervision and staff development.

Conclusion

To what extent are supervision and staff development autonomous and separate specialties? In what ways can each be defined as an integral part of the other?

Because staff development has emerged as a field in its own right, does this mean that it is no longer an aspect of supervision? Instead of making a clean—and I believe somewhat academic—split between two fields of practice, the situation might more correctly be viewed with use of a Venn diagram:

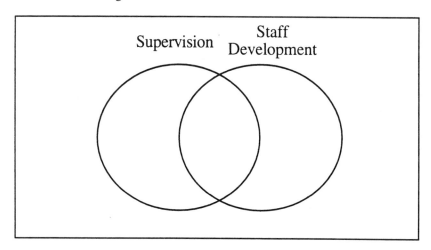

Shared Goals and Delivery Systems

As depicted, supervision and staff development as fields of educational endeavor are neither inclusive nor exclusive. They can—and should—overlap as needs and local preferences dictate.

Is supervision only staff development?   No.
Does supervision include staff development?   Yes.
Is staff development a way for supervision to be accomplished?   Yes.

The generalities expressed here may stand in sharp contrast to any example. There are bad practices that carry labels of "supervision" as well as bad practices occurring as "staff development."

When desired results occur, as with Carol, Myrna, Jim, and Barbara, the ideas, ideals, and people under the umbrellas of both terms have collaborated. The overlap seems clear in theory and in practice. The potential for positive results from avoiding the creation of separate camps is appealing.

Carol, Myrna, Jim, and Barbara cared not at all about supervisory or staff development labels. Their concentration was on their teaching, their students, and themselves as individuals and professionals. Perhaps we can learn from their experience.

Energy needs to be focused on getting the work of both supervision and staff development done in a way that serves teachers and students. At a time when downsizing is prevalent, semantic arguments used to protect specialized entities seem inappropriate.

The commonalties in purpose and delivery systems indicate that a merger may be better than a split. The result: super development.

Super development? The term effectively captures the shared goals and similar approaches to delivery. It also implies excellence (super) and change over time (development). Further, it responds to the needs of the real people who run schools. People like Carol, Myrna, Jim, and Barbara are busy, often overworked, and simultaneously bright and multitalented. To provide appropriate professional activities is not easy.

Ron Brandt (1994) recently wrote that "The challenge remains to make continuous learning an integral part of every educator's life" (p.2). Continuous learning is, and can be, facilitated by the continuity—as opposed to fragmentation—of opportunity in staff development and supervisory endeavors.

References

ASCD (1995). Strategic plan for the Association for the Supervision and Curriculum Development. *Educational Leadership*, Alexandria, VA: Association for Supervision and Curriculum Development.

Brandt, R. (1994). Establishing staff development as a professional function in "reflections on 25 years of staff development." *Journal of Staff Development*, 15(4), 2.

Burnham, R. M. (1976). Instructional supervision: Past, present and future perspectives. *Theory into Practice, 15,* 301–305.

Burton, W. H. (1922). *Supervision and the improvement of teaching.* New York: D. Appleton-Century.

Dillon-Peterson, B. (1994). Twenty-five years of staff development—reflections from NSDC's "mom" in "reflections on 25 years of staff development." *Journal of Staff Development, 15*(4), 2–3.

Eisner, E. W. (1982). An artistic approach to supervision. In T. J. Sergiovanni (Ed.), *Supervision of teaching* (pp. 53–66). Alexandria, VA: Association for the Supervision and Curriculum Development.

Glickman, C. G. (1985). *Supervision of instruction: A developmental approach.* Newton, MA: Allyn & Bacon.

Goldsberry, L. (1984). The realities of clinical supervision. *Educational Leadership, 41,* 12–15.

Griffin, G. S. (1991). Interactive staff development using what we know. In A. Lieberman & L. Miller (Eds.), *Staff development for education in the 90's: New demands, new realities, new perspectives* (2nd ed.). New York: Teachers College Press.

Harris, B. M. (1975). *Supervisory behavior in education* (2nd ed.). Englewood Cliffs, NJ: Prentice-Hall.

Lieberman, A., & Miller, L. (1992). Professional development of teachers. In M. Alkin et al. (Eds.), *Encyclopedia of educational research* (6th ed.), (pp. 1045–1051). New York: Macmillan.

Marks, J. R., Stoops, E., & King-Stoops, J. (1985). *Handbook of educational supervision: A guide for the practitioner* (3rd ed.). Newton, MA: Allyn & Bacon.

McNeil, J. D. (1982). A scientific approach to supervision. In T. J. Sergiovanni (Ed.), *Supervision of teaching* (pp. 18–34). Alexandria, VA: Association for the Supervision and Curriculum Development.

Oliva, P. F. (1984). *Supervision for today's schools* (2nd ed.). New York: Longman.

Sparks, D. (1995). NSDC's mission puts students at the center of staff development. *The Developer.*

Sullivan, C. G. (1980). *Clinical supervision: A state of the art review.* Alexandria, VA: Association for the Supervision and Curriculum Development.

Sullivan, C. G., & Fulton County Expert Teachers (1995). *Expanding the skills of expert teachers.* Presentation to the Georgia Staff Development Council.

Wood, F. H., & Thompson, S. R. (1993). Assumptions about staff development based on research and best practice. *Journal of Staff Development, 14*(4), 54.

Is Staff Development Supervision? *No*

Gary A. Griffin

I am concerned in this essay with staff development as something other than supervision. Unlike some authors, I do not see staff development as subsumed under or within supervision (see, e.g., Glickman, Gordon, & Ross-Gordon, 1995). Rather, I have come to believe that staff development is a completely different approach to school improvement than is supervision as I have come to know that term over several decades. In fact, the recent past has convinced me that staff development, with school restructuring as its means and its goal, is the only way that we can break the tight grip of mediocrity and status-quo orientations that characterize so many of our nation's schools.

First, I indulge myself in a fragmented memoir focused on supervision that, because of its trajectory over time, may help to frame the remainder of the essay. Next, I argue for a conception of staff development that takes into serious account some of the important lessons we have learned about school improvement over the past several decades. Last, I suggest a set of conditions that seem to me to be necessary when promising engagement with staff development occurs.

Recollections Related to Supervision: A Personal Journey

My experience with the concept and practice of educational supervision began, as did most educators', during my student teaching semester. This took place at UCLA in the mid-1950s. Coming as it did at the conclusion of a lengthy period of "studenting," there seemed to me nothing untoward with having someone older and wiser provide direction for my forays into learning to teach. Similarly, when I began full-time teaching in a beachfront community in Southern California, I was receptive to being visited periodically by supervisors of art, reading, mathematics, social studies, physical education, and the like. (I taught multiple subjects in an elementary school.) In fact, I welcomed these visits because they gave me an opportunity to "show off," in most instances, or learn something in others.

Over time, however, and particularly after the teacher next door and I traded classes a few times (just for something different to do and think about in our teaching), I came to the realization that I was learning a good deal more about my craft from my teacher colleagues than I was from my supervisor colleagues. This mini-epiphany, I am sorry to say, had little lasting effect because I was also enrolled in a graduate program at the time and immersed in the myriad "strategies" for supervision that formed one of the program's several strands of content about teaching and schooling. It appears that I was neither clever enough nor sufficiently self-analytic to resolve the tensions between the submerged and unvoiced notion that teacher colleagues were very influential on my teaching practice and the claims made by supervision experts who were engaging me with models of supervision developed in colleges and universities across the nation.

A decade later, I was fortunate to be appointed as a professor at Columbia University Teachers College. One of my first teaching assignments was a seminar on supervision. As is often the case, that seminar was less an occasion for thinking through the fundamental premises of the primary topic than a time devoted to gathering together already-known ways of thinking about it. (I offer a belated apology to those first groups of gifted educational professionals, including one of the co-editors of this book, who spent 18 Tuesday evenings with me each semester as we "learned" extant models of supervision.)

My first real break from the existing canons of supervision came in the mid-1970s when I worked with others at developing and understanding the consequences of implementing the Interactive Research and Development process (Tikunoff, Ward, & Griffin, 1981). This knowledge-production approach placed teachers, researchers, and staff developers/teacher educators together in parity-laden situations and charged them with working collegially on an important schooling issue according to their particular experiences and areas of expertise. The intention, of course, was to demonstrate that teachers' ways of knowing about schooling can be as important sources for coming to grips with the problems and concerns about educating children as university-based scholars' views had been. What my colleagues and I discovered during the implementation of the strategy was that, while the findings of the studies were meaningful and important, the process of inquiry and collaboration itself was seen by all concerned as the most important feature of the shared experience. In particular, teachers found valuable and rewarding the strategy's insistence upon the validity of teacher views and understandings.

A series of linked opportunities to become involved in school improvement efforts pervaded the next 15 years. I directed a coordinated set of three national studies aimed at understanding how prospective, novice, and experienced teachers are influenced to teach as they do (Griffin, 1986). I became involved with the NEA Mastery in Learning Project and its successor, the NEA National Center for Innovation, the work of which rested on the belief that teachers working together could and should come together to decide on the nature and intended consequences of their work (Barrett, 1992; Griffin, 1992). I was a founding executive board member of The Holmes Group and spent considerable time thinking anew about how schools and universities could join in creating what have come to be called professional development schools. I studied schools that had engaged in restructuring activities for five or more years (Griffin, 1995), and I am currently studying a national sample of 14 schools that have made considerable and serious changes in how they do the important work of teaching and promoting learning while, at the same time, they are successfully moving schooling into new times with new demands.

Assumptions about Staff Development and Supervision

And what have I come to believe as a consequence of this journey that began almost 40 years ago? The central belief that has come about for me is that *typical supervision models assume that important knowledge is privileged knowledge.* That is, through sets of circumstances such as graduate degree programs, certification of administrators and supervisors, the persistence of status stratification in educational organizations, and the like, we have created settings where it is widely accepted that some persons (administrators and supervisors) possess knowledge and skill that others (teachers) do not and, perhaps, should not possess. If one accepts this view, then supervision as typically practiced is not only normal but desired. All that needs to be done is to ensure that such privileged knowledge is distributed in some sort of humane way to those who don't possess it. (I use the word "humane" to deflect typical horror stories about how supervisors and administrators are sometimes reported to interact with their teacher colleagues.) Thus, the supervisor finds ways (strategies, models, plans, whatever) to convince teachers that a "new" way of teaching has more advantages than current practice has. The supervisor, then, *holds* the privileged knowledge and devises an institutionalized seduction (some say implementation) strategy to convince teachers to *use* that knowledge. (It goes without saying that the privileged knowledge is important; otherwise, the larger organization wouldn't invest in ensuring its presence in the organization.)

Similar to the view about privileged knowledge, experience and observation of practice have led me to believe that *shared meaning is more powerful than compartmentalized meaning.* By this statement, I hope to convey the belief that a community is held together and sustained in large measure as a consequence of the sometimes (but not necessarily) painful process of coming to grips with what is believed to be so, what is believed to be necessary, and what is believed to be possible. This core of beliefs and understandings is often assumed in conventional school settings but seldom realized where hierarchical systems of privileged knowledge and the concomitant privileged power are present. This notion of core beliefs is not the same as uniformity. Uniformity allows no room for deviation, whereas the very concept of "core" suggests that the central understandings are surrounded and buttressed by other views, often idiosyncratic and unique, that are carried and made public by individuals in community.

Another lesson I have taken from my own experience and from the wise words and deeds of valued colleagues is that *"knowledge" related to teaching and schooling is always mutable and open to serious question and equally serious revision.* What is "known" today in this place may have no authority tomorrow in another place. What is believed to be so for this group of students does not fit another group of students. What "works" with this group of teachers is not even vaguely relevant to that group of teachers. And so on. In terms of supervision, the point of this realization is that even if one were to accept the concept of privileged knowledge, it is unlikely that the knowledge held by a few would be helpful to the many who are not intimately connected with the built-in baggage that comes with that knowledge in the form of assumptions, underlying premises, political and other power dimensions, and the like.

As is suggested immediately above, I have also come to understand the *considerable influence that context plays in any institutionalized approach to improvement activity.* Schools get better at what they do, I believe, because there is a carefully designed fit between a deep and serious understanding of the immediate context and a willingness to think about how that understanding ought to be acted upon. This way of thinking denies a large part of the applicability of generalized ways of approaching "problems." The idea that a teaching strategy, for example, is or should be helpful across most or all teaching situations—an assumption underlying many centralized supervision approaches—seems to me to be untenable in light of recent years' revelations regarding the impact of context features on learning, teaching, and schooling.

The last point I will make here, the last lesson from my recollected journey, as it were, is my firm belief that *school improvement will take place to the degree that what is determined to be a positive course of action is homegrown.* This homely metaphor seems particularly apt to me because it evokes an image of community (home) and an assumption that knowledge and understanding are evolutionary and developmental (grown) rather than fixed and externally validated. This does not mean that ideas and approaches and suggestions from outside the school environment are not or should not be considered. But, as the concept of mutual adaptation reminds us, ideas from outside the school are reshaped in many of the same ways that settings are influenced by the outside idea. Ideally, school professionals engage in making meaning together in community *and* in shaping to their needs the ideas that enter the community as a consequence of the insiders' sense of appeal, possibility, and promise.

How do these understandings support my views that supervision is not the same as staff development and that staff development is essential to school improvement? Of course, it might be argued that nothing that has appeared here is explicitly definitive in terms of staff development and therefore exclusionary to supervision. I believe, however, that staff development has come to mean a system in which education professionals grow together in community toward some commonly held perspective, whereas supervision assumes that there are persons in the community whose privileged knowledge and power positions set them apart, more frequently above others. Staff development, to me, flattens the organizational structure, spreading authority and acknowledged expertise horizontally rather than hierarchically, as I believe conventional supervision does.

Certainly, there are times and occasions in any organization that call for the expertise and authority of one or more members over one or more other members; the initiation of newcomers comes to mind as an example. As a general principle, however, studies of staff development, school restructuring, school improvement, and teacher leadership have convinced me that shared authority, shared expertise, and shared expectations as a consequence of staff development opportunities are preferable to conventional supervision approaches involving top-down strategies designed to realize top-down expectations.

Because this volume was designed as a stimulus to thinking about central school improvement features, I am not as uncomfortable with presenting a set of complex issues so boldly as I might be in other circumstances. Although text is one of the most controlling of media, my position here may cause (incite?) others to reconsider or strengthen positions in opposition to what I present here. Nonetheless, it is reasonable for anyone to ask how my argument might look in practice.

Staff Development Features Not Commonly Found in Supervision Models

Three large-scale studies of teacher education (aimed at understanding programs designed for preservice, novice, and experienced teachers) resulted in what was called the Research in Teacher Education (RITE) framework for clinical teacher education (Hoffman & Edwards, 1986). This framework was developed empirically, but it is supported both intuitively and philosophically. In other words, the features of the RITE proposal were derived from re-analysis of the findings of the three large-scale studies *and* are consonant with a coherent view of learning to teach. The features, taken together, provide us with a way of thinking about staff development that seems to me to be very different from patterns of supervision that are typically practiced (and written about) in the United States. I will present each of the features and suggest how it demonstrates this difference.

The defining feature of this way of thinking about staff development is that the work of the school is determined in very large measure by the context of the school itself. This real-life approach to determining what is important and what should be expected in a school flies directly in the face of most supervision strategies that specify how and under what conditions school change should move forward (the several steps or stages of clinical supervision come to mind). If one takes the position that school itself is the richest and most powerful source of understandings about school issues and that the way the school *is* and what it *has been* and *may be* should evolve naturally out of school persons making meaning together, few supervision approaches are sufficiently adaptive to accommodate this defining feature. In fact, my experience with and observation of supervision as a practice (as well as supervision as theories and proposals for action) lead me to believe that it is the school that must be adaptive to some external expectations for change.

Working from the defining property and directly linked to it is the requirement that staff development be context sensitive. This feature of the RITE framework demands that those in the school—those who are most familiar with its problems and possibilities—are far more appropriate designers and implementers of change than is the typical supervisor who may or may not have a serious understanding of the school as a place for teaching and learning. This feature also acknowledges that there is a "wisdom of practice" that accrues to a schoolplace and that this body of current and historical lore can have a powerful influence on how a school does or does not move forward in positive ways. I assume that most schools can be truthfully characterized as places in which the educational professionals are both wise about their work and thoughtful about problems and issues that need attention. Although it is possible to identify exceptions to this rule, there is no evidence of which I am aware that says that even these places can be "turned around" as a consequence of hierarchically organized requirements for change.

The RITE framework also requires that staff development be *purposeful and articulated.* Goals of schools and intentions of teachers need to be uncovered, examined, critiqued, reviewed. This approach to purposes, and making meaning about them in sensible ways, must evolve from the school community itself to satisfy the feature of context sensitivity; moreover, it is directly opposed to purposes that are formulated within a deficit model of teaching and schooling, as so many supervisory intentions seem to be. Somehow, supervision has come to mean correcting rather than inventing, bringing recalcitrant teachers into the fold rather than ensuring that teachers in community work together to determine how they will (or, in some cases, will not) move forward. School and classroom purposes are so often in conflict and ambiguous that creating community through staff development such as proposed here seems an important direction to take.

Staff development is most effective when it is *participatory and collaborative.* These features of community are self-evident, but too often, it seems to me, supervision approaches are more aligned with convincing others to think and do as the supervisor thinks and does. In a truly participatory environment, where teachers and others come together seriously and expect all to contribute to the school-level debate about what counts, there is far more likelihood that school improvement will be taken seriously than in an environment where improvement strategies are based on assumptions about compliance and attending to others' expectations.

The RITE framework requires that staff development be *knowledge based*. In the studies that undergird the framework, it was noted that a public acknowledgment of what set of understandings supported staff development was related to the success of the development work. All too often, however, there is little attention given to the knowledge upon which a move for change is based. (Knowledge here, of course, includes the wisdom of practice that resides in the school as well as more conventional research and theoretical knowledge.) A strong reason for giving attention to knowledge in this context is to promote the ongoing habit of critique and review, of peeling away the layers of meaning that can accrue to relatively simple ideas. Attending to knowledge and its many guises helps staff development participants become more critical of their own and others' notions about what is desirable and what is not. This attention is seldom seriously acknowledged or anticipated in conventional supervision situations.

A feature of staff development that is central to successful school improvement is that the development work be *ongoing*. This feature fits nicely with the expectation that the work also be context sensitive. For an activity to be truly ongoing rather than fitfully engaged in, it must be embedded deeply in the place and people it is meant to influence. There are already too many complaints about typical "inservice" or "supervisory" practices being fragmented, unconnected, and so on, for me to indulge in my own here. Staff development, almost by definition, requires a continuity over time and a sense of "paying attention" that can only be accomplished by school professionals working in community rather than in layered, top-down, authority manifestations of interaction.

Staff development, according to the RITE framework, must also be *developmental*. There must be attention given not only to how the participants develop their views, practices, and expectations during the ongoing interactions but also to how the staff development work itself develops and grows as a consequence of the school community's efforts. This attention to growth and change, it seems to me, is better accomplished as a kind of self-study by participants in staff development than by conventional evaluation procedures engaged in by someone external to the community, as is typical supervisory practice. Staff development that is undertaken seriously must focus on sets of expectations and the ways teachers and others move toward them that are best understood by the participants themselves.

The last feature of the RITE model is that staff development is *analytic* and *reflective*. These conditions, of course, are implicit in the other features presented here. But the specific attention to analysis and reflection calls our intention to the importance of knowing one's path and paying attention as it is followed. Blind or partially sighted adherence to a goal of supervision qua supervision simply will not fit in the emerging conceptions of school improvement. Richardson's (1994) edited volume on how teachers can come to better understand their own practice demonstrates the power of reflection and analysis to bring to the forefront of consciousness teachers' underlying assumptions about practice. Philosophers have encouraged us to be more preoccupied with *why* we do what we do and think as we think. Similarly, staff development rooted in a belief in creating a sense of self and community (as well as self in community) promotes analysis and reflection as everyday ways of being and knowing, whereas conventional supervision seldom calls for participants to systematically critique and review their work as a matter of course.

The framework presented here depends for success on all of the features being present at the same time and in the same place. Staff development carried forward with all of the pieces of the framework in place looks very different from supervision, and is both empirically and intuitively more likely to result in deep and meaningful school change than might be expected from engagement with large numbers of supervision strategies in practice and in the literature. It is this necessary condition that all of the elements be attended to in a comprehensive manner that sets this approach to staff development apart from supervision as I have come to know it.

References

Barrett, P. (Ed.). (1992). *Doubts and certainties: Working together to restructure schools.* Washington, DC: National Education Association.

Glickman, C., Gordon, S., & Ross-Gordon, J. (1995). *Supervision of instruction: A developmental approach* (3rd ed.), Needham Heights, MA: Allyn & Bacon.

Griffin, G. A. (1986). Clinical teacher education. In J. Hoffman & S. Edwards, (Eds.), *Reality and reform in clinical teacher education* (pp. 1–24). New York: Random House.

Griffin, G. A. (1992). Learning from the "new" schools: Lessons for teacher education. In L. Darling-Hammond, G. Griffin, & A. Wise (Eds.), *Excellence in teacher education: Helping teachers develop learner centered schools* (pp. 24–31). Washington, DC: National Education Association.

Griffin, G. A. (1995). Influences of shared decision making: Conversations with five teachers. *Elementary School Journal, 96*(1), 29–46.

Hoffman, J., & Edwards, S. (Eds.). (1986). *Reality and reform in clinical teacher education.* New York: Random House.

Richardson, V. (Ed.). (1994). *Teacher change and the staff development process.* New York: Teachers College Press.

Tikunoff, W., Ward, B., & Griffin, G. (1981). Interactive research and development as a form of professional growth. In K. Howey, R. Bents, & D. Corrigan, (Eds.), *School-focused inservice: Descriptions and discussions* (pp. 187–214). New York: Random House.

Postnote

Is Staff Development Supervision?

Since its inception, public schooling has been concerned chiefly with ensuring quality programming. Most often quality has been measured by levels of student achievement. Teachers were viewed as having the most direct influence on children, and thus efforts at enhancing their professional development gained momentum. Traditionally, the function, process, and practice of supervision were mainly concerned with ensuring quality standards. For some, conventional supervision with its reliance on oversight and teacher evaluation proved inadequate and thus evolved into staff development, which was viewed as a more effective paradigm for achieving instructional excellence. Although staff development is no longer viewed as something that is only necessary for teachers, current discourse clearly differentiates staff development from supervision. Inclusion of this issue in this volume calls this assumption into question and challenges readers to explore the relationship between, and fundamental purposes of, supervision and staff development.

Review Questions for

The Yes Response:

1. How does Dr. Sullivan differentiate between supervision and staff development?
2. How would Sullivan respond to the arguments presented by Griffin?
3. According to Sullivan, has the link between staff development and student achievement been formally established? Is such a link possible?
4. Do you concur with the author that "the fields of supervision and staff development coincide"?
5. According to Sullivan, how in fact did staff development emerge "as a field in its own right"?
6. React to Sullivan's Venn diagram depicting the relationship between supervision and staff development.
7. How do you think Carol, Myrna, Jim, and Barbara would respond to Sullivan's conception of the relationship between the two fields?

The No Response:

1. Why is staff development, and not supervision, the only way, according to the author, that "we can break the tight grip of mediocrity and status-quo orientations that characterize so many of our nation's schools"?

2. How has Dr. Griffin's "personal journey" influenced his views about the relationship between supervision and staff development? What specific factor(s) do you think have influenced his position in this chapter?

3. React to the author's five lessons or beliefs that have emerged as a result of his unique experiences. Do these beliefs resonate with meaning for you? If so, how? If not, explain.

4. How does Griffin differentiate between supervision and staff development?

5. Have your experiences with staff development been "participatory and collegial," as Griffin suggests they should be?

6. Griffin's assumptions about supervision influenced his views that supervision is essentially coercive and nonparticipatory. Is this an accurate assessment from your experience? Is it ever possible for "supervision" to be collegial and participatory?

7. Could staff development as framed in the RITE proposal be adopted in your school/district? Explain.

For Further Research

1. ASCD (1981) and the National Society for the Study of Education (1983) published yearbooks on staff development. How is staff development defined in each text and how has our understanding of staff development evolved since 1981? Also, what is the relationship between staff development and supervision as discussed in these texts?

2. Conduct a literature review of the research conducted on staff development. See, for example, Firth (1977) and Mazarella (1980).

3. The *Journal of Staff Development* is a periodical singly devoted to the study and practice of staff development. Conduct a content analysis of this journal indicating various topics addressed and how the field has evolved into its current state.

4. Read Gordon and Nicely's (in press) chapter on the relationship between supervision and staff development. Contrast their views with those of the authors in this volume.

5. How would Griffin react to the Issues 1, 3, 5, 6, and 7 in this volume. Document your reasons.

6. Research the National Staff Development Council's Standards for Staff Development. What is the National Staff Development Council? How does it define staff development? Describe and react to the standards it has established.

7. Interview three staff developers regarding their views on the issue highlighted in this chapter. Interview three practitioners responsible for supervision and ascertain their views as well.

8. Identify several successful staff development programs. Research programs that exist in the League of Professional Schools, the Coalition of Essential Schools, and the Comer Schools. What characteristics do these programs have in common? Can such a program be developed in your school/district? If not, discuss the reasons why.

9. Compare Professor Griffin's views of supervision and staff development in this chapter with his chapter in Lieberman and Miller (1991). Have his views changed? What does Griffin mean by "interactive staff development?"

10. Review and discuss the significance of the various chapters in Lieberman and Miller (1991) for staff development. How is supervision treated by other authors?

11. Much recent work has been conducted on efforts to restructure schools. Discuss the role of staff development and supervision regarding professionalizing teaching and restructuring schools. See, for example, Lieberman (1988). Has systemwide staff development been successful in changing the culture and structure of schooling?

12. Read Chapter 18 in Glickman, Gordon, and Ross-Gordon (1995), and describe their view of staff development. How would these authors respond to the debate of issues presented in our book? Select some of the exercises at the end of their chapter as a substitute assignment for any of the above questions.

13. Read Chapter 15 in Sergiovanni and Starratt (1993) and describe their view of staff development. How would these authors respond to the debate of issues presented in our book? How do Sergiovanni and Starratt differentiate among inservice, staff development, and renewal? According to the authors, what does supervision have to do with teacher development and renewal?

14. Arredondo, Brody, Zimmerman, and Moffett (1995) argue that supervision can be collaborative. Read their account and describe how Griffin would react.

References

Arredondo, D. E., Brody, J. L., Zimmerman, D. P., & Moffett, C. A. (1995). Pushing the envelope in supervision. *Educational Leadership, 53*(3), 74–78.

ASCD. (1981). *Staff development/organizational development.* B. Dillon-Peterson (Ed.). Alexandria, VA: Association for Supervision and Curriculum Development.

Firth, G. R. (1977). Ten issues on staff development. *Educational Leadership, 35,* 215–220.

Glickman, C. D., Gordon, S. P., & Ross-Gordon, J. M. (1995). *Supervision of instruction: A developmental approach.* Boston: Allyn & Bacon.

Gordon, S. P., & Nicely, R. F. (in press). Supervision and staff development. In G. R. Firth & E. Pajak (Eds.), *Handbook of research on school supervision.* New York: Macmillan.

Lieberman A. (Ed.). (1988). *Building a professional culture in schools.* New York: Teachers College Press.

Lieberman, A., & Miller, L. (Eds.). (1991). *Staff development for education in the '90s: New demands, new realities, new perspectives*. New York: Teachers College Press.

Mazarella, J. A. (1980). Synthesis of research on staff development. *Educational Leadership, 38*, 182–185.

National Society for the Study of Education. (1983). *Staff development*. Chicago: The University of Chicago Press.

Sergiovanni, T. J., & Starratt, R. J. (1993). *Supervision: A redefinition* (5th ed.). New York: McGraw-Hill.

Issue 9

Should There be National Standards in the Preparation of Supervisors?

✦ ✦ ✦ ✦

YES—Gerald R. Firth, University of Georgia
NO—Helen M. Hazi, West Virginia University

✦ ✦ ✦

Issue Summary

YES: Gerald Firth, co-editor of the *Handbook of Research on Supervision*, argues that it is unlikely that a "profession of educational supervision" is possible without an agreement on "appropriate standards for preparation programs of school supervisors." Dr. Firth supports his belief in standard setting by presenting ten compelling arguments for your consideration.

NO: Helen Hazi, professor of educational administration at West Virginia University, asserts that "standards, any kind, are often presumptuous, dogmatic, and illusory." She begins her essay by placing standard setting for supervision within the larger context of the nationwide standards movement and argues that the process of standard setting in general is flawed and problematic. Her personal experiences with attempts at setting standards for supervision have strengthened her conviction that the task is impossible and not particularly desirable.

Guiding Questions

1. What might be some advantages and disadvantages of having national standards?
2. What personal and professional characteristics should instructional supervisors have?
3. How will the adoption of national standards affect the practice of supervision?
4. Who should be involved in the process of developing standards?
5. How will standards contribute to improving teaching, learning, and the quality of life in schools?
6. What arguments for or against federally imposed standards can you think of that are not raised by the authors in this chapter?

Should There Be National Standards in the Preparation of Supervisors? *Yes*

Gerald R. Firth

Introduction

No common agreement exists on the nature of educational supervision, the role of a school supervisor, or the expectations of performance by a school supervisor. Consequently, debate exists on the appropriate standards for preparation programs for school supervisors. The *field of educational supervision* must reach agreement on these matters if there is to be any hope of having a *profession of educational supervision*. In the statement that follows, ten arguments are raised and discussed that speak directly to the critical need for identification of national standards that can guide the preparation and subsequent service of those who would be called *school supervisors*.

District Expectations and Standards Are Ambiguous and Erratic

Clearly, supervision has not fared well when local school districts have been allowed to determine the preparation needed for positions given supervisory titles and/or supervisory responsibilities. In fact, very often titles are meaningless in terms of duties assigned. Moreover, positions with the same title in different districts often entail widely different duties; positions with different titles in different districts often entail the same or similar duties. The absence of any widely held set of expectations for the school supervisor has encouraged superintendents with little understanding or appreciation for the work of school supervisors to create, transform, or even eliminate their positions. They have—often with little thought or reason—placed them in the central office, on cluster teams, or at individual schools and assigned them as line or staff personnel, or even left unaddressed their place in the chain of command. Moreover, they have held school supervisors accountable for purpose or program or performance. No position can achieve identity or project a consistent image under such varied, volatile, and vulnerable conditions. One can only imagine how the role of superintendent, principal, or counselor would have advanced if subjected to such ambiguity.

The lack of precision in the description of the school supervisor's role and functions makes the position the easiest to redesign, reassign, or eliminate when budgets must be pared. The actual history of school supervision since its inception in Colonial America demonstrates that supervisors thrive only when financial resources are ample. Because there is no common agreement on their role and functions—

and consequently no agreement on how to prepare them for their positions—school supervisors are viewed as "nice to have"—but not necessary!

The well established role and functions of Her Majesty's Inspectors (HMI) in England stand in sharp contrast to the widely varying roles of school supervisors in the United States (Edmonds, 1962). In England, some 200 individual HMIs operate with tremendous autonomy as they evaluate schools and exact compliance; indeed, they are viewed as an elite force. Their royal reports commonly make or break an educational program, whether that program be an emerging innovation or an established offering. The counsel of HMIs is sought, valued, and heeded. They are well paid, well respected, and well utilized. They are above politics, economics, and bureaucracies—they answer only to the crown. They are the products of academic programs with uniform standards; every English school official knows what skills and knowledge to expect from them. In this country the anticipated performance should be no less.

State Standards Are Ambiguous and Erratic

The standardization of educational supervision when left to the state is no better. Despite the growth of professional standards commissions, much of the decision making about education rests in the hands of lay citizens at the state and district levels. Members of district boards of education, by whatever means they are selected, elected, or appointed, are charged with representing the concerns of the state in a particular jurisdiction. The phrase "local board of education" is used to distinguish such bodies from the state board of education. In practice, however, lay citizens at both levels exert influence on the standards for preparation of school supervisors. State boards of education achieve this end indirectly through certification standards; district boards do so directly through employment. In neither case do those professionals who are most knowledgeable regarding the work of school supervisors, including those so employed, have any influence on the standards governing their licensure and—by extension—their preparation.

The criteria for preparation of educational personnel, from teachers through superintendents, are established by state boards of regents for higher education and/or particular colleges and universities. These bodies are separate and independent of the state boards of education which control certification. Nevertheless, preparation programs at all institutions of higher education in a given state are influenced by the state's licensure requirements faced by individuals seeking admission to practice. Even the most renowned schools of medicine or law would feel compelled to explain any low percentage of satisfactory ratings earned by their students on the state-administered medical examination or bar examination. Less prestigious professions would be even more attentive to such measures. In education, however, preparation programs for teachers and leadership positions too often precisely mirror the state determined certification requirements. Such requirements represent the legally accepted minimum for individuals to be allowed to accept positions in that state. While it is certainly possible for educational institutions to require higher standards of their graduates than those dictated by state authority, neither public nor private colleges or universities could add requirements or standards without risking loss of "market share." Therefore, standards of preparation for school supervisors in the state's institutions of higher education most frequently reflect the same standards as those required to obtain a license in the same state (Shafer & Mackenzie, 1965). Because few states impose written or oral examinations in education, as is common in other professions, the standards for preparation are too often the same as the legal minimum for certification. Distressingly, the final determination to award licensure follows the favorable review of the applicant's college transcript by a clerical employee of the state education department, who has no background in any of the material on which he or she is passing judgment.

When standards, norms, and requirements are established state by state, it is difficult to avoid the influence of partisan politics. Approval of preparation programs in school supervision and in education generally is subject to such bias when teams that impose standards on institutions within a state are composed of individuals who themselves are practitioners or representatives of related agencies. In short, a *supervision profession* cannot be realized on a state-by-state basis.

Program Specialization Requires National Standards

If preparation programs for school supervisors were clear, independent, and separate, the problem would be complex enough. Most often, however, school supervisors are prepared in postgraduate programs in colleges of education along with other leadership personnel, including principals, superintendents, and curriculum directors, to name only a few. Moreover, many individuals enroll together in the same courses in supervision, curriculum, instruction, administration, and other fields. Such simultaneous and generic preparation operates on the assumption that the various leadership roles are more alike than different. The situation conveys the impression that anyone who pursues such a program successfully can serve equally well in any of several leadership roles. Further endorsement of this omnibus character of leadership preparation is provided by a certificate that allows individuals to qualify for several roles simultaneously. Even completion of master's, specialist, and doctoral degrees too often fails to demand specialization except in the form of a few elective courses that distinguish the transcript of one student from another. In many cases the individual student merely qualifies for general leadership certificates at successively higher levels.

State approval for preparation programs to allow college endorsement for certification typically is granted following evaluation by a visiting team from the state education department. Such evaluations often are coordinated with those focused on regional accreditation for the institution visited. The representative(s) of the state education department are also members of the regional team or consultant(s) to it. This situation allows those associated with the state board of education through the state department of education to exert still more influence on preparation programs technically under the jurisdiction of the state board of regents. During the evaluation visit that influence is felt directly at the operational level rather than remotely at the policy level. In summary, program specialization must be free of parochial basis and be guided by national standards.

Accreditation Is Best Served by National Standards

The very common American phenomenon of voluntarily seeking approval of individual preparation programs at institutions of higher education by responsible, nationally recognized agencies requires constant support and protection. Incursion, involvement, and/or interference by government on the traditionally sovereign campus of the university is a threat to institutions, individuals, and ideas. History provides many frightening examples of control—social, political, and financial—by ministries of education and/or other government agencies in other countries. In contrast, universities in the United States have turned to external bodies with appropriate expertise in various fields to judge programs of preparation. Involvement with such evaluation groups preserves the free exchange of thought, opinion, and fact. It brings nationwide recognition and acceptance of those programs deemed worthy of accreditation.

Rare at the local school district level, except in large, metropolitan systems of education, internal assessment processes are routine within virtually every institution of higher education. These processes are augmented by external audits conducted by state, regional, national, and occasionally international organizations, associations, and/or agencies. Mayor and Swartz (1965), reviewing assessment procedures for teacher education specifically, found that national accreditation, rather than imposing rigid requirements, actually contributed to increased flexibility in state requirements. They reached the conclusion that national accreditation would do much more to stimulate than to stifle improvement and innovation needed in preparation programs for education. Accreditation of preparation programs is essential for the professionalization of school supervision. That accreditation is meaningful only when measured against national standards.

Education Associations Accept National Standards

The evolution of national accreditation in education resulted from a need for similar criteria recognized by institutions engaged in the preparation of teachers. The early efforts of the North Central Association of Colleges and Schools in 1915 led to the establishment of the American Association of Teachers College (AATC) in 1917, which began accreditation a decade later. The AATC merged in 1948 with two other organizations to form the American Association of Colleges for Teacher Education (AACTE). The AACTE promoted the creation of a broad-based body—the National Council for Accreditation of Teacher Education (NCATE)—to which it transferred the accrediting function in 1954. The NCATE is the only organization officially recognized by the U.S. Department of Education to perform this function.

So strongly supported was this development that, as Firth (1959) reported, institutions and organizations in education abandoned any other approach to national appraisal of preparation programs in education. The NCATE currently comprises representatives of 28 constituent organizations in its membership. It was designated by the Association for Supervision and Curriculum Development (ASCD) in 1963 as the appropriate organization to approve preparation programs for curriculum directors and instructional supervisors. ASCD has conducted several operations to prepare standards for separate approval of both of these leadership specializations in education. The mechanism is in place to effect accreditation based on national standards and guided by the education associations. Those who wish to establish a *supervision profession* must choose and support the opportunities that these standards provide.

Leadership Organizations Endorse National Standards

Organizations that represent teachers both generally, particularly the National Education Association, and in their subject and/or grade level specializations endorse national standards of preparation. Interstate compacts and certification reciprocity are based on the premise that teacher preparation throughout the country is more alike than different. The same logic should apply to specializations among leadership roles—superintendent, principal, curriculum director, and instructional supervisor.

ASCD has urged the identification of standards for those leadership roles based on nearly 50 years of experience in representing aspirants, incumbents, and alumni of such positions. In concert with the American Association of School Administrators (AASA), a campaign was initiated by ASCD in 1959 to "professionalize" the roles of instructional leaders. In 1961, they joined forces with the National Association of Secondary School Principals (NASSP), the National

Association of Elementary School Principals (NAESP), and the University Council for Educational Administration (UCEA). Each of these organizations has influenced, contributed to, and/or undertaken efforts to provide national standards for preparation programs. All are involved directly as constituent members of the National Council for Accreditation of Teacher Education and indirectly as constituent members of the National Policy Board for Educational Administration. The work of ASCD, independently and in collaboration with other national professional organizations, has focused on national standards for program accreditation. ASCD also advocates specialty board certification at the national level separate and distinct from basic licensure at the state level (Firth, 1986, 1987).

The education associations have championed the cause and provided the framework within which preparation and certification can be based on national standards. To become the *profession* of supervision, the *field* of supervision must follow their lead.

Practitioners of Instructional Supervision Advocate National Standards

Countless inquiries directed to practitioners of school supervision have revealed strong and consistent support for national standards. These inquiries have been conducted by institutions, organizations, and agencies; have been the focus of many master's theses, specialist in education projects, and doctoral dissertations; and have been reported and supported by many individual authors, researchers, and/or investigators.

A series of councils, committees, and/or commissions within ASCD focused on instructional supervisors and curriculum directors. Whether these groups focused on either or both specializations, Bartoo (1976), Christensen (1976), and Sturgis (1978) found that practitioners preferred that professional accreditation of preparation programs occur at the national level. With nationally accredited programs of preparation in place, those same practitioners urged that certification or licensure of individuals occur at the state level. They also urged that they participate actively and continually in developing, applying, and/or enforcing standards. ASCD produced guidelines for approval of preparation programs for curriculum directors in 1977–78 and revised them in 1982–83 with expectation of their implementation through NCATE. In 1988, respective ASCD teams sought to develop NCATE criteria for instructional leaders, curriculum directors, and instructional designers. The project was unsuccessful because the standards proposed by the three teams did not distinguish the competencies required by the respective specializations.

The study of preparation programs by Pajak (1989) and a team of doctoral students at the University of Georgia identified in their review of the literature 101 proficiencies in 12 categories for preparation of instructional supervisors. Nine separate but related dissertation studies that evolved from that research effort validated the significance of these proficiencies for various positions engaged in instructional leadership. Several master's theses, specialist projects, and/or doctoral dissertations at various universities throughout the country have recommended separate programs for instructional supervisors and curriculum directors based on periodic surveys of practitioners in the field. Practitioners, writers, researchers, and advocates have published many articles urging the adoption of national standards for preparation programs. A sampling of these published in issues of *Educational Leadership* have been compiled into a single volume, *Supervision: Emerging Profession* (Leeper, 1969). Practitioners have registered their belief in and support for the identification of national standards for the *profession* of supervision. Scholars and practitioners representing the *field* of supervision must respond through their organizations, particularly ASCD.

Practitioners of Other Leadership Specializations Endorse National Standards

Current efforts to improve preparation programs for educational leadership in general and for instructional supervision in particular are channeled through the National Policy Board for Education Administration. Constituent members include ASCD, AASA, NASSP, and NESSP, each of which has generated respective criteria for instructional supervisors and curriculum directors (ASCD), superintendents (AASA), secondary principals (NASSP), and elementary principals (NAESP).

The AASA once planned to restrict membership to individuals who held the title of superintendent, who had received their academic preparation at an NCATE-approved institution, and who had earned, at a minimum, the sixth-year, or specialist, degree. Such qualifications also have been considered from time to time by other leadership organizations. It would seem plausible for associations focused on a particular position such as elementary principal, rather than those seeking to attract a diverse membership, such as ASCD, to hold to such requirements. The efforts of at least four former ASCD presidents to make that organization "a home for supervisors" have been unsuccessful because such a large proportion and number of other leadership positions are represented among its membership. However, the assignment of professional responsibility for accreditation of preparation programs at the national level and for certification to practice at the state level is clearly preferred by all these leadership specializations. The preference for such a division of responsibility is evidenced by inquiries of institutions, organizations, and agencies; by master's theses, specialist projects, and/or doctoral dissertations; and by authors, researchers, and/or investigators.

Such consistency in response should strengthen the resolve to place the responsibility for approving preparation standards in the hands of national-level organizations or agencies. Again, the practitioners of the several leadership specializations have spoken. The need is for national standards that will guide preparation by universities and performance by practitioners.

Established Professions Utilize National Standards

Criteria advanced as essential to the acceptance of an occupation as a profession invariably include an extensive period of specialized preparation (Carr-Saunders, 1928; Flexner, 1951; Lieberman, 1956; Firth, 1959; Dull, 1981; Hart & Marshall, 1992). Such programs have been approved by members of the profession through appropriate organizations and serve as a rite of passage for acceptance as a practitioner.

Medicine, considered the premier profession, owes much of its prestige to the Flexner Report (1910), which brought about control of the preparation of physicians through the professional accreditation of medical schools. Much the same circumstance elevated dentistry to professional status following the Gies Report (1926). One sine qua non of a profession is control of practitioner preparation. This has been the case for architecture, business administration, engineering, law, medicine, nursing, pharmacy, physical therapy, psychology, public accounting, and social work. Without control of practitioner preparation, those who long for a profession of supervision wait in vain. National standards for preparation and service must be adopted.

So important are such preparation programs that they create for each specialization a distinct culture, complete with its own language patterns, behavior norms, and governance structure. The identity of the individual is molded to the image expected by the public. Each profession utilizes a national organization not only to accredit programs of preparation but also to monitor continually the performance of its members. Boards composed of practitioners preside over admission to the profession through licensing at the state level, often involving an examination prepared by the same organization, and over suspension or revocation of licensure when the conduct of a member is judged to be unacceptable in terms of the code of ethics developed by members of the profession. It is this monitoring of performance that enables the profession to obtain and maintain the trust of particular clients and the public at large. The success of such efforts rests on the foundation of national standards for preparation and service.

Professionalization of Instructional Supervision Demands National Standards

Virtually every statement of aspiration to professionalize education in general (Firth, 1959; Hart & Marshall, 1992; Lieberman, 1956) and/or school supervision in particular (Frymier, 1969; Hartsig, 1966; Leeper, 1965; Mackenzie, 1961; Ogletree, 1965) has identified the need for national standards for approval of preparation programs.

The National Commission on Teacher Education and Professional Standards (NCTEPS, or TEPS) was established by the National Education Association in 1946. As an outgrowth of these efforts, NEA supported the project on New Horizons in Teacher Education and Professional Standards in 1959. The project's final report, published in 1961, stated that accreditation of preparatory programs was the keystone supporting all other standards and their enforcement— the core of the professional standards movement. The report urged completion of an approved program of preparation at an institution of higher education approved by the National Council for Accreditation of Teacher Education (Lindsey, 1961).

Every study of established professions—from Carr-Saunders (1925) through the Research Division (1938) to Yff (1992)—in which comparisons or contrasts have been made, has implied, interpreted, or imagined that education must emulate the established professions for a variety of reasons, some altruistic but most pragmatic. Lieberman (1956), Firth (1959), and Hart and Marshall (1992) provide convincing evidence that education in general and specializations such as school supervision in particular must mirror established professions in regard to national standards for preparation programs. Shafer (1965) related the Flexner approach symbolically and operationally to the efforts of an ASCD commission to professionalize the roles of instructional supervisor and curriculum director. The professionalization of school supervision can be achieved only if and when national standards for preparation and service are established, circulated, accepted, and implemented.

Summary

National standards are essential for the preparation of professional school supervisors for the following reasons separately and collectively:

1. Standards for preparation of school supervisors that have only local credibility will continue to invite uncertainty, vulnerability, and dependency.
2. Standards generated at the state level will continue to hold preparation programs captive to certification requirements for school supervisors imposed by lay boards, whose members too often act on the basis of political expediency and without benefit of counsel from professionals in education.
3. Only through application of national standards is it possible to create preparation programs in school supervision that recognize the unique needs and opportunities for service by that profession.

4. The application of national standards for accreditation of preparation programs by the National Council for Accreditation of Teacher Education can shape the professionalization of school supervision at the state and regional levels.

5. The use of national standards to guide the preparation of school supervision is a logical and essential extension of a concept accepted in education for over 75 years.

6. National standards in school supervision have been advocated, endorsed, and proposed by leadership organizations for nearly 50 years.

7. Practitioners in the field recognize the necessity for national standards in school supervision to preserve, protect, and promote professionalization of that specialization.

8. Practitioners in other positions of leadership in education recognize the importance of national standards in the preparation of school supervisors as well as the roles in which they serve.

9. All studies comparing and contrasting professions urge practitioners of education in general and of school supervision in particular to develop national standards for influencing, if not controlling, preparation programs.

10. Identifying national standards as the basis for accreditation of preparation programs will allow school supervision to attain the hallmark of an established profession.

References

Bartoo, E. (1976). Who is the curriculum worker? In C. A. Speiker (Ed.), *Curriculum leaders: Improving their influence*. Washington, DC: Association for Supervision and Curriculum Development.

Carr-Saunders, A. M. (1928). *Professions: Their organization and place in society*. Oxford: The Clarendon Press.

Christensen, D. J. (1976). The curriculum worker today. In C. A. Speiker (Ed.), *Curriculum leaders: Improving their influence*. Washington, DC: Association for Supervision and Curriculum Development.

Dull, L. W. (1981). *Supervision—school leadership handbook*. Columbus, OH: Charles W. Merrill Publishing Company.

Edmonds, E. L. (1962). *The school inspector*. London: Routledge & Kegan Paul.

Firth, G. R. (1959). *Professional self-discipline of public school personnel*. Unpublished doctoral dissertation, Teachers College, Columbia University.

Firth, G. R. (1987, March). Messages from the president—Recognition by professional organizations: A better way to clear up role confusion. *ASCD Update*, 2.

Firth, G. R. (1986, September). Messages from the president—specialty recognition options available to school leaders. *ASCD Update*, 2.

Flexner, A. (1910). *Medical education in the United States and Canada*. New York: Carnegie Foundation for the Advancement of Teaching.

Flexner, A. (1951). What are the earmarks of a profession? In B. O. Smith (Ed.), *Readings in social aspects of education*. Danville, IL: Interstate Printers and Publishers.

Frymier, J. R. (1969). The supervisor and his professional identify. In W. H. Lucio (Ed.), *The supervisor: New demands, new directions*. Washington, DC: Association for Supervision and Curriculum Development.

Gies, W. J. (1926). *Dental education in the United States and Canada.* New York: Carnegie Foundation for the Advancement of Teaching.

Hartsig, B. A. (1966). Professionalization of supervisors and curriculum workers. *Educational Leadership, 24,* 268–271.

Hart, S., & Marshall, J. D. (1992). *The question of teacher professionalism.* Paper presented at the annual meeting of the American Educational Research Association (ERIC Document and Reproduction Service No. ED 349 291).

Leeper, R. R. (1965). *Role of supervisor and curriculum director in a climate of change.* Washington, DC: Association for Supervision and Curriculum Development.

Leeper, R. R. (1969). *Supervision: Emerging profession.* Washington, DC: Association for Supervision and Curriculum Development.

Lieberman, M. (1956). *Education as a profession.* Englewood Cliffs, NJ: Prentice-Hall.

Lindsey, M. (Ed.). (1961). *New horizons for the teaching profession.* Washington, DC: National Education Association, National Commission on Teacher Education and Professional Standards.

Mackenzie, G. N. (1961). Role of the supervisor. *Educational Leadership, 19,* 86–90.

Mayor, J. R., & Swartz, W. D. (1965). *Accreditation in teacher education: Its influence on higher education.* Washington, DC: National Commission on Accrediting.

Ogletree, J. R. (1965). Professionalization of supervisors and curriculum workers. *Educational Leadership, 23,* 153–155.

Pajak, E. F. (1989). *Identification of supervisory proficiencies project.* Athens, GA: Department of Curriculum and Supervision, University of Georgia.

Research Division. (1938, September). Statutory status of six professions. *Research Bulletin, 16*(4), Washington, DC: National Education Association.

Shafer, H. T. (1965). What does the Flexner report say to ASCD? *Educational Leadership, 23,* 235–238.

Shafer, H. T., & Mackenzie, G. N. (1965). Securing competent instructional leaders. In R. R. Leeper (Ed.), *Role of supervisor and curriculum director in a climate of change.* Washington, DC: Association for Supervision and Curriculum Development.

Sturgis, A. W. (1978). *Certificating the curriculum leader and the instructional supervisor.* Washington, DC: Association for Supervision and Curriculum Development.

Yff, J. (1992). *Analysis of standards used by specialized accrediting bodies in ten professions.* Washington, DC: National Council for the Accreditation of Teacher Education.

Should There Be National Standards in the Preparation of Supervisors? *No*

Helen M. Hazi

At issue is the notion of standards, and I take the position contrary to my colleague Gerald Firth. While I may oppose standards, I do favor quality, program renewal, and responding to the needs of our clients. I oppose all the other things that are entangled with standards—such as the pursuit of professionalization and the notion of a knowledge base, as I hope to make clear later in this essay. I oppose standards because of the process used to set them and because standards are often presumptuous, dogmatic, and illusory. I oppose standards because the field of supervision is in transition and would find it difficult, if not impossible, to come to consensus on standards. In laying out my argument, I first present background to show that supervisory standards are part of a larger nationwide standards movement and to argue that standard setting comes at a time when supervision is most vulnerable.

Background

Ravitch (1995) traces the use and meaning of the word *standards*. Its earliest use was as " 'a conspicuous object (as a banner) formerly carried at the top of a pole and used to mark a rallying point esp. in battle or to serve as an emblem' " (p.7). A standard is "both a goal (what should be done) and a measure of progress toward that goal (how well it was done)" (p.7). The history of standards, says Ravitch,

> is a history of people agreeing on ways to improve materials, processes, and products and communicating that information to people who need to know it. Much of that development has occurred in response to changing technology or as a result of wars or disasters. (p. 8)

The disaster that prompted the current standards movement and its various waves was precipitated by *A Nation at Risk* (National Commission on Excellence in Education, 1983) that told of a national crisis of confidence in schooling. This policy document, in turn, spawned other interest groups with their own documents that subsequently indicted the preparation of teachers and administrators (e.g., National Policy Board for Educational Administration (NPBEA), 1989).

A discussion of standards for supervisors occurs at a time in which standard setting is a popular nationwide movement designed to bolster public confidence in education. One wave of this movement focuses on articulating what public school students should know and be able to do in various subject areas by certain grade levels (Diegmueller, 1995). Since 1991 thousands of educators involved in a dozen national disciplinary projects in the content areas (and in parallel projects at the state level) have produced reams of standards. "If schools nationwide would only raise their expectations for all students by setting rigorous standards, the premise goes, then learning and achievement would surely blossom" (Diegmueller, 1995, p.4). This movement has come propitiously a decade after *A Nation at Risk,* breathing new life into school reform in the midst of waning public confidence that the quality of schooling can be improved.

Another wave of this movement has engulfed teachers and administrators through the work of different groups. One group is the National Board for Professional Teaching Standards (NBPTS). The thrust of this project, started in 1987, has been "to elevate teaching by codifying what expert teachers should know and be able to do" (Bradley, 1995, p. 1). NBPTS advocates voluntary national board certification for teachers. Another group, the National Council for Accreditation of Teacher Education (NCATE), has been working in partnership with subject area groups to develop new performance-based standards that "will express the knowledge and skills teacher candidates should have, rather than the content of courses that education schools should offer" (Bradley, 1995, p.16). Yet another group, the National Policy Board for Education Administration (NPBEA), founded in 1988, was convened to advance professional standards for educational leaders and to similarly establish voluntary national board certification for school administrators (NPBEA, 1989). The effort to develop supervision standards rides on this wave of the standards movement and is located within NPBEA's and NCATE's activities to improve the preparation standards of educational leaders.

It is also important to keep in mind that this standard setting comes at a time when the field is "in transition" (Glickman, 1992). In his preface to the ASCD 1992 yearbook aptly titled *Supervision in Transition,* Glickman writes:

> Most activities or programs that I, and others, have clearly articulated in the past as "supervisory" or "supervision" are not called by that name by today's risk-taking practitioners. Instead they use terms such as coaching, collegiality, reflective practitioners, professional development, critical inquiry, and study or research groups. Practitioners shun the word "supervision" to describe the what and why of their actions. (p. 2)

There have been calls from the field to abolish supervision (Starratt, 1992; see Issue 1), to find substitutes for it (Sergiovanni, 1992a), to imagine schools where supervision will no longer be needed (Sergiovanni, 1992b), and to move into a new paradigm (Gordon, 1992).

This state of "traveling incognito," which Glanz and Hazi (1995) choose to call the current period, is due to the plethora of problems that has haunted the field. Some of the problems have been "ahistoricism, blurred boundaries, multiple purposes, absence of a theoretical framework to guide practice, conflicting theories, archaic methods, vestiges of authoritarian practices, eclecticism at its worst, a penchant for the practical, and unpopular acceptance" (Glanz, 1995). Instructional supervision travels incognito "in disguise and invisibly in law, in job title, in certification, and in practice" (Hazi & Glanz, 1995).

Thus, the move to standard setting occurs at a time when the field of supervision is most in dispute about its purposes and directions. Members of the field have not called for these standards. Rather, they have been asked to respond to standards already drafted by others.

Professionalization

Standards symbolize quality and are usually discussed in association with the concept of knowledge base, which in turn is entangled in arguments for professionalization. Taking a trait approach to the professions (a popular sociological explanation of the occupations and their evolution), one mark of a "genuine" profession is the claim to possession of a body of knowledge that is not possessed by the non-professional (Howsam, Corrigan, & Denemark, 1976, 1985). Once there are high standards, the logic goes, then education will be considered to be a profession—and not a semi-profession (e.g., Etzioni, 1969)—with the dignity, respect, and salary afforded other professions, such as law and medicine. This reasoning became popular during the 1970s (e.g., Howsam et al., 1976, 1985; Shanker, 1985) and has come in vogue once again (e.g., Bradley, 1995; Sykes, 1991).

Professionalization, however, is problematic. Groups periodically tackle the knotty question of whether they are a profession to control competition, to build channels for individual achievement, or to promote an economic monopoly over services (Abbott, 1988). Occupational groups typically critique their standing according to a specific list of criteria. This list usually includes such criteria as a specialized (abstract) body of knowledge that cannot be applied in a routine fashion (but requires the exercise of independent judgment), specialized schools that convey this knowledge, a rigorous system of examination and licensing meant to exclude those unqualified, and a code of ethics, to name a few (e.g., Caplow, 1954; Carr-Saunders & Wilson, 1934).

The trait approach to professionalization, however, has been dysfunctional and hegemonic. This approach to thinking about professions views an occupational group in abstract time and in isolation rather than in relation to others. Those claiming professional standing usually possess these requisite criteria. Law and medicine are used as a basis of comparison to include or exclude an occupation. If one disliked social work or chiropractic, one easily found some trait excluding it from the prestigious ranks of the professions (Abbott, 1988).[1] One trait, among others, that relegated teaching to the classification of semi-profession was that it had "a preponderance of women" (Howsam et al.,1976, 1985, p. 9). This kind of reasoning creates a seductive and "artificial status hierarchy" that benefits only the few (Burbules & Densmore, 1991b).

Professionalization as an ideology has limited utility in a postmodern world. It is a hegemonic concept that undermines democracy, equity, and cultural diversity. It also serves to further distance clients who already distrust educators. Additional negative consequences of professionalization within the education ranks include the under-representation of minorities; professionalization for the few; greater standardization, rationalization, and deskilling; and diverting attention and resources away from more pressing concerns such as better communications with parents and community. Invoking professionalism only serves as a shield to protect educators from the public (Burbules & Densmore, 1991a, 1991b).

Codification of a Knowledge Base

Codification of a knowledge base, attempted in a postmodern time,[2] is problematic. It represents nothing more than a consensus of the beliefs of those people brought to the table at that time. It does not represent "the" objective, value-free, "right" view of what knowledge is worth knowing and communicating to those future supervisors. Different people at the table would produce different knowledge bases because their views are shaped by their past and present education and experiences.

Those with the most difficulty in a postmodern world are the objectivists who want to enforce a single official reality structure. They want to "rebuild consensus, to get a core of standard values and beliefs in place in every American mind" (Anderson, 1990, p. 4). The pursuit of a knowledge base in education (and supervision) in the 1990s is the pursuit of a single official reality structure that appeals to those in search of certainty in an uncertain, complex, and uncontrollable postmodern world. Thus, standard setting can be viewed not only as a public relations technique but also as a control strategy.

Donmoyer (1995) provides a perspective on early and contemporary attempts at knowledge codification in both teaching and administration. He reminds us that Thorndike (1910), an educational psychologist with a social engineering orientation, promised that a knowledge base would help educators to avoid the political control and corruption found in schools of the early twentieth century and, with faith in science, to predict and control events, just like engineers and other scientists. While reformers generally succeeded in minimizing political influence, they failed to provide a knowledge base of precise, cause–effect formulas for practice. The search for a knowledge base for three-quarters of this century has been dominated by the process-product paradigm, which seeks to correlate teacher behavior with student learning. "The role of research was to discover and validate formulas for practice, and practice, itself, was often thought of in terms of systems, techniques, routines, and standard operating procedures" (Donmoyer, 1995, p. 5). When research did not yield the hoped for answers, then the field was regarded as "a very young science" that would eventually produce the answers with time and better science. This did not seem to stymie the search for a knowledge base, however, since "it was Thorndike's notion of a knowledge base . . . not the actual existence of one, which was instrumental in promoting the cause of profession control" (Donmoyer, 1995, p. 5).

This Thorndikian hold on research was not broken until the mid-1970s with the introduction of new lines of research such as teacher thinking from cognitive psychology. Donmoyer (1995) says that "today knowledge is more likely to be seen as a heuristic to guide practice rather than as a source of formulas which dictate what professionals are to do" (p.8). "Those who attempt to articulate a knowledge base to ground a professional community," says Donmoyer (1995), "must be either consciously or unconsciously engaged in the process of perpetuating an illusion" (p. 15).

One of the early attempts at developing standards and codifying knowledge for the field was by A. W. Sturges and Gerald Firth (ASCD, 1982–83). Their document revising 1977–78 ASCD standards included standards and guidelines for evaluating preparation programs for curriculum leaders.[3] Their approach was broad-based and process-oriented, and resembled the approach taken generally when accrediting programs in higher education. Another effort by Pajak (1989) was a knowledge codification effort funded by ASCD. Pajak extracted "knowledge, skills, and attitudes" (or KSAs) that appeared at least twice in articles, reports, and textbooks and that were associated with highly effective supervisory practice. These "proficiencies" were then subjected to vote by 12 categories of outstanding instructional leaders and resulted in 12 dimensions of supervisory practice with 239 proficiencies. The project's intent was to provide a basis for identifying standards of practice which would then lead to voluntary, national certification in supervision through ASCD. It was hoped that these standards "could simultaneously improve practice, restore public confidence, and enhance the prestige of the education profession" (Pajak, 1989, p. 1). This project would also help "to meet the profession's responsibility for defining the discipline of supervision" (p. 2) because "an agreed upon body of knowledge and skills along with a set of shared values and attitudes are the hallmarks of a profession, and distinguish a professional from a nonprofessional" (Pajak, 1989, p. 149).

Instead of advocating separate national certification in supervision, (as was assumed when the Pajak's Project was funded), ASCD joined forces with other national professional associations for administrators in the NPBEA, as previously mentioned. The NPBEA refocused its efforts to develop a common set of guidelines for the NCATE accreditation of programs in educational leadership.[4] It was this effort that produced content standards in the form of 85 statements of essential KSAs in 11 knowledge and skill domains integrated into 4 broad areas: (1) strategic leadership, (2) organizational leadership. (3) instructional leadership, and (4) political and community leadership (NPBEA, 1994). These 85 KSAs are for a generic administrator and are based on the assumption that there is no difference in the roles of superintendent, principal, and central office supervisor.

The Standard-Setting Process

The process of articulating standards is problematic. While it may be described as consensus building, it is a process of control and dominance that gives the illusion of inclusion, objectivity, and collaboration. The final point in this argument was learned as a result of two experiences at standard setting. The first occurred in 1984 when West Virginia developed the first customized competency test for instructional supervisors. The second occurred in 1995 when I reacted to the fifth draft of the proposed NCATE standards for supervisors. In the former I was chair of the state advisory committee; in the latter I was one of over 100 professors invited to participate two years after the process had already begun. Both experiences were unsettling, despite attempts to voice my concerns about each (Hazi, 1985; Hazi, 1995).

In the first experience the task was to revise, add, or delete items from a list of 120 objectives. An item was included based on criteria such as job-relatedness (as measured by a survey of state practitioners), significance, accuracy, and whether it could be measured by a multiple-choice item. This was called the test of inclusion. The test development company framed the task, the amount of time we met, and the key questions we addressed. We never did talk about our disparate definitions of supervision or what skills would be required of those in the role. There was not enough time. We became fixed on the task of interpreting and revising the wording of each objective. Anyone who questioned the task was viewed as a deviant (Hazi, 1985).

Yet the test of inclusion was influenced by those who showed up for the meetings. Since the majority of the committee was composed of practitioners, the diversity of one's practice became an unspoken rationale for inclusion or exclusion of an item.[5] Those who consistently attended meetings had a better understanding of the history of previous meetings and decisions. As people floated in and out, previous decisions were revisited and redecided,[6] and the loudest, most convincing argument that withstood criticism seemed to be the real test of inclusion of an objective (Hazi, 1985). The lessons of the first experience were patience, persistence, and endurance.

The second experience was very different. Although NPBEA was formed in 1988, it did not get down to the business of standards until 1993. Faculty who trained supervisors (and curriculum directors) were not invited to participate in the process until the spring of 1995, when we were asked to react to an already conceptualized fifth draft document. Our representatives at the table were staff members of ASCD who solicited input from the Council of Professors of Instructional Supervision (COPIS) and the professors of curriculum at ASCD's annual meeting.

Not having participated in the process, one can only react to a document as if one has just entered a conversation already in progress. One must surmise how the writers got to this place and what decisions must have been made along the way. One must read messages in the "subtext" of the document to reveal the logic and ask a lot of questions. Still, reading and reacting to the document represents only a vicarious experience in standard-setting. The lesson learned from this experience was that you had to be there to understand and benefit from the process.

I also learned about the dilemma of standard-setting. On one hand, standard-setting most benefits the people who participate in the process. It gives them the opportunity to articulate their beliefs, examine taken-for-granted assumptions, and define what is most important in promoting quality. The process allows its participants to engage in a transformative experience in which they critically examine what they do and come to a different understanding about that when they are through. The process of standard-setting—not the standards—is the key to promoting quality. The standards, the result, are a mere representation of what was discussed over a series of meetings. On the other hand, an effort such as standard-setting is an impossible task. It can rarely be totally inclusive of various groups and ideas in these postmodern times; nor is it feasible to completely encapsulate a field of knowledge by arbitrarily identifying some standards. The problem is that we have not yet imagined new ways to ensure quality and progress without standardization in a postmodern world.

A quote from Donmoyer (1995) seems an apropos conclusion:

> According to postmodern scholars, the world will always consist of a cacophony of voices talking past each other. In such a world, the idea that discourse and deliberation can lead to consensus about a course of action to be pursued is considered, at best, romantic and, at worst, dangerous. (p. 24)

Endnotes

1. An example is the American Medical Association's illegal conspiracy and boycott against chiropractors as "an unscientific cult" starting in the 1960s. "In 1990, the U.S. Supreme Court let stand a federal district court decision and an appellate ruling finding the AMA tried to destroy a competitor." It took a 15-year lawsuit against the AMA (and an undisclosed settlement) for doctors to be able to refer patients to chiropractors ("After 15-year fight, AMA gives OK to chiropractors," 1992).

2. Postmodernism is characterized by a relativistic world view in which there is no one fixed truth, but multiple competing and socially constructed views of reality. With the birth of a global culture, there has been a breakdown of old ways of belief, a single way of looking at the world. Not only do individuals have choices in religions, but they also have choices about stories of what the universe is like and who are the good guys and bad guys. There is no one neutral, objective view of reality (although some may choose this view). Science is not omnipotent and objective, but is another form of reality construction (Anderson, 1990).

3. The eight areas for the standards included professional studies (e.g., curriculum, instruction, and supervision); supporting fields; practicum; resources and facilities; organization and governance; faculty; student services; and evaluation, program review, and planning (ASCD, 1982–83).

4. NCATE requires that preparation programs be based on some knowledge base: "The unit ensures that its professional education programs are based on essential knowledge, established and current research findings, and sound professional practice. . . ." (Gideonse, 1989, pp. 37–38).

5. Indeed, job title has been the most troublesome of the field's problems. It has been documented by Spears (1953) that supervisors masqueraded under a miscellaneous array of titles, avoiding "supervisor" because of the stigma attached to the term. Supervisors had been responsible for teacher rating which quickly degenerated to finding fault with teacher behavior.

6. According to Dick, Watson, and Kaufman (1981), the result of a consensus approach is a "conglomerate" of items with no interrelationship. What gets included is the result of "consensus, good judgment, and conventional wisdom" (p.9). It becomes difficult to add items that are "not in vogue or well understood" and difficult to delete items that are "institutionalized but useless."

References

Abbott, A. (1988). *The system of professions: An essay on the division of expert labor.* Chicago: The University of Chicago Press.

After 15-year fight, AMA gives OK to chiropractors. (1992, January 9). *Chicago Sun-Times*, p. 3.

Anderson, W. T. (1990). *Reality isn't what it used to be: Theatrical politics, ready-to-wear religion, global myths, primitive chic, and other wonders of the postmodern world.* San Francisco: HarperSanFrancisco.

ASCD (1982–83). *Evaluating graduate programs preparing curriculum leaders: Standards & guidelines.* Alexandria, VA: Association for Supervision and Curriculum Development.

Bradley, A. (1995, April 5). Signs abound teaching reforms are taking hold. *Education Week*, pp. 1,16,17.

Burbules, N., & Densmore, K. (1991a). The limits of making teaching a profession. *Educational Policy*, 5(1), 44–63.

Burbules, N., & Densmore, K. (1991b). The persistence of professionalism: Breakin' up is hard to do. *Educational Policy*, 5(2), 150–157.

Caplow, T. (1954). *The sociology of work*. Minneapolis: University of Minnesota.

Carr-Saunders, A. P., & Wilson, P. A. (1934). *The professions*. Oxford: Oxford University Press.

Dick, W., Watson, K., & Kaufman, R. (1981). Deriving competencies; Consensus versus model building. *Educational Researcher, 10*(8), 5–13.

Diegmueller, K. (1995, April 12). Running out of steam. In struggling for standards, a special report. *Education Week*, pp. 1–70.

Donmoyer, R. (1995, April). *The very idea of a knowledge base*. Paper presented at the annual meeting of the American Educational Research Association, San Francisco.

Etzioni, A. (1969). *The semi-professions and their organization: Teachers, nurses, social workers*. New York: Free Press.

Gideonse, H. (1989, January). *Relating knowledge to teacher education: Responding to NCATE's knowledge base and related standards*. Washington, DC: American Association of Colleges for Teacher Education.

Glanz, J. (1995). *The tao of supervision: Taoist insights into the theory and practice of educational supervision*. Unpublished manuscript.

Glanz, J., & Hazi, H. (1995). *Supervision traveling incognito: Implications for supervision and administration*. Unpublished manuscript.

Glickman, C. (Ed.), (1992). *Supervision in transition: The 1992 ASCD yearbook*. Alexandria, VA: Association for Supervision and Curriculum Development.

Gordon, S. (1992). Paradigms, transitions, and the new supervision. *Journal of Curriculum and Supervision, 8*, 62–76.

Hazi, H. (1985). *Minimum competency testing in West Virginia: A case of missing identity for instructional supervisors*. Paper presented at the annual meeting of the American Educational Research Association, Chicago.

Hazi, H. (1995, January 22). Memo to members of COPIS re: COPIS and the NCATE document.

Hazi, H., & Glanz, J. (1995). *Supervision traveling incognito: A historical-critical analysis*. Unpublished manuscript.

Howsam, R. B., Corrigan, D. C., & Denemark, G. W. (1976, 1985). *Educating a profession: Reprint with postscript 1985*. Washington, DC: Bicentennial Commission on Education for the Profession of Teaching of the American Association of Colleges for Teacher Education.

The National Commission on Excellence in Education. (1983). *A nation at risk: The imperative for education reform*. Washington, DC: Superintendent of Documents, U.S. Government Printing Office.

NPBEA. (1989, May). *Improving the preparation of school administrators: An agenda for reform*. Charlottesville, VA: National Policy Board for Educational Administration.

NPBEA. (1994, November). *Proposed NCATE curriculum guidelines: Advanced programs in educational leadership for superintendents, principals, curriculum directors and supervisors* (5th draft). Charlottesville, VA: National Policy Board for Education Administration.

Pajak, E. (1989). *Identification of supervisory proficiencies project: Final report*. Athens, GA: University of Georgia, Department of Curriculum & Supervision.

Ravitch, D. (1995). *National standards in American education: A citizen's guide*. Washington, DC: The Brookings Institution.

Sergiovanni, T. (1992a). Why we should seek substitutes for leadership. *Educational Leadership, 49*(5), 41–49.

Sergiovanni, T. (1992b). Moral authority and the regeneration of supervision. In C. Glickman (Ed.), *Supervision in transition: The 1992 ASCD yearbook* (pp. 203–214). Alexandria, VA: Association for Supervision and Curriculum Development.

Shanker, A. (1985). *The making of a profession*. Washington, DC: American Federation of Teachers, AFL-CIO.

Spears, H. (1953). *Improving the supervision of instruction*. New York: Prentice-Hall Inc.

Starratt, R. J. (1992). After supervision. *Journal of Curriculum and Supervision*, 8, 77–86.

Sykes, G. (1991). In defense of teacher professionalism as a policy choice. *Educational Policy*, 5(2), 137–149.

Thorndike, E.L. (1910). The contribution of psychology to education. *The Journal of Educational Psychology*, 1, 5–12.

Postnote

Should There Be National Standards in the Preparation of Supervisors?

The adoption of national education goals has been a major impetus for the development of national standards for many disciplines. National standards have broad support nationwide because of increasing pressures for accountability as well as the perceived need to achieve world-class skills, excellence, and equity in the nation's schools. The impetus for standards in the preparation for supervisory positions is particularly strong. The issue for many is not "if there will be standards established" but which ones are most suitable in order to adequately prepare future school leaders. Despite the support for national standards, there is much disagreement about what the standards should be, who establishes them, and a host of other urgent concerns. National dialogue on the efficacy of national standards is likely to continue. We hope this chapter can provoke and further stimulate discourse on this critical and controversial issue.

Review Questions for

The Yes Response:

1. Why does Dr. Firth contend that developing national standards for supervisors is critical "if there is to be any hope of having a *profession* of educational supervision?" Do you agree or disagree? Explain.
2. React to Firth's 10 arguments in favor of national standards. Which arguments are the most convincing? least convincing?
3. Why does Firth question the viability of state standards for preparing educational personnel? Why does he maintain that "partisan politics" interferes with standard setting at a state level, and why wouldn't such concerns be prevalent with federally imposed standards?
4. How would Firth counter Hazi's arguments? Do you find his arguments convincing? Explain.
5. How would the establishment of national standards affect you as a practitioner?

The No Response:

1. Dr. Hazi asserts that standard setting in supervision is premature in that the field is currently beset by a plethora of problems. What problems currently beleaguer the field of supervision? Why would these problems interfere with standard setting?
2. How is standards setting "viewed as a public relations technique" and "also as a control strategy?" Do you agree? Explain.

3. Should there be separate standards for different supervisory positions such as superintendent, principal, and central office supervisor? Explain.

4. What fundamental assumptions underlie the postmodernist thinking that supports Hazi's assertions? How would Firth counter these postmodernist claims?

5. How do you think Hazi's experiences with standard setting affected her views on national standards? Have you ever been in the position of developing standards? Describe your experiences.

6. How would Hazi counter Firth's assertions? Do you find her arguments convincing? Explain.

For Further Research

1. What specific knowledge, skills, and attitudes (KSAs) can be identified for superintendents, curriculum directors, supervisors, and principals? Are the roles of supervisor and curriculum director different from those of principal and superintendent? If so, should the difference be reflected in preparation programs? What might be the consequences of promoting "generic" standards for all administrative roles?

2. Read Daresh's (in press) chapter, "Preparation Programs in Supervision." How does Daresh conceptualize this issue? What factor(s) influence the establishment of national standards? Do you think that universities that have adopted national standards would necessarily prepare you any better as a supervisor than a university that has not accepted these standards? Explain.

3. Interview at least five educators on their views about national standards. Compare their views with the authors' in this chapter as well as your own.

4. What are the effects of the supervision standards movement on the content, structure, and processes of supervisor education? To what extent is the standards movement consistent with other goals of supervisor education programs? Would national standards bolster supervision's prestige in your school/district/community?

5. Should graduate students be required to demonstrate specific competencies prior to certification? Should supervisor education require national board examinations for certification? Why or why not?

6. Write a report describing what competencies all supervisors should have. How could you ensure that all graduates demonstrate these competencies?.

7. Much controversy exists regarding developing and adopting national standards in general. Consult the following critics and

supporters, and assess their arguments for standards setting: Bain (1995), Eisner (1994), Gandel (1995), Gardner (1994), and Goodman (1994).

8. What might be the consequences of promoting "generic" standards for all administrative roles? Would this result in a "generic" administrative certificate, and is this appropriate? Would these KSAs ultimately appear in a single test?

9. Write an overview of standard setting in general. What lessons can we learn about competency and standard-driven instruction from other disciplines that have already established national standards?

10. Write a history of the rise of national standards. Consult Ravitch (1995), for example. How are current concerns about national standards linked to past efforts? How have significant ideas, events, and people influenced or informed current conceptions of this issue? What are some of the social, economic, philosophical, and political forces that influence this debate? What can we learn from history that might help us develop a perspective on the national standards issue?

11. Conduct a literature review on standard setting and compare different views on the issue.

12. What vested interests does ASCD have in establishing standards for supervisory positions? What about other national organizations?

13. How will standards contribute to improving teaching, learning, and the quality of life in your school/district?

14. Consult the following sources and react to their views in setting national standards: Alexander (1993), Apple (1993), Costa (1993), Darling-Hammond (1994), Eisner (1993), Flood and Lapp (1993), Greene (1994), Ladson-Billings (1994), Miller (1995), Porter (1994), and Ravitch (1993). How would each of these authors react to the arguments set forth by Firth and Hazi?

15. Consult the proposed NCATE Curriculum Guidelines prepared by the National Policy Board for Educational Administration (1994) (your professor can readily provide copies for you) and discuss the following: How were draft guidelines formulated? What rationale is presented for establishing new standardized guidelines in the preparation of supervisors (seven factors)? Name and discuss the five broad shifts in the knowledge and skills required of educational leaders today according to the document. What assumptions guided the development of these guidelines (nine assumptions)? Assess the efficacy of the specific curriculum guidelines.

16. Read the following authorities about their views on national standards: Apple (1992), Ravitch (1995), and Sarason (1993). Compare and contrast their views. What issues and questions do these authors raise that help us clarify and possibly resolve this controversial issue?

References

Alexander, F. (1993). National standards: A new conventional wisdom. *Educational Leadership, 50,* 9–10.

Apple, M. W. (1992). Do the standards go far enough? Power, policy, and practice in mathematics education. *Journal for Research in Mathematics Education, 23,* 412–431.

Apple, M. (1993). The politics of official knowledge: Does a national curriculum make sense? *Teachers College Record, 95,* 222–241.

Bain, R. (1995, February 7). The world-history standards: A teacher's perspective. *Education Week.*

Costa, A. (1993). How world-class standards will change us. *Educational Leadership, 50,* 51–55.

Daresh, J. C. (in press). Preparation programs in supervision. In G. R. Firth & E. Pajak (Eds.), *Handbook of research on school supervision.* New York: Macmillan.

Darling-Hammond, L. (1994). National standards and assessments: Will they improve education? *American Journal of Education, 102,* 478–510.

Eisner, E. (1993). Why standards may not improve schools. *Educational Leadership, 50,* 22–23.

Eisner, E. (1994). Do American schools need standards? *School Administrator, 51,* 8–15.

Flood, J, & Lapp, D. (1993). Clearing the confusion: A closer look at national goals and standards (issues and trends). *Reading Teacher, 47,* 58–61.

Gandel, M. (1995). Not all standards are created equal. *Educational Leadership, 5,* 16–21.

Gardner, H. (1994, September 7). The need for anti-babel standards. *Education Week.*

Goodman, K. (1994, September 7) Standards not! *Education Week.*

Greene, M. (1994). The arts and national standards. *Educational Forum, 58,* 391–400.

Ladson-Billings, G. (1994). A critique of national standards. *Educational Leadership, 50,* 4–8.

Miller, R. (Ed.). (1995). *Educational freedom for a democratic society: A critique of national educational goals, standards and curriculum.* Brandon, VT: Resource Center for Redesigning Education.

National Policy Board for Educational Administration. (1994, November). *Proposed NCATE curriculum guidelines.* Unpublished document.

Porter, A. (1994). National standards and school improvement in the 1990's: Issues and promise. *American Journal of Education, 102,* 421–449.

Ravitch, D. (1993). Launching a revolution in standards and assessments. *Phi Delta Kappan, 74,* 767–772.

Ravitch, D. (1995). *National standards in American education.* Washington, D.C.: The Brookings Institution.

Sarason, S. B. (1993). *The case for change: Rethinking the preparation of educators.* San Francisco: Jossey-Bass.

Issue 10

Should Educational Supervision Be Influenced by Business Management Practices?

✦ ✦ ✦ ✦

YES—Francis M. Duffy, Gallaudet University

NO—Edward Pajak, University of Georgia

✦ ✦ ✦

Issue Summary

YES: Professor of administration and supervision, Frank Duffy outlines a new model of supervision, "Knowledge Work Supervision," that is derived in large measure from business management theory. Dr. Duffy insists that supervisors who work with individual teachers cannot effect significant improvements in student achievement without attention to the systematic application of business management practices district-wide. These ideas, argues Duffy, can powerfully transform "supervision from what it is to what it could be."

NO: Professor Ed Pajak counters Duffy's claims that educational supervision should be influenced by business ideology. Dr Pajak emphasizes that the process of education is not a "production system," and given its personal interactive quality, business procedures are inappropriate to and incompatible with education. Pajak explains that early supervision based on democratic practices "provided an effective counterpoint and barrier to unwarranted intrusion of business management practices and ideas." The author believes that educators too readily embrace business-inspired practices with little, if any, reluctance. He concludes by elucidating five steps that "I think would help to move the practice and study of supervision in education forward."

Guiding Questions

1. What are the benefits of drawing on business management theories to aid the practice of supervision in schools?
2. What are some disadvantages of applying business management practices to supervision?
3. To what extent are principles and practices of business management in private industry, for example, applicable to public schools in general?
4. Can principles derived from other disciplines and fields such as the military have relevance and applicability for supervision?
5. Which of the two essays do you find most persuasive? Why?
6. What aspects of Duffys' and Pajaks' thinking make most sense to you?

Should Educational Supervision Be Influenced by Business Management Practices? *Yes*

Francis M. Duffy

Is there a profession or discipline that has not begged, borrowed, or stolen ideas and methods from other professions or disciplines? Lawyers are trained in communication and theater arts. Metaphors from the "new sciences" are leaping into our management lexicon with rapidity and power. Should educational supervision be exempt from this kind of influence?

Those who answer "no" to the question posed in the title of this essay would not argue against supervision borrowing ideas from psychology, communication theory, or the human relations movement. Those suggesting that notions of community building should influence supervision would be smothered with hugs and kisses—they would be exalted for suggesting that supervision be influenced by diversity and multicultural concepts. But God forbid they suggest that business management practices should influence supervision. "What does business have to do with schooling?" the antagonists would pule. Anything derived from or related to business is disparaged intensely in some education circles.

Leave the circles of disparagement and go into the hallways, offices, and classrooms of schools. In the context of real-world schooling, supervisory practice is, rightfully so, influenced by business management practices. Consider the notion of preparing and managing a department budget—business idea. Reflect on linking all computers in a school as a "local area network" so teachers can enter their grades from desktop terminals and thereby facilitate the reporting and mailing of grades—business idea. Visualize supervisors employing principles of organization development as advocated by Pajak (1982)—business idea. Ponder supervisors crafting mission and vision statements for their departments, teams, or schools—business idea. Imagine supervisors developing their teams into high-performing work units—business idea. Work teams—business idea. Can you imagine the practice of school supervision without the influence of business management practices? Can you think of other examples?

New Supervision Born of Business Management

An example of a new educational supervision model evolving from business management is sketched below. In the business world there are ideas that have power and meaning for school supervision. These ideas are found in the literature on knowledge work, sociotechnical systems design, business process reengineering, quality management, and organization development. This new model of supervision, born of business management, represents a shift in the way educational supervision is thought about and practiced. The model is called *Knowledge Work Supervision*® (Duffy, 1995).

Before reading about Knowledge Work Supervision, please reflect on two questions: What if the focus of supervision were to shift from an examination of individual teacher behavior to an examination and improvement of three sets of key organizational variables: work procedures, social architecture, and the school district's relationship with its environment? (In 1982, Pajak argued for a similar shift in supervisory perspective.) What if supervision could be transformed from twice-a-year performance evaluation (which, by the way, is the predominant model of supervision used in schools) into a process for designing high-performance schools (Duffy, 1996)?

Knowledge Work Supervision (hereafter referred to as KWS) can produce the shifts mentioned to in the above questions. It is a systemic and systematic means to redesign the anatomy (structures), physiology (flow of information and webs of relationships), and psychology (beliefs and values) of a school district. The paradigm of Knowledge Work Supervision is portrayed in Figure 1.

The vision for KWS is that it develop into a supervisory process that helps a school district *become a high performing learning organization that applies its collective knowledge to create and deliver educational services that have true value for* all *students and parents.* The model was constructed by reviewing business literature in several interrelated areas: sociotechnical systems design (e.g., Trist, Higgin, Murray, & Pollack, 1965; Pasmore, 1988, 1993), knowledge work (Drucker,

Figure 1:   The Paradigm of Knowledge Work Supervision

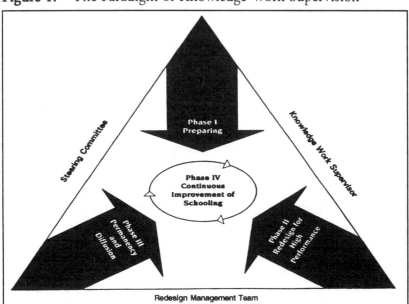

1969, 1985, 1993), quality improvement (e.g., Crosby, 1979; Deming, 1982; Juran, 1989), business process reengineering (Hammer & Champy, 1993), and organization development (e.g., Argyris & Schön, 1974, 1978; Burke, 1982). My real-world experiences as an organization development consultant to businesses like State Farm Insurance, the Association for Supervision and Curriculum Development, and the U.S. Departments of Energy and Agriculture also contributed to the design of this model of organizational renewal.

The Structure of Knowledge Work Supervision

Remember that KWS examines and improves work procedures, social architecture, and the district's relationship with its environment. Thus, it is essentially an organizational redesign process. KWS has four phases, each with multiple steps. The paradigm is also cyclical, so that at the completion of Phase 4 the process recycles back to Phase 1. The cycle continues for the life of the school district because KWS is a never-ending process of becoming. The four phases are briefly described below.

The paradigm is powered by three key players: a steering committee providing strategic leadership, school-based redesign management teams providing tactical leadership for the redesign work, and knowledge work supervisors (retrained, reskilled administrators and supervisors) skilled in the process of organizational redesign.

Phase 1: Preparing

Phase 1 supervisory activities are:

Step 1.1:   Build support for the redesign project.
Step 1.2:   Identify a starting point.
Step 1.3:   Establish a contract.
Step 1.4:   Form a steering committee.
Step 1.5:   Engage the steering committee in open systems planning.
Step 1.6:   Engage the steering committee in redefining the mission and vision of the school district.
Step 1.7:   Establish a change management structure and process.

These supervisory activities focus on preparing to redesign a school district for high performance. Failure to complete this phase or shortcutting the preparation process usually results in a failed redesign effort. This conclusion is supported by Kotter (1995), who identifies eight errors made by organizations engaged in redesign efforts—errors that result in failure.

Steps 1.1–1.3 are conducted by a small group of influential administrators, supervisors, and teachers who see the need to redesign their school district. These people build support for KWS, identify a school or cluster of schools that will begin the process (the school that begins the process is called the *target school*), and develop a contract with teachers and administrators from the target school.

The steering committee established in Step 1.4 is composed of representatives from a cross-cut of district personnel (administrators, supervisors, teachers, and, most important, the superintendent). It provides broad strategic leadership for KWS, which includes examining the district's relationship with its environment (Step 1.5) and defining (or redefining) the district's mission and vision (Step 1.6).

The last step of Phase 1 is the formation of a redesign management team (RMT) within the schools that begin the process. The RMT is a structure already in place in many school districts in the guise of school improvement teams. The RMT, in collaboration with the knowledge work supervisor, becomes the driving force behind the KWS process by providing tactical leadership for redesigning work procedures and work relationships. The RMT manages the KWS process within its respective school, thereby increasing the likelihood that improvements will "stick."

Phase 2: Redesigning for High Performance

Phase 2 supervisory activities are:

Step 2.1(a):   Diagnose the work processes of the target school(s).
Step 2.1(b):   Diagnose the social system of the target school(s).
Step 2.2:   Develop proposals to redesign the target school(s).
Step 2.3:   Develop an implementation plan.
Step 2.4:   Implement selected proposals.
Step 2.5:   Evaluate the process and outcomes of the redesign effort.

Step 2.1(a) examines the work processes of the target school(s). In school districts, which are knowledge organizations, there are two key knowledge work processes. The most important is classroom teaching. Classroom teaching is not a step-by-step work process (like making a toaster), but instead is nonlinear. The nonlinear nature of teaching is reflected in how a teacher teaches. When she is on her feet her mind is racing. She has her objective(s) in mind. New examples of the points she is trying to make pop into her head. Students ask questions that take her off course temporarily. She returns to her original direction when a story that reinforces her points comes to mind. She looks at the clock and realizes that she must bring the lesson to a close. Before closing she makes one last point that was triggered by a student's question during the first minute of class—a full 44 minutes earlier.

The second knowledge work process in schools is a step-by-step, linear process that supports classroom teaching. It is the instructional program, kindergarten through twelfth grade. Students must progress through this grade-by-grade work system. Certain requirements must be satisfied before the student can progress to the next higher grade. This sequential work process continues until students graduate.

To diagnose these two work systems, the RMT and knowledge work supervisor determine where errors are made or identify where they could be made. To examine the linear instructional program, a program audit is conducted. Policies, procedures, information flow, and so on, are examined to identify errors. To examine nonlinear classroom teaching, the RMT and knowledge work supervisor identify topics teachers need to be thinking and talking about in order to teach effectively. They also figure out who the teachers should be exchanging information with and assess the quality of the forums for these exchanges. Finally, the RMT and knowledge work supervisor take a look at any device or procedure supporting classroom teaching and assess its quality and effectiveness (e.g., the lesson planning process, administrative procedures, and computer networks). This kind of analytic process is called *deliberation analysis* and was first articulated by Pava (1983).

Step 2.1(b) examines the social architecture of the target school. The biggest oversight in current organizational improvement models (e.g., school improvement efforts, business process reengineering, and total quality management) is that they do not try to improve the social architecture of an organization. The social architecture is a web-like structure of roles, required skills, relationships, beliefs, values, and perceptions. The social architecture and the work processes interact at a significant level. The social architecture maintains the work system—if improvements are made only in the work system, the redesign effort will fail. The social architecture and the work system must be improved simultaneously to increase overall organizational effectiveness.

The most important outcome of Phase 2 is the implementation of a comprehensive proposal to redesign the target school(s). Steps 2.2 through 2.5 accomplish this goal. The results of the environmental analysis (completed in Phase 1 by the steering committee) and data from diagnosing work procedures and work relationships are analyzed to identify significant ways to improve the target school(s). This analysis results in a comprehensive redesign proposal having sufficient breadth and depth to effect lasting improvements in the work system, social architecture, and environmental relationships. The proposal must also be clearly and powerfully aligned with the school district's vision statement.

Phase 3: Achieving Permanence and Diffusion

Supervisory activities for this phase are:

Step 3.1:   Conduct "double-loop" learning seminars.
Step 3.2:   Gain commitment to the changes that have been made.
Step 3.3:   Allocate rewards for desired behaviors.
Step 3.4:   Diffuse the changes to other parts of the organization.
Step 3.5:   Detect and correct deviations from the desired outcomes.

There is an old French saying that applies to school improvement efforts of the past and present: "Plus ça change, plus c'est la même chose." It translates as "The more things change, the more they stay the same." This cynicism is reflected in statements like "Didn't we do this last year?" or "I thought we solved that problem!" or "If we hang on long enough, this too shall pass." Obviously, if a school district really wants to improve its performance level, it doesn't want to suffer from the change–revert back–change again–revert back again syndrome. District personnel want their hard work, emotional commitment, and energy to pay off with permanent improvements. Permanent improvements are effected by completing Steps 3.1 through 3.3, which are designed to anchor the improvements to the district's culture and other deep organizational structures.

After redesign improvements are completed in the target school(s), a second round of KWS is initiated. Lessons learned from the first round are used to redesign other target schools. New RMTs are chartered and trained by knowledge work supervisors with assistance from the original RMT(s). This spreading of the redesign improvements is called diffusion (Step 3.4).

Knowledge Work Supervision, as described above, recycles until the entire district is redesigned for high performance. Once the entire district is redesigned, the steering committee, RMTs, and knowledge work supervisors identify and correct deviations from desired outcomes (Step 3.5). Redesign improvements are frequently compared to the district's vision statement, which contains design criteria. If improvements are moving away from the vision, they are brought in line. This kind of alignment is critical to the long-term success of KWS.

Phase 4: Continuous Improvement of Schooling

The supervisory activities for this phase are:

Step 4.1:   Supervise system boundaries.
Step 4.2:   Seek opportunities for continuous improvement.

There are invisible system boundary lines between grades, levels of schooling, and the district and its environment. Information passes through these boundaries. The quality and quantity of information and cross-boundary relationships among people need to be managed to ensure effective organizational performance. Knowledge work supervisors are specifically responsible for supervising the boundaries (Step 4.1).

After the entire district is redesigned for high performance, the RMTs, which remain active (although with rotating membership), and knowledge work supervisors seek ways to make incremental improvements in their schools' environmental relationships, work processes, and social architecture (Step 4.2). This kind of fine-tuning is important because it helps the district eliminate glitches in improvements made. The tools and methods of quality management are useful during this phase. Continuous improvement flows for a predetermined period of time (e.g., for five years). At the end of that period, KWS recycles back to Phase 1 to search for significant ways to improve work procedures, work relationships, and the relationship of the district with its environment.

Some "loving critics" of the proposed paradigm raise a legitimate question: "What happens to those individual teachers who need intense, direct supervisory assistance to improve *their* teaching?" My answer is "Engage them, as individuals, in clinical supervision, peer supervision, cognitive coaching, or some other model designed to help individual teachers!" The proposed paradigm does not preclude the use of supervisory tools and methods to help individual teachers; in fact, knowledge work supervisors should be expected to help coordinate the provision of direct supervisory assistance to selected teachers as needed. However, don't think that traditional supervision will improve instruction throughout an entire school district by correcting the teaching of individual teachers, one at a time.

Conclusion

All disciplines, professions, and fields of endeavor are influenced by concepts and practices from other disciplines, professions, and fields. This cross-disciplinary "seeding" is an important source of creative, status-quo–shattering, paradigm-shifting ideas. Educational supervision is also influenced by other disciplines, such as psychology and human relations. Business management practices are, and should continue to be, important sources of cutting-edge ideas for transforming supervision from what it is to what it could be.

In this essay, a new model of educational supervision that evolved from business practices was portrayed. It is called *Knowledge Work Supervision.*® The KWS model looks complex because it is. It must be complex, because school districts are complex organizations. The model views a school district as a system and provides techniques to improve all pieces of the system—not just the curriculum, the length of the school day, or the classroom behavior of individual teachers. It offers a systematic way to examine critical variables that affect the performance of an entire district. KWS looks like it takes time because it does take time. There are no quick fixes for real school improvement. If a district goes for the quick fix, it is going for failure.

If applied consistently and with patience, Knowledge Work Supervision, which is a process of continual organizational renewal, will move a school district toward higher levels of organizational performance. Case studies on redesigning business organizations using similar models confirm this conclusion. Although a school district may not perfectly achieve its new vision through KWS (because that vision, according to chaos theory, is a moving target), the cyclical nature of KWS ensures that the district will move continually toward that vision.

A systemic and systematic model of supervision informed by principles of organizational redesign is needed to raise a district's level of performance. Nothing less will improve the entire system—nothing! Don't be fooled by popular prescriptions for quick-fix improvements. Don't be stuck in the supervisory traditions of the past or present— they don't work well (Duffy, 1994). And, remember, if you keep on doing what you are doing, you will continue to be what you have always been.

References

Argyris, C., & Schön, D. (1974). *Theory in practice: Increasing professional effectiveness.* San Francisco: Jossey-Bass.

Argyris, C., & Schön, D. (1978). *Organizational learning.* Reading, MA: Addison-Wesley.

Burke, W. W. (1982). *Organization development: Principles and practices.* Boston, MA: Little, Brown.

Crosby, P. B. (1979). *Quality is free: The art of making quality certain.* New York: New American Library.

Deming, W. E. (1982). *Out of crisis.* Cambridge, MA: The MIT Press.

Drucker, P. F. (1969). *The age of discontinuity: Guidelines to our changing society.* New York: Harper & Row.

Drucker, P. F. (1985). *Management tasks, responsibilities, practices.* New York: Harper & Row.

Drucker, P. F. (1993). Professionals' productivity. *Across the Board, 30,* 50.

Duffy, F. M. (1994). *Designing high performance schools through instructional supervision.* Presentation to the annual conference of the Council of Professors of Instructional Supervision, Fordham University, New York.

Duffy, F. M. (1995). Supervising knowledge work. *The NASSP Bulletin, 79*(573), 56–66.

Duffy, F. M. (1996). *A practical guide to designing high performance schools.* Delray Beach, FL: St. Lucie Press.

Hammer, M., & Champy, J. (1993). *Reengineering the corporation: A manifesto for business revolution.* New York: HarperCollins.

Juran, J. M. (1989). *Juran on leadership for quality.* New York: The Free Press.

Kotter, J. P. (1995). Leading change: Why transformation efforts fail. *Harvard Business Review, 73,* 59–67.

Pajak, E. F. (1982). Organization development: Implications for supervision. *Planning and Changing, 12,* 245–54.

Pasmore, W. A. (1988). *Designing effective organizations: The sociotechnical systems perspective.* New York: John Wiley & Sons.

Pasmore, W. A. (1993). Designing work systems for knowledge workers. *Journal of Quality and Participation, 6,* 78–84.

Pava, C. H. P. (1983). *Managing new office technology: An organizational strategy.* New York: The New Press.

Trist, E. L., Higgin, G. W., Murray, H., & Pollack, A. B. (1965). *Organizational choice.* London: Tavistock Publications.

Should Educational Supervision Be Influenced By Business Management Practice? *No*

Edward Pajak

Practices and theories derived from business management have long inspired authors in the field of educational supervision (e.g., Sergiovanni & Starratt, 1971; Alfonso, Firth, & Neville, 1975). Such influence could easily be interpreted as a healthy sign of vigor and versatility in our field because exciting developments and original thinking frequently occur at the boundary or interface of two or more cultures, traditions, or world views.

Unfortunately, ideas from the business world are too often adopted by educators wholesale, or are adapted only slightly without careful consideration of the factors that make schools and supervision in schools unique. The extent to which ideas and practices borrowed from business management are taken for granted among educators today makes the question "Should business management influence supervisory practice?" seem almost nonsensical. An understanding of how we arrived at this dependency on the business world is necessary before we can begin to talk about alternatives. Indeed, other possibilities and choices do exist.

Supervision Rooted in Democratic Principles

Early in the twentieth century, school supervision in the United States began to develop an identity that was closely related to "the democratic motive of American education" (Elliott, 1914, p. 2). Edward C. Elliott distinguished "administrative efficiency," which demanded "centralization of administrative power" defined by law, from "supervisory efficiency," which required *"decentralized, cooperative, expert,* supervision" (p. 78). Administrators stifled the individuality of teachers and children, Elliott argued, when they misapplied administrative control to the work of teachers and the accomplishments of students. The "ideal of supervision," he boldly stated, "should be striving for the preservation and enlargement of the professional identity of each teaching unit . . . service to children through service to teachers" (p. 3).

Authors of supervision texts published during the 1920s repeatedly referred to the importance of democratic leadership (e.g., Ayer & Barr, 1928; Barr & Burton, 1926; Burton, 1927; Stone, 1929) and invoked John Dewey's combination of democracy and scientific thinking as guiding principles for supervision in education (Department of Supervisors and Directors of Instruction (DSDI), 1934). Dewey's definition of scientific problem solving differed greatly from that of Bobbitt and other advocates of measurement and should not be confused with scientific management (McKernan, 1987; McNeil, 1982). When

Dewey (1929) called for the application of the scientific method to the solving of educational problems, he was referring to reflective inquiry as a guide to practice. His notion of consciously reasoned cooperative problem solving, rather than the rules generated by science, became the defining tenet of supervisory leadership in education (Pajak, 1993).

In the early 1930s, publications of the National Education Association's Department of Supervisors and Directors of Instruction, one of ASCD's forebears, called for greater involvement by teachers in decisions related to instruction, as well as group deliberation and experimentation in solving problems (DSDI, 1932, 1933, 1934). Barr, Burton, and Brueckner (1938) drew heavily on this body of literature and announced in the Preface to their influential 1938 textbook, *Supervision,* that democratic supervision was intended to introduce responsible leadership that would rely on scientific reason and experimentation for direction. Thus, democratic principles, firmly rooted in the philosophy of education, for many years provided an effective counterpoint and barrier to unwarranted intrusion of business management practices and ideas. However, history was soon to be rewritten.

Revisionist History

The most commonly repeated version of the development of thought in educational supervision during the twentieth century is generally attributed to William H. Lucio (Sergiovanni, 1975; Anderson, 1986), who claimed in a 1967 ASCD publication entitled *Supervision: Perspectives & Propositions,* that supervision theory early in this century was heavily influenced by Frederick Taylor's 1911 book, *The Principles of Scientific Management.* Partly in reaction to the severely technical nature of Taylor's prescriptions, according to Lucio's account, supervision next fell under the spell of the "human relations" school of management during the 1930s. The "human relations" perspective, based on the research of Elton Mayo and his associates, emphasized the importance of satisfying workers' psychological and social needs.

School supervision followed industry, Lucio (1967) contended, in the mistaken notion that high morale would result in high productivity. Lucio next described how dissatisfaction with the results of emphasizing the interests of individuals over those of the organization led management theorists like Chris Argyris and Douglas M. McGregor to try to reconcile the scientific management and human relations viewpoints. The research and theory of Argyris and McGregor, Lucio proposed, held promising applications for supervision in schools.

Curiously, this account seems to have represented a major intellectual departure for Lucio, who only five years before (Lucio & McNeil, 1962) had described the history of supervisory thought with *no mention whatsoever* of Frederick Taylor or Elton Mayo. Instead of praising the work of Argyris and McGregor, he had advocated that supervision be directed by "reason and practical intelligence," a position he refer-enced liberally with citations of John Dewey (1910, 1927) and George S. Counts (1954).

Although other authors had already begun introducing concepts from business management into the supervision literature (e.g., Fos-ter, 1964), Lucio (1967) was the first to place educational supervision within a historical context linked to business management theory. Anyone who does a careful reading of the supervision literature prior to the mid-1960s, however, will discover that Lucio's 1967 version of the evolution of supervision in education is highly questionable (Pajak, 1993).

Supervision Is *Not* Administration

The impact of Frederick Taylor's industrial logic on *educational ad-ministration* in the early twentieth century has been well chronicled (Callahan, 1962). While it would be inaccurate to suggest that Taylor's work had no effect on educational supervision, its impact continues to be vastly overestimated (e.g. Gitlin & Smyth, 1989). As early as the mid-1920s, Barr and Burton (1926) noted in their text, *The Supervi-sion of Instruction*, that Franklin Bobbitt's adaptation of Taylor's principles of scientific management to education "has never been espe-cially popular and seems to have had little influence" (p. 75).

According to Callahan and Button (1964), the reason that scien-tific management failed to influence supervision was that "the problems of supervision and of teaching method were not readily amenable to investigation in the management frame of reference nor with the tech-niques available" (p. 90). The field of supervision distinguished itself from administration during the 1930s by aligning itself instead with the process of curriculum development and "a new organization, the Association for Supervision and Curriculum Development" (Callahan & Button, 1964, p. 90).

On the positive side, Lucio's (1967) revision of supervision history opened the field to new perspectives on the organization of schools, motivation of teachers, and leadership (Sergiovanni, 1975). A most unfortunate outcome, however, is that the wealth of literature in the tradition of progressive educational philosophy that had given unique focus and direction to supervision in education was soon abandoned by most authors in the field (Pajak, 1993). A result is that practitioners today seem to readily embrace business-inspired practices with little, if any, reluctance.

The image of the educational leader as "corporate visionary" took hold during the 1980s as the federal government championed busi-ness interests while reducing funding for educational programs. The *Nation at Risk* report (National Commission on Excellence in Educa-tion, 1983) blamed schools for failing to develop the human resources needed by American industry to compete successfully in the international marketplace. Heavily influenced by the literature of business management and by legislation at the state level, educational leadership became viewed in terms of behaviors, usually displayed by principals, who shaped school culture by manipulating symbols and rituals that conformed to personal visions of what schools might become (Pajak, 1993).

In the 1990s, terms borrowed from business management such as *site-based management*, *empowerment*, and *participative decision making* permeate articles that appear in journals like *Educational Leadership* and represent practices that are often highly regarded by many practitioners and authors. The work of W. Edwards Deming is a recent example of how ideas from business management can quickly establish an influence on thinking and practice in our field. While the rebirth of participative structures in schools might be cause for celebration, it is important to note that today's practices, having originated in the business management literature, are divorced from educational philosophy. They are also naive in reflecting a simplistic "one best way" of thinking about practice.

Another difficulty with the "generalized business orientation" that prevails in educational administration is that it is "neither well defined nor internally consistent" (Kliebard, 1988, p. 31). Indeed, the usual approach is to apply "prefabricated solutions to preconceived problems" without inquiring or allowing for the "conflicting goals of education." Change for its own sake is the overriding consideration as school administrators become preoccupied with demonstrating that their schools are at least as innovative as those in neighboring districts (Kliebard, 1988).

Toward Comparative Inquiry?

Elsewhere, I have argued for a more deliberately comparative inquiry in educational supervision as an alternative to the uncritical importation of constructs that originate in noneducational contexts (Pajak, 1990). Careful comparative inquiry might avoid the common error of focusing on superficial similarities of behaviors exhibited by leaders in very different organizational realities and prematurely concluding that supervision in disparate situations is identical.

Organization theory is one framework that might be useful in conducting comparative inquiry in supervision (Pajak, 1990). In a seminal study of organization structure and process, Lawrence and Lorsch (1967) pointed out that "the essential organizational requirements for effective performance of one task under one set of economic and technical conditions may not be the same as those for other tasks with different circumstances." Thus, we ought to carefully ponder whether a successful supervisor or supervisory technique in a business setting would be equally successful in an educational setting that differs substantially in its goals, technology, product, and reward system. Whether business managers would perform well in an educational context may not be immediately evident, but perhaps better ways of asking the question are needed. For instance:

- What kinds of supervision are most successful in different organizational contexts?
- What kinds of supervision are most successful in schools of different sizes and in schools with different kinds of organizational environments?

The first question might help us avoid the trap of uncritically adopting an idea or practice from another field of study into our own. The second question has the advantage of helping us avoid generalizations about the one best way to supervise or teach, and the common practice of simply imitating what neighboring schools are doing. Both questions together might also help us to better understand educational supervision and make more informed decisions about supervisory practice (Pajak, 1990).

Organization theorists have only recently come to recognize, and attempt to account for, the inherent ambiguity and unpredictability of the techniques employed in schools, and the fact that processes and events within schools are very likely to be influenced if not largely determined by unplanned and uncontrollable factors (Pajak, 1989). During the 1970s organization theorists began describing schools as "loosely coupled" systems (Weick, 1976), a perspective that contrasts sharply with the more traditional view of schools as "tightly coupled" bureaucracies. The concept of loose coupling refers to the weakness or relative absence of control, influence, coordination, or interaction between parts or events within an organizational system. The term *loose coupling* has been used in reference to relationships between elements or subsystems within an organization (Glassman, 1973) as well as between events within organizational processes (March & Olsen, 1976).

A number of characteristics exhibited by schools contribute to the phenomenon of loose coupling, which makes them less rational and presumably more difficult to lead than other types of organizations. For one thing, the goals that schools pursue are multiple and shift frequently. Indeed, it has long been noted that schools are expected to be all things to all people and to respond immediately whenever society changes direction.

Another factor contributing to loose coupling in schools is that the techniques educators employ tend to be unpredictable in their consequences. Teachers cannot guarantee that all students will learn from a particular assignment, for example, even if students follow directions and do exactly as they are told. Educators can at best hope to create a set of conditions under which learning is likely to occur. But the results are never entirely certain because of uncontrollable psychological and contextual influences (Pajak, 1989).

In addition to ambiguous goals and unpredictable techniques, schools exhibit other traits that tend to make their structures and processes loosely coupled. These include a structural pattern that is compartmentalized, learning outcomes that defy easy measurement, frequent turnover among students and staff, and turbulence caused by social, political, and economic forces (March & Olsen, 1976; Weick, 1976).

The term "organized anarchy" has been used to describe the way in which organizations respond to the chronic condition of "ambiguity" that results from shifting or poorly defined goals, unpredictable technologies and environments, unclear relationships among events, and changing patterns of participation (March & Olsen, 1976, p.12). A secondary school principal once described his job to me as trying to "coordinate bedlam," which neatly captures the reality faced by leaders in many types of organizations and highlights the urgent practical need to reduce ambiguity and uncertainty.

Because the processes and techniques that educators employ are generally unpredictable in their consequences, supervision in schools is very complex. For example, a teacher cannot guarantee that all students will learn what is taught, even if the students do exactly what is prescribed for them. Likewise, a supervisor cannot ensure teacher success. A variety of uncontrollable psychological and environmental factors inevitably intervene. Teachers and supervisors are essentially limited to creating a set of conditions under which learning is more likely to occur (Pajak, 1989). Results in schools are never entirely certain.

A school is very much *unlike* a steel mill, therefore, where certain proportions of iron, coke, and lime, when combined at a predetermined temperature and pressure, can be counted on to produce a particular grade of steel every time. A school is in many ways more like a brokerage firm, which provides information and advice in the form of general recommendations based on experience and informed hunches about what clients should do. Neither the brokerage firm nor the school can predict specific outcomes with any degree of certainty because of the volatility of the environment and the fact that decisions are ultimately made by the client (Pajak, 1989).

Bottery (1994) proposes six distinctions between nonprofit organizations and those engaged in commercial enterprise, which imply differences in how such organizations are best managed. These distinctions neatly call attention to some of the important limitations of applying business management principles to supervision in schools:

1. Business organizations rely more on material incentives to motivate people, while schools rely on intangible rewards like prestige and personal satisfaction.
2. Business organizations seek economic profit, while schools "break even" financially.
3. Business organizations exist in a competitive environment, while schools adhere to a cooperative ethos.

4. Business organizations can redefine their mission according to changes in market conditions, while schools are confined to a specific mission.
5. Business organizations are characterized by hierarchy and delegation of work, while schools are more commited to equality, collegiality, and participation.
6. Business organizations pursue fewer goals and answer to fewer constituents, while schools pursue and answer to (sometimes contradictory) goals and constituents.

Where Do We Go from Here?

The following are five suggestions that I think would help to move the practice and study of supervision in education forward:

1. *Re-embrace the legacy of supervisory practice grounded in the philosophy of John Dewey.*   The absence of an agreed-upon purpose in educational supervision opens the door to almost any idea, goal, or procedure that comes along. The field of supervision in education must distinguish itself from the narrowly focused canons of business practice and recommit itself to principles of democracy, reason, and collaboration, all aimed at improving the quality of life and learning for students.

2. *Distinguish educational supervision from administration, but remain open to emerging ideas that are consistent with supervision.* Scholars and practitioners of supervision should distance themselves from the traditional culture of educational administration, which tends to encourage change for the sake of change instead of change in a purposive direction (Kliebard, 1988) for the benefit of students. Some authors in educational administration have begun questioning many basic assumptions of their own field (e.g., Maxcy, 1994, 1995). Others have proposed new ways of viewing administrative work (e.g., Beck, 1994) that are compatible with Elliott's (1914) slogan of "service to children through service to teachers."

3. *Re-establish ties with the curriculum field.*   The absence of agreed-on purpose is also true of the curriculum field (Kliebard, 1988) and, indeed, is a fundamental problem in public education today. Curriculum and instruction are inseparable processes. Richer and more frequent dialogue is needed between the fields of curriculum and supervision, which seem somehow to have forgotten that they share a common history and function. For example, meaningful discussion of the paradoxical simultaneous trends of decentralization of school governance and centralization of curriculum and testing could result. Site-based, participative management appears to be benign and even progressive to most authors and practitioners in educational supervision, although

some have questioned its motives (Hargreaves & Dawe, 1990). While local control may affect the working conditions of teachers, the influence on learning in the classroom has been questioned by some curriculum scholars as actually exaggerating social inequities (Pinar, Reynolds, Slattery, & Taubman, 1995).

4. *Consider multiple sources of practices and ideas to enrich and enliven supervisory practice and theory.*   Ideas and practices from supervision in settings other than business, such as health and social service contexts, are almost entirely overlooked by authors and practitioners in our field. Rational models of organization may fit the traditionally stable goals, technologies, and environments of some businesses and government agencies. But "natural" or "organic" systems may more closely approximate the dynamic realities of service agencies such as hospitals and other organizations in the nonprofit sector that focus on bettering the human condition. Such organizations exhibit less formalized roles and fewer gradations in status and specialization, and value equality in decision making (Scott, 1992). Comparative study of supervision in these organizations might lead to the importation of more appropriate practices in schools.

5. *Remain skeptical of all externally developed ideas before they have been carefully examined and their merit proven in particular educational contexts.*   Again, the idea of change for the sake of change has to be abandoned. We in supervision ought to be less willing to embrace ideas from outside education without carefully considering their appropriateness for schools. Much comparative empirical and ethnographic research in educational supervision is needed before we can make informed decisions about best practices. We are likely to find that successful supervisors and teachers are not all alike nor, indeed, are all schools.

In conclusion, both practitioners and scholars in supervision should be wary of ideas that smack of one-size-fits-all thinking and solutions to educational problems that are mechanistically rational. Most basically, the question should always be asked: "Does this practice directly serve the best interests of students, or does it distract our attention and efforts from this primary purpose of our profession?"

References

Alfonso, R. J., Firth, G. R., & Neville, R. F. (1975). *Instructional supervision: A behavior system.* Boston: Allyn & Bacon.

Anderson, R. H. (1986). The genesis of clinical supervision. In W. J. Smyth (Ed.), *Learning about teaching through clinical supervision.* London: Croom Helm.

Ayer, F. C., & Barr, A. S. (1928). *The organization of supervision: An analysis of the organization and administration of supervision in city school systems.* New York: D. Appleton.

Barr, A. S., & Burton, W. H. (1926). *The supervision of instruction.* New York: D. Appleton.

Barr, A. S., Burton, W. H., & Brueckner, L. J. (1938). *Supervision: Principles and practices in the improvement of instruction.* New York: D. Appleton-Century.

Beck, L. G. (1994). *Reclaiming educational administration as a caring profession.* New York: Teachers College Press.

Bottery, M. (1994). *Lessons for schools? A comparison of business and educational management.* New York: Cassell.

Burton, W. H. (1927). *Supervision and the improvement of teaching.* New York: D. Appleton.

Callahan, R. (1962). *Education and the cult of efficiency.* Chicago: University of Chicago Press.

Callahan, R., & Button, H. W. (1964). Historical change in the role of the man in the organization: 1865–1950. In D. E. Griffiths (Ed.), *Behavioral science and educational administration* (pp. 73–92). Chicago: University of Chicago Press.

Counts, G. S. (1954). *Decision making and American values in school administration.* New York: Cooperative Program in Educational Administration.

Department of Supervisors and Directors of Instruction. (1932). *Supervision and the creative teacher.* Fifth Yearbook of the Department of Supervisors and Directors of Instruction. New York: Teachers College, Columbia University.

Department of Supervisors and Directors of Instruction. (1933). *Effective instructional leadership.* Sixth Yearbook of the Department of Supervisors and Directors of Instruction. New York: Teachers College, Columbia University.

Department of Supervisors and Directors of Instruction. (1934). *Scientific method in supervisory programs.* Seventh Yearbook of the Department of Supervisors and Directors of Instruction. New York: Teachers College, Columbia University.

Dewey, J. (1910). *How we think.* Boston: D.C. Heath.

Dewey, J. (1927). *The public and its problems.* New York: Henry Holt.

Dewey, J. (1929). *The sources of a science of education.* New York: Horace Liveright.

Elliott, E. C. (1914). *City school supervision.* New York: World Book.

Foster, R. L. (1964). Poise under pressure. *Educational Leadership, 22*(3), 149–154.

Gitlin, A., & Smyth, J. (1989). *Teacher education: Educative alternatives.* Philadelphia: The Falmer Press.

Glassman, R.B. (1973). Persistence and loose coupling in living systems. *Behavioral Science, 18*, 83–98.

Hargreaves, A., & Dawe, R. (1990). Paths of professional development: Contrived collegiality, collaborative culture, and the case of peer coaching. *Teaching and Teacher Education, 6*(3), 227–241.

Kliebard, (1988). Fads, fashions, and rituals: The instability of curriculum change. In L. Tanner (Ed.), *Critical issues in curriculum* (pp. 16–34). Chicago: The University of Chicago Press.

Lawrence, P. R., & Lorsch, J. W. (1967). *Organization and environment: Managing differentiation and integration.* Boston: Division of Research, Harvard Business School.

Lucio, W. H. (1967). The supervisory function: Overview, analysis, propositions. In W. H. Lucio (Ed.), *Supervision: Perspectives and propositions* (pp. 1–11). Washington, DC: Association for Supervision and Curriculum Development.

Lucio, W. H., & McNeil, J. D. (1962). *Supervision: A synthesis of thought and action.* New York: McGraw-Hill.

March, J. G., & Olsen, J. P. (1976). *Ambiguity and choice in organizations.* Bergen, Norway: Universitetsforlaget.

Maxcy, S. J. (1994). *Postmodern school leadership: Meeting the crisis in educational administration.* Westport, CT: Praeger.

Maxcy, S. J. (1995). *Democracy, chaos, and the new school order.* Thousand Oaks, CA: Corwin Press.

McKernan, J. (1987). Action research and curriculum development. *Peabody Journal of Education, 64*(2), 6–19.

McNeil, J. D. (1982). A scientific approach to supervision. In T. J. Sergiovanni (Ed.), *Supervision of teaching* (pp. 18–34). Alexandria, VA: Association for Supervision and Curriculum Development.

National Commission on Excellence in Education. (1983). *A nation at risk: The imperative for educational reform.* Washington, DC: U.S. Government Printing Office.

Pajak, E. (1989). *The central office supervisor of curriculum and instruction: Setting the stage for success.* Needham Heights, MA: Allyn & Bacon.

Pajak, E. (1990). Do we need "comparative supervision?" A response to Duffy's "Supervising for results." *Journal of Curriculum and Supervision, 6,* 41–44.

Pajak, E. (1993). Change and continuity in supervision and leadership. In G. Cawelti (Ed.), *Challenges and achievements of American education* (pp. 158–186). Alexandria, VA: Association for Supervision and Curriculum Development.

Pinar, W. F., Reynolds, W. M., Slattery, P., & Taubman, P. M. (1995). *Understanding curriculum.* New York: Peter Lang.

Scott, W. R. (1992). *Organizations: Rational, natural, and open systems.* Englewood Cliffs, NJ: Prentice-Hall.

Sergiovanni, T. J. (1975). Beyond human relations. In T. J. Sergiovanni (Ed.), *Professional supervision for professional teachers* (pp. 1–8). Washington, DC: Association for Supervision and Curriculum Development.

Sergiovanni, T. J., & Starratt, R. J. (1971). *Emerging patterns of supervision: Human perspectives.* New York: McGraw-Hill.

Stone, C. R. (1929). *Supervision of the elementary school.* Boston: Houghton Mifflin.

Taylor, F. W. (1911). *Principles of scientific management.* New York: Harper & Row.

Weick, K. E. (1976). Educational organizations as loosely coupled systems. *Administrative Science Quarterly, 21,* 1–19.

Postnote

Should Educational Supervision Be Influenced by Business Management Practices?

Raymond Callahan (1962) has called our attention to the effects of adopting business management practices in education. Notwithstanding some of Callahan's critics, we in education seem fascinated and quite ready to apply theories and concepts from other disciplines, professions, and fields. Educators should consider the reasons for their interest in the transfer of business practices to their educational context. Is this a matter of perceived "identical elements," or are the principles of business management practice understood to have general applicability? Adopting business practices may or may not make sense. Only by first carefully considering the impact that business practice may have on teaching, learning, and curriculum should a decision be made one way or the other. What impact does business management practice have on supervisors?

Review Questions for

The Yes Response:

1. In your estimation, what does business have to do with schooling?
2. Can you imagine the practice of school supervision without the influence of business?
3. Can you think of examples in which supervision has been influenced by business management practices?
4. What does Dr. Duffy mean by "knowledge organizations?" Is your school a "knowledge organization?"
5. Imagine that you are a new superintendent and you hired Duffy Associates or adopted their model. What would your school look like in two years? What benefits would accrue by adopting Duffy's business model? What would be the role of supervision in such an organization?
6. Duffy states that "redesigning business organizations using similar models" to KWS have had positive effects. What positive effects are likely, and could these effects be realized in schools?
7. How would John Dewey react to Duffy's proposals?

The No Response:

1. According to Dr. Pajak, how have we arrived at a "dependency on the business world"? How are schools currently dependent on business?
2. How does Pajak's historical evidence lend credence to his position?

3. How does Pajak's discussion of organizational theory lend credence to his position?
4. Pajak makes five recommendations—what is your reaction to his suggestions? What would supervision look like in your school/ district if Pajak's recommendations were implemented?

For Further Research

1. A provocative and lively debate ensued in the *Journal of Curriculum and Supervision* (1990) that, in part, influenced the inclusion of this issue in our book. How business practices can shed light on supervisory practice was the issue under debate in 1990. Reexamine that debate in light of the current exchange in this chapter. Has Duffy altered his position? Compare Professor Pajak's comments in 1990 with his remarks in this chapter. In your estimation, should business practices influence supervisory practice? If so, describe how.
2. Describe loosely coupled organizations versus tightly coupled bureaucracies. Give examples of each. Compare Alfonso's (see Issue 1) discussion of loosely coupled organizations with Pajak's discussion in this chapter.
3. Pajak explains that "ideas from the business world are too often adopted by educators wholesale . . ." Provide historical evidence for this assertion. Refer, in part, to Callahan's (1962) work.
4. Compare Dewey's (1929) understanding of science as applied to education with Bobbitt's (1913) conception of science. For a discussion on this comparison see Glanz (1991) and Pajak (1993). See also McNeil (1982).
5. Write a paper explaining the history of educational supervision and the emergence of business management theory.
6. Research W. Edwards Deming's model and describe its potential for instructional supervision.
7. Read Everhart (1995) and explain how Pajak and Duffy might react to Everhart's thesis.
8. Invite one or more professionals from business to your class to discuss how business practices might positively influence supervisory practice in schools.
9. Interview a supervisor who is currently involved with a business/ school collaboration project.
10. Seymour Sarason (1983, 1995) is highly critical of the business influence in education. Consult his works and explain why, according to Sarason, educational reform is doomed to failure if we uncritically adopt a business ideology. Specifically, see his comments about Avishay (1994). Compile a list of other scholars who are either pro or con business in regard to education/supervision. Consult, for example, *Journal of Curriculum and Supervision* (1990) as well as other sources. Compare Fullan's (1993) and Sarason's views.

11. Read Post and Killian's (in press) chapter, "Scientific Dimensions of Supervision," for current views of the relationship between science and supervision.
12. Would Dr. Duffy support Total Quality Management (TQM)— why or why not?
13. Would Duffy support Snyder's proposals in Perspective 3?
14. How can the KWS model be used to change a school that practices traditional supervision to one in which shared decision making is employed?

References

Avishay, B. (1994). What is business's social impact? *Harvard Business Review*, 40–46.

Bobbitt, F. (1913). Some general principles of management applied to the problems of city school systems. In *Twelfth Yearbook of the National Society for the Study of Education, Part I, The supervision of city schools* (pp. 7–96). Chicago: The University of Chicago Press.

Callahan, R. E. (1962). *Education and the cult of efficiency.* Chicago: The University of Chicago Press.

Dewey, J. (1929). *The sources of a science of education.* New York: Liveright.

Everhart, R. B. (1995). Is business the business of American education? *Kappa Delta Pi Record, 1,* 30–33.

Fullan, M. (1993). *Changing forces: Probing the depths of educational reform.* Bristol, PA: Falmer Press.

Glanz, J. (1991). *Bureaucracy and professionalism: The evolution of public school supervision.* New Jersey: Fairleigh Dickinson University Press.

Journal of Curriculum and Supervision. (1990). 6(1).

McNeil, J. D. (1982). A scientific approach to supervision. In T. J. Sergiovanni (Ed.), *Supervision of teaching* (pp. 18–34). Alexandria, VA: Association for Supervision and Curriculum Development.

Pajak, E. (1993). Change and continuity in supervision and leadership. In G. Cawelti (Ed.), *Challenges and achievements of American education* (pp. 158–186). Alexandria, VA: Association for Supervision and Curriculum Development.

Post, D. M., & Killian, J. E. (in press). Scientific dimensions of supervision. In G. R. Firth & E. Pajak (Eds.), *Handbook of research on school supervision.* New York: Macmillan.

Sarason, S. B. (1983). *Schooling in America: Scapegoat and salvation.* New York: Free Press.

Sarason, S. B. (1995). *Parental involvement and the political principle: Why the existing governance structure of schools should be abolished.* San Francisco: Jossey-Bass.

Issue 11

Is Clinical Supervision a Viable Model for Use in the Public Schools?

✦   ✦   ✦   ✦

YES—Robert H. Anderson, University of South Florida
NO—Noreen Garman, University of Pittsburgh

✦   ✦   ✦

Issue Summary

YES: Robert Anderson, TECO Energy Chair in Education at the University of South Florida and president of Pedamorphosis, Inc. asserts that clinical supervision is indeed a useful model for facilitating a better understanding of the "analysis of learning and how teachers help it to happen." Acknowledging some of the criticisms leveled against it, Anderson maintains that the legitimacy of clinical supervision is greatest within the context of collegial partnerships developed as supervisors work with "teams" of teachers.

NO: Noreen Garman, a student of Morris Cogan who along with Robert Goldhammer was instrumental in popularizing clinical supervision, critiques four interpretations of clinical supervision as presented at an AERA conference in 1992. These versions, although slightly different from one another, all represent, according to Garman, "a functionalist view of clinical supervision." Professor Garman asserts that clinical supervision conceived from a functionalist perspective is not viable for use in schools. The author ends her essay by explaining "a few principles" of clinical supervision that may contribute to a more meaningful understanding and practice of supervision in schools.

Guiding Questions

1. What is clinical supervision?
2. What are the chief characteristics of clinical supervision that differentiate it from other models of supervision?
3. Have you ever used or been involved with clinical supervision?
4. What obstacles might impede successful implementation of a clinical model in your school/district?
5. What are the advantages and disadvantages of clinical supervision?
6. What aspects of Andersons' and Garmans' thinking make sense to you? Do you have trouble accepting any of their arguments? If so, which ones?

Is Clinical Supervision a Viable Model for Use in the Public Schools? *Yes*

Robert H. Anderson

The Language of the Debate

Dealing with this issue calls for an up-front examination of several terms. *Viable*, ordinarily, is synonymous with such concepts as survivability, practicability, and perhaps even usefulness. The term is usually employed to indicate that a particular idea or scheme can in fact be made to work, that it is possible, that it will (or can) accomplish its purpose, or that there are few forces or conditions that can prevent it from succeeding or happening. Within the context of this debate, presumably I would have to prove that clinical supervision can or should be made to work, whereas Noreen Garman would have to argue/demonstrate that the possibilities or the necessities for its employment in a public school context are very limited.

Next we must look at the term *model*. The editors doubtless have in mind an archetypical system or pattern for the examination and improvement of teaching procedures, in particular the several-stage approach introduced in the seminal writings of Robert Goldhammer and his mentor Morris L. Cogan. *Model*, however, also connotes excellence, as for example when one speaks of a model wife or husband or of a particularly admirable behavior or artifact that sets high standards for other such acts or things. Perhaps in this debate we may assume that it is the feasible implementation of an approach or method rather than presumed or alleged excellence ("imitate-ability") that is being debated.

Why the question focuses upon the public schools, as opposed to nonpublic schools, may also be examined. Again, we might estimate or even conclude that the editors have limited the debate issue by examining only that school context most dominated by fiscal constraints or even historical resistances. I for one will not address this as an issue, since it seems clear to me that the professionals in nonpublic schools have neither more nor less need for the benefits of clinical supervision than those who are paid with tax dollars.

This leaves us with the term *clinical supervision*, for which no doubt there are a great many legitimate definitions. Few of these, however, vary to any significant extent from the Goldhammer/Cogan approach. It is appropriate, of course, to observe that many decades have gone by since those two giants first used and explained the term. There may indeed be other, and possibly even better, terms and approaches that we could be debating. But this is not our assignment.

Within the framework of our debate, first let me observe that I am now, and I have always been, comfortable with a simple explanation: Each teacher has needs or goals; the supervisor (or colleague, for that matter) seeks to provide assistance to teacher(s) in meeting those goals; in each specific instance, the person who will do the teaching makes information about his or her plans and intentions available to the person who will be providing such assistance; a teaching or equivalent event then occurs, to which the assister is witness; there follows a time for both the person who "taught" and the person who watched to reflect upon what happened; and then finally there is a conversation during which these separate views are examined for the dual purpose of understanding what actually occurred and then building toward future understandings and events.

This is only a sketchy definition. Within it there remains plenty of room for deep inquiry and discussion, multiple actors, lengthier or shorter sequences, complex connections with concomitant pedagogical and dialogical events, and longer-range commitments to high performance that translate into greater pupil learning. But again I am second-guessing the editors by presupposing that it is, in particular, the sequenced approach combining a presumably expert witness with a presumably receptive performer (not really the right word) that Dr. Garman and I are expected to chew on.

Also to be acknowledged, as doubtless the rest of this volume will amply document, is that debates rage over the very legitimacy of supervision in any and all forms. This includes arguments about supervision as an administrative or evaluating activity that affects ratings and even employment, as contrasted with supervision as a helping (or some would say, facilitating) activity more closely related to staff development than to staff management. While the clinical-supervision "cycle," as it has come to be known, might sometimes be followed when there is administrative decision making to be served, I strongly believe that this is not what we are debating. It is only the growth-oriented function that I am willing to argue in this statement. When an administrative officer goes through the process of talking with a teacher, visiting the teacher at work, and subsequently conferring with that teacher in a judgmental context, something different is happening, and neither Dr. Garman nor I would choose to take sides as to the viability of such practice. This is, however, not to say that administrative or judgmental behavior is wrong or ineffective. I simply do not see it as related to our debate.

Perhaps with this introductory comment on the record, I can now move toward persuading the reader that clinical supervision, as defined above and within the "helping" context, is not only a viable model for schools but a truly useful form of professional service and behavior.

Sources of Basic Information

Since some readers may not be fully conversant with the many dimensions of clinical supervision (CS), I note that they can profitably turn either to the two basic works (Cogan, 1973; Goldhammer, 1969, and later editions with Anderson and Krajewski) or to chapters or sections on clinical supervision in nearly all recent texts on supervision (notably Oliva, 1993, pp. 474–504, and Glickman, Gordon, & Ross-Gordon, 1995, pp. 287–310). A particularly broad review of CS's many landscapes, involving 27 authors, is available in Anderson and Snyder (1993). Within these and other sources, CS is usually described as a hands-on, classroom-centered, supportive or developmental activity in which the supervisor (who can be either a superordinate or a peer) plays essentially a teaching/helping/coaching role and does not engage in the process to assist the school administration in making personnel decisions. (See Issue 5.)

The events within a CS cycle, as already noted, invariably involve some sort of preparatory discussion, observation of an episode of professional activity (teaching), and subsequent analysis. Some definitions limit these events to three, most refer to five, and at least one (Cogan's) refers to eight. There is, however, close agreement on the nature and purposes of the steps or activities. In the literature there is a wide range of viewpoints concerning both philosophy and methodology. Nonetheless, there is not much disagreement among scholars and practitioners on how CS usually functions, and most seem to accept as typical the 5-stage sequence associated with the Goldhammer version: preobservation, observation, analysis and strategy determination, postobservation, and postconference analysis. Also fairly well accepted in most discussions is that although the CS approach is basically one on one, variants are possible in which more than one person's work is being observed and analyzed and/or more than one person is playing the role of observer/analyst.

How the Pedagogical World Has Changed

When CS was first described to the world, the usual school situation was characterized by individual teachers working mostly alone in their self-contained classrooms. Understandably, the primary effort by CS protagonists was to promote a teacher-friendly, help-oriented relationship between the individual teacher and a "supervisor" who participated with the presumable intent of helping the teacher to examine daily practice. This scenario remains common, but as self-containment becomes, increasingly, an anomalous working situation (not only in education but in all professional fields), there has been a shift in the direction of collegiality/partnership/groupwork and a concomitant shift in perceptions of how professional skill and knowledge can best be shared, examined, and improved.

When we examine the viability of clinical supervision, therefore, it is necessary or at least advisable to perceive it as an exchange among equals rather than as an exchange between persons occupying different roles. Even a concept such as "mentoring"—which like CS has long implied that one professional possesses a somewhat higher (or at least different) level or type of skill and knowledge, and seeks to share it with another professional in need of such nurturing—takes on a new meaning when equal-rank workers interact.

This notion might be stated simply: In every group of workers there is inevitably a range of talents and backgrounds, and although homogenization of the group is by no means an ultimate goal it is highly appropriate for each worker to share his or her special talents and insights with the other workers, in the interest of increasing the effectiveness and success of the total group. It is within this view that CS takes on a powerful dimension, since workers in continuous and close contact with each other are both more likely to engage in helping behaviors and more inclined to be receptive to such exchanges.

The term *supervision* is probably less appropriate as a label for such exchanges than is a phrase such as "collegial support." However, all of the positive ideas associated with supervision are likely to be operative. And although it may seldom be used or even come to mind, the word *clinical* remains relevant since (as Cogan noted) it is within a "hands-on," "live" context that the observers and discussants are sharpening their understandings of what can and should be done to enhance learning. One might therefore legitimately conclude that the conversations and other exchanges that attend collegial support in a team (or equivalent) situation are appropriate illustrations of clinical supervision at work.

The Leadership Role

Often teams or other working groups have designated or de facto leaders, and so what follows may be pertinent to their leadership activity as well. For the moment, however, it seems useful to indicate how principals, department heads, directors, and supervisors can best utilize their talents and energies in the interest of furthering the pedagogical skills and insights of teachers.

Not so long ago, as was noted at the beginning, such furtherance was promoted largely through one-on-one, hands-on supervision. This was so expensive of time that very little such supervision actually occurred: Even with the best of motivation, a supervisor or principal could visit only so many classrooms and could set aside only so much time for the accompanying conversations and reflections. It is primarily this reality that has caused critics to question the viability of the CS model. A great idea, critics may have said, but who really has time to implement it?

Some critics have also questioned the justifiability of a system that seemed to presume a deficiency of professional virtue and autonomy on the part of the person being supervised, while ascribing greater levels of such virtue to the supervisor. Who is to say, they argued, that X is a lot smarter (or whatever) than Y?

In this debate I am prepared to grant the general legitimacy of these arguments, although it is not all that difficult to locate principals and supervisors who have truly admirable qualifications for providing supervision and whose work with appreciative classroom teachers is performed with great skill. It is also possible to show how these supervisors manage to prioritize their workloads and find (ample?) time for supervisory work. Viability comes into question not because CS is a poor idea but because school districts are sometimes less than diligent or successful in employing good people and in arranging good working conditions for them. That this happens all too seldom is to be regretted, but it should not be a reason for concluding that CS is not viable.

CS, defined as a helping function housed within actual classroom situations, is indeed viable. Given the time-restraining conditions that prevail, however, what can be done to promote the helping function (and therefore growth in skill among the workforce)? I think that supervisors can help CS to become more widespread by reducing, if not eliminating, their efforts to work one on one with teachers and by concentrating upon helping teams and other work groups to acquire the interaction and communication skills that can lead to instructive insight and exchange. Spending time with groups of teachers as they meet to plan and discuss their work, showing them how they could implement CS cycles within their daily schedules and routines, joining them in their conferences, helping them to analyze episodes of teaching (both individual and group), and steering them to useful published or media materials that will increase their awareness of the necessary and the possible—all such activities can be extremely helpful to teams as they move beyond managerial, scheduling, and other matters toward the analysis of learning and how teachers help it to happen.

Although our assigned debate topic does not require us to offer empirical or other evidence to support or dispute the effectiveness of CS, after reviewing the most recent texts and articles on this topic I feel safe in reporting that CS appears to make at least some positive difference in the professional effectiveness of both teachers and supervisors. Garman (1982) herself notes that the role of the supervisor in CS is that of a friend, confidante, and respected colleague, and she further observes that CS embraces four concepts: collegiality, collaboration, skilled service, and ethical conduct. These, I strongly agree, form an excellent definition of the elements that are important to the success of CS. In their absence, of course, all thought of legitimacy or viability must go down the tube. But it is in an optimistic mood that we should consider the motivation of CS participants, and within that mood we can surely expect that good things will happen.

References

Anderson, R. H., & Snyder, K.J. (1993). *Clinical supervision: Coaching for higher performance.* Lancaster PA: Technomic.

Cogan, M. L. (1973). *Clinical supervision.* Boston: Houghton Mifflin.

Garman, N. B. (1982). The clinical approach to supervision. In T. J. Sergiovanni (Ed.), *Supervision of teaching* (pp. 35–52). Alexandria, VA: Association for Supervision and Curriculum Development.

Glickman, C. D., Gordon, S. P., & Ross-Gordon, J. M. (1995). *Supervision for instruction: A developmental approach.* Boston: Allyn & Bacon.

Goldhammer, R. (1969). *Clinical supervision: Special methods for the supervision of teachers.* New York: Holt, Rinehart & Winston.

Oliva, P.F. (1993). *Supervision for today's schools.* New York: Longman.

Is Clinical Supervision a Viable Model for Use in the Public Schools? *No*

Noreen B. Garman

It is indeed an honor to be invited to join the discussions with thoughtful supervision scholars and practitioners in this volume. I appreciated the opportunity to choose the position I would argue but my decision was disturbing. I have spent a good deal of my professional life practicing, teaching, and writing about clinical supervision. I studied with Morris Cogan and later became his colleague when I joined the faculty here in Pittsburgh. We even co-taught a course the year his book came out, and although his version of clinical supervision was born in a preservice MAT program, his rhetoric was fashioned for public school use. It is difficult to contradict one's roots!

Perhaps I am most disturbed by the way in which the question is framed. The press into a yes/no posture is really to engage in an either/or discussion and this is never very comfortable for academics. I really don't want to say "no" to the question, but rather I want to give a resounding "it depends." Most significant, however, the language of the question betrays an instrumental interpretation of clinical supervision, which forces me to argue against instrumentalism. My esteemed colleague, Robert Anderson, has argued well that the instrumental version of clinical supervision is viable. Since I cannot accept the instrumental perspective, it may be that we will be comparing disparate concepts (as in comparing apples and radial tires.)

It is quite amazing to me that interpretations of clinical supervision in the supervision discourses have continued with such vitality since the discipline's early roots at Harvard in the 1950s. (I've often remarked in casual conversation, "When all is said and done, there is more said than done in clinical supervision.") From time to time supervision scholars have lamented the popularity of the specialty, while students in supervision classes continually ask, "Are there examples of clinical supervision being used in schools presently?"

Morris Cogan's book came out in 1973, and I can remember vividly the reception for him. I was a novice assistant professor, asked to review his book for the occasion. Among other things I asked, "Does clinical supervision have much of a future?" (Many of us, including Morris, had considerable doubts.) Almost two decades later, in 1992, I was a discussant on an AERA panel entitled, "Isn't it High Time to Bury Clinical Supervision?" Given the span of time associated with the rise and fall of educational ideas, I thought at the time that this one had experienced quite a robust life. Meredith Gall, Allan Glatthorn, Frances Rust, and Lee Goldsberry were the presenters. Their commentaries are typical of the discourse related to our current discussion. As I listened to their arguments, I asked, "What are the presenters' views on the disposition of clinical supervision? Do they come to bury this thing or to praise it?" Most of all I wondered, "What do the presenters mean by clinical supervision? Just what is this it, in their perspectives, that should be abandoned?"

Meredith Gall, however, came to praise it and to argue that we need to keep clinical supervision because we have, for the most part, traditional teachers doing mediocre teaching; that there is precious little clinical supervision going on now (research showed that 112 minutes per teacher per year average); that teaching is a solo endeavor; that teachers teach for long periods of time without inspection by administrators; that preservice teachers get more counseling than clinical supervision; and that, given all of these conditions, clinical supervision is one of the best methods we know about for improving the situation. In other words, conventional wisdom tells us that clinical supervision helps teachers.

Allan Glatthorn, on the other hand, suggested that we bury part of clinical supervision, especially the part where administrators and supervisors observe and confer with competent, experienced teachers. A sharply modified version is okay for student teachers, novice teachers, and marginally competent tenured teachers. He wanted to see teachers observing each other, working in a variety of ways. Otherwise, he claimed, clinical supervision is dysfunctional.

Frances Rust disagreed with Glatthorn. She interpreted Cogan's model of clinical supervision as too restrictive for teacher education programs, especially in light of the call for teacher education reform. "*It* is not the one I would choose for supervisors working to prepare teachers that we would like to become collaborative, reflective and scholarly. The question becomes not whether to bury clinical supervision, but how to move the field beyond it."

As Lee Goldsberry contemplated the demise of supervision, he said, "The victim is the function of supervision and the crime suspects are time (or rather the lack of it) for supervision and *preparation* (or rather the lack of it) for the supervisor." In lamenting the sorry state of supervision in the schools he said, "Perhaps the surest way to kill a craft is to prepare no one to do it well." He proposed that there be a "stay of execution for *it*" by arguing that the schools are in a shabby state of affairs and practitioners need to think seriously about the purposes and consequences of education.

At the AERA meeting, then, it seemed that clinical supervision had one praise, one partial bury, one bury, and one stay of execution. However, the question remained, What is this thing, this *it*, they were considering as viable? Gall claimed that it has a flexible structure. "The only fixed components are the preconference, observation, and postconference." In Gall's version these three events are the essence of clinical supervision. Glatthorn's interpretation of clinical supervision is, he said, seriously flawed in its obsession with method and in its typical application. He mentioned the primary focus on teaching techniques as an obsession and argued for a focus on learning instead. When I heard him articulate the obsession with method, I agreed with his statement, but later in his presentation he offered yet another method, which he called "learning centered supervision." His point was confusing. He also equated clinical supervision to what school administrators do when they hold two observations and two conferences. He echoed the popular complaint that the original behaviors and techniques of clinical supervision have been co-opted by administrators for the annual personnel evaluation of teachers.

Rust used the Cogan approach as her referent to clinical supervision, recognizing that his book was published in 1973. She focused on the one-to-one tutorial as a model that she feels is inappropriate for collaboration and reflective practice. (Gall's version tended to construe clinical supervision as a tutorial.) Furthermore, Rust suggested, "its emphasis on scheduled observations, pre and post observation conferences and development of classroom observation data focuses on the 'front stage' behaviors of teaching, while the backstage behaviors are missed." Goldsberry construed supervision as a function and the supervisor as a superordinate attending to the subordinate's techniques for accomplishing a job. The supervisor intervenes to produce better overall performance. This version is grounded in a functionalist perspective complete with the traditional bureaucratic hierarchy.

As we hear the voices of my colleagues, there are four versions of clinical supervision being critiqued. In each case, however, the scholars accepted a functionalist view of clinical supervision. Likewise, the question posed here (Is clinical supervision a viable model for use in public school?) suggests that there is some common notion of clinical supervision in the guise of a model. Dr. Anderson assumes in his argument that "it is the feasible implementation of an approach or method . . . that is being debated." I would argue from an interpretivist postition that it is not possible to determine the feasibility of an abstract, generic model or method because it lacks contextual stories about a lived experience. We would need to begin by asking whose interpretation of clinical supervision we are considering. Is it that of authors, Robert Anderson, John Smyth, Madeline Hunter, and Patricia Holland, who represent various world views in their writings; or is it that of elementary principal Jacqueline Gregory, who interprets Hunter as she lives out each supervisory encounter with her teachers; or is it that of English teacher Kathy Ceroni, who describes her painful experience with her supervisor?

How can we then know the meaning of clinical supervision? Perhaps we can remind ourselves of at least two ways of getting to meaning. One is *definitional knowing* and the other is *discursive knowing*. In the first we can seek a definition of an idea or a concept and gain a singular sense of the meaning. In discursive knowing we recognize that meaning is reflected in the discourses regarding the concept under consideration. Thus, the meaning of clinical supervision is socially constructed through members of the clinical supervision community as we continue to take a stance and a counter stance in the ongoing dialogues that represent our practice in both thought and action.

For purposes of this essay, then, I reject the notion that we can debate the feasibility of clinical supervision in the abstract. We can, however, recognize the significance of ideas within the discourses associated with clinical supervision. For instance, the discussion carried on at AERA provides a context where scholars presented critiques of their interpretations of clinical supervision. By providing my own commentaries to their critiques, I can engage in the discourse and perhaps continue the debate.

Glatthorn mentioned in his presentation that clinical supervision (I suspect he meant the classic Cogan interpretation) is being used by administrators to conduct the annual personnel evaluations of teachers. I agree with him that what Gall described as "the fixed components . . . preconference, observation, and post-conference" have been co-opted and made legitimate as the standard practice for administrative accountability. For years clinical supervision scholars have tried to disassociate themselves and their versions from the evaluative function of administrators. Administrators, on the other hand, continue to name their duty and claim that it is really clinical supervision for the purpose of improving instruction. In Pennsylvania, as in other states, the Department of Education sanctioned an approach through executive training workshops that resemble the Gall "components." I have argued that this notion of clinical supervision, whether touted as the improvement of instruction or as personnel evaluation, has served for several years to define the perimeters of teaching. By this I mean that teaching is seen as an individual act within the bounds of the classroom. As we expand our notion of schools as learning communities, we also need to expand our notion of teaching to include schoolwide and even community duties. As Rust suggested, the current practice focuses on front stage behaviors of teaching while the backstage behaviors are missed.

Because clinical supervision has been closely associated with teacher evaluation, educators complain that there is a ritual nature to the classic "model" thaty they have been taught. Supervisors, required by state mandate to give teachers a once-a-year appraisal of their performance, visit classrooms and generally meet with teachers about the results of their contact. This has created a tradition mixed with strong images about the supervisor's visitation. Perennial doubts echo from teachers, who say, "What does the supervisor know about teaching in my subject area and the way I'm supposed to teach kids on a day-to-day basis? One or two visits won't tell anything!" Good feelings are the result of affirming gestures, like "At least someone in the front office will see what I'm doing!" or "Somebody cares about my classes." Teachers who have been around for a while often report that good ratings give them a sense of esteem; still, they admit that in-class visitation is largely ceremonial and doesn't much change the way they teach their students. The ritual of the visitation is clearly recognized by those who have been a part of the school culture. Teachers tolerate and accommodate to being scrutinized and judged. Supervisors adjust their sense of uneasiness as they pretend to know what good teaching is and prescribe future improvement. The whole experience is made tolerable through its ritual nature. It is not taken too seriously in its literal form, since ritual has a figurative meaning ascribed to the culture. With this version of a clinical–supervision-like set of events already in the culture of schools, it is difficult to image that the vision of clinical supervision presented by Dr. Anderson can replace it.

For both Gall and Goldsberry supervision represents a hierarchical situation with superordinates and subordinates. Both lament the fact that there is not enough time given to supervisory visitations. Goldsberry also laments the fact that supervisors lack appropriate training and skill. Although Cogan and Goldhammer do not use these terms for the supervisor and the teacher, it is clear that, in their versions, the supervisor is expected to have special skills associated with the events of clinical supervision. Issues of power and manipulation are embedded in the discourse. The supervisor has the evidences of teaching, the supervisor conducts the conference, and the teacher is in the high-risk situation as he or she becomes vulnerable to the observation and judgment. Henry St. Maurice (1987) analyzes several versions of clinical supervision in light of these social and political power "regimes." He suggests that Cogan's model resembles facets of clinical psychology and as such indicts the kind of control that the clinical supervisor would employ. He cites recent reports by teachers from inside the classroom that provide vivid testimony that teachers' power is not in balance with the supervisors'. "These imbalances," he says, "are not the results of oversights by harried administrators, but rather the articulations through 'human engineering' of regimes of bureaucratic power." He attributes this to the "technology of clinical supervision," which explicitly subordinates human relations to effective instruction. Moreover, the issue of teacher agency is an important one (agency in the sense that teachers are "agents" of their own professional development.) In St. Maurice's interpretation of clinical supervision, teachers are stripped of their professional agency.

I have presented several critiques of various interpretations of clinical supervision. I would add these to the no argument. Nevertheless I want to end with a few statements of "it depends." First, there is the issue of a cultural place for a version of clinical supervision. Over the years supervision has been a practice that is part of three groups of people in three different environments: the preservice teachers in education programs, the induction teachers who are in their novice phase of entrance into the profession, and the maturing professionals who are seasoned practitioners. I suggest that a 1990s version of clinical supervision such as Robert Anderson described is viable for preservice and inductive teachers. It is assumed that supervision is an important part of their educational programs. Professional development and accountability are taken for granted. It is the third group, the mature professionals, who are not easily able to accommodate to supervision as a means of professional growth for the reasons that I have suggested above. The question is, can those involved in the culture of the public school make a place for an educative version of clinical supervision?

I am impressed with Robert Anderson's carefully crafted description of the participants who are mutually engaged in working toward good ends. The "assister" is a witness and "there follows a time for both the person who 'taught' and the person who watched to reflect upon what happened . . ." His language suggests that there is a modicum of equality within the relationships. Furthermore, he broadens the working configurations, suggesting that supervisors may want to eliminate their efforts to work one on one with teachers, concentrating on helping teams and other work groups. In my own practice in the schools I have concentrated on working with study groups of teachers and administrators. Andrew Hargreaves (1991) points out that collegiality is rapidly becoming one of the new orthodoxies of educational change. He suggests that there are two broad types of collaborative working arrangements and relationships between teachers and their colleagues, depending on the kind of administrative control and intervention that is excercied in each case. He describes these first, as collaborative working relationships initiated between teachers and their colleagues and, second, contrived collegiality, which is bureaucratically contrived and administratively controlled forms of cooperation. It is clear that contrived collegiality can present challenges (and, at times, problems) to those who espouse clinical supervision.

For me, clinical supervision is embodied in a few principles. First of all, it is about people—acting with their hearts and minds toward understanding each other; it is directed toward the personal rather than the institutional (to personal practice rather than institutional programs). The practice is discursive, with emphasis on the nature of the discourses among the participants and their authentic educative relationships. Those engaged strive for a deep sense of compassion and wit. Clinical supervision has a moral/ethical dimension that serves to guide the encounters, and a critical dimension that continues to challenge the pretense of certitude. Most important, the meaning of clinical supervision is embodied in the individual stories fashioned from genuine dialogue, honest introspection, and the willingness to struggle toward wisdom in practice. Is it reasonable to hope that colleagues in public schools will work together with a conscious effort to make their schools the best places for all kids to learn and love? It depends!

References

Hargreaves, A., (1991). Contrived collegiality: The micropolitics of teacher collaboration. In J. Blase (Ed.), *The politics of life in schools: Power, conflict, and cooperation.* Newbury Park: Sage.

St. Maurice, H. (1987). Clinical supervision and power: Regimes of instructional management. In T. Popkewitz (Ed.), *Critical studies in teacher education: Its folklore, theory and practice.* London: The Falmer Press.

Postnote

Is Clinical Supervision a Viable Model for Use in the Public Schools?

Few educational models have received the acclaim and attention that the clinical supervision model has. Developed at Harvard by Morris Cogan, Robert Goldhammer, and Robert Anderson in the 1950s, clinical supervision has embraced the notion that cooperative planning and collegial working relationships between supervisor and teacher can influence instruction in positive ways. Variously defined and implemented, clinical supervision remains the most widely recognized model. Our authors in this chapter have presented provocative viewpoints regarding the efficacy and usefulness of clinical supervision. How do you account for the difference of positions in this chapter? What are the author's central assumptions regarding the goals of clinical supervision? Can clinical supervision be successfully implemented in your school?

Review Questions for

The Yes Response:

1. What assumptions does Dr. Anderson make at the outset of his article that form the basis for his argument?
2. How does Anderson's definition of clinical supervision differ from traditional methods of supervision you have experienced?
3. React to Anderson's essential thesis about the viability of clinical supervision.
4. Has Anderson persuaded you that clinical supervision as defined in this essay, "is not only a viable model for schools but a truly useful form of professional service and behavior"?
5. Anderson acknowledges some of the criticisms of clinical supervision. What would those who criticize clinical supervision say about Anderson's assertion that clinical supervision is still viable in the public schools?
6. Anderson suggests that the "pedagogical world has changed" by moving away from traditional self-contained settings in which teachers work alone to collegial teams or groups of teachers. It is within this latter arrangement that Anderson seems to suggest that clinical supervision is most viable. Do you agree or disagree that the "pedagogical world has changed"? Has your "pedagogical world changed?" Would clinical supervision work in your school? Why or why not?

The No Response:

1. Why is Dr. Garman uncomfortable about addressing our question in this chapter?

2. Are there any good examples of clinical supervision being used in schools presently?
3. Summarize each of the four versions of clinical supervision discussed by Garman and note her reactions to each. Describe your reaction to each version. With whom do you agree and disagree? React to Garman's position regarding these "functionalist" views. How would each presenter at AERA respond to Garman's critique?
4. React to Garman's statement that "Teachers who have been around for a while often report that good ratings give them a sense of esteem; still, they admit that in-class visitation is largely ceremonial and doesn't much change the way they teach their students."
5. What is "good" teaching?
6. Garman quotes Hargreaves' description of "two broad types of collaborative working arrangements and relationships between teachers and their colleagues." Which type is most prevalent in your school? Which type would be more conducive to clinical supervision? Is such collaboration really possible in your school? Explain.
7. Is it reasonable to hope that colleagues in public schools will work together in a conscious effort to make their schools the best places for all kids to learn and love?

For Further Research

1. In your opinion, is the supervision of instruction in nonpublic school settings similar or dissimilar to supervision as practiced in public schools? Would clinical supervision have greater, fewer, or the same problems being implemented in private schools? Interview individuals who work in private schools to ascertain their experiences with supervision in general and with clinical supervision in particular.
2. Clinical supervision has been criticized. Review the nature of this criticism. Do you agree or disagree with these criticisms?
3. Examine the efficacy of clinical supervision in preservice settings. What is the role of supervision in preservice settings? What are the potential benefits of using clinical supervision in preservice settings? What are the real limitations on supervisors' time and energies, and how might these affect supervisors' interactions with preservice teachers?
4. Examine why Hunter (1986) believed that the pre-observation phase in the clinical supervision cycle was a waste of time. What's your reaction to Hunter's assertion?
5. Describe what clinical supervision is to someone who has no idea what it is. Be as specific as possible.
6. Set up a role-playing situation for a pre-observation conference and a post-observation conference. Discuss key elements of each aspect.

7. Conduct an interview with a supervisor who practices clinical supervision. Discuss your findings. Conduct an interview with a teacher who has experienced clinical supervision. Discuss your findings.

8. Write a report comparing Cogan's (1973) conception of clinical supervision with Goldhammer's (1969). How has the Goldhammer, Anderson, and Krajewski (1980) text advanced Goldhammer's original model?

9. Recently, developments in clinical supervision were reviewed in an issue of *The Teacher Educator, 30*(3). Examine the articles in that issue and note how each author might approach or view the issue addressed in this chapter. What are some specific problems or difficulties that arise when implementing clinical supervision?

10. According to some authorities, clinical supervision can be used to enhance instruction within the classroom because supportive supervision softens the hierarchical supervisory relationship by formally distributing authority among members. Consult Poole (1994) and indicate how this distribution of authority is accomplished.

11. Conflicts among advocates of clinical supervision continue. Compare the nature of these conflicts by examining the following sources: Darling-Hammond and Sclan (1992), Garman, Glickman, Hunter, and Haggerson (1992), and Tracy and MacNaughton (1989). What implications about the practice of clinical supervision may be drawn from these analyses?

12. Compare the theory and practice of clinical supervision in non-educational fields, such as counseling and religious studies, with supervision in schools. Consult, for example, Pohly (1993), and Williams (1995). Describe how supervision is defined and practiced. How is clinical supervision as practiced in counseling different from practices of clinical supervision in schools?

13. Acheson and Gall (1987) are advocates of clinical supervision. Describe their conception of clinical supervision and how a clinical model might be effectively implemented in schools.

14. Compare and contrast Acheson and Gall's (1987) application of clinical supervision in schools with Glickman's (1985) developmental model and Costa and Garmston's (1993) approach. How are they similar and dissimilar from one another? Which approach would make sense in your school/district?

15. Read McFaul and Cooper's (1984) critique of clinical supervision in which they question its utility in school settings. What are their underlying assumptions about clinical supervision and why do they think that clinical supervision may not be suited to the realities of schools? React to the responses proffered by Goldsberry (1984) and Krajewski (1984) in that same issue of *Educational Leadership.* In your estimation, can clinical supervision be practically employed in schools? If so, describe how you would go about implementing a clinical program.

16. Clinical supervision as a topic has received noteworthy attention in both *Educational Leadership* and the *Journal of Curriculum and Supervision.* Critique five of the most recent articles published about clinical supervision in each journal.

References

Acheson, K. A., & Gall, M. D. (1987). *Techniques in the clinical supervision of teachers* (2nd ed.). New York: Longman.

Cogan, M. L. (1973). *Clinical supervision.* Boston: Houghton Mifflin.

Costa, A. L., & Garmston, R. J. (1993). *Cognitive coaching: A foundation for renaissance schools.* Norwood, MA: Christopher-Gordon Publishers.

Darling-Hammond, L., & Sclan, E. (1992). Policy and supervision. In C. D. Glickman, (Ed.), *Supervision in transition* (pp. 7–29). Alexandria, VA: Association for Supervision and Curriculum Division.

Garman, N. B., Glickman, C. D., Hunter, M., & Haggerson, N. (1992). Conflicting conceptions of clinical supervision and the enhancement of professional growth and renewal: Point and counterpoint. *Journal of Curriculum and Supervision, 2,* 152–157.

Glickman, C. D. (1985). *Supervision of instruction: A developmental approach.* Boston: Allyn & Bacon.

Goldhammer, R. (1969). *Clinical supervision: Special methods for the supervision of teachers.* New York: Holt, Rinehart & Winston.

Goldhammer R., Anderson, R. H., & Krajewski, R. A. (1980). *Clinical supervision: Special methods for the supervision of teachers* (2nd ed.). New York: Holt, Rinehart & Winston.

Goldsberry, L. F. (1984). Reality—really: A response to McFaul and Cooper. *Educational Leadership, 41*(7), 10–11.

Hunter, M. (1986). Let's eliminate the preobservation conference. *Educational Leadership, 43*(6), 69–70.

Krajewski, R. J. (1984). No wonder it didn't work! A response to McFaul and Cooper. *Educational Leadership, 41*(7), 11.

McFaul, S. A., & Cooper, J. M. (1984). Peer clinical supervision: Theory vs. reality. *Educational Leadership, 41*(7), 4–9.

Pohly, K. (1993). *Transforming the rough places: The ministry of supervision.* Dayton, OH: Whaleprints.

Poole, W. (1994). Removing the 'super' from supervision. *Journal of Curriculum and Supervision, 9,* 284–309.

Tracy, S., & MacNaughton, R. (1989). Clinical supervision and the emerging conflict between the Neo-Traditionalists and the Neo-Progressives. *Journal of Curriculum and Supervision, 4,* 246–256.

Williams, A. (1995). *Visual and active supervision: Roles, focus, technique.* New York: W. W. Norton & Company.

Issue 12

Will Technology Replace the Role of the Supervisor?

✦ ✦ ✦ ✦

YES—Saundra J. Tracy, Butler University
NO—Joyce E. Killian, Southern Illinois University

✦ ✦ ✦

Issue Summary

YES: Dean of the College of Education at Butler University, Saundra Tracy argues that as technology's potential is realized, supervisors' roles will shift dramatically. She bases her position on three premises: (1) that technology, if utilized properly, can "replace many of the current roles performed by persons called supervisors;" (2) that many roles heretofore performed by supervisors can be played by teachers, thus enhancing teacher empowerment; and (3) once these roles are shifted from supervisors to teachers, "supervisors will be freed to assume new roles that will maximize their overall impact."

NO: Professor Joyce Killian, acknowledging the benefits and utility of technology in helping supervisors more effectively carry out their responsibilities, argues that "technology will not replace the role of the supervisor." She argues the limitations of "tool technology" and then presents "a case for why those technological applications promoted as potential replacements for central supervisory roles are unequal to the task." She offers a cautionary note by setting some ground rules to guide supervisors in making decisions about using technology.

Guiding Questions

1. What is technology?
2. How does technology influence supervision?
3. In what ways is teaching with technology affecting classroom instruction?
4. What are the advantages and disadvantages of technology for supervision?
5. What factors are likely to guide effective technology-based supervision?
6. How can technology facilitate classroom observations?
7. How might technology result in a reconceptualization of supervisors' roles?

Will Technology Replace the Role of the Supervisor? *Yes*

Saundra J. Tracy

Why Technology Will Replace the Role(s) of the Supervisor

At the risk of alienating the many instructional supervisors who labor diligently to improve teaching and learning in schools, I argue in this essay that technology can be an even more potent catalyst to accomplish the functions long associated with these positions. Such a radical contention does not mean that the *position* of instructional supervisor will soon disappear, although there are indications that this already may be happening for other reasons (ASCD, 1993; Costa & Guditus, 1984; Tracy, 1993). Rather, I contend that the roles supervisors carry out will shift dramatically as technology's potential is realized. Those who take exception to this point of view will surely point out that there are few examples of this realized potential. While this is true, we must not let a focus on what is limit our vision of what can be. Barker (1988) states that the primary question that should be asked as a field seeks a new paragidm is "What do we believe is now impossible to do in our field, but if it could be done would fundamentally change the field (for the better)?" There is a great deal of evidence that technology is the key to the next supervisory paradigm shift.

The significance of technology in effecting dramatic supervisory change is built upon three hypotheses. The first is that if technology is tapped to its fullest, something that has rarely occurred in education, it can replace many of the current roles performed by persons called supervisors. Second, technology will allow teachers to assume a number of these roles, thus merging the roles of teacher and supervisor into one. This will occur primarily as teachers are empowered to be more self-directed in the analysis and improvement of instruction. Third, as these roles are transferred from supervisors to teachers, supervisors will be freed to assume new roles that will maximize their overall impact.

The term *supervisor* often is applied to a wide range of positions and responsibilities in schools. However, two common functions of these positions are improvement of instruction and monitoring of the curriculum. Both roles generally involve direct one-on-one interaction with teachers and observation of instruction. These common supervisory roles will serve as examples of the potential of technology to transform supervision as we know it today.

Tapping Technology's Full Potential

There actually are multiple new technologies that are changing the ways teaching and learning are carried out in schools. Barbee and Ofeish

(1990) believe that the microcomputer is at their heart. They state that "it has made possible the creation, delivery, and management of learning environments that provide textual, audio, video and graphical stimuli to the learner and over which he or she has control" (p. 17). Consider the supervisory implications of tapping the potential of this computer technology as a teaching and learning tool.

The Saturn School in St. Paul, Minnesota, is an excellent example of how computer technology has served as the catalyst to dramatically alter the roles of all participants in this learning environment (Bennett & King, 1991). Built on the assumption that all students must assume responsibility for their own learning, computers play an integral role in fostering student self-direction. Hopkins (1991) contends that computer technology provides students and teachers tools for addressing five broad outcomes: (1) individualizing learning, (2) encouraging group interaction, (3) managing and coordinating learning, (4) fostering student expression, and (5) assisting students in knowledge production. In this technology-rich environment, teachers rarely carry out the role of information disseminator to large groups of students. Basic skills instruction generally is accomplished via drill, practice and simulation software, or integrated learning systems. Thus, skills instruction is both individualized and self-directed.

Group interaction can be increased through network access, by which students respond to each other as well as by the many projects developed by pairs or small groups of students using technology. In the Saturn School example, students' and the teacher's computers are connected via keyboards with small text windows so that the teacher and/or students can share information and request responses. The teacher can see all of the students' responses, adjust instruction accordingly, and maintain a record of student performance. In other settings, networking allows students to work with partners sometimes many miles from the local classroom. Networks also can afford numerous external players the opportunity to be partners in classroom learning—parents, community resource persons, peers in other places, and teachers with special skills regardless of assigned classroom or geographic location.

Similarly, technology allows the management and coordination of learning to no longer be merely a function of the teacher. At the Saturn School, students develop their personal growth plans and record progress using computer technology, then demonstrate to teachers and parents what they have learned—again often using the computer to assist in organizing, documenting, and presenting learning. The national trend toward student portfolios lends itself to this type of technological management—shifting responsibility for the management of learning from just the teacher to teacher and student.

Computer technology also opens almost limitless possibilities for students to express themselves in unique ways and produce their own personal knowledge. Simple multimedia authoring tools allow students to develop creative ways to demonstrate their learning. Access to worldwide databases brings resources previously inaccessible to student desktops. Video productions, brilliant graphics, and synthesized music are all ways students can explore, create, and find answers to questions. Of course, computer technology also affords students a powerful way to express ideas and, as mentioned earlier, to critique each other's work.

This technology also can have a significant impact on a teacher's life in the school setting. Peterson and Allen (1992) cite a number of examples of computer uses teachers can adapt to assist them in improving their instruction. Like students, teachers can easily develop their own portfolios via computer. Statistical packages allow teachers to analyze student test performance and predict needed areas of improvement. Combined with district data, teachers may measure their group's progress against the district population. An "instrumented" classroom unobtrusively observes instruction and offers teachers a wealth of feedback that prior to technology was limited to the occasional supervisory visit (Burke, 1993). Video data can be computer-analyzed for patterns of teacher behavior not easily noticed from a single observation.

Among the other technologies significantly influencing education, distance learning technologies rank high. In a 1990 report, the Office of Technology Assessment noted that between 1987 and 1988, the number of states reporting involvement in distance education increased from ten to more than two-thirds. Today virtually all states are exploring or are directly engaged in it. Distance learning utilizes a variety of technological tools, including satellites, compressed digital video, and full-motion analog video. Some examples illustrate the power of these technologies to transform the teaching and learning environment and its supervision.

Distance learning erases the traditional boundaries of the classroom. The "classroom" may be multiple sites many miles apart. It is not limited to the school building or even the local community. Students who can see and interact with each other quickly forget the distances that separate them. The "teacher" may be the traditional classroom teacher whose talents are shared across buildings in a single school district or whose class is disseminated to several districts. For example, in central Indiana, a finite math class whose small enrollment is cost-prohibitive for a single high school is shared among four school districts, affording students opportunities they would not have if instruction were constrained by physical location. This scene is repeated in numerous states for a variety of special offerings.

But who is the teacher in distance learning? In one Pennsylvania classroom, the "teacher" is also a student. A French teacher supervises instruction as students learn Japanese from a distant instructor via satellite. This teacher facilitates discussions, coordinates projects and assignments, and provides resources for learning. She also plays the role of student, learning Japanese at the same time as her "class." In another setting, students in a high school science lab eagerly interact with a scientist at a local research center who is demonstrating how tests are conducted to determine the safety and effectiveness of potential prescription drugs. The local teacher joins in the discussion and monitors the experiments the students are carrying out during these interactions. The researcher displays chemical formulas that students can complete or alter on a jointly manipulated white board. Data from the experiments also are exchanged.

Students are not the only ones benefiting from this distance learning technology. Later in the day, three chemistry teachers, each the only chemistry teacher in his or her school district, work on a new unit on acid rain. They are joined via technology by a professor from the regional university. Each agrees to "observe" another during the implementation of the unit and the video postconference to analyze its effectiveness. In addition, a group of preservice science teachers from the university have asked to view one of the lessons and discuss the teacher's instructional decisions after the lesson.

While these uses of computer and distance learning technologies may sound futuristic to some, they are increasingly common in schools all across the country. They illustrate the dramatic effect these technology-driven changes in the teaching and learning environment are having on the roles of teachers and supervisors in these settings.

Transferring the Supervisory Role to the Teacher

Instructional technologies such as those just described can fundamentally alter the role of the teacher in the classroom. This transformation begins with the students' roles, which change as dramatically in these new learning environments as the teacher's (Wasley, 1991). As students utilize the tools of technology they become active rather than passive learners, controlling their own learning rate and style. Emphasis shifts from remembering information presented by a teacher to finding, organizing, and making sense of the wealth of information accessible via technology (Hopkins, 1991). The traditional information dispenser role of the teacher is assumed by other sources of information. The teacher's role as organizer of information is given over to the student. Even the teacher's feedback role often is carried out by other students, resource persons, or software.

The transfer of many of the traditional teaching roles to the student opens the way for the teacher to take on new roles such as those traditionally assigned to supervisors. Contrast the supervisor's functions in a typical cycle of clinical supervision (Goldhammer, 1969; Pajak, 1993; Tracy & MacNaughton, 1993) with this new teaching/learning environment. Stage 1, the preobservation conference, is intended to set the teacher at ease, to help the teacher rehearse the lesson and think through the intended outcomes and instructional methodology. In our technology-rich environment, the teacher discusses what is to be learned, helps students think through how they will access and organize information, and then turns students loose to direct their own learning.

Stage 2 is observation of teaching. Recall the distance learning classroom where the teachers and students are observers and participants in the learning process. Or follow a teacher in the Saturn School as he or she moves from student to student, observing and collecting information to assist the students in their learning, much as the traditional supervisor gathers information during a classroom observation.

Now let's shift to stage 3, analysis and strategy. Goldhammer (1969) believes that teachers can improve teaching if they better understand the reality of what goes on in the classroom. Classroom data can be used to identify behavior patterns unique to the individual teacher. Similarly, teacher coaches or facilitators in these new learning environments look for patterns of student behavior that facilitate or inhibit learning. Since much student learning occurs individually or in small groups, the teacher can focus on the unique behaviors related to directing and organizing learning, and develop strategies for sharing this information with the student(s). The goal, as in Goldhammer's cycle, is for the student to use the information to increase the effectiveness of his or her own behaviors—in this case learning rather than teaching behaviors. The teacher may rely on the data analysis of student learning behavior generated by the computer to find learning patterns and thus revise instruction.

Goldhammer's stage 4 is the well-known supervision conference. According to Goldhammer, the strategy the supervisor uses in this conference is likely to affect not only the teacher's knowledge but also his or her feelings about him- or herself, about teaching, and about the supervisor and supervision. Translated into the new teaching/learning environments, the manner in which the teacher carries out the learning facilitator role, giving feedback to students, has major ramifications on how students feel about directing their own learning, what knowledge they gain, and how they generally react to the roles in this new environment.

Finally, Goldhammer promoted a fifth stage of postconference analysis in which the role of the supervisor is critically examined. Translating this stage into our high-tech environments, many observers note an increased self-reflectiveness on the part of teachers (Dwyer, Ringstaff, & Sandholtz, 1991). Teachers routinely speculate about the causes of changes they see in their students and their roles in these changes—analogous to the supervisor's analysis of supervision.

Another significant factor in the changing roles of teachers and supervisors is the transition to a feedback-rich environment. In the past, the teacher was the main provider of feedback to students and the supervisor the main provider of feedback to teachers. However, in these new environments, technology records and manages information on learning decisions. When the classroom is extended beyond the bounds of the four walls and "teachers" include scientists, parents, and teachers in far away settings, feedback on teaching and learning is no longer limited to the supervisor/teacher relationship. Opportunities for feedback are constant and ongoing. The teacher need not wait for the anticipated visit by the supervisor to gain additional insights on what is happening in the classroom. In summary, the traditional supervisory role as envisioned by Goldhammer and others may no longer be the major approach to improving instruction.

New Roles for Supervisors

Let's return to the question asked at the beginning of this essay: What do we now believe is impossible that would fundamentally improve the field of supervision? Starratt (1992) contends that 80 to 90 percent of current supervisory activity in schools focuses on performance evaluation that is tolerated simply because it has been around so long. There is no research that shows that supervision as generally practiced or as it might ideally be practiced leads to sustained and substantial improvement in instruction (see Issue 3). He concludes that technology as well as a number of other factors make teaching today so different from what we think, that supervision will have to be replaced by different varieties of support personnel. One interpretation of Starratt's radical conclusion is that the traditional supervisory roles must be replaced by new ones—regardless of the name we give to these positions.

Based on the changes already noted in the teachers' roles, four probable new or enhanced roles for those persons we presently call supervisors are: (1) as a guide to accessing information, (2) as a link to human resources, (3) as an organizational coordinator of instructional improvement activities, and (4) as a technology advocate and support person. Although each of these may sound quite similar to current supervisory roles, the actual functions differ.

Supervisors routinely describe their role as one of resource provider (Pajak, 1989). Traditionally, resource providers found information on conferences and workshops and materials such as articles and books and shared them with interested teachers. They were the gatherers, sorters, and disseminators of information. But in our technology-rich teaching and learning environments, where a wealth of information is at the teacher's fingertips, what is needed is not a supervisor who *provides* resources but one who can assist the teacher with how to *access* them. The teacher's new responsibility as resource gatherer is enhanced by support from the supervisor on sources and methods of resource access.

Isolation of teaching in the self-contained classrooms means that teacher-to-teacher interaction, if and when it occurs, tends to happen within one department or school. District-wide supervisors sometimes expand this circle to include teachers across the school district. Technology, on the other hand, redefines what it means to link human resources involved in instruction. We earlier described the variety of persons involved in instruction in these new environments unlimited by location or affiliation. Supervisors in these settings must expand the range of their networks to include, at the least, the broader communities in which they work and ideally the even wider national educational arena. For example, knowledge of the extensive human resources in a given field at an area university allows for potential linkages to augment the human resources in the local high school.

Supervisors also have traditionally played a coordinator role for the improvement of instruction. Typical tasks associated with this role are planning workshops, establishing district committees to tackle problems, and monitoring curriculum implementation, among other activities. The major task in the transition of this role is to help teachers avoid duplication of efforts. Much of this role can conceivably be played out via technology using management systems and network communication, much like teachers use to facilitate student learning in the classroom.

Finally, supervisors in the new supervisory paradigms must be technology advocates and support persons. This does not imply that supervisors should assume a technician role. Rather, they will need to ask pointed questions about technology's capacity to solve instructional issues, then determine what technological resources and support systems are necessary to fully tap technology's potential.

Benefits of a Technology Transformation

The technology scenarios painted here represent many of the espoused outcomes for instructional supervision. In these examples, technology happens to be the tool that brings these outcomes about. Teacher and supervisor time is used more efficiently and effectively to maximize what each can do best. Students and teachers become more self-directed learners, with teachers reflecting on and being responsible for improving their own practice. The impetus for instructional improvement occurs at the level where change is most likely and most needed—in the classroom.

Could these desired supervisory ends be accomplished without technology? Most likely they could. However, deeply rooted and significant change usually results from the introduction of some type of significant stimulus for change. In a personal conversation with this author, Shanker (1990) stated that technology is this catalyst for dramatically altering teaching and learning as we know it today. One might add that as such it is also the catalyst for transforming instructional supervision. With no other tool as potentially powerful as technology on the horizon, we should carefully consider how to harness its power for achieving teachers' and supervisors' mutual goals of radically improving student learning in today's schools.

References

Association for Supervision and Curriculum Development (1993). Supervision reappraised. *ASCD Update, 35*(6), 1, 3, 8.

Barbee, D. E., & Ofeish, G. D. (1990). *A report on the nationwide "State of the Art" of instructional technology.* (Unpublished report).

Barker, J. A. (1988). *Discovering the future: The business of paradigms* (2nd ed.). St Paul, MN: ILI Press.

Bennett, D. A., & King, D. T. (1991). The Saturn School of tomorrow. *Educational Leadership, 48*(8), 41–44.

Burke, R. L. (1993). Role of technology in facilitating personnel evaluation. *Journal of Personnel Evaluation in Education, 7*(3), 235–238.

Costa, A., & Guditus, C. (1984). Do districtwide supervisors make a difference? *Educational Leadership, 41*(6), 84–85.

Dwyer, D. C., Ringstaff, C., & Sandholtz, J. H. (1991). Changes in teachers' beliefs and practices in technology-rich classrooms. *Educational Leadership, 48*(8), 45–52.

Goldhammer, R. (1969). *Clinical supervision: Special methods for the supervision of teachers.* New York: Holt, Rinehart & Winston.

Hopkins, M. (1991). The Saturn School: Technology's cutting edge. *Principal, 71*(2), 16–19.

Office of Technology Assessment (OTA), U. S. Congress (1990). *Linking for learning: A new course for education.* Washington, DC: OTA.

Pajak, E. (1989). *Identification of supervisory proficiencies project: Final report.* Athens, GA: University of Georgia, Department of Curriculum and Supervision.

Pajak, E. (1993). *Approaches to clinical supervision: Alternatives for improving instruction.* Norwood, MA: Christopher-Gordon Publishers.

Peterson, K. D., & Allen, J. E. (1992). Uses of microcomputers in school teacher evaluation. *Journal of Research on Computing in Education, 24*(3), 392–398.

Shanker, A. (1990). A personal conversation with Al Shanker on the role of technology in restructuring American education, Washington DC.

Starratt, R. J. (1992). A modest proposal: Abolish supervision. *Wingspan, 8*(1), 14–19.

Tracy, S. J. (1993). The overlooked position of subject area supervisor. *Clearing House, 67*(1), 25–30.

Tracy, S. J., & MacNaughton, R. (1993). *Assisting and assessing educational personnel: The impact of clinical supervision.* Boston, MA: Allyn & Bacon.

Wasley, P. A. (1991). From quarterback to coach, from actor to director. *Educational Leadership, 48*(8), 35–40.

Will Technology Replace the Role of the Supervisor? *No*

Joyce E. Killian

Technology Will Not Replace the Role of the Supervisor

Tool technology has streamlined many school routines. By taking over all or part of such tasks as attendance taking, parental notification, and calculation of grades, it has freed teachers and administrators to spend their time on more professional tasks. Supervisors in schools have likewise reaped benefits of efficiency from technology. They can, for instance, write reports of observations and conferences with a word processor and keep track of staff development needs with a database. But while tool applications can benefit supervisors by giving them time for more important tasks, they have not and will not replace their central role. This essay will develop two major arguments in support of the contention that technology will not replace the role of the supervisor. First, I will argue the limitations of tool technology with respect to the central role of supervision. Second, I will present a case for why those technological applications promoted as potential replacements for central supervisory roles are unequal to the task.

The Benefits and Limitations of Tool Technology in Supervision

Years ago, when I began teaching high school English, much of my time was spent at the typewriter preparing materials on dittoes. When I finished typing, I edited my errors by scraping away the waxy substance of the ditto's under page with a razor. Next morning before class, I primed the ditto machine, clamped the master onto its round metal drum, and if the fluid levels and pressure were functioning properly, cranked the appropriate number of handouts for my day's classes.

Today companies that sell conventional typewriters have gone out of business. And today, like most teachers, I compose, revise, and edit my handouts on a word processor. I don't touch hard copy until the finished page leaves the printer. My computer's word processing program, my office's laser printer, and my department's Risograph, with its automatic page counting and collating features, are *technological tools* that help me to accomplish the paper production aspect of my job much more efficiently than I did in the past. But does this technology change the kind of teacher I am? Only to the extent that I choose to use the "found" time in professional enterprise.

As a high school English teacher, I also occasionally used a grammar textbook. The text contained several writing activities that supported my writing workshop approach and many exercises that reinforced editing skills that I was trying to teach. Other sections of the text that were incompatible with my own teaching goals I did not use. In more recent years I have come to use software just as selectively as I have long used textbooks. Even when I take my entire class to the computer lab to work through a simulation, the computer remains my tool in achieving the goals that I have set for that day; it does not *replace* any of the fundamental roles that I play in the classroom.

In supervision, just as in teaching, the selective use of computer software as the best tool for a task has the potential to free supervisors to spend some of their time on more professional efforts. Properly used, technology will remain the servant of the supervisor, neither changing nor replacing his or her central supervisory role of working with teachers toward instructional improvement. This assignment of technology to servant status is critical in conceiving the role of technology in supervision, for as our infatuation with the benefits of technology increases, so will our temptation to use this technology in ways that shift the locus of control and that are not compatible with what many supervisors believe about good supervisory practice.

As a Word Processor during Observations

Because word processing serves supervisors well in keeping track of data and transcribing notes of observations, it may seem only a minor extension to take the laptop into the classroom. A supervisor with good keyboarding skills can type faster than she or he can write, and in-class data entry eliminates an intermediate step. As Kuralt (1987) notes, taking the computer into the observation allowed him to have a complete transcription of classroom interaction for the teacher prior to the post-observation conference, giving both the opportunity to be better prepared for a collegial post-conference.

But efficiency should not be the primary criterion for extending the computer's use in supervision. There are other equally or more important questions to ask: Will the use of the computer change the conditions of the classroom observation or its follow-up conference? Will the attention to the computer limit what the supervisor sees in the environment, particularly the more subtle cues? Will computer use in some way change the relationship between the "observer" and the "observed?"

There is evidence that the answer to some of the above questions may be yes. Presence of a computer may affect the climate of the observation, and its use may be perceived as invasive. Kuralt (1987) notes that although the effect wore off quickly, at least initially the computer seemed too intrusive and mechanical for classroom observations. The clicking sounds of the keyboard made both students and teachers wonder about his purpose. He also notes that the level of his keyboarding skills caused him to look at the keyboard frequently. He downplays this obstacle, however, and concludes that occasional scanning allowed him to gather data effectively.

Teachers, too, have concerns about computer use during observation. Hazi (1989) recalls an incident in which a supervisor's use of a computer during a classroom observation resulted in a formal complaint. She recounts her conversation with a New Jersey supervisor who recently had a grievance filed against her for the use of a laptop to assist in "script taping." The teacher's association claimed that the computer was disruptive, distracting, and intimidating and that it restricted the supervisor to monitoring only the audible components of the classroom environment. Although use of the laptop did not violate the contract, the supervisor was asked to discontinue it.

Thus, even at the first point where the computer crosses over from the supervisor's office into the classroom, it can become more than a servant of the supervisor, affecting teachers' and students' attitudes and behavior during the observation and possibly limiting the visual data collected.

As a Tool for Collecting and Analyzing Observational Data

Another supervisory tool application, the customized observation program, allows the user to record a classroom event with the convenience of a preprogrammed single keystroke in place of text. Once data are collected with the customized software, the same program can be used to streamline synthesis, display, and storage of those data. Reed, Toth, and Reed (1987) describe the use of the Computerized Observation System (COS) to document preservice and inservice teacher performance. Using the COS on a portable computer, observers were able to record and analyze both high and low inference measures of classroom interaction. Observers also had the option of including a narrative to elaborate details of the context of the observation.

While customized observational software applications like the COS have the potential to transform data into more succinct and user-friendly formats, such applications also raise concerns. In the conclusion of their report on the implementation of the COS, Reed, Toth, and Reed (1987) note an intrusive effect of the computer and its user. They speculate that the computer's distracting effect on students reduced the likelihood that the observer saw the teacher performance optimally. Technology proponents, however, often ignore the potential drawbacks of observational software. Burke (1993), for example, in a discussion of the role of technology in personnel evaluation, speculates that an "easily constructed . . . instrumented classroom" would in fact reduce "intrusive" management interventions. In his high-tech scenario, electronic technology would be put to work to "very unobtrusively record classroom interaction data, summarize it, and provide valuable feedback to teachers on their performance, in many cases, in 'real time'" (p. 237). Software design considerations and problems with teacher acceptance in Burke's scenario are nonexistent.

Tool applications of computers in supervision raise two additional concerns, the first related to teacher perception and the second to validity. To the extent that teachers perceive that computer-generated data are being used to help them reach mutually agreed-on goals for improvement, such efforts are likely to be accepted merely as a supplement to good supervision. But to the extent that teachers perceive the data will be used for the sake of comparison or ranking, or for decision making about their advancement or retention, such efforts will be met with resistance. Because computer software has the potential to facilitate the expansion of district- and statewide quantification, its applications to teacher supervision and evaluation may receive particular scrutiny.

A final concern about observational software is that it will promote supervisory practices that focus solely on easily measurable classroom behaviors, ignoring more complex but potentially more important interactions. Computerized versions of observational systems will suffer no more or less from validity weakness than did their nontechnological predecessors, but their computer-generated "hard" data may have the added impact of being perceived as more correct.

Technological "Replacements" for Central Supervisory Roles

In addition to the tool applications of the computer to supervision, there are a host of other technological applications that have been suggested as aids to or replacements for some of the central roles that supervisors play. These range from some currently feasible applications to futuristic models. Real or conceived, however, what they have in common is that each has potential to affect the quality of the relationship between the teacher and the supervisor and thus to compromise supervisory practice.

Messenger Applications and Distance Conferencing

As online services are added to the computers available to both teachers and supervisors, they will increasingly be tapped for their power as efficient and patient messengers. Suggestions for such use appear most often in the literature on preservice supervision, probably because problems related to the distance between campus and school placement sites have historically hindered supervisors' efforts to maintain close and ongoing contact with the field-experience students they supervise. Whether preservice or inservice, however, in situations where there is distance between supervisors and teachers, technological applications like wide area networks, electronic mail, and bulletin boards, as well as fax machines, may be used to supplement direct supervision. Such applications can be particularly effective in keeping both parties apprised of schedule changes and meeting dates and in providing information. Nevertheless, what distance technology cannot provide is an acceptable substitute for the face-to-face contact between student and supervisor.

Research on resistance to distance learning in higher education in general provides evidence of why such substitution in supervision will prove unsatisfactory. Hansen and Perry (1993) observe that both students and instructors resist technology if they fear that it will reduce or replace their direct contact with one another. In general they note a fear among learners of "going electronic" because of their sense that computers will depersonalize the educational process (p. 50). These problems seem to be borne out by studies that suggest a problem with personal motivation and with a higher dropout rate for courses delivered by distance education (Verduin & Clark, 1991).

A principle of the effective instructional message design also suggests why online conferencing will not substitute for direct personal contact. This principle holds that, in comparison with all forms of media, face-to-face communication is more effective in promoting acceptance than mediated communication, particularly in difficult cases (Bednar & Levie, 1993). In their discussion of this principle, Bednar and Levie note that factors related to the physical presence of the speaker enhance the effectiveness of a message. First, the message is more likely to be understood because the speaker can tailor delivery to cues received during the interaction. Second, face-to-face communication overcomes one of the major obstacles to media campaigns: it increases the probability that the message will be attended to.

Instructional Design Systems: the Computer as "Learning Center"

Other proposed uses of computers in the supervisory process involve using the computer as "teacher." One such application is that of simulation with interactive feedback. A teacher with classroom management problems, for instance, might view a simulation of an interaction between a teacher and a disruptive child. The teacher at the computer chooses among several possible responses to the child's behavior, and the program then branches to show the consequences of that response. Such a simulation certainly has value in letting teachers experiment with management techniques without projecting the consequences onto real children, but it has potential only as a tool mutually selected by the teacher and the supervisor to meet perceived needs.

Other computer-as-teacher applications are programs designed to provide information to teachers and, in some cases, to provide feedback about their success in retaining that information. While such programs may serve well in conveying material that is predominantly informational, they have several documented shortcomings, among them excessive fragmentation, a basically "closed" nature, and a tendency to promote passive rather than active learning (Merrill, Li, & Jones, 1990). The reasons that such applications will have only limited application to supervision are also apparent in Hannafin's (1992) discussion of the limitations of instructional design systems. He notes that the internal, learner-directed processes, which are essential to successful learning, are not well accomplished by present instructional design systems. Until design perspectives broaden to include more experience, inquiry, manipulation, and prediction, instructional systems will have little to offer supervision.

Artificial Intelligence (AI) and Expert Systems

Among the most futuristic of proposed technological applications to supervision are artificial intelligence and its subcategory, expert systems. An expert system is an artificial intelligence program that to a degree imitates human expertise. A rule-based, if-then logic allows the computer program to examine data and make recommendations based on logic and criteria established by experts (Peterson, 1990).

A system developed by Peterson illustrates how such a program can be applied to teacher evaluation. Peterson's purpose was to compare the decisions made by a computer expert system with those made by a panel of experts whose performance in teacher evaluation had already been documented. He reports high levels of agreement between a computer expert system and similar decisions by human experts on the judgments of 12 school-teacher performance dossiers: "DOSSIER demonstrated a capacity to make defensible promotion decisions and rankings on teacher performance data. . . . It discriminated as well as the better human judges in this simulation task" (p. 138).

Peterson does not advocate the application of an expert system like DOSSIER to the teacher evaluation process. Rather, he sees its greatest value in what it can help us to learn about how experts think about teacher quality. But although Peterson cautions that this expert system was not designed to replace the necessary human professional judgments, others may not recognize the limitations of such narrow, rule-based systems for actual practice. Certainly there will be some who will take the view that if expert systems can predict as well as the experts, then why not use them for that purpose? It is important for supervisors to understand, therefore, that like many complex predictive formulas, expert systems work well on average but are not uniformly valid for the individual case, especially the exceptional one. Nor can they factor into their decision making any information not known in advance. Take, for instance, the case of a teacher recently named her state's "teacher of the year." She can be passed over for promotion by the logic that controls DOSSIER if she does not have recent scores above the fiftieth percentile on one of three nationally normed exams.

Other practical applications of artificial intelligence to supervision will occur only after considerably more sophisticated tools are available for analyzing human speech and digitized images. The early optimism that linguists had about generating rule-based speech by computer has been tempered by an increased understanding of the complexity of the rules that govern our language and the abundance of exceptions. Anyone who has tried to edit with a computerized grammar or style checker knows just how limited such applications are. Even programs that can "translate" script or voice into word processing have not worked very well, as the introduction of Apple's error-prone Newton "transcription pad" testifies. Nor will computers soon be able to pass judgment on images received from camera or videotape. In terms of direct application to the observation process, there is little likelihood that the computer will be used for the direct gathering of data in the near future, as even low inference measures of observation are far beyond current artificial intelligence capabilities. While years of development on an AI program called WISARD (Aleksander & Burnett, 1987) allow it to judge whether a digitized image is smiling or frowning, this is still a long way from making such distinctions as whether a child is "on task" or whether a teacher's nonverbals are consistent with her message. Thus, the task of recording data about teacher performance will remain a human supervisory function for the foreseeable future.

Setting Some Standards for the Use of Technology in Supervision

Supervisors who put technology to use in tool applications may well find time that they did not have before—time that, if spent observing in classrooms and working individually and collectively with teachers, may make them better and more effective supervisors. Like teachers, supervisors may use integrated software to help them handle the paper load more efficiently. They may also take advantage of scheduling programs and calendars to help them plan for visitations and conferences. They may use databases to customize district-level expectations for performance and staff development, creating a sort of supervisory "IEP" for individual teachers. They almost certainly will use word processors for keeping track of all conferences and records of classroom observations and both formative and summative evaluation of teachers.

However, because not all present and proposed uses of technology are equally positive in their potential, some ground rules should guide supervisors in making decisions about their adoption.

- First, and at an absolute minimum, proposed technology must do no harm. This rules out strategies perceived by any party as intrusive, disruptive, or likely to distort data collection.
- Second, technology should be chosen to support, not supplant, existing satisfactory supervisory practices. Teachers and supervisors must retain the responsibility for deciding the questions that should be asked about practice. Only after those questions are formulated should they decide whether technological tools can help them in the process.
- Third, the complexity of the proposed technology must match the complexity of the supervisory task. Traditional systematic observation instruments have at best captured only some of the

important information about the complex interactions that go on in a classroom. Computerized versions deserve the same skepticism about the extent of their validity.

- Finally, the proposed technology must support a face-to-face relationship between a teacher and supervisor. While some "messenger" functions of the computer may increase effective communication, substitutes for direct personal contact between teachers and supervisors depersonalize the experience and minimize the potential for professional growth.

A lesson from supervision in business and industry serves well to explain why I end this chapter on such a cautionary note. For several years now, employers in a variety of work settings have capitalized on technology's potential to let them electronically supervise the speed, accuracy, and on-task behavior of employees. But while videocameras and embedded computer devices have demonstrated great precision in monitoring the work of data entry clerks and postal employees, gains in productivity have been offset by increases in absenteeism and reports of job stress and burnout. The lesson that we might learn from such efforts is that just because technology *can* be used for a given supervisory task doesn't mean that it *should.* Ensuring quality in the future of supervision is just as likely to involve rejecting new technology as it is to involve jumping on the bandwagon.

References

Aleksander, I., & Burnett, P. (1987). *Thinking machines.* New York: Knopf.

Bednar, A., & Levie, W. H. (1993). Attitude-change principles. In M. Fleming & W. H. Levie (Eds.), *Instructional message design* (pp. 283–304). Englewood Cliffs, NJ: Educational Technology Publications.

Burke, R. L. (1993). Role of technology in facilitating personnel evaluation. *Journal of Personnel Evaluation in Education, 7,* 235–238.

Hannafin, M. J. (1992). Emerging technologies, ISD, and learning environments: Critical perspectives. *Educational Technology Research and Development, 40*(1), 49–63.

Hansen, E., & Perry, D. (1993). Barriers to collaborative performance support systems in higher education. *Educational Technology, 33*(11), 46–52.

Hazi, H. (1989). *How have supervisors fared amidst the current reform movement?* Paper presented at the fall conference of the Council of Professors of Instructional Supervision, State College, PA.

Kuralt, R. C. (1987). The computer as a supervisory tool. *Educational Leadership, 44*(7), 71–72.

Merrill, M. D., Li, Z., & Jones, M. K. (1990). Limitations of first generation instructional design. *Educational Technology, 30*(1), 7–11.

Peterson, K. D. (1990). DOSSIER: A computer expert system simulation of professional judgments on schoolteacher promotion. *Journal of Educational Research, 83,* 134–139.

Reed, T. M., Toth, F. D., & Reed, M. M. (1987, February). *Computerized observation system (COS) for field experiences.* Paper presented at the annual meeting of the American Association of Colleges of Teacher Education, Washington, DC.

Verduin, J. R., & Clark, T. A. (1991). *Distance education.* San Francisco: Jossey-Bass.

Postnote

Will Technology Replace the Role of the Supervisor?

Technological advancements and innovations dramatically affect many aspects of our society. Developing technology is beginning to alter the delivery of instruction and will most certainly accelerate dramatically in the immediate future. As the use of technology expands at unprecedented rates, the need to carefully consider the role and judicious use of technology becomes essential. How are schools using technology to enhance their educational programming? How are distance learning, the Internet, computer-based instruction, and other multimedia technologies being utilized? What impact do these technologies have on the supervision of instruction?

Review Questions for

The Yes Response:

1. What is your reaction to Dr. Tracy's three premises?
2. Which of the techniques used in the Saturn School in St. Paul, Minnesota, can be adopted in your school/district?
3. To what degree has your school/district been technologically influenced in terms of (1) individualizing learning, (2) encouraging group interaction, (3) managing and coordinating learning, (4) fostering student expression, and (5) assisting students in knowledge production?
4. How can computer technology assist you as a teacher/supervisor?
5. In what ways do you foresee technology altering your role as a teacher or supervisor?
6. How might technology alter traditional supervisory roles and responsibilities?
7. How might technology alter teacher evaluation in your school/district?
8. In what ways might technologies be negatively used?
9. Tracy cites "four probable new or enhanced roles" for supervisors. Which of these roles is most relevant to you as a teacher/supervisor?
10. What indications have you seen that current models of supervision of instruction are becoming obsolete in light of emerging new technologies?

The No Response:

1. In what way is technology currently used in your school/district?
2. Does technology replace any of the fundamental roles that you play in the classroom?
3. Dr. Killian describes the use of word processors during observa-

tions. Have you ever been observed with one or have you ever used a laptop to observe a teacher? What are the advantages and disadvantages of using a word processor to observe teachers? If you use one, what ground rules might you first agree on with the teacher?

4. Have you ever used computers to collect and analyze observational data? How have computers assisted in this process?
5. What is your reaction to Killian's assertion that distance learning does not provide face to face contact between supervisor and teacher and is likely to be resisted?
6. Have you ever experienced an online conference as described by Killian?
7. What are potential risks of using artificial intelligence and other futuristic technological applications?
8. Killian ends her essay by highlighting some ground rules for using technology. What is your reaction to these ground rules?
9. Killian suggests that we educators often hop on the bandwagon and are too easily influenced by the latest innovations without scrutinizing their potential. What is your opinion? Provide evidence to back up your position.

For Further Research

1. Write a paper on these two questions: Which factors influence implementation of technology across schools and districts? What roles do schools, districts, states, and the federal government play in helping teachers adjust to the challenges and opportunities presented by new technologies?
2. Using computers and various technologies is increasingly common in schools throughout the world. Conduct a literature review that documents how these technologies are currently employed in schools.
3. Examine the history of technology and how technological advancements have affected teaching and learning since the turn of the century.
4. Reed, Toth, and Reed (1987) describe the Computerized Observation System (COS) to record and analyze classroom interaction. Research its usefulness. Are there any other kinds of customized observational software that can assist instructional supervision?
5. Conduct a survey of teachers/supervisors about their knowledge of various technologies and their willingness to incorporate new technologies.
6. What specific skills do you as a supervisor need to have to be "technologically competent?" Consult, for example, Bozeman and Spuck (1991), Kearsley and Lynch (1992), and Lauda (1994).
7. React to the position argued by some that most schools are impervious to change and will not be fundamentally altered by the

increasingly popular use of computers and other technologies.

8. Read King (in press) for a more complete discussion of the role of technology in supervision. Describe how futuristic technological applications might be employed in your school.

9. Assume you have been asked by your superintendent to conduct district-wide staff development on technology. Consult Bailey and Lumley (1994) and design a staff development program.

10. Computer scientist Joseph Weizenbaum wrote 18 years ago in his book *Computer Power and Human Reason*: "We must learn the limitations of our tools as well as their power. Even in its most advanced state, the computer is not, and never can be, a panacea for human problems or a substitute for our own, uniquely human judgement." Which of the authors in this chapter would more likely concur with Weizenbaum's statement? Why? Explain why you agree or disagree with his statement.

References

Bailey, G. D., & Lumley, D. (1994). *Technology staff development programs: A leadership sourcebook for school administrators.* New York: Scholastic.

Bozeman, W. C., & Spuck, D. W. (1991). Technological competence: Training educational leaders. *Journal of Research on Computing in Education, 23,* 514–529.

Kearsley, G., & Lynch, W. (1992). Educational leadership in the age of technology: The new skills. *Journal of Research on Computing in Education, 25,* 50–60.

King, J. M. (in press). Technology, computers, and telecommunications. In G. R. Firth & E. Pajak (Eds.), *Handbook of research on school supervision.* New York: Macmillan.

Lauda, D. P. (1994). Responding to the call for technological literacy. *NASSP Bulletin, 78,* 44–48.

Reed, T. M., Toth, F. D., & Reed, M. M. (1987, February). *Computerized observation system (COS) for field experiences.* Paper presented at the annual meeting of the American Association for Colleges of Teacher Education, Washington, DC.

Part Two

Perspectives on Critical Issues

✦ ✦ ✦ ✦

"After all, it all depends on your perspective"
—*Anonymous*

✦ ✦ ✦

Presented in this section of the book are various perspectives or viewpoints on important issues affecting the theory and practice of supervision. Consideration of these views is extremely relevant to any principled analysis of supervision in schools. Answers to questions posed in this section explore alternate ways of thinking about supervision, expanded ways of practicing supervision, the impact of the school organization on the work of supervisors, legal impediments to the supervisor/teacher dyad, and issues of diversity. Although not necessarily controversial, these and other issues challenge us to consider the multifaceted and complex nature of educational supervision. As you read these perspectives on critical issues ask yourself these key questions:

- What is the fundamental or specific issue addressed?
- What facts and opinions does the author cite to support her or his view?
- Can you summarize each view concisely?
- How do social, political, economic, cultural, philosophical, historical, legal, and other factors affect the issue?
- Do you agree or disagree with the author's conclusions? Explain.
- Can you suggest another way of viewing this issue?

The Perspectives

How Can We Move Toward a Community Theory of Supervision? Wrong Theory/Wrong Practice.

Is Supervision More Than the Surveillance of Instruction?

What is the New Supervisory Role in an Age of Complexity?

How Does the Law Affect Educational Supervision?

Why Is Advocacy for Diversity in Appointing Supervisory Leaders a Moral Imperative?

Perspective 1

How Can We Move Toward a Community Theory of Supervision? Wrong Theory/ Wrong Practice

✦ ✦ ✦ ✦

Thomas J. Sergiovanni, Trinity University

✦ ✦ ✦

Perspective Summary

Lillian Radford Professor of Education and Administration at Trinity University and distinguished scholar of educational supervision, Thomas J. Sergiovanni advances his theory of a community school and discusses its implications for supervision in schools. Dr. Sergiovanni maintains that current practice in supervision has yielded, at best, minimal gains in teaching and learning because the theory upon which supervision is based is flawed.

Guiding Questions

1. What assumptions does the author make about current theory and practice of supervision?
2. What is a community theory of supervision?
3. How does the traditional view of supervision contrast with the author's community view?
4. Could the author's suggestions for reform be implemented in your school?
5. What changes would be necessary to implement a community theory of supervision?

How Can We Move Toward a Community Theory of Supervision?

Thomas J. Sergiovanni

If the validity of supervisory practice depends on its governing theory, then we may have stumbled across the reason that our present supervisory practices remain legitimate and persist over time, even though they seem not to affect things very much.[1] New standards are provided, new models of supervision and evaluation emerge, new training programs are created to help principals and other supervisors improve their practice. But once in place, little of this supervision seems to affect the lives of teachers, their practice of teaching, or the learning of their students very much for very long. In *The Limits of Science* the Nobel Laureate, Peter Brian Medawar (1984) hinted at this problem when he stated, "No process of logical reasoning—no mere act of mind . . . can enlarge the information content of the axioms and premises or observation statements from which it proceeds" (p.79). His thought provides the basis for the *Law of Conservation of Information*, which states that no matter how refined a theory, model, or image of supervision becomes, and no matter how carefully it is translated into practice, this refinement cannot enlarge the basic premises upon which the theory, model, or vision rests.

The *Law of Perceptual Limits* holds that theories, models, and visions of supervision function as much like walls as they do like windows. As windows they are intended to help expand our view of things, resolve issues that we face, provide us with answers, and give us a better basis for functioning as researchers and practicing professionals. But because reality is mind dependent, these would-be windows function as walls that blind us to other views of reality, other understandings, and other alternatives. As Eisner (1985) explains:

> Theory is both an asset and a liability. It is an asset because it provides guidelines for perception: it points us in directions that enable us to see. But it is also a liability, because while it provides windows through which we attain focus, it creates walls that hamper our perceptions of those qualities and processes that are not addressed by the concepts we have chosen to use. Our theoretical frameworks function as templates for perception. Every template conceals some part of the landscape just as it brings other parts to our attention. (p.261)

Once the walls of theory are constructed, the supervisory realities created within them become scripts that program what we believe and do. The effects of the Law of Conservation of Information and the Law of Perceptual Limits are heightened by the cultural nature of school life. Culture and theory are connected. The heart and soul of school culture is what people believe, the assumptions they make about how schools work, and what they consider to be true and real. These factors, in turn, provide a *Theory of Acceptability* that lets people know how they should behave. Underneath each school culture is a Theory of Acceptability, and every school culture is driven by it. Efforts to change school cultures inevitably involve changing our theories of acceptability.

Let me give you an example of how the Law of Conservation of Information, the Law of Perceptual Limits, and the Theory of Acceptability help create work. It is a story about a teacher and a supervisor at the Crestwood school.

New teachers to Crestwood are assigned a mentor who provides support, helps with problems, and in other ways tries to make that difficult first year of teaching a successful one. When Theresa arrived at Crestwood as a new special education teacher, she was introduced to Arturo by the district's director of elementary education. Arturo had been an outstanding teacher at another school prior to becoming Crestwood's assistant principal the year before.

Theresa and Arturo hit it off from the beginning. They decided to begin their mentoring relationship by having Arturo teach the class for a while. Together they designed the classroom to accommodate his teaching style. Theresa became an "understudy" not only by observing Arturo's teaching but by trying to understand the subtleties of his teaching, his intents, his style, the ways in which he seemed to bring together curriculum, teaching, and learning environments for specific purposes.

From the beginning of their relationship, Arturo and Theresa were engaged in a continuous conversation about what was going on in the classroom. Arturo was interested in having Theresa focus on how he used teaching arrangements and learning designs to influence students' behaviors. He believed that issues of control are best handled informally rather than by direct intervention. Theresa was able to observe firsthand just how this could be accomplished.

Next it was Theresa's turn to take over the class. She understood that what made sense for Arturo might not make sense for her. She had to change the way the classroom was set up and think about teaching and learning arrangements in ways that fit her own style, needs, and intents. As Arturo explains, "Theresa was not lacking in ideas. She decided, for example, that the existing furniture wasn't suitable for how she wanted to work with the students. It happened that too many tables were ordered for one of the kindergarten classes, and I was able to get ten of those tables for Theresa's class. Together with the students the classroom was redecorated and turned into an amazingly lively place. Each student was able to create their own little area, and each was also provided with an aquarium. These aquariums served as living science exhibitions. Students brought such organisms as turtles, tadpoles, spiders, insects, plant life, and algae, and maintained these exhibitions physically, and also by keeping logs of their experiences in working with their mini-museums."

Arturo made frequent informal visits to Theresa's classroom. Each was followed by an open conversation about what was going on, about issues, and about other events that were of interest to Theresa. From time to time Theresa experienced some difficulties with her teaching. On one occasion it was her inability to reach a particular child. On another occasion it was a classroom management problem. In every case issues were dealt with openly. Arturo was also there for her when nonteaching problems arose. "One day Theresa brought a note from a parent for me to read. The parent was very hostile toward her. She wanted my advice as to how to respond. She prepared a response and shared it with me, but I felt that it sounded too defensive. After pointing this out, I suggested she replace a short phrase with one of my own. She was both amused and relieved with the suggestion, and used it with great success. She was very, very appreciative."

Theresa was delighted when Arturo shared with her several of the lesson plan books he had accumulated over the years as well as his daily logs, notes, and boxes of other materials that he had used when teaching. Theresa found these to be a treasury of inspirational and useful ideas. Clearly, Theresa and Arturo were off to a good start in their mentoring relationship.

I wish this story could end here. But shortly before the end of the first semester, the relationship between Theresa and Arturo cooled. In the beginning, it didn't matter that Arturo was the assistant principal. But as time went on, some of the other teachers at Crestwood asked Theresa whether she realized that sooner or later Arturo would be the person who would have to evaluate her. When evaluation time did come, Arturo scheduled a meeting with Theresa and explained the process. The meeting was a "preconference" of sorts that wound up being stressful for Theresa. Arturo did everything that he could to try to make her feel at ease, and he assured her that evaluating with the required state instrument would be little more than a pro-forma process. He was more interested in conducting an evaluation that would serve as a benchmark for where Theresa was and that would be helpful to her as she planned ahead. But Theresa was unconvinced. Two days later she requested that the mentoring relationship be discontinued.

In Arturo's words, "It was obvious that our relationship was changing. I had picked up on a few hints, but I wasn't sure until then. I talked to Theresa and asked her if she would feel comfortable writing me a letter telling me what the problem was from her perspective. 'I want you to be honest with me, and tell me how I might help things get back to where they were.'" Arturo received the following letter:

Dear Arturo:

   Last week I had a chance to discuss a wide variety of classroom frustrations with our associate psychologist when she came by for a meeting. It was valuable, and it made me remember how useful it was talking to you about similar concerns. It's a shame that I have to wait for these visits when your good advice is just down the hall, but I feel uneasy in seeking your counsel in our present respective positions. This is a disappointing aspect of our job relationships, which I'm sure frustrates you as much as me.

Although I still value your advice, I know that your obligations to other teachers and to administrative goals sometimes makes it hard for you to assist me in the way you used to. In your present supervisory position, I feel uncomfortable asking you about the challenges I often face in my classroom. It is difficult for me to share information, and speak in full candor, when I know that I must also maintain a professional level of control and preparation for observation and evaluation.

When we talk about my class, and you offer suggestions or theory, I can't receive your advice in the same casual way I used to. As my supervisor, your suggestion carries more weight, and I must treat it as a directive. You had suggested I post classroom rules. I decided not to. If you advise me to do this now, I would post them the next morning. This seems unfortunate, for we often need to explore several paths before choosing a successful course. I wish we could share a cup of coffee, and have a discussion about my class without thinking about future evaluations. I know that my class would benefit.

Please keep offering what advice you can under the circumstances. I will do my best to talk with you freely, in spite of professional concerns. Let me know if you have any good solutions to this dilemma.

Sincerely,

Theresa

What happened to Theresa? Why did her relationship with Arturo take this all too familiar turn? Theresa learned about the script of schooling and the role this script required her to play. The other teachers at Crestwood were veteran actors who had memorized the script and played their parts so naturally that they didn't think much about it anymore. According to this script, you can't get too cozy with supervisors because they might turn things around on you at evaluation time. Once Theresa became socialized to the norms of the existing culture, she behaved similarly. This script became part of her mindscape of reality.

Though most of us find the events described above regrettable, we are reluctant to challenge some basic assumptions behind the theory that leads us to think about supervision and evaluation in this way. Arturo, we reason, is the assistant principal. Theresa needs to accept that and at the same time trust Arturo enough to know that he will help rather than hurt her, that she will be treated fairly, and so on. Besides, that is what supervisory training is all about—teaching the Arturos to work with the Theresas in such a way that the Theresas accept the offered supervision.

What is not considered by this kind of reasoning is the *why* question. Arturo's obvious competence notwithstanding, why do we assume that teachers should automatically be evaluated by principals or other supervisors? Indeed why do we link supervision to hierarchy, anyway? Is it because our present theories assume that hierarchy equals expertise? In many instances this is indeed the case. After all, knowledge about teaching and learning and the ability to share these insights with teachers are key factors in any good supervisor selection process. But few would argue that one is better able to evaluate everyone else who is lower in the hierarchy just because of her or his position.

The answer to the why question posed above is *because* schools are understood as formal organizations, and what goes on in them is understood as organizational behavior. Supervision borrows its fundamental frames for thinking about how schools should be structured and coordinated, how compliance within them should be achieved, what supervision is and how it works, how teachers should be evaluated, inserviced and helped, and virtually everything else from organizational theory and behavior. Even the theories of human nature and motivation that dominate supervisory thinking and practice are defined by the organizational frame. These theories are built on the simple premise that as human beings we are motivated by self-interest and thus seek to maximize our gains and cut our losses.

How Organizational Theories Work

The phrase "to organize" provides a good clue to how organizational thinking forces us to think about schools. To organize means to arrange things into a coherent whole. First, there has to be a reason for organizing. Then a careful study of each of the parts to be organized needs to be done, and a plan needs to be developed that enables the parts to be arranged according to the desired scheme. As the plan is followed, it becomes important to monitor progress and make corrections as needed. Finally, when the work is completed, the organizational arrangements are evaluated in terms of original intents. Organizational thinking prizes rationality, and thus schools understood as formal organizations must keep up the appearance of being rational in order to maintain legitimacy. As a result, as Meyer (1984) points out, schools develop explicit administrative and supervisory structures and procedures that give a convincing account that the proper means–ends chains are in place to accomplish the purposes.

Organizing schools into departments and grade levels, developing job descriptions, constructing curriculum plans, and putting into place instructional delivery systems of various kinds are all examples of attempts to communicate to everyone that the school knows what it is doing. Emphasizing rules and regulations and monitoring and supervising teachers are forms and rituals that communicate to everyone that the school is in control. From time to time these rational processes get dressed up with new labels and new language systems ("strategic planning" and "Total Quality Management" are recent examples), but underneath they remain the same. Teachers, in turn, develop similar schemes and efforts to control students.

As suggested in the Crestwood story, there is an assumption in organizations that hierarchy equals expertise. Those higher in the hierarchy are presumed to know more about teaching, learning, and other matters of schooling than those lower, and thus each person in the school is evaluated by the next higher level. Moreover, organizational thinking encourages us to assume that hierarchy equals moral superiority. As teachers move up the ranks into supervisory positions, it is presumed not only that they know more about teaching and learning and other matters of schooling but that they care more as well. That is why those higher in the hierarchy are trusted with more responsibility, more authority, and less supervision. Organizations are creatures of people, but over time they become separated from people by functioning independently in pursuit of their own goals and purposes. This separation has to be bridged somehow. Ties have to be developed that connect people to their work and that connect people to others with whom they work. In schools as organizations, these ties are contractual. Each person acts separately in negotiating a settlement with others and in negotiating a settlement with the school itself that best meets his or her needs.

Self-interest is assumed to be the primary motive in these negotiations. For supervisors to get teachers to do what needs to be done, rewards and punishments must be traded for compliance. Teachers teach the way they are supposed to in efforts to win good evaluations. Good evaluations lead to better assignments and improved prospects for promotion. Teachers who are cooperative get picked to attend workshops and conferences. A similar pattern of trading rewards and compliance emerges in classrooms and characterizes the broader relationships that exist between students and their schools. In this environment, leadership takes the form of bartering. Supervisors and teachers and teachers and students strike bargains within which the former in each case gives the latter something they want in exchange for compliance. Everyone becomes connected to their work for calculated reasons. Students behave as long as they get the rewards they desire. Teachers respond for the same reasons. When rewards are no longer available or valued, less effort is given in return.

In his seminal book, *Leadership in Administration*, Phillip Selznik (1957) pointed out that organizations are made up of standard building blocks that lend themselves to manipulation by administrators and supervisors who are interchangeable across all organizations and whose practices involve the use of generic theories, concepts, and skills. As a result, their roles are generalized to the point that they become similar to parallel roles in other organizations. From an organizational perspective, successfully managing a shoe store, bank, insurance company, auto manufacturer, high-tech corporation, hospital, corporation, day care center, church, volunteer group, civic enterprise, mutual aid society, school, or family requires the same insights, know-how, and skills.

When all enterprises are managed and led the same way, however, none are managed and led very well. Whatever the nature of the enterprise, those that are able to function with integrity and character create structures and engage in activities that are uniquely adapted to their purposes, and that are uniquely adapted to their societal roles. They develop distinctive ways of making decisions, distinctive commitments to their purposes, distinctive ways of operating, and distinctive connections to the people they serve. In Selznick's (1957) words:

> In this way the organization as a technical instrument takes on values. As a vehicle of group integrity, it becomes in some degree an end in itself. This process of being infused with value is part of what we mean by institutionalization. As this occurs, *organization management* becomes *institutional leadership* ... the building of integrity is part of what we have called the "institutional embodiment of purpose" and its protection is a major function of leadership. (pp. 138–139)

Selznick's theory of institutional leadership provides a major breakthrough in understanding the way societies, organizations, and institutions work, and it has much to contribute to how schools should be viewed and how supervision should be practiced within them. Institutional leadership seeks to bring integrity to an enterprise and seeks to transform the enterprise from an organization to an "institution." As the process of institutionalization occurs, schools evolve away from being generic organizations to becoming distinctive communities. This evolution to community provides the school not only with a distinctive character but with a defense of integrity that allows it to develop a distinctive competence.

How Communities Work

How are communities different from organizations? Communities are organized around relationships and ideas. They create social structures that bring people together in a oneness and bind them to a set of shared values and ideas. Communities are defined by their centers of values, sentiments, and beliefs that provide the needed conditions for creating a sense of "we" from "I."

In communities members create their lives with others who have similar intentions. Both organizations and communities must deal with issues of control, but instead of relying on external control measures, communities rely more on norms, purposes, values, professional socialization, collegiality, and natural interdependence. As community connections become established in schools, they become substitutes for formal systems of supervision, evaluation, and staff development.

The ties of community also redefine how empowerment and collegiality are understood. In organizations empowerment is understood as having something to do with shared decision making, site-based management, and similar schemes. Within communities, empowerment focuses less on rights, discretion, and freedom, and more on commitments, obligations, and duties that people feel toward each other and toward the school. Collegiality in organizations results in part from administrative arrangements that encourage or force people to work together, and in part from the team-building skills of principals. In communities, since community members are connected to each other for such moral reasons as mutual obligations, shared traditions, and other normative ties, collegiality is something that comes from within. Members feel compelled to help each other, and to share with each other, because doing so is right and is part of one's job. Communities, as Etzioni (1993) reminds us, speak to their members in moral voices.

A Theory of Community for Schools

In *Building Community in Schools* (1994) I gathered together from many sources ideas, examples, and experiences with community into a framework that could help principals, parents, and teachers struggle to build community. Since community means different things in different disciplines, I proposed that for schools we define the term as follows: collections of individuals who are bonded together by natural will and who are together bound to a set of shared ideas and ideals. This bonding and binding is tight enough to transform them from a collection of "I's" into a collective "we." As a "we," members are part of a tightly knit web of meaningful relationships. This "we" usually shares a common place and over time comes to share common sentiments and traditions that are sustaining.

I then proposed that the concepts *gemeinschaft* and *gesellschaft* could help us to understand this definition and the forms it might take as schools become communities. The use of foreign words can seem pretentious, but this risk is worth taking. *Gemeinschaft* and *gesellschaft* are special words in sociology that communicate a set of concepts and ideas well known in that discipline. When a sociologist, for example, observes that one group of individuals, one town, or one school is more gemeinschaft than another, those familiar with the terms have a detailed image of what is meant.

Gemeinschaft translates to community and gesellschaft to society. Writing in 1887, Ferdinand Tonnies (1957) used the terms to describe the changes in values and orientations that were taking place in life as we moved first from a hunting and gathering society, then to an agricultural society, and then on to an industrial society. Each of these transformations resulted in a shift away from gemeinschaft toward gesellschaft, away from a vision of life as sacred community toward a more secular society. Though gemeinschaft and gesellschaft do not exist in pure form in the real world, they represent two "ideal types," two ways of thinking and living, two types of cultures, two alternative visions of life.

Tonnies (1957) argued that as society moves toward the gesellschaft end of the continuum, community values are replaced by contractual ones. Among any collection of people, for example, social relationships don't just happen, they are willed. Individuals decide to associate with each other, and the reasons they do so are important. In gemeinschaft natural will is the motivating force. Individuals decide to relate to each other because doing so has its own intrinsic meaning and significance. There is no tangible goal or benefit in mind for any of the parties to the relationship. In gesellschaft rational will is the motivating force. Individuals decide to relate to each other to reach some goal, to gain some benefit. Without this benefit there would be no relationship, and once the benefit is lost, the relationship ends. In the first instance the ties among people are moral. In the second instance the ties among people are calculated.

The modern corporation is an example of gesellschaft. Within the corporation relationships are formal and distant, having been prescribed by roles and expectations. Circumstances are evaluated by universal criteria as embodied in policies, rules, and protocols. Acceptance is conditional. The more a person cooperates with the corporation and achieves for the corporation, the more likely she or he will be accepted. Relationships are competitive. Those who achieve more are valued more by the corporation. Not all concerns of members are legitimate. Legitimate concerns are bounded by roles rather than needs. Subjectivity is frowned upon. Rationality is prized. Self-interest prevails.

Gesellschaft values make sense in the corporation and in other organizations such as the army, the research university, and the hospital. But applying the same values to a small African-American church, the family, a social club, the neighborhood, a mutual aid society, the small town, a volunteer social action group, *or the school* raises important questions of effectiveness and goodness.

All social enterprises must solve the connections problem if they are to function effectively. Members, for example, must be sufficiently connected to each other in some way so that they can communicate with each other, understand each other, and coordinate their activities. And members must be sufficiently connected to the enterprise's purposes and values so that, either willingly or unwillingly, they will function to reflect or achieve them.

Gesellschaft enterprises maintain connections by bartering rewards or punishments for loyalty and compliance. Members work for pay or for psychological rewards, and their involvement, as a result, is calculated. As long as they get what they want, they give what they have to. But when they calculate otherwise, their involvement decreases.

Gemeinschaft enterprises, by contrast, do not ignore "what gets rewarded gets done," but strive to go beyond calculated to committed involvement. They strive to develop relationships among people that have moral overtones. They understand the importance of identifying with place and space over a period of time and of providing members with security, sense, and meaning. And they recognize that in the end the ties that bind us together come from sharing with others a common commitment to a set of ideas and ideals.

Tonnies (1957) refers to these ties as community by relationships, community of place, and community of mind. Community by relationships characterizes the special kinds of connections among people that create a unity of being similar to that found in families and other closely knit collections of people. Community of place characterizes the sharing of a common habitat or locale. This sharing of place with others for sustained periods of time creates a special identity and a shared sense of belonging that connects people in special ways. Community of mind emerges from the binding of people to common goals, shared values, and shared conceptions of being and doing. Together the three represent webs of meaning that uniquely connect people by creating a special sense of belonging and a strong common identity.

As schools struggle to become communities, they address questions such as the following: What can be done to increase the sense of family, neighborliness, and collegiality among the faculty of a school? How can the faculty become more of a professional community where everyone cares about each other and helps each other to be together, to learn together, and to lead together? What kinds of relationships need to be cultivated with parents that will enable them to be included in this emerging community? How can the web of relationships that exist among teachers and between teachers and students be defined so that they embody community? How can teaching and learning settings be arranged so that they are more like family? How can the school itself, as a collection of families, be more like a neighborhood? What are the shared values and commitments that enable the school to become a community of mind? How will these values and commitments become practical standards that can guide the lives community members want to lead, what community members learn and how, and how community members treat each other? What are the patterns of mutual obligations and duties that emerge in the school as community is achieved?

Though not cast in stone, community understandings have enduring qualities. They are resilient enough to survive the passage of members through the community over time. They are taught to new members, celebrated in customs and rituals, and embodied as standards that govern life in the community. As suggested by Bellah and his colleagues (1985), enduring understandings create a fourth form of community—community of memory. In time, communities of relationships, of place, and of mind become communities of memory. Being a part of a community of memory sustains us when the going is tough; connects us when we are not physically present; and provides us with a history for creating sense and meaning.

What are the implications of community for how we understand schools, how we arrange for teaching and learning, and how we supervise? These are invitational questions. Answers require that we begin a new conversation within supervisory academic circles and among our colleagues who are working as supervisors in the schools. My guess is that with community as the theory we would have to restructure in such a way that the school itself is not defined by brick and mortar but by ideas and tight connections. Creating communities of relationships and of place, for example, might well mean changing most high schools from large organizations into several small schools rarely exceeding 400 or so students.

The importance of creating sustained relationships would require that students and teachers stay together for longer periods of time. Teaching in 50-minute episodes would have to be replaced with something else. Elementary schools would have to give serious consideration to organizing themselves into smaller and probably multi-aged families. Discipline problems would no longer be based on psychological principles but on moral ones. The use of moral principles would require abandoning such taken-for-granted ideas as having explicit rules linked to clearly stated consequences that are uniformly applied, in favor of the development of social contracts, constitutions, and normative codes.

Inservice and staff development would move from the administrative side of the ledger to the teacher side as part of teachers' ongoing commitment to practice at the edge of their craft. Teachers and supervisors would have to share responsibility for implementing and accountability for sustaining the quality of the various other supervisory functions. Extrinsic reward systems would have to disappear. The number of specialists would probably be reduced and pull-outs would be less common as families of teachers and students, like families of parents and children, take fuller responsibility for solving their own problems. And all of these changes would necessitate the invention of new standards of quality, new strategies for accountability and new ways of working with people—the invention of a new school leadership, in other words.

Implications for Leadership

A *community theory of supervision* takes us to the roots of school leadership. Leadership is generally viewed as a process of getting a group to take action that embodies the leader's purposes (as is typically the case in business organizations) or shared purposes (as should be the case in schools). It is different from commanding or bribing compliance in that it involves influencing others by persuasion, by example, or by tapping inner moral forces. This influence, however, is typically reciprocal. Unless followers are willing to be led, leaders can't lead. Further, groups naturally create norms that constitute a cultural order or way of life. Leaders must be part of that order even as they attempt to change it, or their leadership will be rejected. Faced with either the fear or the reality of rejection, they resort to commanding or requiring compliance. But when they do this, follower commitment is sacrificed and compliance is difficult to maintain over time.

For leadership to work, leaders and followers need to be tied together by a consensual understanding that mediates this pattern of reciprocal influence. In schools, a reciprocal process of leaders and followers influencing each other to action involves not only issues of shared purposes but roles that are connected to moral obligations. Just as teachers, parents, and students have roles linked to moral obligations, supervisors are expected to meet the obligations that come from their role responsibilities as leaders.

It is through morally held role responsibilities that we can understand school leadership in its more traditional sense. School leadership is bound not just to standards of technical competence but, to use Bellah and his colleagues' (1985) distinction, to *standards of public obligation* as well. Standards of public obligation always override technical standards when the two are in conflict. At the root of the leader's role responsibilities we find a commitment to administer to the needs of the school as an institution by serving its purposes, by serving those who struggle to embody these purposes, and by acting as a guardian of the institutional integrity of the school. The first roles of school leaders, as we shall soon discuss, are ministerial ones.

How are ministerial roles embodied in practice? What are the tasks that, for example, principals and other designated supervisors should perform as leaders? The following nine tasks are worth considering:

1. *Purposing*—bringing together shared visions into a covenant that speaks compellingly to principals, teachers, parents, and students with a moral voice.
2. *Maintaining harmony*—building a consensual understanding of school purposes, of how the school should function, and of the moral connections between roles and responsibilities, while respecting individual conscience and individual style differences.

3. *Institutionalizing values*—translating the school's covenant into a workable set of procedures and structures that facilitates the accomplishment of school purposes and provides norm systems for directing and guiding behavior.
4. *Motivating*—providing for the basic psychological needs of members on the one hand and for the basic cultural needs of members to experience sensible and meaningful school lives on the other.
5. *Managing*—ensuring the necessary day-to-day support (planning, organizing, agenda setting, mobilizing resources, providing procedures, recordkeeping, etc.) that keeps the school running effectively and efficiently.
6. *Explaining*—giving reasons for asking members to do certain things and giving explanations that link what they are doing to the larger picture.
7. *Enabling*—removing obstacles that prevent members from meeting their commitments on one hand and providing resources and support that helps members to meet their commitments on the other.
8. *Modeling*—accepting responsibility as head follower of the school's covenant by modeling purposes and values in thought, word, and action.
9. *Supervising*—providing the necessary oversight to ensure that the school is meeting its commitments and, when it is not, to find out why, and help everyone do something about it.

The Role of Supervision

Most of the tasks listed above are understandable. But including the supervising task as part of the responsibilities of leadership may need some explaining. The word *supervision*, for example, has a gesellschaft tinge that conjures up factory images of foremen checking up on workers as in "snoopervision." But supervision was originally a virtuous word that referred to the carrying out of one's stewardship responsibilities. Traditionally stewardship meant overseeing and caring for an institution such as a university, church, or school.

When principals function as stewards by providing for the overseeing and caring of their schools, they are not so much managers or executives as they are administrators. According to *Webster's*, to manage means to handle, to control, to make submissive, to direct affairs, to achieve one's purposes. *Webster's* defines an executive as an individual or group designated to control or direct an organization. *Administer*, by contrast, means to serve, to minister, and to "superintend the execution, use, or conduct of" an enterprise. *Superintend*, in turn, means attending to, giving attention to, having oversight over what is intended. It means, in other words, supervision. As supervisor the principal acts *in loco parentis* in relation to students, ensuring that all is well for them. As supervisor the principal acts as a trustee in relation to parents, ensuring that all is well for them, too. And as supervisor the principal acts as steward, guarding and protecting the school's purposes and structures.

Much of the literature on school supervision tries to provide for the caring and oversight of teaching and learning in schools, but it is hampered by being too connected to the kind of supervision found in gesellschaft organizations. Needed is a new definition of supervision that reclaims its original intent. Instead of looking to business organizations, we might begin this process of reclamation by trying to understand how supervision is defined and how it functions in churches, families, youth associations, mutual help societies, and other gemeinschaft enterprises that have been less influenced by business values. We might, for example, look to pastoral supervision to see what insights might help us to develop a supervision unique to the school.

Kenneth Pohly (1993), Director of the Center for Supervisory Studies of the United Theological Seminary, defines pastoral supervision as "doing and reflecting on ministry in which a supervisor (teacher) and one or more supervisees (learners) covenant together to reflect critically on their ministry as a way of growing in self-awareness, ministering competence, theological understanding, and christian commitment" (p.75). In schools we might read "theological understanding" and "christian commitment" as an idea structure based on teaching and learning and other school issues that translates readily into the traditions and shared values that make up the school's covenant as it becomes a community.

Pohly believes that supervision is pastoral, is a way of doing ministry, is covenantal, is reflective, and is intentional. It is pastoral "in the sense of its shepherding nature, that is, its care-giving. This includes everyone involved—supervisees as well as supervisors. The giving and receiving of care is something in which all supervisory participants engage." It is a way of doing ministry because "it provides a way for persons to engage in the same ministry as colleagues, as co-participants." It is covenantal in the sense that it "occurs within an agreement in which persons say to each other: `This is what we will do together, and for which we will hold one another accountable.' " It is reflective because "it occurs within a supervisory conversation in which the participants reflect critically upon their ministry." And it is intentional, as it seeks to help people understand themselves more clearly, to assist them in developing their competencies, in clarifying their understandings, and in deepening their commitments to the enterprise (Pohly, 1993, pp. 75–76).

Supervision in communities implies accountability, but not in the tough, inspectoral sense suggested by factory images of inspection and control. Instead, it implies an accountability embedded in tough and tender caring. Principals and other designated supervisors care enough about the school, about the values and purposes that underlie it, about the students who are being served, about the parents whom they represent, and about the teachers upon whom they depend, to do whatever is necessary to *protect* school values and purposes on one hand and to *enable* their accomplishment on the other.

In a recent interview Deborah Meier, Co-Director of the celebrated Central Park East Secondary School in New York City, was asked, "What is the role of the principal in an effective school?" (Scherer, 1994) Her response shows how the various ministerial roles of the principal are brought together by supervision understood as an expression of stewardship:

> Someone has to keep an eye on the whole and alert everyone when parts need close- or long-range attention. A principal's job is to put forth to the staff an agenda. The staff may or may not agree, but they have an opportunity to discuss it. I'll say, "Listen, I've been around class after class, and I notice this, don't notice this, we made a commitment to be accountable for one another, but I didn't see anybody visiting anybody else's class. . . . " Paul [Schwartz, Meier's Co-Director] and I also read all the teacher's assessments of students. Once we noticed that the 9th and the 10th math teachers often said the kids didn't seem to have an aptitude for math. We asked the math staff, "How can these kids do nicely in 7th and 8th grade, and then seem inept in 9th and 10th? Are we fooling ourselves in 7th and 8th, or are we fooling ourselves in 9th and 10th? Because they are the same kids." (p.7)

Meier and Schwartz both practice leadership that is idea based. The source of authority they appeal to is the values that are central to the school and the commitments that everyone has made to them. And because of this, their supervisory responsibilities do not compromise democratic principles, dampen teacher empowerment, or get in the way of community building. Both directors are committed to creating a staff-run school with high standards—one where staff must know each other, be familiar with each other's work, and know how the school operates. As Meier (1992) explains,

> Decisions are made as close to each teacher's own classroom setting as possible, although all decisions are ultimately the responsibility of the whole staff. The decisions are not merely on minor matters–length of classes or the number of field trips. The teachers collectively decide on content, pedagogy, and assessment as well. They teach what they think matters . . . governance is simple. There are virtually no permanent standing committees. Finally, we work together to develop assessment systems for our students, their families, ourselves, and the broader public. Systems that represent our values and beliefs in as direct a manner as possible. (p.607)

Of course, principals and other designated supervisors can't be tough about values, standards, role responsibilities, and meeting commitments without also being tender by accepting responsibility for enabling teachers to meet their commitments. Central Park East Secondary School works hard to do just that by providing structures and other arrangements that enable teachers to reflect on their own teaching, and the teaching of their colleagues, and to give each other support (Meier, 1991, p. 144).

Supervision as Pedagogical Leadership

With supervision as an expression of stewardship at the core, the tasks of leadership are brought together when principals and other school leaders practice leadership as a form of pedagogy. *Pedagogy* is not a term in popular use in North America, and when it is used it refers vaguely to instruction, curriculum, or teaching. But the term has deep historical roots and meanings that are worth reviving. Max van Mannen (1991) explains,

> . . . the term *pedagague* derives from the Greek, and refers not to the teacher, but to the watchful slave or guardian whose responsibility it was to lead (*agogos*) the young boy (*paides*) to school. . . . The adult had the task of accompanying the child, of being with the child, of caring for the child. The pedagogue would be expected to see to it that the child stayed out of trouble, and behaved properly. This is a kind of "leading" that often walks *behind* the one who is led. The slave, or pedagogue, was there *in loco parentis*. (p.37)

The pedagogue's job, as a teacher, principal, coach, guardian, slave, or other adult, was to provide the child with a sense of protection, direction, and orientation—a role shared with parents and exercised in their absence. And since this role was so important to the development of the best interest of the child and to the protection of the interests of parents, it implied a form of leadership. "The original Greek idea of pedagogy had associated with it the meaning of *leading* in the sense of accompanying the child and living with the child in such a way as to provide direction and care for his or her life" (van Mannen, 1991, p.38).

Teachers practice a form of pedagogical leadership directly, since in schools they stand first and closest in a caring relationship to children. They have the major responsibility for guiding children academically, socially, and spiritually through the world of childhood to adulthood. Indeed, the process of education in itself implies leadership. Children, as van Mannen explains, must eventually grow out of (*educere*, to lead out of) the world of childhood, and adults must help children grow into (*educare*, to lead into) the world of adulthood (p.38).

Supervisors practice leadership as a form of pedagogy by facilitating this process and by ensuring that the interests of children are served well. A key part of this practice is the ability of the leader to "mobilize" people and community to face their problems and to make progress in solving them (Heifetz, 1994). In this sense the pedagogy they practice is understood as a form of authority that ensures that good decisions are made, that people face up to their responsibilities, and that things work right for children. This pedagogical authority, however, is not authoritarian in the sense that it is exercised simply because principals have more power than teachers or students, but it is authoritative. Its legitimacy comes in part from the virtuous responsibility associated with the supervisor's role.

Endnotes

1. This article is drawn from *Leadership for the Schoolhouse: How is it Different? Why is it Important?* San Francisco: Jossey-Bass, 1996.

References

Bellah, R. N., Madser, R., Sullivan, W. M., Swidler, A., & Tipto, S. M. (1985). *Habits of the heart: Individualism and commitment in American life.* New York: HarperCollins, 1985.

Eisner, E. W. (1985). *The art of educational evaluation: A personal view.* (1985). Philadelphia: Falmer Press.

Etzioni, A. (1993). *The spirit of community rights, responsibilities, and the communitarian agenda.* New York: Crown Publishers.

Heifetz, R. A. (1994). *Leadership without easy answers.* Cambridge, MA: Harvard University Press.

van Mannen, M. (1991). *The tact of teaching: The meaning of pedagogical thoughtfulness.* Albany: State University of New York Press.

Medawar, P. B. (1984). *The limits of science.* New York: Harper & Row.

Meier, D. (1991). The kindergarten tradition in high school. In K. Jarvis & C. Montag (Eds.), *Progressive education for the 1990s: Transforming practice.* New York: Teachers College Press.

Meier, D. (1992). Reinventing teaching. *Teachers College Record, 93,* 594–609.

Meyer, J. W. (1984). Organizations as ideological systems. In T. J. Sergiovanni & J. E. Corbally (Eds.), *Leadership and organizational culture.* Urbana–Champaign, IL: University of Illinois Press.

Pohly, K. (1993). *Transforming the rough places: The ministry of supervision.* Daton, OH: Whaleprints.

Scherer, M. (1994). On schools where students want to be: A conversation with Deborah Meier. *Educational Leadership, 52*(4–8).

Selznik, P. (1957). *Leadership In administration: A sociological interpretation.* Berkeley: University of California Press.

Sergiovanni, T. J. (1994). *Building community in schools.* San Francisco: Jossey-Bass.

Tonnies, F. (1957). *Gemeinschaft und gesellschaft [Community and Society].* (C. P. Loomis, Ed. and Trans.). New York: Harper Collins. (original work published 1887).

Postnote

How Can We Move toward a Community Theory of Supervision? Wrong Theory/Wrong Practice

Dr. Sergiovanni's work over the past several years, of which this piece is representative, has pointed to new ways of conceiving schools. Attempting to create a new paradigm for the theory and practice of supervision, Sergiovanni has expanded our perspectives and shattered what Schutz (1964) calls our "social world as taken for granted" (p. 229). Sergiovanni has laid the groundwork for a new vision of schools and proffers a sense of hope that it is indeed possible to restructure our schools as caring and cooperative communities. Still, his vision will remain unfulfilled unless the language and culture of community are embraced and forged with a new understanding of supervision in schools.

Review Questions

1. What is your opinion of Sergiovanni's claim that supervisory practice doesn't have much effect on educational outcomes?
2. What do the Laws of Conservation of Information and Perceptual Limits, as discussed by Sergiovanni, tell you about the theory and practice of supervision?
3. In your opinion, what does the Theory of Acceptability reveal about efforts to change your school?
4. How does the Crestwood story demonstrate the relationship among the Law of Conservation of Information, the Law of Perceptual Limits, and the Theory of Acceptability?
5. As related in the Crestwood story, describe Arturo's supervisory strategies in working with Theresa. Were his efforts successful? Explain.
6. As a supervisor, how would you have worked with Theresa?
7. React to the event(s) that precipitated the change in Theresa's attitude toward Arturo.
8. If you were Arturo, how would you respond to the letter that Theresa sent?
9. According to Sergiovanni, why did Theresa's relationship with Arturo take a turn for the worse? Explain.
10. A frame is a lens that affects what we see and how we interpret meaning (Bolman & Deal, 1991). According to Sergiovanni, how does the traditional organizational frame influence the way teachers and supervisors relate to one another?
11. How does the organizational frame, as conceived by Sergiovanni, influence you as a supervisor?
12. According to Sergiovanni, how are communities different from organizations?

13. Explain the relationship and difference between *gemeinschaft* and *gesellschaft*.
14. Give an example of an enterprise conceived as gesellschaft. Give one example of an enterprise conceived as gemeinschaft.
15. According to Sergiovanni, collegiality in organizations does not foster shared visions and mutual obligations. How would Professor Pavan (see Issue 7) respond?
16. Sergiovanni maintains that as long as schools are conceived as formal organizations "new labels and new language systems" such as Total Quality Management are ineffective in fundamentally changing schools. How would Professor Snyder respond (see Perspective 3)?
17. In general, what would a "community" school look like?
18. More specifically, what kinds of relationships need to be cultivated so that teachers and principals work toward a professional community? What kinds of relationships need to be cultivated with parents that will enable them to be included in a community school? How will teaching and learning settings be arranged under a community theory of schooling?
19. What would "leadership" look like in a school guided by a community theory? What are the implications for supervision?
20. In the Crestwood story, how might the problems encountered by Theresa and Arturo be resolved under a community theory of supervision?
21. What other changes in schools are likely under a community theory of supervision?
22. How likely are schools to become "communities?"
23. What practical changes are necessary to bring about a new community theory of schooling? of supervision?

For Further Research

1. Compare Covey's (1989) use of "scripting" with the way Sergiovanni uses the term. What does scripting teach us about life in schools?
2. Sergiovanni asserts that extrinsic reward systems aren't necessary under newly constituted community schools. Compare Alfie Kohn's (1993) thesis in *Punished by Rewards* with Sergiovanni's belief in shared values that foster intrinsic rewards. Why would Kohn's ideas find justification within a community school?
3. Sergiovanni bases his thesis on "moral" principles. Describe his conception of supervision as a moral enterprise. See, for example, Sergiovanni and Starratt (1993), and Sergiovanni (1990, 1991, 1992); compare Blumberg (1989) and Tom (1984).
4. Research Selznick's (1957) Theory of Institutional Leadership and explain why Sergiovanni asserts that it "provides a major breakthrough" in the way " . . . schools should be viewed and how supervision should be practiced" within schools.

5. Research Deborah Meier's Central Park East Secondary School (1573 Madison Ave., New York City 10029) and explain why Sergiovanni considers her model of supervision as community theory in action. See Meier (1987, 1992, 1993, 1995). Also see Lieberman, Falk, and Alexander (1995).

6. Read Sergiovanni (1994a) and write a book review. See Mooser (1995). Read Pohly (1993), as quoted and discussed by Sergiovanni, and explore the notion of a "ministry of supervision" and its relevance to supervision as practiced in public schools.

7. Compare Sarason's (1990, 1995) call for a complete restructuring of the way schools are governed with Sergiovanni's reform proposals. Also see Barth (1990), Darling-Hammond (1993), and Fullan (1991).

8. Research the origins of supervision. According to Sergiovanni, the term *supervision* was originally a "virtuous word that referred to the carrying out of one's stewardship responsibilities." He states that a new definition of supervision is needed "that reclaims its original intent." See, for example, Tanner and Tanner (1987) for a similar claim. But compare Sergiovanni's claim with statements made by the following writers, who assert that supervision was anything but "virtuous": Elsbree (1939), Spears (1953), and Glanz (in press). Also see Glanz's *No* response in Issue 6.

9. Explore Sergiovanni's works on organizations and leadership. See, for example, Sergiovanni and Corbally (1986) and Sergiovanni (1994b).

10. Develop a skit in which two principals conduct a post-observation conference with a teacher each has just observed. Role-play how a principal espousing a traditional view of organizations and leadership might confront this teacher and role-play how a principal in Sergiovanni's "community" school might approach the situation. Discuss differences in approaches and implications for supervision in general.

11. For a more global treatment of the "community" concept see Oakes and Quartz (1995). Describe efforts to build "new educational communities." Also, explore possible connections between "caring learning communities" (Cooper & Boyd, 1995; Noddings, 1992; *Phi Delta Kappan, 76*(9)) and Sergiovanni's notions of community.

References

Barth, R. (1990). *Improving schools from within.* San Francisco: Jossey-Bass.

Blumberg, A. (1989). *School administration as a craft.* Boston: Allyn & Bacon.

Bolman, L. G., & Deal, T. E. (1991). *Reframing organizations.* San Francisco: Jossey-Bass.

Cooper, C., & Boyd, J. (1995). Schools as collaborative learning communities. *Cooperative Learning, 15,* 3–7.

Covey, S. R. (1989). *The seven habits of highly effective people.* New York: Simon & Schuster.

Darling-Hammond, L. (1993). Reframing the school reform agenda: Developing capacity for school transformation. *Phi Delta Kappan, 74,* 753–761.

Elsbree, W. S. (1939). *American teacher: Evolution of a profession in a democracy.* New York: American Book Company.

Fullan, M. G. (1991). *The new meaning of educational change.* New York: Teachers College Press.

Glanz, J. (in press). Histories, antecedents, and legacies: Constructing a history of school supervision. In G. R. Firth & E. Pajak (Eds.), *Handbook of research on school supervision.* New York: Macmillan.

Kohn, A. (1993). *Punished by rewards: The trouble with gold stars, incentive plans, A's, praise and other bribes.* Boston: Houghton Mifflin.

Lieberman, A., Falk, B., & Alexander, L. (1995). A culture in the making: Leadership in learner-centered schools. In J. Oakes, & K. H. Quartz (Eds.), *Creating new educational communities: Ninety-fourth yearbook of the national society for the study of education, part I* (pp. 108–129). Chicago: The University of Chicago Press.

Meier, D. (1987). Success in East Harlem. *American Educator, 11,* 34–39.

Meier, D. (1992). Reinventing teaching. *Teachers College Record, 93,* 594–609.

Meier, D. (1993). Transforming schools into powerful communities. *Teachers College Record, 94,* 654–658.

Meier, D. (1995). How our schools could be. *Phi Delta Kappan, 76,* 369–373.

Mooser, E. K. (1995). Review of the book *Building community in schools. Teachers College Record, 96,* 580–582.

Noddings, N. (1992). *The challenge to care in schools.* New York: Teachers College Press.

Oakes, J., & Quartz, K. H. (Eds.). (1995). *Creating new educational communities: Ninety-fourth yearbook of the national society for the study of education, part I.* Chicago: The University of Chicago Press.

Phi Delta Kappan, 76(9). Special section: Youth and caring, 665–721.

Pohly, K. H. (1993). *Transforming the rough places: The ministry of supervision.* Dayton, OH: Whaleprints.

Sarason, S. B. (1990). *The predictable failure of educational reform: Can we change course before it's too late?* San Francisco: Jossey-Bass.

Sarason, S. B. (1995). *Parental involvement and the political principle: Why the existing governance structure of schools should be abolished.* San Francisco: Jossey-Bass.

Schutz, A. (1964). Equality and the social meaning structure. In M. Natanson (Ed.), *Collected Papers II: Studies in social theory.* The Hague: Marttinus Nijhoff.

Selznick, P. (1957). *Leadership in administration: A sociological interpretation.* New York: Harper & Row.

Sergiovanni, T. J. (1990). *Value-added leadership.* San Diego, CA: Harcourt Brace Jovanovich.

Sergiovanni, T. J. (1991). *The principalship: A reflective practice perspective.* Boston: Allyn & Bacon.

Sergiovanni, T. J. (1992). *Moral leadership: Getting to the heart of school improvement.* San Francisco: Jossey-Bass.

Sergiovanni, T. J. (1994a). *Building community in schools.* San Francisco: Jossey-Bass.

Sergiovanni, T. J. (1994b). Organizations or communities: Changing the metaphor changes the theory. *Educational Administration Quarterly, 30,* 214–226.

Sergiovanni, T. J., & Corbally, J. E. (Eds.). (1986). *Leadership and organizational culture: New perspectives on administrative theory and practice.* Urbana, IL: University of Illinois Press.

Sergiovanni, T. J., & Starratt, R. J. (1993). *Supervision: A redefinition* (5th ed.). New York: McGraw-Hill.

Spears, H. (1953). *Improving the supervision of instruction.* Englewood Cliffs, NJ: Prentice-Hall.

Tanner, D., & Tanner, L. N. (1987). *Supervision in education: Problems and practices.* New York: Macmillan.

Tom, A. (1984). *Teaching as a moral craft.* New York: Longman.

Perspective 2

Is Supervision More Than the Surveillance of Instruction?

✦ ✦ ✦ ✦

John Smyth, Flinders University of South Australia

✦ ✦ ✦

Perspective Summary

Internationally recognized expert of instructional supervision and a director of the Flinders Institute for the Study of Teaching at Flinders University of South Australia, John Smyth helps us question many taken-for-granted assumptions underlying the theory and practice of supervision. Provocative, critical, and urgent, Professor Smyth's analysis poses hard-hitting questions for supervision as a field of inquiry and practice. His thesis is that supervision is more than merely the surveillance of instruction and the assessment of how teachers and supervisors perform. Indeed, supervision should be framed as an emancipatory enterprise that aims to inform and shape "curriculum, pedagogy, and evaluation in the interests of improving the life chances of all students."

Guiding Questions

1. What assumptions does the author make about current theory and practice of supervision?
2. Why should supervision be concerned with more than the surveillance of instruction?
3. How do social, economic, cultural, and political factors beyond the classroom affect the process of supervision?
4. What are some of the more critical questions this chapter raises for you as an educator?
5. What is the author's view of the future of instructional supervision?

Is Supervision More Than the Surveillance of Instruction?

John Smyth

Introduction

I want to locate what I have to say in this essay in the realm of the slightly provocative, because I have an uneasy feeling that in its historical development, the field of supervision has indeed moved, as Duncan Waite (1995) so aptly put it, from "humble beginnings to monstrous proportions" (p. 2). In that context, there is a need to stand off at some distance and ask some potentially difficult and possibly quite uncomfortable questions. At least, that is the way I conceive of my role here.

As a further opening caveat, I should also say that I am in the rather unusual situation of commenting on and operating within a context for which there is no such field of inquiry known as "instructional/educational supervision" in my own country. That is not to say that we do not have such processes in Australia, or that I have not contributed to shaping the discourse and practice in this arena internationally, but rather to make the point that when any of us talks about social practices like supervision of instruction, we are doing so from within a historically and culturally constructed context that profoundly shapes what we mean by supervision. In other words, we are dealing with a social and a cultural practice that is not immutable but that is constantly being formulated by historical and contemporary forces, neither of which we can or should take for granted, even if the practices seem natural and commonsensical.

A further point I want to make in framing my contribution to this important international dialogue is that if we want to get to the essence of what we mean by *educational supervision* (or *instructional supervision*—I will use these terms interchangeably), then we may need to step outside of it temporarily in order to be able to see what kind of questions are important for it as a field of inquiry and practice. In almost 30 years as a teacher, teacher educator, academic, scholar, and researcher I have learned some of the most profound things I know when I have moved myself outside of the field I want to analyze and looked at things from another vantage point—by that I mean culturally as well as intellectually. For example, by reading myself into a strange or unfamiliar theoretical perspective I am able to see clearly what the issues are that I am struggling with. I guess I have formed the view that nothing dulls the senses quite like habit, routine, familiarity, or accustomed ways of doing and seeing things. Maxine Greene (1973) summed this up well a number of years ago in her book, *Teacher as Stranger*, when she said:

To take a stranger's vantage point on everyday reality is to look inquiringly and wonderingly on the world in which one lives. It is like returning home from a long stay in some other place. The home comer notices details and patterns in his environment he never saw before. He finds that he has to think about local rituals and customs to make sense of them once more. For a time he feels quite separate from the person who is wholly at home in his ingroup and takes the familiar world for granted. Such a person, writes Alfred Schutz, ordinarily "accepts the ready-made standardized scheme of the cultural pattern handed down to him by ancestors, teachers and authorities as an unquestioned and unquestionable guide in all the situations which normally will occur in the social world." The home comer may have been such a person. Now, looking through the new eyes, he cannot take the cultural pattern for granted. It may seem arbitrary to him or incoherent or deficient in some way. To make it meaningful again, he must interpret and reorder what he sees in light of his changed experience. He must consciously engage in inquiry. (pp. 267–268)

This rather lengthy quote is by way of making my overarching point in this chapter that processes, procedures, practices, and fields of inquiry like instructional supervision are not accidental, nor are they innocent—they are dripping with agenda (usually undisclosed), with politics, and with perspectives that are ripe for examination, unmasking, and unveiling, and which when found to be inadequate need to be reconstructed. I have the uneasy feeling that instructional supervision is in this state at the moment.

My Thesis

What would it mean, then, to look wonderingly at educational supervision with a different set of eyes, from a different theoretical and philosophical standpoint? Expressed in a slightly different way, what would it mean if we were to redraw the educational boundaries (to borrow an analogy from Henry Giroux) of educational/instructional supervision in a different way? At the moment, it would be true to say that educational supervision has been shaped by a long and close association with educational management and administration. That history has had palpable effects in terms of shaping what has been possible, what has been included, as well as what has been marginalized, excluded, and silenced so far as supervision of teaching is concerned. It is obviously difficult to strip away the crustaceans of nearly a century of research, scholarship, and practice in a brief chapter like this, and to do so would be to run the risk of gross oversimplification, but there are some points that can be made in terms of what the supervision of instruction has been about historically and what it is up to at the moment.

Perspectives, frames of reference, points of view, or habits of mind, as Jack Mezirow (1991) reminds us, are deeply implicated in assumptions through which we make interpretations of the world, form unquestioned positions about it, enact language codes, and carry ideologies with us that serve to distort, parcel out, and constrain and maintain views we feel most comfortable with. Those of us who live and work in the field of instructional supervision are no different from other groups in the ways we work to keep the boundaries in place.

Whether we like it or not, and despite the occasional rhetoric to the contrary, instructional supervision has mostly operated to maintain rather than challenge or question the educational status quo. While we have been good at genuflecting in the direction of supervision "for development" or "the improvement of instruction," this has invariably been from within existing structures and frames of reference and vantage points that do not question educational, moral, or social ends but merely the means for getting there. The largely unspoken intent has been to ensure that teaching and learning adhere to some largely unquestioned or uncontested (even unarticulated) norms that are supposedly universally agreed on. In other words, the interests served have tended to be those of institutions, educational systems, and social structures that represent dominant and prevailing points of view about the way schooling is or ought to be. This has become even more so as educational systems and schools have increasingly been pushed by governments around the world to engage in skills enhancement and thus operate largely as annexes to industry in the futile quest to restore flagging international economic competitiveness.

Perhaps I can make the position I am adopting even clearer by reference to what I regard as the major prevailing canons of instructional supervision, at least as they generally tend to be worked out. They might be characterized as follows:

1. It endorses the notion of accountability to school systems, parents, and governments for the expenditure of public monies, assuring various constituencies that funding spent provides "value for money."
2. It is a mechanism for identifying and rectifying incompetent teaching, at the point of production, where remediation is possible.
3. It is hierarchical in the sense that someone lower on the educational totem pole (a teacher) has something "done to them" by someone wiser and higher up (usually a nonteaching administrator), in a context in which the latter is construed as having some kind of (undisclosed) "expertise."
4. It is purportedly objective because the focus is on the teaching, not the teacher; it involves some kind of visitation by the outsider; and there is some kind of mapping of the data collected regarding what transpired in a particular (usually isolated) teaching episode.

5. It claims to be nonjudgmental because of reliance on data collected through in-class observation, rather than focused on traits, attributes, or personal failings.
6. Such processes are, above all, nonpolitical because they are unambiguously focused on "improving instruction."

I could go on at considerable length, but by now you no doubt get my drift. I should say that each (and perhaps all) of the above have some credibility, although limited and constrained. They all seem to be pitching or aiming in what most of us would see as the "right direction"—making schools into more competitive places so that this will spill over into the wider community, and make us economically better as a consequence. But it is precisely the natural, universal, and commonsense nature of such claims that ought to render them, and forms of instructional supervision that derive from them, problematic.

The most prominent question not addressed at all in the scenario of supervision described above, which makes this a dead giveaway, is: "Whose interests are *really* served through this kind of instructional supervision?" Framing it another way, "What is the real agenda behind instructional supervision thus construed?" One answer to this question is to say that such forms of supervision are about a "domesticating" rather than a "liberating" or an "emancipatory" agenda. By this I mean that the real power to change or shape what transpires in education resides or inheres largely in the upper echelons and not at the point of production of teaching and learning in classrooms. I do not want to put too pessimistic a spin on this because I know that teachers and students have very effective strategies for resisting policies and procedures not of their own making or in their own interests. My point is that the larger template of education is increasingly crafted further and further away from teachers and students in classrooms in the form of policies, guidelines, frameworks, directives, national curricula, competencies, standards, benchmarks, and the like, and that supervisors are becoming increasingly complicit in enjoining teachers to work within these in various forms of teamwork, collaboration, participation, partnerships, and site-based forms of management aimed at implementing preformulated agendas. What is interesting about all of these is that we have two simultaneous processes occurring—a concerted push for recentralization of educational policy supposedly to enhance international economic competitiveness, and much chest beating also about school-based management, autonomy, choice, local decision making, and the like. But the significant question still hinges on where the really important decisions are being made, and about that there can be no dispute—not in schools or classrooms! These so-called reforms are not fundamentally about serving the interests of teachers or pupils, even though the rhetoric suggests this to be the case.

Supervision is coming to be the crucial intermediary in this process of brokering national and systems priorities, and repackaging and selling them in more palatable forms at the local level of schools. There is nothing especially new in all of this, for supervisors since the turn of the century have continually been working toward priorities formulated outside of classrooms. What makes the current strain of supervision especially significant is that the wider agenda is not subjected to challenge or question, so that supervisors are becoming unwittingly spot-welded onto the economy as agents of industry and transnational corporations.

Herein lies the major worry, because it throws into high relief the question, "Whom do schools exist for?"

An Alternative Agenda

The difficulty with the discourse and the logic of the international economic marketplace that underpins my view of supervision is that it has a widespread and superficial appeal that is difficult to dislodge. It actually sounds quite compelling! If, however, we were to start from a different position, to see education not exclusively as a commodity or primarily as a handmaiden to the economy, then it may be possible to construe schools and what goes on inside them as having a wider social purpose than merely satiating the economy. It may be possible, for example, to regard schools as having a legitimate role in questioning what kind of society we are creating and having a hand in shaping it through the ways we teach students to be inquiring agents.

For example, if we were to regard supervision as being about working with students, teachers, parents, and community groups to locate schooling *in society*, then supervision would actually look quite different from how it was sketched above (Smyth, 1991). To step somewhat out on a limb, while trying to be quite specific, such an approach to supervision would look somewhat more like this:

1. It would be more about mapping out an agenda from within schools, if you like, identifying an indigenous culture of teaching and schooling according to the collective aspirations of the people inside schools.

2. It would be less about measurement and calibration of what transpires in schools and ranking them against national priorities, and more about artistic and narrative forms of portrayal of locally created experiences and visions of what people in schools are trying to do.

3. The attempt within supervision would be not merely to focus on instructional behavior but to canvass somewhat wider to put the analytic spotlight on the structure, context, and location within which teaching and learning are occurring and to uncover in what ways these are deficient.

4. When teaching and learning "do not work out," questions might be asked, within supervision, about what factors appear to act as impediments or constraints—rather than there being victim blaming of teachers and students.

5. A starting point for this construal of supervision might be asking and answering questions of this kind: "What does teaching/learning/schooling feel like from the perspective of the least advantaged?"

6. Such processes would be less about finding fault with teachers or identifying deficits in learning styles of students, and more about helping sections of the school community identify wider disabling or debilitating sets of circumstances and what might be done about them politically.

7. It would have as a guiding principle the question: "Who is education/schooling *really* for?"

8. Supervision of this kind would have a decidedly "critical" agenda that involves getting at truth and falsity in terms of "exposing those who are duplicitous or dangerous or exploitative or monstrous or weak and who by being so cause harm to us and/or to others" (Newman, 1994, pp. 53–54).

9. Supervision would be much less about producing conformity and compliance and more about "being at the edge, at the moment of truth, face-to-face with the enemy" (Newman, 1994, p. 54).

10. It would provide an opportunity for what Strike (1993) calls "defamiliarization," meaning a chance for reinvigoration and freshness of thought as well as challenging comfortable illusions and the rupture likely to come from a "possible loss of tacit norms and habits of institutional life" (p. 188).

11. The central framing question is "For whom does power work, and how might this be changed in the interests of the least advantaged?"

What I have been arguing in this essay is that it is possible to conceive of supervision in impoverished terms that regard schools and what occurs in them in instrumental or exchange-oriented ways. In either case, the agenda is externally crafted and imposed on schools, and supervision becomes a complicit agent in "doing a number on schools." Alternatively, it is possible to conceive of schools and supervision in more robust terms, in which the "gaze" is not upon the surveillance of instruction and how teachers and students perform, but rather there is a more emancipatory agenda aimed at informing and shaping curriculum, pedagogy, and evaluation in the interests of improving the life chances of all students.

Let's Get More Specific

The apt title of Blumberg's (1980) book, *Supervisors and Teachers: A Private Cold War*, is even more appropriate now than it was over a decade and a half ago. Waite (1995) cites evidence from the Organization for Economic Cooperation and Development that "support personnel" employed in U.S. schools outnumber teachers and a substantial number of those are supervisors. With increasing pressure on teachers to "teach to the test," Waite says, an accompanying disdain of so-called "snoopervision" develops because teachers are individually targeted and blamed as the perception spreads that somehow schools are failing. Labeling teachers as "the problem" and trying to encase them in a supervisory straightjacket produces the not surprising effect that supervisory practices fall into disrepute as far as teachers are concerned. There are even widespread calls for abandoning the concept altogether.

The difficulty seems to be that what started out as a fine ideal and as a way of enabling teachers to share ideas about what we call today "best practice" has become a process by which teachers are converted into "marionettes" (Waite, 1995, p. 5). Where things appear to have come unstuck is in a loss of historical memory as to what the process of educational supervision is supposed to be about. There has been too much infatuation with industrial models of supervision that are totally inappropriate for education (see Issue 10). As long as the focus was squarely on supervision as communicating ideas about innovative practice among teachers and helping them to break down "the walls of privatism" (Fullan, 1982), in the process becoming more perceptive analysts of their own and one another's teaching, then supervision was doing what it was intended to do. Once it took on, wittingly or unwittingly, the role of treating teachers in "teacher proofing" ways (the more recent term is "deskilling"), then supervision began moving in the wrong direction; that is it became preoccupied with surveillance and giving teachers *less* rather than *more* control over their teaching.

Notwithstanding, I am one of the optimists who believe that the process of educational supervision is retrievable but only under conditions dramatically different from what is generally being experienced at the moment. The single most important element in reclaiming supervision has to be a shift in real power back toward teachers. As long as that fails to occur, and as long as supervision is enacted so that individual teachers become the object of supervision, then the process will remain doomed.

In my own current theoretical, practical and research work related to supervision, I am exploring what supervision might look like if it were regarded as a process of self-study by schools committed to re-creating themselves as discursive, critical, and collaborative communities (Smyth, in press). Within this approach, a number of salient features are beginning to emerge. But before I list some of them, it goes without saying that the kind of supervision I am talking about has some clear characteristics—it is voluntary and noncoercive; it eschews notions of hierachy; it is in-class in nature; it involves the collection of a wide range of information about life in classrooms; it is not focused on the alleged deficiencies of the teacher; it is teacher directed in terms of the information to be collected and the colleague to assist in that; ownership of all aspects of the process resides with the teacher; there is a joint endeavor to extract meaning from information about teaching; it is not used for purposes of retribution; it is ongoing; and, as far as possible, it is widespread within the school, becoming the basis for discussion among *all* teachers about the nature of the work of teaching and how it might be changed for the social betterment of children.

Some of the more specific features beginning to emerge from the work I am currently doing include the following:

- A preparedness to endure discomfort.
- A willingness to change social relationships.
- A desire to locate teaching in its broader social/cultural context.
- Seeing how power operates in and through one's own pedagogy.
- Pursuing questions about whose interests are served/denied/silenced through particular pedagogies.
- Questioning assumptions, beliefs, and practices.
- Reconstructing practice on the basis of inquiry.
- Searching for the socially transformative potential in schooling.
- Asking questions about the socially just nature of educational experiences.
- Adopting a process of simultaneously describing, informing, and confronting one's teaching with a view to reconstructing it.
- Deconstructing hierarchies of authority, gender, race, class, disability, and other forms of stereotyping.
- Looking at the familiar differently, for example, extraordinarily re-experiencing the ordinary.
- Challenging conventional practices, ideas, and ideals.
- Making the assumptions, practices, and categories of everyday life problematic.
- Unmasking and unveiling hidden message systems in curriculum, pedagogy, evaluation, and administration.
- Looking at circumstances and seeing how through dialogue and theorizing about them they might be different.
- Understanding the oppressive and undemocratic features of schooling and how they came to be.
- Regarding the work of teaching as being historical, theoretical, and political.
- Seeing teaching as a form of critical intellectual struggle.

Each of these is regarded by teachers as broad orienting touchstones for an approach to supervision that is fundamentally committed to regarding schooling, teaching, and learning as part of a bigger picture of liberation and democratization.

One of the more concrete ways teachers interrogate their classrooms and teach with one another, and in the process move beyond supervision as surveillance, is to intersect directly with the micro-politics of the classroom and how it is constructed by social, economic, cultural, and political structures originating beyond the classroom. Seeing how these wider forces are constructed, worked out, and accommodated in classrooms is an important precursor to resisting, removing, and ultimately reconstructing socially unjust practices. How teachers work with students, students with one another, and the stories and experiences of both, has to be the starting point for any such journey. Questions that have proven useful so far for classroom focus, observation, and supervisory encounters include the following:

- Who talks in this classroom?
- Who gets the teacher's time?
- How is ability identified and attended to here, and what is the rationale?
- How are the unequal starting points of students dealt with here?
- How are instances of disruptive behavior explained and handled?
- Is there a competitive or a cooperative ethos in this classroom?
- Who helps who here?
- Whose ideas are the most important or count the most?
- How do we know that learning is occurring here?
- Are answers or questions more important in this classroom?
- How are decisions made here?
- How does the arrangement of the room help or hinder learning?
- Who benefits and who is disadvantaged in this classroom?
- How is conflict resolved?
- How are rules determined?
- How are inequalities recognized and dealt with?
- Where do learning materials come from?
- By what means are resources distributed?
- What career aspirations do students have, and how are they manifested?
- Who determined standards, and how did they arrive at them?
- How is failure defined and to what is it ascribed ? Who or what fails?
- Whose language prevails in the classroom?
- How does the teacher monitor his or her agenda?
- How does the teacher change oppressive structures in the classroom?

- What is being measured and assessed in this classroom?
- Who do teachers choose to collaborate with and under what circumstances? (Smyth, 1995).

These questions, or ones like them, are important probes that teachers are able to use to uncover not only how power works in the classroom but also the manner in which oppressive structures external to the classroom come unwittingly to have a life of their own in classroom practices.

Conclusion

This essay explored the question of whether supervision is more than surveillance and opted for an answer along the lines that supervision has become sidetracked from the main event by those who would have it tarnished by affiliation with an outmoded industrial model of quality control and who regard it as a convenient control technology. I have explored an alternative to or counterview of the prevailing orthodoxy that suggests supervision need not be this way at all. For it to be different, however, I argue that it will require a quite different basis that is located much more in the lifeworlds of teachers and students and in the struggle for a more just, equitable, and democratic world. But the starting point has to be the classroom, and with bigger questions about what is socially just about schooling and what it exists for than hitherto occupied by the economically minded and opportunistic reformers, who have captured supervision largely under the guise of a supposedly benign managerialism—which it never is, of course.

References

Blumberg, A. (1980). *Supervisors and teachers: A private cold war* (2nd ed.). Berkeley, CA: McCutchan.

Fullan, M. (1982). *The meaning of educational change.* New York: Teachers College Press.

Greene, M. (1973). *Teacher as stranger.* Belmont, CA: Wadsworth.

Mezirow, J. (1991). *Transformative dimensions of adult learning.* San Francisco: Jossey Bass.

Newman, M. (1994). *Defining the enemy: Adult education in social action.* Sydney: Stewart Victor Publishing.

Smyth, J. (1991). *Teachers as collaborative learners: Challenging dominant forms of supervision.* London: Open University Press.

Smyth, J. (1995). *Some possible candidates for classroom observation by socially critical teachers and colleagues.* Adelaide: Flinders Institute for the Study of Teaching.

Smyth, J. (in press). The socially just alternative to the "self-managing school." In D. Corson (Ed.), *International handbook of educational leadership and administration.* Netherlands: Kluwer Academic.

Strike, K. (1993). Professionalism, democracy, and discursive communities: Normative reflections on restructuring. *American Educational Research Journal, 30*(2), 255–275.

Waite, D. (1995). *Rethinking instructional supervision: Notes on its language and culture.* London: The Falmer Press.

Postnote

Is Supervision More Than the Surveillance of Instruction?

Dr. Smyth's penetrating analysis has raised critical questions that challenge us to consider many complex and perplexing issues that inform supervisory discourse in the field as well as influence the practice of supervision in schools. Smyth, not unlike Sergiovanni, rouses dialogue, stimulates thinking, and helps us expand our taken-for-granted assumptions about the theory and practice of supervision. Smyth reminds us that supervision should not be seen merely as a technical process to be managed by specialists but as an emancipatory and liberating process involving the "lifeworlds of teachers and students and the struggle for a more just, equitable, and democratic world."

Review Questions

1. What does Smyth mean when in describing "instructional supervision" he states "we are dealing with a social and a cultural practice that is not immutable but that is constantly being formulated by historical and contemporary forces . . ." Specifically, why is supervision a social and cultural practice? Further, what historical forces have shaped supervision and what contemporary forces continue to influence discourse in the field?

2. Summarize Smyth's position on the state of the field of instructional supervision. Do you concur with his analysis? Explain why or why not.

3. Smyth maintains that "educational supervision has been shaped by a legacy of a long and close association with educational management and administration." What are the consequences of this association for the field of supervision? Is supervision administration? Do administrators supervise?

4. What is your reaction to Smyth's six major prevailing canons of instructional supervision? Do they make sense to you? To the extent that you concur with any or all of his canons, provide examples from your experience to support his contention.

5. How would Smyth react to the concept of school-based management? What questions would he raise about the role of supervision in such a school?

6. According to Smyth, what role(s) should supervisors or those concerned with supervision play in schools? How do his suggestions raise the level of discourse about supervision as a process, professional practice, and field of study?

7. What would the "ideal" school look like according to Smyth? What role would supervision play in such an ideal school?

8. Is Smyth optimistic about the future of supervision? What does he propose to help move beyond the "surveillance of instruction?"

9. Smyth states that "[T]he single most important element in reclaiming supervision has to be a shift in real power back toward teachers." How would this shift help to reclaim supervision? What organizational factors need consideration to effect such a change? What are the consequences of this "shift in power back toward teachers" for the way supervision might be conducted in schools? Under this scenario, would supervisors who weren't teachers be necessary? Explain.

10. How would Glanz (Issue 6) respond to Smyth's "emancipatory conception of supervision?" As a teacher/supervisor how do you react to his views about the emancipatory nature of supervision?

11. Smyth poses many provocative questions near the end of his essay. These questions aim to "uncover not only how power works in the classroom but also the manner in which oppressive structures external to the classroom come unwittingly to have a life of their own in classroom practices." How do the questions that Smyth poses attempt to achieve the aforementioned objective?

For Further Research

1. Dr. Smyth used the terms *instructional* and *educational* interchangeably to describe supervision. Are the two terms synonymous? Research how other authorities in the field refer to supervision. What distinctions are made between the terms, and what is your understanding of these differences?

2. In question 7 above we asked you to consider an "ideal" school according to Smyth's view. We believe each author in this textbook would have his or her own conception of an ideal school and the role supervision would play. How are the authors similar or dissimilar? With which authors do you most agree? With which authors do you most disagree?

3. Smyth presents six provocative questions near the end of his chapter. Examine a classroom in your school/district based on these questions. How do the answers help to "uncover not only how power works in the classroom but also the manner in which oppressive structures external to the classroom come unwittingly to have a life of their own in classroom practices?"

4. Smyth is a noted authority in the field of instructional supervision. Research some of his previous work. What themes do you discern in his writings? How have his views changed? Compare Smyth's work with Starratt's or Sergiovanni's. Similarities? Differences?

5. Compare Smyth's (1991) views about instructional supervision with his analysis presented in this chapter. How do his views on collegiality compare with those presented by Pavan in Issue 7?

6. Conduct an ethnographic study of a district, school, and/or class-room using Smyth's questions posed near the end of his perspective statement.

References

Smyth, J. (1991). Instructional supervision and the redefinition of who does it in schools. *Journal of Curriculum and Supervision, 7,* 90–99.

Perspective 3

What is the New Supervisory Role in an Age of Complexity?

✦ ✦ ✦ ✦

Karolyn J. Snyder, University of South Florida

✦ ✦ ✦

Perspective Summary

Professor Snyder's contributions to the School Management Institute at the University of South Florida, her scholarship on productive schools and educational supervision, and her work with school districts are recognized nationally and internationally. In this perspective statement Snyder presents a mosaic of the work of teachers and supervisors in this postmodern age, where they confront a society characterized by ambiguity, uncertainty, and imperfect information. To address the ambiguity and chaos that is part of contemporary educational reality, Snyder identifies "world-class standards—quality standards" for work/learning teams and supervisors. Her "Education Quality System" combines the dimensions of visionary leadership and management which provide the conditions for the stages of work-team development: awareness, transition, and transformation. After defining the stages and the "performance areas for the team" Snyder notes the importance of systems thinking and information systems for the supervisor's major task—"human resource development." The author continually reminds us that our attention and efforts must always consider "the students who are being served and their learning environment."

Guiding Questions

1. How would you distinguish between the modern and postmodern world as these concepts relate to educational processes and responsibilities?
2. In a world beset by fractionating cultures and communities how would the development of "work teams" help schools meet their responsibilities?
3. How is it possible for supervisors to help schools, individuals, and groups of teachers respond to this "age of complexity:" at-risk populations, the global village, conditions of chaos, and the new marketplace?
4. If a school is a "social system," what are its responsibilities to meet the changes and challenges that accompany new technology and alternative value systems?
5. Given the author's interpretation of the complexities of the postmodern world, what changes in supervisory roles and functions are anticipated for the work of supervisors?

What is the New Supervisory Role in an Age of Complexity?

Karolyn J. Snyder

In this postmodern age of complexity and rapid change, social, governmental, and business agencies around the globe are transforming their cultures of work. Many have already come to grips with the inability of traditional programs, with their linear structures, to meet the challenges of the times, and they are reinventing every feature of work life and its supervision. Schools, like all other institutions today, function within a postmodern landscape of instability, irregularity, and unpredictability (Elkind, 1995), and in response they, too, are redesigning systems of work. World-class work standards are now emerging to guide institutions through this transition to an altogether new form of work and its environment.

The purpose of this chapter is to explore the complexity of the work environment for teachers and other school-based professionals, and then to offer an *Education Quality System* for supervisors to guide the development of high-performing work teams for a new age of professional behavior. When teams, which are the building blocks of organizations, are encouraged to explore and take risks, they naturally use a range of information, their own talents, and available resources to invent and pilot new programs and services (Snyder, Acker-Hocevar, & Snyder, 1995). Teams that work within an environment that supports invention tend to thrive, as do their students. If the role of supervisor is to survive at all in the redesign of schooling, supervisors must add energy to the professional learning of work teams that address the daily complexities of this postmodern era.

It is my belief that the problems in education today have little to do with the complex challenges of our postmodern society, except for the declining financial levels for education. The problem, I believe, relates to outdated systems of professional work and to redefinitions of supervision and control. Current supervisory practices too often continue to be compliance driven, and they are out of step with current schooling realities. The paradox of unpredictable schooling conditions and control-oriented supervisory practices presents a huge barrier to the transformation of schools into viable social institutions. We need to abandon *control* as a guiding principle and recognize that complexity and irregularity are the norms today. What can be controlled is the development of team progress over time to world-class status.

In the pages that follow I hope to build a case for the new role of supervisor as one that adds value to the continuous development of work teams, which function interdependently within a dynamic school environment. I begin by exploring the complexity of schooling in the postmodern era, with emphasis given to at-risk populations, the global village, new work proficiencies, and chaos theory as a new lens for supervising work teams. Questions about the new work of schools and of supervisors are discussed as they relate to a context of complexity. Finally, an *Education Quality System* for work teams is provided as a set of world-class standards. The Quality System serves as a guide for the development and empowerment of work teams, which I believe is the new work of supervisors. I hope the reader will gain fresh perspectives on the current challenges teachers face and gain insights into developing world-class professional work teams.

The Age of Complexity

The postmodern era is characterized by ambiguity and uncertainty as many organizations, including schools, respond to changing conditions and new demands. In this section I examine the complexities of disparate forces of influence on schools which in the aggregate are forcing the demise of work traditions of the past 100 years. Let us first consider a few features that add to the complexity of schools today.

At-Risk Populations

The label *at-risk* has emerged recently as a generic term for students who fail to make adequate progress in school and are either retained in grade or referred to special programs (Karweit, 1988). As we have witnessed a growth in school services and programs over the last several decades, there seems to be little doubt that the range of student needs has grown increasingly complex and has now surpassed the ability of most schools to respond with much success. As one dramatic example, the advent of the "inclusion" movement signals the end of century-old practices of *adding* more programs and services to those designed for "normal" populations.

Hodgkinson (1991, 1993) tells us that from 30 to 40 percent of all students are at risk of failing in school, largely because of the restrictive social, economic, physical, emotional, intellectual, and cultural conditions in which they live. Twenty-five percent of these students live in poverty, and 33 percent have the deck stacked against them. At-risk students typically come from urban or rural settings and from one-parent families that are economically and socially deprived. Transportation and health care services, housing, security, and family systems are unstable, at best, in urban settings. Social factors that tend to foster at-riskness include having a single parent and belonging to a low-income family, often being home alone, and having parents of low education and limited English. At-risk medical factors are somewhat different, but are found within the same population. They include fetal alcohol syndrome, a drug-addicted mother, no medical care during pregnancy, teenage mothers, and being a victim of child abuse.

Because of the social conditions of these youth, many during the teen years seek escape and become pregnant, commit crimes, and attempt to or do commit suicide. Juvenile crime is also on the rise. Unless community agencies work together with schools, this segment of the population is doomed to continue the cycle of poverty, welfare, drugs, and time in jail. Consequently, the social environment of crime will worsen for us all.

What, then, is the function of schooling within at-risk neighborhoods? The difficulty in meeting these described needs is now so great that schools themselves, in some states, are being labeled "at-risk schools." Perhaps our definitions of "normal" are outdated as well as our criteria for determining progress and success. Or perhaps our conceptions of professional work are worn out. One wonders what it will take for educators to boost the life chances of at-risk students. To be certain, responding well is beyond the capacity of individual teachers; they must now be enabled to work in teams, with assistance from school leaders and the district office, and within systems of work that are designed for their success.

The Global Village

Schools can no longer be viewed as social institutions that "do their own thing," for schooling is vitally linked to national social and economic conditions and to the United State's role in the global marketplace. The continuous explosion of technology and the emergence of new industries are altering the nature of work altogether, and this will affect the life chances of many high school graduates. Furthermore, in anticipation of the future many schools have moved beyond a *high school graduation* mission and are now considering *preparation to contribute to communities of the twenty-first century* as the new purpose of schooling.

Some international industries have surfaced in the last few decades that present schools with new challenges. These include microelectronics, biotechnology, new materials science, telecommunications, robotics, and computers and software. How can schools be expected to prepare youth for these new industries given the lack of adequate knowledge about them as well as time-worn systems of teaching and learning and the declining levels of educational funding? The quality of our responses to these and other career challenges not only is of interest to each community but has a national economic impact as well. In a recent speech MIT economist Lester Thurow remarked that the nineteenth century belonged to the British economically, while the twentieth century belonged to the Americans. Already, he predicts, the twenty-first century will belong to the Japanese and the Germans; Americans rank only 11th to 13th on current international measures of productivity. Unless we accept a continued downward swing, schools must play a vital role in the revitalization of our new national role in the global village.

What new forms of schooling will it take to prepare students for a new age of work? Some schools are already exploring the changing realities of the complex and dynamic workplace that students will face as adults (Snyder, Acker-Hocevar, & Snyder, 1994). Teachers and supervisors together are reaching out to their communities and becoming familiar with the dramatic changes in the world of work. Consequently, they are transforming their approaches to curriculum as well as to the structures and systems for learning.

If schools are to prepare students to help shape the global village, then a fundamentally new vision of schooling will be required of leaders, along with the kind of systemic change that can endure and continue over time. The twentieth century models and metaphors of schooling simply won't work. It is time for us to get our management and supervision heads out of the sand and face, head on, the realities of today as well as the projections of tomorrow.

New Marketplace Requirements

Becoming concerned with the declining status of the United States in the global marketplace, the U.S. Department of Commerce launched a study to determine basic job requirements for today's workplace. The report of the Secretary's Commission on Achieving Necessary Skills (SCANS, 1992) provided the education industry with a realistic picture of the marketplace today. *Basic work competencies* now include (1) the use of multiple resources to address challenges; (2) interpersonal skills to work with others in various kinds of work teams; (3) the use of multiple information bases for problem solving and decision making; (4) understanding of social, organizational, and technological systems of work to manage and improve performance; and (5) the use of technology in performing tasks. In addition, competent workers in high-performing workplaces need (6) the traditional basic skills of reading, writing, arithmetic, and speaking; (7) thinking skills for learning, reasoning, inventing, making decisions, and solving problems; and (8) the personal qualities of responsibility, self-esteem and self-management, sociability, and integrity.

In addition to the basics listed above, the technology revolution is causing us all to alter how we retrieve and store information, communicate with others around the globe, search for information, and design new systems of work. How students learn in this technologically driven world, what they learn, and how they demonstrate both their knowledge and the new workplace "know-how" remain a primary challenge for schools and school districts. Almost nothing in schools of the future will function as it did in decades past, *"for the times, they are a-changing."*

Chaos Theory

The new Theories of Chaos and Complexity provide a useful frame for addressing current conditions of schooling. Over the last 50 years, scientists from many fields of the natural sciences have observed that the natural order is not entirely logical, orderly, predictable, or linear, but rather complex and filled with variation and randomness. Within the natural order, however, there are patterns that can be observed as natural change unfolds (Gleick, 1987).

The story of *Jurassic Park* (Crichton, 1990) poignantly illustrates how linear thinking and planning models, along with high-powered technology, can fail to account for all variables within complex natural environments and so ultimately fail to serve their purpose. In the story, a new theme park, Jurassic Park, is built on an island off the coast of Costa Rica and features genetically re-engineered and living dinosaurs. This amazing creation resulted from the owner's vision, which is shared by all workers and based on the most advanced computer technology in the world; new technological systems guide scientists to re-engineer the birth of dinosaurs and to monitor and manage their habits in a controlled park environment.

However, neither the park owners nor their workers pay close enough attention to daily patterns of life; they believe all variables in the management system of the park have been anticipated. Eventually, unforeseen and disastrous outgrowths of this novel environment lead to the death and destruction of many workers, as well as the park owner. The Costa Rican government eventually destroys the park. This disaster might have been prevented, however, if the designers had recognized the virtual impossibility of controlling all variables in their dinosaur park and had watched for what might occur unexpectedly. Had they embraced Chaos Theory, as they were challenged to do, perhaps the park would have thrived.

What can we learn about the new laws of complexity from the sciences that might be useful in guiding change within natural school environments? Scientists over the last 50 years were troubled by assumptions about predictability and order in natural science. Within their own fields they began observing the natural patterns that evolved, most of which could not be explained by theories of predictability and objectivity or by linear frameworks. Eventually scientists began to share what they were observing with others. Gleick (1987) wrote a landmark book, *Chaos*, that introduced the history of "chaos" to the public. He reported how each scientist found the natural order (like the weather) to be irregular, discontinuous, erratic, complex, and filled with sudden leaps and jagged edges; yet it contained strong regular patterns. Scientists found that nonlinear equations and fractal geometry could explain much of this natural phenomenon. However, within these natural environments, which they eventually called "chaos," the scientists observed that regular patterns exist and repeat themselves over time.

As a result of continued scientific explorations, a new law of complexity soon replaced the time-worn laws of regularity and controllability within the sciences. Roger Lewin (1993), in his book

Complexity: Living on the Edge of Chaos, concludes that scientists earlier believed that outside forces direct life, and hence objectivity and predictability became guiding scientific principles. Now chaos scientists understand that collections of internal energy guide self-regulation and regeneration within the natural environment. The process of change, which is chaotic and predictably random in its natural state, has the potential to progress toward a dysfunctional turbulence unless internal energy forces offset that tendency.

The New Work of Schools

Chaos? Complexity? Dynamic natural systems? What do these notions have to do with schooling and supervision? And should such speculation even be permitted? "Jurassic" management, argues Gunter (1995), is leading schools into decline. She contends that education managers need to break free from the seduction of stability in order to create an appropriate future for schooling. Open debate and opportunities for teachers to self-organize within their teams can lead naturally to more responsive forms of teaching and learning. Chaos Theory challenges us to consider the natural social environment of schools and raises questions about being able to control the context and predict student success or failure. It now seems that the best chance we have of making sense out of a school's social complexity is to constantly examine the students who are being served and their learning environment.

Paying attention to the natural patterns that exist in each school, and building collective energy for and commitment to the success of students, provides a practical backdrop for vision building, planning, program redesign, and professional development. By studying the "deep patterns" within a classroom and a school, the right kinds of changes can be anticipated to offset the negative effects of complexity. Today a strong and knowledgeable staff, using a range of information and resources, is a good bet for altering learning conditions and their effects. And building strong professional learning teams, in my view, is the new work of supervisors.

Perhaps the greatest difficulty is to acknowledge the natural chaos that exists within schools in this postmodern era and to ask new questions. For example, how can we develop new professional energy systems that offset the negative tendency for things to fall apart or just fail? Gunter (1995) argues that people will not learn if they are subject to the control of a strong (outdated) value system, but will learn if they know how to recognize and respond to disorder and ambiguity. A school district superintendent recently shared an observation with me: When schools move boldly toward the edge of chaos (the unknown), novel and creative success patterns emerge. Living dangerously, near the edge of chaos, is certainly upside-down thinking from the traditional patterns of school supervision.

A prerequisite for learning how to function on the edge of chaos is *systems thinking,* a way of life in which professionals focus on a common vision and a few operational goals as they work together in teams that function interdependently. In a study of 28 schools (Snyder, Acker-Hocevar, & Snyder, 1994), my colleagues and I learned that when leaders and other professionals are grounded in systems thinking, such patterns as team teaching, integrated curriculum and continuous progress systems, nongraded structures (K–12), inclusion programs, multi-age student groupings, and working more with entire families as well social agencies and community business, *all* quite naturally evolve as forms of energy in the school environment.

The New Work of Supervisors

A question remains: Are supervisors needed any longer? If so, in what capacity? Traditional supervisory practices of helping and evaluating individual workers are no longer useful except with respect to contract decisions. Assumptions about *correctness* and *predictability* within schools tend to reinforce supervisory practices such as top-down management, dominance over workers, providing professional freedom to work in isolation, holding a linear view of change, and harboring faulty perceptions that things are improving. Linear programs and processes are not capable of dealing with the natural ambiguities of schooling today. Professional recognition of the new ways of knowing and working has led many educators to disrupt the status quo and its systems of work. The primary supervisory task is to develop professional learning communities, in work teams, that not only acquire new knowledge and skills but also learn how to study and respond exceptionally well to their natural work and learning environments.

Supervisors and other professionals who recognize the nonlinear patterns in the school environment, and who assume that multiple interpretations and meanings naturally permeate improvement efforts, are likely to succeed in their work. Systems thinking can become a norm as professionals work within and across teams, role groups, and institutions (Snyder, Acker-Hocevar, & Snyder, 1995). Social constructivism (figuring it out together) will necessarily become the norm for dialogue and decision making. And so building the energy mass, school by school and team by team, is also the new work of the supervisor. Then we can have meaningful debates about the quality of teaching and learning, for teachers will be more distinctly responsible for student progress and success.

Developing World-Class Professional Work Teams

How can supervisors help teams to thrive on chaos and yet develop new response capacities? In this section I identify world-class standards for guiding the professional development of many school work teams, such as teaching teams, departments, grade-level teams, multi-age teams, service teams, and support teams. The quality standards that are presented here are designed for work teams to use in guiding their own growth, with the supervisor advancing that quest. Work teams in schools typically are professionals who work in close proximity and share common job responsibilities. Within the twentyfirst-century workplace, however, teams are likely to be accountable not only for working together cooperatively but for advancing over time the success and satisfaction of their students. It is especially within this context that supervisors will function. Their survival may depend on how well and to what extent they add value to the work of professional teams and to the quality of their services.

The Education Quality System

In 1994, Michele Acker-Hocevar and I developed an *Education Quality System* (EQS) in partnership with 13 school districts in Florida. The purpose of the EQS, which is explained in two unpublished documents and has been validated for its content (Acker-Hocevar, 1994), is to guide the direction of change within education institutions under the umbrella of quality management principles. After extensive research into the quality writings as well as education reform trends, we created a quality management model (see Figure 1), and then a *change process* model, as a diagnostic tool for benchmarking change over time as institutions progress from unresponsive bureaucratic practices to those that are increasingly responsive to needs.

The *Education Quality System* model is characterized by systems of continual improvement that are driven by customer success and satisfaction criteria, which drive six interdependent work culture features: visionary leadership, strategic planning, systems thinking, information systems, human resource development, and quality services. Educators may not be accustomed to viewing students as customers. Nevertheless, this concept is central, I believe, to reversing the focus and purpose of work and its continual improvement. An accompanying diagnostic tool enables educators to identify the location of their institution on the bureaucratic-quality continuum. (For further information about this system, see Acker-Hocevar, 1996.)

In this essay, the focus is the development of high-performing work teams rather than the school as an organization—hence the emphasis on a work team version of the EQS. As teams begin to address their own development needs, they will naturally progress through three stages: awareness, transition, and transformation.

In the *awareness stage,* the work team performs primarily according to traditions and policy guidelines. In this learning stage, the focus of work is on service improvements and professional development, with the beneficiaries being the students and administrators that the teams serve. The team leader typically makes policy decisions and responds to requests for information that relate to policy, while others

Figure 1:   Education Quality System*

engage in their routine work. Systems of work are idiosyncratic as members learn how to work together within the school organization's traditional culture. The objective of work in the awareness stage is to more adequately meet legal requirements, with principals and district supervisors assessing areas of need. Quantitative information is generated periodically to determine progress against norm-referenced criteria and to identify compliance with established policy. However, team members are engaged in professional development programs in which the emphasis is on quality work cultures and systems thinking and also on new knowledge and skill bases for responding to the emerging job requirements.

In the *transition stage,* the change process is well under way, moving work patterns from compliance systems to those that are more responsive. The focus for improvement is the team's programs and services that will benefit customer groups both internal and external to the team. Team leaders and administrators still tend to make policy decisions, but there is team member input in specific situations. Some parents and students, or other customer groups, can make occasional recommendations for improvement to the team. The team is beginning to gather not only quantitative data but also qualitative information from customers about the appropriateness of programs and services and their structures. This information is used periodically to guide improvement decisions. The outcome of the transition stage is the team's growing awareness of the function of integration as a goal for all programs and services, both within and across the unit. The team is learning how to study its own context for learning and working and is making adjustments to its programs. Yet its work is still controlled by district and school policy guidelines and decisions, so experimentation exists only within allowable limits.

In the *transformation stage,* the team has developed the capacity to study and learn about its students or clients and to make continuous adjustments to programs and services. The interdependence of programs and services has become a way of life, as the team responds to the complexities of students and to the challenges of preparing them for the twentyfirst-century world. The focus of work is on continual systemic improvement and professional learning that better meets the needs of those being served. The result is that the team has developed a capacity for continuous self-renewal. Customers (students, parents, community members, other professionals) make recommendations to the team for improvement, and this information is aggressively sought by the team. Both qualitative and quantitative data are gathered to inform continuous improvement directions, with the tendency to rely more and more on qualitative information. Learning is what the team does as it seeks to meet the needs of those being served.

High-Performing Work Team Standards

The work of supervisors will be to facilitate the development of strong learning teams—those that have the capacity to continuously study and refine the processes of work, programs, and their effects. In this section the EQS standards for work teams are introduced by describing each of the six *performance areas* for the team that are identified in Figure 1. The standards listed below are characteristic of work teams in the transformation stage, whereas the work of supervisors is to facilitate the team's growth toward these high levels of performance. (Although I will focus on school-level teams, the reader should consider the concepts as generic and use them as world-class benchmarks for work teams within any level of the education enterprise and its institutions.) Currently these new standards are being piloted by numerous types of work teams, so the instrumentation is still in a developmental phase. For purposes of this essay, the standards can function as a general guide for team development and for the work of supervisors.

1. Visionary Leadership.   *A vision for the work team's future, as defined by understanding customer long-term needs and expectations, guides work and has positive effects upon the direction of change for different populations.* The team shapes a vision over time, which is changed and modified as the needs of customer groups and environmental conditions are altered. Programs and services are aligned with the team's vision, while its strategic plan translates the vision into action. The team develops the internal capacity to support its own change efforts and to constantly align programs with the vision.

2. Strategic planning.   *A comprehensive plan for achieving the vision of the work team is shaped with and for customer groups. A quality management system guides continuous improvement to benefit different customer groups.* The team's vision of new futures for its clients guides the continuous assessment of their needs. Data are consistently used as a basis of dialogue for planning, whereas institutional resources are aligned with the strategic plan. New funding patterns are aggressively sought to enhance the team's work for the benefit of customers, according to its plan.

3. Systems thinking and action.   *Services of the work team are interdependent, with each other as well as other teams, to provide the energy for work and to stimulate cooperation among customers and suppliers.* All services are integrated and function interdependently within the team, while programs are aligned with school goals. Barriers to work progress are identified and removed to facilitate the work of the team, while piloting new ideas and programs becomes a way of life. Teams routinely

generate customer data for improving their services, while networks and partnerships evolve to foster new systems of work. Team members receive continuous support and recognition from the school for their contributions to customer groups.

4. Information Systems.   *Information systems are created to identify data and trends about changing conditions, different customers' needs, and the effects of services. Information influences the continual improvement process by making the necessary data available to team services for revision.* The team gathers multiples sources of customer data to assess the impact of its services. Both quantitative tools and qualitative data gathering are used to generate reliable information to guide improvement efforts. Included in the system is regular feedback on services. The work team uses communications networks for sharing and exchanging information with customers, suppliers, and workers.

5. Human resource development.   *A comprehensive professional development system enhances the capacities of team members to anticipate and respond to emerging demands in relation to the team's vision.* Team members engage in continuous individual and organizational development to enhance their performance and effects on customers. Training programs are sought that will help them meet new job demands and refine current job skills for increasing customer success and satisfaction. Coaching and mentoring systems are used to assist employee performance and to advance innovation and development. The team is also proactive in improving members' health, safety, and job satisfaction while they demonstrate continuing optimism for meeting and exceeding customer needs.

6. Quality services.   *Services are the processes, programs, and interventions that are designed to achieve the team's vision and to exceed the needs and expectations of customers.* Data that have been gathered confirm that all services strive to meet or exceed the changing needs of customer groups. Customers and suppliers function interdependently with the team. Services are measured over time in relation to the vision and purpose and to their effects upon customer groups.

7. Customer success and satisfaction.   *Customer-generated data from multiple sources are gathered regularly to assess the extent to which customer needs are being met and also to align systems improvements and innovations with the new information.* Data on team performance document trends of success and satisfaction for all customer groups. The team responds quickly to emerging needs and challenges of different groups and demonstrates a commitment to continual improvement.

New Supervisory Skills

The context for high-performing work teams is critical to their success. It is possible, although rare, for a work team to succeed within a traditional school context of routine structures, programs, and services with their regular complexities. It is far more likely that work teams will thrive in a school environment that is driven by a vision for the student populations, one that is shaped by the staff. When the school's strategic plans reflect this vision the planning of each work team is consistent with, and advances, the organization's priorities. In this context, the energy system for managing forces within the school's complex environment is harnessed to offset that natural tendency toward turbulence and dysfunctionality.

Systems thinking, school-wide, enables work teams to function interdependently in striving for upward trends in student success, and predictably it will enhance the work of any individual work team. Information systems that are generated school-wide, by teams, inform decision makers about patterns of success and difficulty within the school's own natural environment. Work teams have many professional development needs in common, and having a school-wide professional development system encourages collaborative learning and risk taking within and across work teams. By routinely studying the quality of programs and services school-wide, and the success patterns of students, teachers, and others aid the advancement of a strong learning community—one that encourages continuous improvement everywhere. In time, staff resistance and political agendas lose their power within a culture united around a few common goals. The success of all students must become the banner as the professional staff selects a few improvement targets each year and then works in teams interdependently toward those educational, rather than political or bureaucratic, goals.

The new job of supervisors is to study continuously the natural and complex work environments of teams. With a grounding in the quality literatures and a commitment to developing high-performing teams, the supervisor uses the same set of EQS standards to guide the team's work. The *supervisor's vision* relates to the future performance capacities of each team, given their changing job requirements. The *supervisor's strategic plan* translates the vision of high-performaning teams into action, a plan that reflects the goals of each work team. Teams can be linked interdependently with other teams, professionals, networks, and partnerships, with the supervisor facilitating this kind of *systems thinking* in action. *Information systems* are designed to gather routine data about the performance of teams and used to assist them in their continuous improvement process.

The supervisor's major task is *human resource development*, that is, anticipating the numerous ways in which the team's knowledge and skill bases can be enhanced to respond to changing conditions. *Supervisory services* are designed to help teams realize their vision as they respond to the growing complexity of the learning environment. The supervisory work objective is to meet and *exceed the needs of the client—the team*. And so data will show evidence of rises in team performance, with the supervisor demonstrating responsiveness and commitment to world-class standards for a new century, and to the success and satisfaction of each school work team. This is the new work of supervisors.

Conclusions

The rising complexity of school life is causing teachers and other professionals to respond in new ways to meet the changing needs of students. If schools are to survive as social agencies, teachers will require that new systems of work be designed for their success and that support structures be invented to assist them in their work and continuous growth. The work of supervisors, in the age of complexity, is to facilitate the team's responsiveness to the students they serve. Since all role groups in educational institutions now are facing the unknown and literally reinventing the systems of work, world-class standards that are based on the quality literatures, such as EQS, are the safest bet for helping teams with the new "right things." The old compliance and control ambitions of supervisors now must be shed altogether and be replaced by a system of team self-development and empowerment. If the complexity within each school and its teams is to be successfully addressed at all, teachers must be released to respond in natural ways to the students they serve. Supervisors play a vital role in adding value and energy to the work of teams and their development over time as they adjust and respond to complexity and ambiguity.

References

Acker-Hocevar, M. (1994). *The education quality system content validation.* Unpublished doctoral dissertation, University of South Florida, Tampa.

Acker-Hocevar. M. (1996, January). Conceptual models, choices, and benchmarks for building quality work cultures. *NASSP Bulletin, 80*(576): 78–86.

Crichton, M. (1990). *Jurassic park.* New York: Ballantine Books.

Elkind, D. (1995). School and family in the postmodern world. *Phi Delta Kappan, 77,* 8–14.

Gleick, J. (1987). *Chaos: Making a new science.* New York: Penguin Books.

Gunter, H. (1995). Jurassic management: Chaos and management development in educational institutions. *Journal of Educational Administration, 33,* 5–20.

Hodgkinson, H. (1991). Reform versus reality. *Phi Delta Kappan, 73,* 9–16.

Hodgkinson, H. (1993). American education: The good, the bad, and the task. *Phi Delta Kappan, 74,* 619–623.

Karweit, N. (1988). *Effective elementary programs and practices for at-risk students.* Paper presented at the annual meeting of the American Educational Research Association, New Orleans.

Lewin, R. (1993). *Complexity: Life on the edge of chaos.* London: Phoenix.

Secretary's Commission on Achieving Necessary Skills (SCANS). (1992). *Learning a living: A blueprint for high performance: A SCANS report for America 2000, part I.* Washington, DC: Department of Labor.

Snyder, K. J., Acker-Hocevar, M., & Snyder, K. M. (1994, April). *Organizational development in transition: A schooling perspective.* Paper presented at the annual meeting of the American Educational Research Association, New Orleans.

Snyder, K. J., Acker-Hocevar, M., & Snyder, K. M. (1995, September). *Chaos theory as a lens for advancing quality schooling.* Paper presented at the annual conference of the British Educational Management and Administration Society, Oxford University, Oxford, U.K.

Postnote

What is the New Supervisory Role in an Age of Complexity?

Dr. Snyder's systems view of an increasingly complex sociocultural world environment challenges educational supervisors to understand their work as service to students and the enrichment of their learning environments. This challenge will require some risk taking and a release from antiquated supervisory procedures and frames of thinking. If supervisors are to be part of the process of reconceptualizing supervision, they will have to build work teams that become learning communities possessing commitment, energy, and professional/technical skills. These teams will help to promote "quality work cultures" necessary for the transformation of schools. The twenty-first century will certainly usher in a complex and challenging age for supervision. Will supervisors adapt and reconceptualize their work?

Review Questions

1. How might you develop a "world-class professional work team" in your school/district? What organizational constraints or obstacles might you encounter?
2. Describe the belief system(s) necessary to develop "world-class professional work teams." What philosophical and/or cultural changes might be necessary to develop such a model?
3. What new forms of schooling will it take to prepare students for a new age of work, according to the author?
4. How does Chaos Theory provide a useful frame for addressing current conditions of schooling?
5. How might Chaos Theory help explain life in your classroom/school district?
6. How might Chaos Theory help you reframe or rethink some taken-for-granted assumptions about education/schooling?
7. According to Snyder, how can supervisors build strong professional work/learning teams?
8. Develop a scenario in which your work team progresses through three stages: awareness, transition, and transformation. How can this be accomplished?
9. What does Snyder mean by "visionary leadership?" Have you ever been influenced by a visionary leader? Explain.
10. Why is customer satisfaction so important in Snyder's system?
11. What new, specific skills will supervisors of the future need to work in an "age of complexity?"

For Further Research

1. Explore the organizational theories developed and discussed by Alfonso, Firth, and Neville (1975) and explain how these theories might inform any attempt to implement change(s) in schools specifically related to supervision.
2. How would Sergiovanni (see Perspective 1) react to Snyder's proposals? Similarly, how would Smyth (see Perspective 2) and Duffy (see Perspective 10) react to Snyder's thesis?
3. In your own school setting, are there any impediments to establishing Snyder's "professional work teams?" If so, describe how you as the superintendent would establish a working environment conducive to some of the reforms advocated by Snyder.
4. According to some authorities, the infatuation with "quality" issues in education is part of a conceptual and theoretical frame that is embedded in earlier practices involving scientific management. Examine the historical connection between, for example, Total Quality Management (TQM) and the rise of scientific management in the early decades of this century. Consult English (1994). How does this historical relationship inform current attempts to establish "work teams?"
5. To what extent does organizational climate affect the work of supervisors? Conduct a literature review of the relationship between organizational climate and school effectiveness. How do the results of this research relate to Snyder's proposals?
6. Conduct a literature search of TQM and discuss its advantages and disadvantages.
7. W. Edwards Deming (1986) taught the Japanese 40 years ago that "quality always leads to increased productivity." React to this statement. Do a literature review of Deming's work. (See e.g., Walton, 1986). How would Snyder react to Deming's proposals?
8. Compare this chapter with Snyder's views in Snyder (1988) and Johnson, Snyder, and Johnson (1995).
9. Alfonso, Firth, and Neville (1984) say that efficient supervisors have three kinds of skills: human, managerial, and technical. How do you think these authors would react to Snyder's call for quality in supervision? What skills would Snyder identify in "efficient" supervisors?
10. How do bureaucratic organizational structures influence the supervisor's role? What organizational structures permit the most efficient and effective instructional supervision?
11. Read Slattery's (1995) exposition of postmodernism and curriculum discourse and describe what supervision would look like in a postmodern world. Would Snyder concur with the postmodernist perspective framed by Slattery and others? Explain.

12. Consult volume 9 of *Wingspan*, which is devoted to quality issues and edited by Dr. Snyder. Compare Snyder's essay with the "Quality Revolution" described in *Wingspan*. How do other authors in *Wingspan* address this issue?

13. See January, 1996 issue of *NASSP Bulletin* guest edited by Drs. Snyder and Krajewski. Compare articles in that issue with Snyder's position in this chapter.

References

Alfonso R. J., Firth, G. R., & Neville, R. F. (1975). *Instructional supervision: A behavior system*. Boston: Allyn & Bacon.

Alfonso, R. J., Firth, G., & Neville, R. F. (1984). The supervisory skill mix. *Educational Leadership, 41*, 16–18.

Deming, W. E. (1986). *Out of the crisis*. Cambridge: The MIT Press.

English, F. W. (1994). *Theory in educational administration*. New York: HarperCollins.

Johnson, W. L., Snyder, K. J., & Johnson, A. M. (1995). Leadership for productrive schools: A Texas study. *Record in Educational Leadership, 15*(1), 42–46.

Slattery, P. (1995). *Curriculum development and the postmodern era*. New York: Garland.

Snyder, K. J. (1988). *Managing productive schools*. San Diego: Harcourt Brace Jovanovich.

Walton, M. (1986). *The Deming management method*. New York: Perigree Press.

Wingspan. (1994, March). Welcome to the quality revolution, *10*(1). (Published by Pedamorphosis, Inc., P.O. Box 271669, Tampa, FL 33688-1669)

Perspective 4

How Does the Law Affect Educational Supervision?

✦ ✦ ✦ ✦

Nicholas Celso, III, Kean College of New Jersey

✦ ✦ ✦

Perspective Summary

As an attorney and coordinator of graduate programs in educational administration, Nicholas Celso has had extensive experience in working with school districts and teachers on legal aspects of educational leadership and management. In this perspective statement he examines aspects of school organization, the concept of the supervisor as an agent of the state, and the dilemma of legal codes and prescriptions for supervisors who are attempting to eschew "traditional Weberian bureaucracy" for an approach that is collaborative, decentralized, and inquiry oriented. He sees the law as a "potent force" in the professional relationships of the supervisor and laments some of its consequences for the development of trust, collaboration, and shared governance. Dr. Celso provides interesting case study references and offers some rules of "supervisory self-preservation."

Guiding Questions

1. What is the role of the law in American education?
2. How does the law help to define the rights and responsibilities of supervisory personnel in education?
3. To what extent does "case law" help to create a framework for the role of the educational supervisor?
4. How does the law "as a mode of influence" on human behavior advance justice and morality in educational decision making?
5. How do the legal obligations and duties of the supervisor affect the development of a collegial and collaborative relationship between teachers and supervisors?

How Does the Law Affect Educational Supervision?

Nicholas Celso, III

Introduction

There are potent forces at work that impede the proper evolution of modern[1] models of humanistic, collaborative, decentralized, inquiry-oriented systems of educational supervision[2] in America's public schools. Well-described examples of such models include, but are not limited to, "clinical supervision" (Cogan, 1973), "human resources supervision" (Sergiovanni & Starratt, 1983, 1993), "developmental supervision" (Tanner & Tanner, 1987), and "artistic supervision" (Eisner, 1982, 1991). A thrust away from the old and neoscientific views of supervision (see Sergiovanni & Starratt, 1993) is commonly embraced by these models. Typically, they reject Theory X (McGregor, 1960) assumptions about teachers; production-function, factory-like accountability and quantification of teaching–learning, and top-down, authoritarian lines of authority. As Glickman (1992) has suggested, ". . . supervision, as a term derived from its industrial roots of closely inspecting the work of employees, is . . . antithetical (and also a bit disgusting) to . . . [today's school staff members]" (p. 2). In short, although there are a variety of competing definitions of educational supervision (Oliva, 1989), there appears to be growing consensus that sound supervisory practices must depart from traditional Weberian bureaucracy (Weber, 1947) and progress toward professional systems of shared decision making and mutual problem solving, from monitoring to leadership and, ultimately, to self-direction.

The myriad of internal and external forces that directly or indirectly affect public education generally and supervision particularly are well described in the literature. MacKenzie (1964), for example, has described a system of internal and external participants who exercise control over certain sources of power and influence to change the schools. Rubin (1982) has observed that as ". . . any other endeavor in the public arena, supervision is subject to the ebb and flow of policy and politics" (p. 170). Tanner and Tanner (1987) have indicated that ". . . supervisors . . . not only are under constant pressure and influence from various bodies representing conflicting interests, but find themselves shifting their priorities in successive epochs in accordance with the dominant wave of a particular period" (p. 274). Similarly, Sergiovanni and Starratt (1993) have noted that "supervision often is defined by criteria extrinsic to the moral qualities of teaching and learning" (p. xviii).

Among the factors influencing the implementation of modern supervisory practices is the organizational structure of the schools.

Sergiovanni and Starratt (1983) have observed that ". . . educational concerns are very much influenced by broader characteristics that make up the school's organizational subsystem" (p. 27). Firth and Eiken (1982) have argued that ". . . the choice of organizational structure [in a school or district] provides the linkage between the views regarding administration and the expectations for supervision. If changes are sought in supervisory practice, the values and assumptions implicit in the organizational structure of schools must first be altered." More to the point, they suggest that "the impact of the bureaucratic structure of the school district on the supervision of instruction is direct, strong and, in many instances, immediate" (p. 153).

Bureaucratic structure fosters uniformity, routines, and standard operating procedures, unlike the professional organization, which encourages creativity, diversity, and uniqueness. There is characteristically an emphasis in bureaucracies upon efficiency, specified skills, and task orientation, whereas professional systems promote achievement of broader goals, professional competence, and client orientation. Additionally, bureaucracies require authority derived from fixed positions through superordinate–subordinate staff relationships, as opposed to professional organizations, in which authority emanates from recognized personal competence that is situation specific and flexible. Furthermore, in bureaucratic structures there is an allegiance to legalistic rules and regulations, whereas professional systems are characterized by loyalty to recognized professional standards (Sergiovanni & Starratt, 1983).

But what forces cause any given school or school district to adopt and/or maintain a bureaucratic structure? Is it simply a matter of conscious decision making, or do subtle pressures coalesce to shape and force such systems? Although long recognized (e.g., MacKenzie, 1964) as a source of influence, the impact of the "Law"[3] on educational supervision recently has gained increased attention.

Hazi (1994), for example, has provided an insightful analysis of a public school district besieged by labor-relations problems emanating directly from legislated school reform efforts. Among other things she observed that "The combination of reform initiatives and state evaluation law . . . [had] created a legalistic vise for teacher accountability . . . school reform initiatives and the threat of evaluation law combine[d] to create a justifiable paranoia among teachers" (p. 211). Hazi concluded that "supervisory technique became a matter of protection for some administrators and teachers . . . [that] partly explain[ed] why practitioners easily overlooked collegiality and trust for the sake of models and techniques" (p. 213).

Hazi's case study provides strong support for the proposition that the "Law" is a driving force behind the inability of schools to break away from anachronistic bureaucratic proclivities. Although her analysis focuses mainly on the observation/evaluation function of the supervisor, the manifestation of underlying legal pressure is, in fact, much more pervasive in its day-to-day incarnation in the schools, touching upon virtually every supervisory function, including recruitment, hiring, assignment, transfer, promotion, staff development, discipline, dismissal, and curriculum development.

The "Law," in its most comprehensive sense, is a potent force that molds and shapes the practice and evolution of school supervision by superimposing a contextual paradigm in which recourse to litigation, grievances, arbitrations, and unfair labor charges increasingly is becoming the problem-solving mechanism of choice. In such a system, aspirations of mutual trust, respect, collaboration, collegiality, and shared governance are rendered impotent at the outset and must seem to the battle-weary little more than unattainable ideals of the uninitiated—simply mellifluous rhetoric wafting down from the ivory tower. The purpose of this exposition is to illustrate, with some level of specificity, the manner in which the "Law" affects the practice of educational supervision, in the broadest sense of that term.[4]

The Supervisor as State Agent

Public education clearly is a state function. Although the day-to-day operation of the schools has been delegated by the individual states to a variety of local, county, and regional boards of education, the state remains ultimately responsible and largely in control. Consequently, school districts are deemed to be public employers and their employees are said to operate "under color of state law." As a result, the entire range of federal, constitutional, employment, and labor laws that apply to state governments apply with equal force to the public schools and their employees. Public school supervisors are thus deemed to be agents of the state, acting under color of state law (*Vail v. Bd. of Ed.* (1983/1984)).

Perhaps the most immediate consequence of the supervisor as a state agent is the applicability of the Due Process clause of the Fourteenth Amendment to educational supervisors. As a result, their acts and omissions in the course of fulfilling their assigned duties may be deemed to have infringed upon a teacher's constitutionally protected liberty or property interests. The Due Process clause protects individuals against infringement by the state of their life, liberty, and property.

Liberty and property interests are judicially defined.[5] In the context of school supervision, they generally denote, respectively, the right to seek and obtain employment in one's chosen profession and the right to continued employment. The relative degree to which public school teachers enjoy these rights tends to vary according to their tenured or nontenured status.

Acquisition of tenure or continuing contract status generally signifies the attainment of an enforceable property right to continued employment. This means that any reduction in rank, compensation, and employment status generally is subject to specific, legislatively prescribed "causes." The causes, which vary from state to state, usually are couched in terms such as inefficiency, incompetence, immorality, unbecoming conduct, and just cause, and they include the right to an adversarial pretermination hearing and impose a burden of proof on the supervisor seeking to undertake corrective or disciplinary action.[6]

Adversarial Hearings and Collegiality: Oil and Water

The credibility of the supervisor is likely to be subjected to judicial scrutiny whenever an adverse employment decision is recommended regarding a tenured teacher. Although courts generally are reluctant to substitute their judgment for a supervisor's, they will receive and examine controverting evidence and set aside the challenged decision if, in their view, it is improper. The case of Everett Ames (*Ames v. Bd. of Ed.*, 1994) is illustrative.

Ames had been employed by a local board of education for 12 years and had achieved tenure pursuant to Kansas law. Under the governing state statute, tenured teachers are subject to nonrenewal upon proper notice and a hearing. Accordingly, the board notified Ames that his teaching contract would not be renewed because of "inadequate teaching and communication techniques over an extended period of time with basic resistance to change." (*Ames v. Bd. of Ed.*, 1994, pp. 233–234).

Ames requested and was granted a full evidentiary hearing before a "due process hearing committee." The committee found that Ames probably possessed inadequate teaching and communication techniques but did not possess a basic resistance to change. It also concluded that the state's statutory evaluation procedures had not been followed. The hearing committee therefore concluded that nonrenewal was improper. The school board nonetheless refused to reinstate Ames.

Upon subsequent appeal to the courts, the Kansas Court of Appeals ordered Ames' reinstatement. Although the supervisor's appraisal of Ames' ineffectiveness as a teacher was accepted, his removal from the classroom was set aside because of noncompliance with prescribed statutory evaluation procedures as well as the Hearing Committee's judgment that Ames was not resistant to change.

The decision in *Ames* (1994) illustrates the willingness of the courts to return inadequate teachers to the classroom despite their supervisor's judgments.

Similar legal challenges occur in the context of nonrenewal recommendations regarding nontenured teachers. Ohio's law is illustrative.[7]

In the case of *Naylor v. Bd. of Ed.* (1994), the Ohio Supreme Court ordered the reinstatement of a nontenured teacher, despite her teaching performance deficiencies, because the board and her supervisors failed to adhere to state procedural requirements.[8]

Deborah Naylor had been employed for three years as a ninth grade English and reading teacher at the time of her notice of nonrenewal. Had she been reemployed, she would have acquired continuing contract status under Ohio law. In three evaluations conducted during her third year of teaching, her evaluator cited one or more areas in need of improvement in teaching performance. As a result, the board determined that the interests of the school district would be better served by not permitting Ms. Naylor to attain continuing contract status and so advised her in response to her demand for a statement of reasons.[9] Exercising her statutory right, Ms. Naylor demanded a hearing before the board. Ohio's statutes require that such hearings be held in executive session (i.e., closed to the public) unless both the teacher and the board agree otherwise. Both the teacher and the board may be represented by an attorney, and a verbatim record may be taken by either party at its expense. In addition to presenting evidence at the hearing, Ms. Naylor wished to examine and confront (i.e., cross-examine) witnesses. The board, however, refused to permit her to call any witnesses (*Naylor v. Bd. of Ed.*, 1994).

Following her nonrenewal, Naylor appealed. The Ohio Supreme Court held that nontenured teachers who are notified of nonrenewal are entitled to receive a "clear and substantive" explanation of the reason for nonrenewal as well as a more formal, adversarial hearing before the board which includes confrontation and examination of witnesses on the record. Additionally, the Court found fault with Naylor's supervisor in that she did not adhere to state statutory evaluation requirements[10] by failing to provide specific recommendations for improvement for each deficiency noted and the means by which the teacher could obtain assistance. Finally, in ordering Naylor's reemployment, the court stated that the state statutes upon which it relied are remedial in nature and must be liberally construed in favor of teachers (630 N.E. 2d 162).

Like the *Ames* decision *Naylor* manifests a continuing judicial trend to exalt procedural compliance with rules and regulations over underlying substantive teaching inadequacies. Even though every reviewing tribunal agreed that Ames was probably ineffective as a teacher, the determination to nonrenew his contract nonetheless was set aside. Likewise, the *Naylor* Court never reached the issue of whether Naylor ought to be returned to the classroom given her performance deficiencies. The message is loud and clear: Incompetent teachers who assert a legal challenge to their supervisors' recommendations based on procedural technicalities stand a reasonably good chance of succeeding in the litigation arena.

As in Ohio, nontenured teachers in New Jersey who are not offered reemployment have a right to appear before the local board of education to attempt to "convince the members of the board to offer reemployment . . . [by] present[ing] witnesses on his or her behalf" (NJ Adm. Code 6:3-4.2(c),(g), 1995). Unlike Ohio, however, New Jersey's Open Public Meetings Act (1995) gives the teacher the right to compel the hearing into public whether or not the board agrees to do so. Once the teacher does so (as many do) it is not unusual to see the teacher's observations, evaluations, and even his or her supervisor publicly dissected and assailed. In the heat of the onslaught of personal attacks that often occur at such meetings, as well as the customary efforts of the local teachers union to discredit "administration" in any way possible to save the teacher's job, any aspirations of collegiality, trust, and mutual respect must seem as remote as a blizzard on a midsummer's day.

Promoting Teacher Potential and Potential Liability

Supervisors who are sued are exposed, together with their employers, to substantial monetary damages[11] and the distress, disruption, and uncertainty of lengthy litigation, as well as to potential damage to their personal reputations.

In *Lee v. Sch. Dist. No. 51-4* (1992), for example, a nonrenewed teacher sued, claiming that his principal's recommendation not to offer continued employment was based on illegal age discrimination. This case presents a good example of recourse to federal law as a basis upon which to sue a supervisor.

Robert Lee's principal had been newly assigned to the school at which Lee had been teaching from some 20 years. Although Lee's earlier evaluations had been generally satisfactory, the principal immediately detected problems with "classroom atmosphere." He labeled Lee's teaching as "sterile and blah" and cited needed improvement in four out of seven categories (pp. 326–327).

Despite some apparent improvement in the following years, Lee eventually became the object of an intense pattern of classroom visitation during the year in which he turned 65. Following observations by the principal on six consecutive school days, Lee was informed in a conference that his questioning and instructional management techniques were deficient. He was required to submit weekly lesson plans, and it was suggested that Bloom's Taxonomy be incorporated into his questioning techniques.

The assistant principal followed up by visiting Lee's classroom 12 to 15 times. He detailed Lee's performance minute by minute (perhaps using scripting). Lee was provided with two "assistance" plans, specifying a lack of instructional competence and providing several specific suggestions for improvement. Ultimately, Lee was informed that his reemployment would not be recommended because of (1) inadequate lesson preparation (2) poor relationships with parents and students, and (3) inappropriate handling of student problems and needs.

Lee arranged to be reviewed by an independent evaluator. However, when he received results that were not favorable to him he resigned. Mr. Lee even signed an agreement releasing the district from all claims in return for payments of $5,000 per year in four annual installments.

When the district replaced Lee with a younger teacher, he sued in federal court, alleging age discrimination under the Age Discrimination in Employment Act of 1967. At the ensuing jury trial, Lee's supervisors were not permitted to provide testimony about the oral complaints they had received from parents and students because they were not memorialized in written form and made part of the school's business records. In the absence of this corroborating evidence, the jury found that Lee's supervisors were motivated by willful age discrimination. The court awarded damages totaling approximately ninety thousand dollars[12] and upheld the jury's verdict of willful age discrimination because the number of classroom visits appeared to be a ploy to force Lee into early retirement.

However, as the dissenting judges noted, "the [classroom] visits in question were made after Lee received the notice of nonrenewal, at a time when Lee had expressed his determination to contest . . . the decision and both sides were preparing for the hearing afforded under state law" (p. 325).

In their apparent anticipation of imminent litigation, Lee's supervisors so closely monitored his performance that the jury viewed their efforts as harassment leading to constructive discharge, predicated upon discriminatory motives.

In addition to mounting recourse to the courts for the alleged constitutional and civil rights violations exemplified by the foregoing cases, there is an alarming propensity for suits against supervisors (and their school districts) to be couched in terms of tortious conduct, such as "intentional infliction of severe emotional distress" and "malicious interference with contract." Such suits commonly seek punitive damages. Although she did not succeed in proving such charges, Phylis Wagoner (Wagoner v. Bd. of Ed, 1994) certainly cannot be accused of not trying.

Wagoner had taught for 11 years as a high school physical education and health teacher. She was reassigned[13] by her principal to the role of ISS (in-school suspension) coordinator when he became " 'concerned that she was not doing an effective job of teaching basic skills to the students' and because the principal felt that the reassignment 'would improve the overall school program' " (p. 122).

Ms. Wagoner complained to the board and the superintendent about the reassignment and new working hours and informed her principal and the board that she would work "regular" hours. She was suspended for insubordination but subsequently reinstated upon appeal. One month later, she resigned (pp. 121–122).

In the suit that followed, Ms. Wagoner alleged that she had suffered "severe emotional distress, had been on medication for depression and anxiety, and had been diagnosed . . . as having a major psychiatric disorder" (p. 122). She sued for intentional infliction of severe emotional distress, constructive discharge, and malicious interference with contract, seeking punitive damages from her principal as well as the superintendent and board.

Wagoner procured an expert[14] who, among other things, stated on her behalf that "defendants' treatment of plaintiff was an 'extreme departure from the normal operation of a public school program' " and that the reassignment was not "motivated by a legitimate educational purpose" (p. 122). Among Ms. Wagoner's specific allegations were that (1) her supervisor told her to throw away her health and physical education materials because she would never need them again; (2) her new assignment placed her away from other faculty members and in a small room with high humidity and temperatures; (3) a student who had once pushed her was returned to her class; (4) her supervisor "stared" at her for "minutes at a time" while she taught; (5) she was assigned after-school and Saturday work hours; (6) she was asked to accompany students on a skiing trip in order to improve her evaluation; (7) she was told that she had the worst job in the school; and (8) she was denied the opportunity to attend workshops in her area.

The underlying truth or falsity of Ms. Wagoner's allegations was never ascertained because her complaint was summarily dismissed by the court because she could not meet her burden of making out a prima facie case.[15]

Although Ms. Wagoner's suit eventually was dismissed[16] because she could not satisfy the appropriate legal criteria, the case again underscores the risk involved in reassigning a teacher who is not performing adequately in her supervisor's judgment. If Wagoner's principal is to be believed, Ms. Wagoner simply was not teaching effectively. His motive for reassigning her was to "improve the overall school program" (p. 122). He was more concerned with the well-being of the students than with Ms. Wagoner's. Her response was to resign and sue everyone for monetary damages. If the principal was correct, this case vividly portrays the risks associated with his willingness to reassign a teacher in a manner that would benefit the overall educational program.

The Supervisor and Labor Relations Disputes

Supervisors increasingly must view themselves as likely defendants not only in the courts but in labor relations disputes involving teachers' unions as well. In such matters, it is not simply teacher versus supervisor but the teachers' union versus the supervisor.

A rising tide of unionism begun in the private sector during the mid-nineteenth century has now swept the nation, fully saturating both the private and public sector. With only a handful of exceptions, some form of collective negotiation concerning the terms and conditions of teacher employment is either permitted or required in most of the states (Valente, 1987; Yudof, Kirp, & Levin, 1992). Depending on permutations of local law, the terms and conditions of employment that are subject to the collective bargaining requirement may include salary, class size, workload, teacher evaluation procedures, transfer, discipline, inservice training, reduction in force, and dismissal procedures, as well as participation in a wide array of policymaking and service delivery matters bearing directly on the day-to-day operation of the schools (see Valente, 1987).

The impact of teacher unions upon the public schools has been pervasive. Kerchner and Mitchell (1988), for example, have described teacher unionism, together with school desegregation and categorical funding, as one of the three major structural changes in public education since World War II. According to Kerchner and Mitchell, the evolution of teachers' unions may be understood as progressing through three distinct stages: (1) the "Meet and Confer" generation, (2) the "Good Faith Bargaining" generation, and (3) the "Negotiated Policy" generation (p. 396). Each generation is characterized by different attributes.

The meet-and-confer generation is "predicated on the assumption that both sides are committed to defining and solving mutual problems using educational effectiveness as the criterion for each decision" (p. 397).

The good-faith-bargaining generation is epitomized by the belief that it has become "legitimate for teachers to represent their own welfare interests, and to explicitly bargain with management over economic and procedural due process questions" (p. 397). In this phase, there is an emphasis on contractual rights, work rules, and grievance adjudications.

In the negotiated-policy generation, everyone acknowledges that teacher negotiations are substantially and directly concerned with the ways in which schools will be run; the patterns of authority and social interaction in the buildings; the definition of what will be taught, for how long, and to whom; and the determinations of who has the right to decide how planning, evaluation and supervision of instruction will be carried out. (p. 398)[17]

The progression of unions from one stage to another may be viewed as movement away from bureaucratic toward professional school structures, from authoritarianism toward shared governance. But if the experience of one state (New Jersey) is characteristic of the national state of affairs, then this movement appears to have become stalled at the second stage. The manner in which the good-faith-bargaining phase, in turn, impedes implementation of professional supervision is amply illustrated by New Jersey's Employer–Employee Relations Act. (See generally, NJ Stat. Ann. 34:13A-5.1 *et seq.*, 1995).

In New Jersey, teachers have a state constitutional right to organize and bargain collectively. The state legislature, too, has promulgated a comprehensive statutory scheme governing public sector labor relations that requires, among other things, that local school boards meet and "negotiate in good faith" with the teachers' union regarding grievances, disciplinary disputes, and other conditions of employment, exclusive of the standards or criteria for employee performance (NJ Stat. Ann. 34:13A-5.3, 1995). The law also mandates negotiation of written grievance and disciplinary review procedures by which the union may appeal "the interpretation, application or violation of policies, agreements, and administrative decisions . . ." (NJ Stat. Ann. 34:13A-5.3, 1995). Under a series of recent amendments to the law, all disciplinary actions are subject to binding arbitration, in which the burden of proof is on the employer (NJ Stat. Ann. 34:13A-29, 1995). Moreover, disciplinary transfers are illegal, so a supervisor's recommendation to transfer, as well as his or her evaluation of a teacher, is readily vulnerable to attack through a prescribed regulatory procedure[18] or the mandated grievance/arbitration process, and may be subject to final determination by a third party under standards of review[19] that have nothing to do with the educational well-being of the students or the school.

The case of Sharon Cleghorn (*In the Matter of Burlington Twsp. Bd. of Ed.*, 1994) is an example. In accordance with the state-prescribed teacher evaluation regulations,[20] she received her annual teacher review and professional development plan. In it, she was rated "unsatisfactory" in performance of "professional responsibilities." The rating stemmed from allegations that Cleghorn had directly involved a student in a personal matter involving her spouse, who was a teacher in the same school district. Allegedly, Ms. Cleghorn asked a student to encourage another student, one of the alleged victims of sexual assault charges pending against Cleghorn's spouse, to drop the charges. The narrative portion of the evaluation criticized her for ignoring "appeals and directives by administrators" to refrain from such action.

Cleghorn challenged the evaluation as predominantly disciplinary and sought binding arbitration. The school board argued that the disputed comments were proper, in that her in-school conduct was both unprofessional and unethical. However, the State Public Employment Relations Commission determined that the contested portions of the annual review were predominantly disciplinary, in that they did not "touch upon her teaching performance" (p. 72).

The determination by the Public Employment Relations Commission demonstrates the line of demarcation it has drawn to distinguish evaluation from discipline: If comments relate to "teaching performance" they are evaluative; if they are not "designed to enhance teaching performance," they are disciplinary.[21] Of course, it is the Commission, an agency designed specifically by the state legislature to "make policy and establish rules . . . concerning [public] employer–employee relations" (NJ Stat. Ann. 34:13A-5.2, 1995), that determines on a case-by-case basis, fueled by ongoing union arbitration demands, what comments properly relate to teaching performance and thus may be included in an evaluation report.

Again, the message is loud and clear: Any teacher wishing to challenge the contents of his or her evaluation report need only enlist the union's support to file the necessary grievance and demand for arbitration. Indeed, once the disputed evaluation is characterized as disciplinary, the law requires the presence, if requested, of a union representative at any post-observation conference between the teacher and supervisor. (*NLRB v. Weingarten* (1979); see also *In re Twsp. of East Brunswick* (1982)). Moreover, any supervisor who believes, apparently as did Ms. Cleghorn's, in a more holistic approach to supervision—one, for example, that requires that attention be paid to "the process of classroom life," including the precise manner of social interaction between teacher and students (Eisner, 1982, p. 66)—must be prepared to defend him- or herself for having strayed onto that hazardous terrain.

The Supervisor as a Survivor

In a system dominated by recourse to the courts, administrative agencies, and labor arbitrators, the rules of supervisory self-preservation are relatively simple:

1. Be prepared at all times to be sued, notwithstanding the noblest of intentions.
2. Follow the rules, regulations and procedures carefully; do not attempt to be creative or to deviate from standard operating procedures.
3. Do not spend inordinate amounts of time observing teachers in the classroom; this may be viewed as harassment.
4. Document everything. Be sure to keep detailed written records, especially those concerning any complaints pertaining to teachers. They may become important evidence later.
5. Know and follow the collective bargaining agreement. Check it first before attempting to do anything.
6. Understand that your concerns about putting the needs of students first and foremost may be subordinate to the legal rights of teachers.
7. Confine your improvement suggestions to specific in-class, instructional activities. Avoid involvement in the more nebulous matters of interpersonal relationships and qualitative inquiry. Stick to the job description.

Failure to adhere to any of the suggestions may result in improved supervision but at great personal cost.

Endnotes

1. According to Anderson, " . . . [s]upervision has only recently reached a point where its theoretical and research basis commands respect and attention. Most of the books and articles dealing with supervision prior to the mid-1980's or thereabouts were generally regarded within the academic community as 'out of the mainstream' of significant educational inquiry" (Anderson, 1993, p. xiii).

2. Carl Glickman's description of the modern theories is illustrative: "Most activities or programs that I, and others, have clearly articulated in the past as 'supervisory' or 'supervision' . . . use terms such as *coaching, collegiality, reflective practitioners, professional development, critical inquiry*, and *study or research groups* (emphasis in original) (Glickman, 1992, p.2).

3. One of the greatest sources of its vitality, as well as confusion for the educational practitioner, is the dynamic and disparate nature of "the Law." The law is derived from many sources, including federal and state constitutions, statutes, regulations, and administrative and court decisions. The resulting amalgam, subject to certain rules of interpretation and constitutional and jurisdictional restrictions, constitutes the law, which itself is ever changing and susceptible to ongoing further revision. Space limitations do not permit an exhaustive analysis of the multifaceted aspects of the law and their respective impact upon educational supervision. Likewise, the complicated and sometimes conflicting differences between and among the states mitigate one's ability to generalize except on issues of federal law and common, national trends. Although federal constitutional, statutory, and regulatory precepts apply uniformly to all of the states, there remains significant variation among the states' respective constitutions, statutes, regulations, and case law. For the purposes of this analysis, therefore, the laws of individual states are discussed in tandem with the federal law whenever necessary in order to provide the needed level of specificity.

   Under the provisions of the Tenth Amendment to the U.S. Constitution, the authority to govern public education, not having been expressly delegated to Congress, is reserved to the states. Thus, every state has promulgated a comprehensive scheme of statutes setting forth the school laws (for a detailed listing, see Valente, 1987). In many cases, an individual state's school laws include administrative regulations promulgated by a state board of education. Such regulations, when properly adopted, generally have the force of law—for example, failure to adhere to them can result in the imposition of sanctions. Violations of the school laws may be adjudicated in a court of law and/or before a specified state agency or officer, depending upon varying procedures among the states.

   Although not primarily responsible for the public schools, Congress occasionally will enact legislation, often remedial in nature, that has a direct impact upon the schools. Usually, this legislation provides financial assistance to the schools in return for compliance with the practices specified in the act. Perhaps the best known example of such legislation is Title I of the Elementary and Secondary Education Act of 1965 (presently renamed and amended as the Improving America's Schools Act), which provides federal aid for basic skills improvement programs serving educationally disadvantaged students. In addition to laws aimed exclusively at the schools, Congress has adopted a myriad of legislation involving other matters which bear directly upon educational supervision.

Redress for alleged violations of federal laws usually is sought through the federal courts and various specialized administrative agencies established for this purpose. A notable example is the Equal Employment Opportunities Commission (EEOC), through which an aggrieved individual first must process his or her claim of any alleged civil rights violation.

The continual interaction of all of the foregoing produces the "Law," in its most comprehensive form, that ineluctably shapes and influences educational supervision.

4. Reference throughout this exposition to "supervisors" does not necessarily apply only to individuals whose job title identifies them as such, but rather denotes any role incumbent who is responsible for routine performance of any recognized supervisory function. In this respect, Oliva (1989) has explained,

> . . . *educational* supervision suggests responsibilities encompassing many aspects of schooling, including administration, curriculum, and instruction . . . *instructional supervision* narrows the focus to a more limited set of responsibilities. . . . *Administrative supervision* covers the territory of managerial responsibilities outside the fields of curriculum and instruction. *General supervision* is perceived by some as synonymous with *educational supervision* and by others as that type of supervision that takes place outside of the classroom (emphasis in original). (p. 8)

The lack of agreement on a clear definition of educational supervision is likely due, in part, to the complexity of the process of supervision, the emergence of a variety of competing models, and the external sources of influence on the supervisory process. It is not the purpose of this exposition to explore the various countervailing views but rather to address the manner in which one source of influence—the "Law"—brings pressure to bear on the still emerging profession and practice of educational supervision, in a sense that encompasses all of the functions described by Oliva.

5. Under guidelines established by the U.S. Supreme Court in *Board of Regents v. Roth,* (1972), and *Perry v. Sindermann* (1972), a school teacher's expectation of continued employment rises to the level of a protected property interest under state statutes and administrative regulations that grant tenure, or continuing contract, status.

Unlike tenured teachers, their nontenured colleagues generally are considered to be probationary and to have no constitutionally protected property interest in continued employment. Accordingly, in most states they can be discontinued for any reason that is not intrinsically illegal (e.g., gender discrimination) or otherwise arbitrary, capricious, or unreasonable (See Endnote 8).

6. In New Jersey, for example, a tenured teacher cannot be dismissed or reduced in compensation except for inefficiency, incapacity, conduct unbecoming a teaching staff member, or other just cause, and then only after a formal, adversarial hearing before an administrative law judge. (NJ Stat. Ann. 18A:28-5; 6-10 (1995)).

In South Carolina, teachers must advance to Level III of a three-level process to acquire continuing contract status; Level I is a provisional contract given to first-year teachers; Level II is an annual contract granted when a teacher is viewed as having satisfactorily completed provisional or Level I status. Attainment of continuing contract status at Level III signifies attachment of procedural due process protection. S.C. Code Ann. §59-26-10 *et seq.*(1995).

Compare *Kramer v. Newman* (1993/1993), in which pretermination procedures consisting of the opportunity to respond to charges of corporal punishment during several meetings with school district officials afforded sufficient due process to uphold tenure dismissal.

7. Despite the general inapplicability of the property interest prong of the Due Process clause to continued employment claims of nontenured teachers, state statutes and regulations increasingly provide procedural due process mechanisms by which employment decisions of supervisors can be subjected to judicial review. These procedural mechanisms typically take the form of prescribed evaluation procedures, required statements of reasons, and some type of termination hearing.

8. As a general rule, nontenured teachers are held to be probationary and may be discharged for no reason or for any reason that is not intrinsically illegal (e.g., gender discrimination). *Chambliss v. Foote* (1976/1977/1978).

   Because of their probationary status, nontenured teachers typically are thought to have no vested property right to continued employment and consequently are not generally entitled to a pretermination hearing. Essentially, they serve as at-will employees (see, e.g., *Castro v. New York City Bd. of Ed.* (1990/1991), although they are protected from employment decisions that are arbitrary, capricious, and unreasonable. Especially because a nontenured teacher is likely to seek reemployment in another school district, he or she enjoys a significant liberty interest. It is well established that the right to pursue one's career and secure future employment is a protected liberty interest that cannot legally be impaired by adverse action of a supervisor that has no basis in fact. See, for example, *Bogard v. Unified Sch. Dist. No. 298* (1977), in which it was decided that improper dismissal impaired valuable liberty interest to obtain other employment, and *Morris v. Bd. of Ed. of Laurel Sch. Dist.* (1975), in which nonrenewal reasons offered by the superintendent were held to be unfounded, violating liberty interest.

9. In Ohio, as in other states (e.g., New Jersey: NJ Stat. Ann. 18A:27-3 1995), a nonrenewed nontenured teacher may demand a statement of the reason(s) for nonrenewal.

10. Compare similar cases in other states in which failure to adhere to statutory evaluation procedures did not constitute a basis to set aside nonrenewal determinations: *Dore v. Bedminster Twsp. Bd. of Ed.* (1982), and *Schofield v. Richland County Sch. Dist. No. 1* (1994); see also *Amarillo Indep. Sch. Dist. v. Meno* (1993), overturning the state education commissioner's determination that current year evaluations of nontenured teachers must be considered before nonrenewal.

11. Some states, such as New Jersey NJ Stat. Ann. 18A:16.6 (1995), provide statutory indemnification for employees who are sued for acts and omissions arising in the course of performing their duties. However, when a supervisor is sued for something like intentional infliction of severe emotional distress or a civil rights violation, his or her employer likely will disavow responsibility to indemnify by claiming that the challenged act was unauthorized and outside the scope of assigned duties. Additionally, under the doctrine of "respondent-superior," the employer may be liable for the wrongdoing of the employee. However, vicarious liability may not extend to any intentional wrongdoing. Thus, where a supervisor is found to have committed an intentional transgression, such as infliction of severe emotional distress, monetary punitive damages may be assessed against him or her individually. See, for example, *Picogna v. Cherry Hill Bd. of Ed.* (1994/1995/1996), (in which $50,000 in punitive damages was initially assessed individually against a superintendent whose evaluations and related actions in support of a termination recommendation were found to

be tortious in nature. Although the amount of the damages was vacated on appeal and returned to the trial court for reevaluation, the supervisor's liability was affirmed).

12. The district court awarded $22,140 for back pay, $39,664 for front pay, $18,332 for attorney's fees, and $10,000 for liquidated damages. The Circuit Court of Appeals upheld most of the lower court's ruling, but returned the case for reconsideration of the liquidated damages portion of the award (981 F. 2d 320).

13. In matters of assignment and transfer there generally is no vested legal right. Teachers usually do not have an enforceable legal entitlement to any particular assignment, and supervisors retain the managerial prerogative to transfer them freely for legitimate educational reasons. However, this does not preclude the legal challenge of a transfer based on the teacher's exercise of a constitutional or civil right. Thus, where a school counselor who complained about a special education program was transferred, partly in retaliation for her comments, the transfer was invalidated as a violation of her right to free speech under the First Amendment (*Bernasconi v. Tempe Elem. Sch. Dist. No. 3* (1977/1977)). Similarly, when a high school teacher was suspended for four days and transferred because of an altercation with a student, a federal appellate court held that his due process rights were violated because he was not allowed a meaningful opportunity to be heard, to present witnesses, and to cross-examine witnesses against him. *Montgomery v. Carr* (1993).

   See also *Booher v. Hogans* (1978/1978) (in Tennessee, teachers enjoy no constitutionally protected right to any specific job assignment); *Keppler v. Hindsdale Twsp. H.S. District* (1989) (a transfer does not implicate property interest); *Thomas v. Smith* (1989) (no liberty interest is attached to a transfer between schools in the same district); and, *Raposa v. Meade Sch. Dist. 46-1* (1986).

14. The trial court ultimately disqualified the opinion as inadmissible because Wagoner's "expert" was not qualified in the subject areas in which his affidavit purported to offer expert opinions (Wagoner, 1994). However, his statements are nonetheless instructive.

15. Where a plaintiff cannot demonstrate that his or her allegations, if true, would meet the elements of proof required for any given cause of action, a court will dismiss the suit without a trial.

16. Compare *Picogna v. Board of Education* (1994/1995), discussed in Endnote 11.

17. Consider the current thrust toward site-based management within the context of this stage.

18. Upon the filing of a "Petition for Contested Transfer Determination" with the state's Public Employment Relations Commission, the Commission will determine, either on the papers or through an evidentiary hearing, whether or not the challenged transfer is "predominantly disciplinary" in nature. If so, the transfer will be nullified (NJ Adm. Code 19:18-1 *et seq.* (1995)).

19. Many collective bargaining agreements will contain a "just cause" clause that comes into play under such circumstances. The typical just cause clause provides that ". . . no teacher shall be reduced in rank, compensation or otherwise deprived of any professional advantage without just cause."

   Invocation of the just cause provision subjects a supervisor's decision to an arbitrator's scrutiny under the collective bargaining agreement's grievance procedure. In that event, if he or she can be persuaded that the supervisor's decision was not just, it may be reversed. In most "just cause" contractual arbitrations, the burden of proof will shift to the responding party—in other words, the supervisor actually may have to prove that his or her decision was educationally viable, supportable, and documentable.

20. Nontenured teachers in New Jersey must be observed a minimum of three times, and tenured teachers at least once, annually, pursuant to statute (NJ Stat. Ann. 18A:27-3.1 (1995)). The corresponding state board of education regulation (NJ Adm. Code 6:3-4.1 (1995)) also mandates with substantial specificity the procedural aspects of the teacher observation process, including the following requirements:

    1. For a minimum observation duration of at least "one class period in a secondary school" and "one complete subject lesson" in an elementary school.
    2. That the evaluation be in written form.
    3. That the written evaluation assess the teacher's "total performance," including, but not limited to, areas of strength, weakness, and needed improvement, based on the *job description*, as well as on *pupil progress and growth*.

    New Jersey's teacher-evaluation regulation is characteristic of the thrust toward duties-based evaluation suggested by Scriven (1990), who observed that, among other things, the criteria generally used for summative evaluation are not legally supportable. By using a list of job duties (i.e., a job description), he suggested, supervisors can determine at least that teachers are performing their required duties.

    New Jersey's law also is characteristic of the current national trend to legislate evaluation procedures as well as evaluation instruments (Sergiovanni & Starratt, 1993). In fact, more than half the states have enacted laws and/or administrative regulations governing teacher evaluation (McCarthy & McCabe, 1992).

21. See *Holland Twsp. Bd. of Ed. and Holland Twsp. Ed. Ass'n.* (1986). In the Cleghorn decision (*In The Matter of Burlington Twsp. Bd. of Ed.*, (1994)), the Commission did indicate that if the allegations are true, the arbitrator may not second-guess the ratings based on them (20 NJPER at 74, ftn. 2). Nonetheless, the point remains that the state's legislation interjects an outside party—an arbitrator—into the teacher evaluation process based on the commission's view of what is related to teaching performance and what is not.

References

Age Discrimination in Employment Act of 1967, 29 U.S. Code Ann., §621 *et seq.* (West 1995).

Amarillo Independent School District v. Meno, 854 S. W. 950 (Tex. Ct. App. 1993).

Ames v. Board of Education, Unified School District No. 264, 864 P.2d 233 (Kan. Ct. App. 1994).

Anderson, R. H. (1993). Foreword. In T. J. Sergiovanni & R. J. Starratt (Eds.), *Supervision: A redefinition.* New York: McGraw-Hill.

Bernasconi v. Tempe Elementary School District No. 3, 548 F. 2d 857 (C. A. Ariz. 1977), *cert.* denied 98 S. Ct. 72, 434 U. S. 825 (1977).

Board of Regents v. Roth, 408 U. S. 564, 92 S. Ct. 2701, (1972).

Bogard v. Unified School District No. 298, 432 F. Supp. 895 (D. C. Kan. 1977).

Booher v. Hogans, 468 F. Supp. 28 (D. C. Tenn. 1978, *aff'd* 588 F. 2d 830 (1978).

Castro v. New York City Board of Education, 777 F. Supp. 1113 (S. D. N. Y. 1990), *aff'd* 923 F. 2d 844 (2d Cir. 1990), *cert.* denied 111 S. Ct. 992 (1991).

Chambliss v. Foote, 421 F. Supp. 12 (D. C. La. 1976), *aff'd* 562 F. 2d 1015 (1977), rehearing denied 567 F. 2d 390 (1978), *cert.* denied 99 S. Ct. 127 (1978).

Cogan, M. L. (1973). *Clinical supervision.* Boston: Houghton Mifflin.

Dore v. Bedminster Township Board of Education, 449 A. 2d 547 (N. J. App. Div. 1982).

Eisner, E. W. (1982). An artistic approach to supervision. In T. J. Sergiovanni (Ed.), *Supervision of teaching* (pp. 53–66). Alexandria, VA: Association for Supervision and Curriculum Development.

Eisner, E. W. (1991). *The enlightened eye: Qualitative inquiry and the enhancement of educational practice.* New York: Macmillan.

Firth, G. R., & Eiken, K. P. (1982). Impact of the schools' bureaucratic structure on supervision. In T. J. Sergiovanni (Ed.), *Supervision of teaching* (pp. 153–169). Alexandria, VA: Association for Supervision and Curriculum Development.

Glickman, C. D. (1992). Introduction: Postmodernism and supervision. In C. D. Glickman (Ed.), *Supervision in transition—1992 Yearbook of the Association for Supervision and Curriculum Development* (pp. 1–3). Alexandria, VA: Association for Supervision and Curriculum Development.

Hazi, H. M. (1994). The teacher evaluation–supervision dilemma: A case of entanglements and irreconcilable differences. *Journal of Curriculum Supervision, 9,* 195–216.

Holland Township Board of Education and Holland Township Education Association, 12 NJPER 824, PERC NO. 87–43 (¶ 17316 1986).

In the Matter of Burlington Township Board of Education and Burlington Township Education Association, 20 NJPER 71, PERC No. 94–77 (¶ 25031 1994).

In re Township of East Brunswick, 8 NJPER 479, PERC No. 83–16 (¶ 13244 1982)

Keppler v. Hindsdale Township High School District, 715 F. Supp. 862 (N. D. Ill. 1989).

Kerchner, C., & Mitchell, D. (1988). The changing idea of a teachers' union. In M. G. Yudof, D. L. Kirp, & B. Levin (Eds.), *Educational policy and the law* (3rd ed.) (pp. 396–398). St. Paul, MN.: West Publishing Company.

Kramer v. Newman, 840 F. Supp. 325 (E. D. Pa. 1993), *aff'd* 16 F. 3d 404 (1993).

Lee v. Rapid City Area School District Number 51–4, 981 F.2d 316 (8th Cir. 1992).

Mackenzie, G. N. (1964). Curricular change: Participants, power, and processes. In M. B. Miles (Ed.), *Innovations in education* (pp. 399–424). New York: Teachers College Press.

McCarthy, M. M., & McCabe, N. H. (1992). *Public school law: Teachers' and students' rights* (3rd ed.). Boston: Allyn & Bacon.

McGregor, D. (1960). *The human side of enterprise.* New York: McGraw-Hill.

Montgomery v. Carr, 848 F. Supp. 770 (S. D. Ohio 1993).

Morris v. Board of Education of Laurel School District, 401 F. Supp. 188 (D. C. Del. 1975).

Naylor v. Cardinal Local School District Board of Education, 630 N.E. 2d 725 (Ohio 1994).

New Jersey Open Public Meetings Act, NJ Stat. Ann. 10:4-6 *et seq.* (1995).

NLRB v. Weingarten, 420 U. S. 251 (1979).

Oliva, P. F. (1989). *Supervision for today's schools* (3rd ed.). New York: Longman.

Perry v. Sindermann, 408 U. S. 593, 92 S. Ct. 2694 (1972).

Picogna v. Cherry Hill Board of Education, No. A-2380-73, Slip op. (N. J. App. Div. Sept. 7, 1994), *cert.* granted 139 NJ 443 (1995), *rev'd* in part and vacated in part, No. A-18, Slip op. (N.J. Supreme Ct. Feb. 22, 1996).

Raposa v. Meade School District 46-1, 790 F. 2d 1349 (8th Cir. 1986).

Rubin, L. (1982). External influences on supervision: Seasonal winds and prevailing climate. In T. J. Sergiovanni (Ed.), *Supervision of teaching* (pp. 170–179). Alexandria, VA: Association for Supervision and Curriculum Development.

Schofield v. Richland County School District No. 1, 447 S. E. 2d 189 (S. C. 1994).

Scriven, M. (1990). Can research-based teacher evaluation be saved? *Journal of Personnel Evaluation in Education, 4,* 19–32.

Sergiovanni, T. J., & Starratt, R. J. (1983). *Supervision: Human perspectives* (3rd ed.). New York: McGraw-Hill.

Sergiovanni, T. J., & Starratt, R. J. (1993). *Supervision: A redefinition* (5th ed.). New York: McGraw-Hill.

Tanner, D., & Tanner, L. (1987). *Supervision in education: Problems and practices.* New York: Macmillan.

Thomas v. Smith, 897 F. 2d 154 (5th Cir. 1989).

Vail v. Board of Education of Paris Union's School District, 706 F.2d 1435 (7th Cir. 1983), *aff'd.* 104 S. Ct. 2144 (1984).

Valente, W. D. (1987). *Law in the schools* (2nd ed.). Columbus, OH: Merrill.

Wagoner v. Elkin City Schools' Board of Education, 440 S.E.2d 119 (N.C. App. Ct. 1994).

Weber, M. (1947). *Theory of social and economic organization.* A. M. Henderson & T. Parsons (Trans.). Glencoe, IL: Free Press.

Yudof, M. G., Kirp, D. L., & Levin, B. (1992). *Educational policy and the law* (3rd ed.). St. Paul, MN: West Publishing Company.

Postnote

How Does the Law Affect Educational Supervision?

Professor Celso has made good on his promise to consider "with some degree of specificity" the legal dimensions of school supervision—not as the final arbitrator but as a "source of influence" in the development of supervisory practice. He indicates awareness of the complicated "internal and external forces" that confront educational organizations: accountability, diversity, bureaucracy, ever present procedural technicalities, and increased tensions associated with unionization. His message concerns the law as a realistic guide to the professionalization of the duties and responsibilities of teachers and supervisors.

Review Questions

1. How does Dr. Celso define supervision, and how does this definition influence his view of the legalities associated with supervision?

2. What rationale does Celso provide for discussing the impact of the law upon educational supervision? Is his rationale convincing? Why or why not?

3. What are some of the "potent forces," internal and external, that Celso refers to as factors that impede "the proper evolution of modern models" of supervision?

4. Celso references the importance of "organization structure" in the design of supervisory programs. In what way(s) does school organization or structure affect supervision?

5. In what sense does the "Law"—the legal mandates and precedents related to education—make a difference in the philosophy and practice of supervision?

6. Given that public education is a responsibility reserved for the states, and given that supervisors are state agents, how do such legal traditions shape and affect the way(s) supervisors and teachers work together?

7. Examine the outlines of the *Ames* and *Naylor* decisions as reported by Celso. Provide your interpretation of the court decisions in these cases and indicate how you would have changed the way in which the supervisor or school board worked with the grievant.

8. Offer your position/ideas on what Celso refers to as the "judicial trend to exact procedural compliance with rules and regulations over underlying substantive teaching inadequacies" in the review of teaching performance in the courts.

9. Critique the supervisory processes and the court decisions in the *Lee* and *Wagoner* cases. How do these cases correspond to

collaborative "inquiry-oriented" supervision? Do they tend to confirm the continued strong presence of Weberian bureaucratic supervisory practices? Explain your position.

10. Celso considers the "impact of teacher unions as pervasive" where teachers in some states have a "constitutional right to organize and bargain collectively" and where local schools are required to "negotiate in good faith" on a range of conditions of employment. What in your judgment has state-mandated collective bargaining done to the development of the supervisory process?

11. Examine Celso's "rules and regulations of supervisory self-preservation." What model of supervision do these rules and regulations represent? What combination of circumstances prompt these admonitions? Given such circumstances is there an alternative approach to self-preservation? How do we get beyond self-preservation to mutual risk taking and the conditions required for collaborative, inquiry-oriented systems of educational supervision? What price leadership?!

For Further Research

1. Compare Celso's analysis of the influence of the law in supervision with Hazi's (in press) analysis.

2. Discuss why many school systems have adopted a bureaucratic organizational framework and discuss how bureaucracy influences supervisory practice. Would legal issues raised by Celso differ in nonbureaucratic organizations? Explain.

3. Compare and contrast Celso's definition of supervision with other authors' in this text: Waite, Sergiovanni, Griffin, and Starratt, among others. How does Celso's definition of supervision inform his discussion of the law of supervision?

4. Have you been personally involved in or do you have knowledge about a case in which a tenured or nontenured teacher was subject to nonrenewal or termination? Describe the case. What effect did the case have on supervisory practice in your school/district?

5. If you were the supervisor involved in the *Ames* case, how would the ultimate outcome have affected your ability to supervise teachers in that school? Explain.

6. Celso describes the New Jersey Open Public Meetings Act that gives the teacher the right to publicly air a post dismissal hearing before the Board of Education. Such public hearings, according to Celso, are likely to preclude future attempts at "collegiality, trust, and mutual respect." How would Pavan (see Issue 7) react to such a situation? Can "collegiality, trust, and mutual respect" ever prevail in a climate of litigation?

7. What is your reaction to a proposal that would eliminate separate teacher and supervisor unions in favor of establishing one union for both teachers and supervisors? What is the likelihood

that such a proposal could be implemented in your district/city?

8. What is the impact of teacher unionism on the practice of supervision?

9. Have you ever been involved in a grievance hearing? Describe the experience. What was the outcome? What consequences do grievance hearings have for the practice of supervision?

10. React to Celso's seven "survival" rules for supervisors. Which rules have you violated? Which rules make the most sense to you? Has Celso's perspective statement convinced you to be more conscious of the legal ramifications of practicing supervision? If so, how?

11. Legal issues are often not addressed in the field of supervision. What other issues, not discussed by Celso, would be of concern to practitioners? Conduct a literature review on the law and supervision. Discuss your findings.

12. Many legal issues raised by Celso as they relate to teacher evaluation have been raised, albeit differently in some instances, by other legal scholars. Consult the work of individuals such as Joseph Beckham, Robert Stephens, and Perry Zirkel. Compare and contrast their views with the perspective presented by Celso. Also, consult the following publications and conduct a literature review of legal aspects related to educational supervision: *West's Education Law Reporter, School Law Bulletin, Journal of Legal Education, Principal, NASSP Bulletin, American School Board Journal, Journal of Law and Education,* and *School Administrator.*

Reference

Hazi, H. M. (in press). Legal considerations in supervision. In G. R. Firth & E. Pajak (Eds.), *Handbook of research on school supervision.* New York: Macmillan.

Perspective 5

Why Is Advocacy for Diversity in Appointing Supervisory Leaders a Moral Imperative?

✦ ✦ ✦ ✦

Carl D. Glickman and *Ronald L. Mells,* University of Georgia

✦ ✦ ✦

Perspective Summary

Noted scholar and director of the Program for School Improvement in the College of Education at the University of Georgia, Carl Glickman, with his colleague Ron Mells, a former assistant principal, address the issue of diversity in selecting individuals for leadership positions. In this perspective statement they affirm that advocating diversity is unquestionably a moral imperative. They extend discussion of this issue by affirming that a "school or district should not simply look diverse (ethnically, culturally, or racially); it should as well be used to lend perspectives and gain the richest information possible on how to best educate both minority and majority students." In this essay, each author presents an experience that has shaped his viewpoint about the importance of achieving diversity in educational settings. They conclude by indicating that the very foundation of American democracy is inextricably entwined with the attempt to embrace and achieve diversity.

Guiding Questions

1. In what sense is advocacy for diversity a moral imperative?
2. Should your school/district adopt an affirmative action policy to hire new supervisory personnel? Why or why not?
3. In what ways do school systems reinforce bigotry, inequality, and repression?
4. How do school systems promote equality, justice, and empowerment?
5. What steps, if any, should be taken to facilitate the representation of minority group members in supervisory positions?
6. Do current hiring patterns in your district promote equality, opportunity, and justice, or do they reinforce bigotry, inequality, and repression?

Why Is Advocacy for Diversity in Appointing Supervisory Leaders a Moral Imperative?

Carl D. Glickman and *Ronald L. Mells*

On being invited to respond to the question "Why is advocacy for diversity in appointing supervisory leadership a moral imperative," the two of us sat together to sketch out some thoughts. The question of whether advocacy for diversity should be a moral imperative has a simple answer: Why yes, of course! The hiring, staffing, and advancement of educators in instructional leadership positions should reflect the diversity of America. However, the answer to why diversity is a moral imperative is much more profound. Diversity of personnel in a school or district should not simply look diverse (ethnically, culturally, or racially); it should be used as well to lend perspectives and gain the richest information possible on how to best educate both minority and majority students. Thus, there is a much higher moral purpose to diversity in education. Inclusion rather than exclusion represents this higher moral purpose.

We, the co-authors, work together. We both have supervisory leadership roles, and our common work is to implement collaborations among higher education and public schools that aim to sustain educational renewal in a democratic direction. The two of us are of different religions, races, and regional backgrounds. Neither one pretends to speak for or be a single representative of any particular cultural group. Instead, we address this question as individuals from our own unique backgrounds. First, you will hear from Ron, then Carl, and at the end from both of us.

Ron

Recently I met with a group of education officials to discuss school reform efforts in their state. Serving a population of 71 percent White, 27 percent African-American, and 1.7 percent Hispanic, many of these state officials are in positions to influence policy and program development that dramatically affects all of the state's school-age children. Excluding my presence, ethnic diversity among this group was absent. Moreover, my presence as an African-American was happenstance rather than a deliberate attempt to exercise the idea of inclusion.

Later that night, my thoughts focused on the informal school reform meeting with representatives from various state offices and organizations. I began to realize that I had experienced a situation that my father made me aware of during childhood. He said, "Son . . . I want you to know that white folks are planning for us while we are still sleeping." To me, this state-level meeting (of well-intentioned educators) reflects the notion espoused by my father, Robert L. Mells, and other African-Americans in my community. The intentions of these educators seem sincerely focused on improving the educational system for all students in the state. However, their failure to include in the discussion individuals of different racial, cultural, and ethnic perspectives can lead them to adopt unfounded assumptions that will influence the development and implementation of policies that are inherently flawed. When discussions take place among public officials who can influence the development of educational policies affecting the lives of African-Americans, or any other minority, representation of the group's culture is critical.

It should come as no surprise that developing policies without the input of those being affected by them can be viewed as short-sighted. Policymakers should include in their deliberations the meanings behind quantified data. In most cases, access to this type of information can only come from individuals who are part of the target population to be served. If policymakers would operate under the democratic principle of inclusion, educational policy and programs would reflect in design a sensitivity to cultural norms and attitudes of the target population. By using this approach, they could increase their chances of realizing positive outcomes from their policy decisions.

An episode from my tenure as a school administrator serves as an illustration of incomplete policy decisions when individuals who represent an insider's view are not part of the process. I served as the assistant principal in a large urban high school with a population of 1,200 students in grades eight through twelve. African-Americans made up about 98 percent of the student body. I had the responsibility for maintaining a safe and orderly school environment. Students' concerns accounted for much of my time. In the area of student conflict, I had to deal with many incidents involving fights among students. The majority white school district in which my school was a member, provided an approach to guide school administrators in their decision making when dealing with problems of student fights.

At the beginning of each school year, students attending our school were given a discipline brochure. They were required to sign for the brochure as proof of receivership. Lessons were taught by teachers on the possible consequences for various types of infractions of the rules. Students were then required to take a test to determine their level of understanding about the rules and consequences. Additionally, I met with all students from each grade level to address their questions and reinforce the need to reduce the number of student fights.

Even though the system wide discipline brochure detailed various student infractions and possible consequences, each school had a great deal of latitude in administering the regulations. In my school, the principal upheld the district policy on fighting by insisting that all students involved in a fight—regardless of the circumstances that led up to it—get a minimum of three days out-of-school suspension. This three-day suspension would apply to a student even if the student was only defending himself/herself from the student who initiated the confrontation. So, from late August to the Christmas break, I vigorously approached the problem of fighting among students by applying the prescribed method. This reactive approach to student discipline began to consume more and more of my time and energies.

As my days at school became more inundated with phone calls to parents explaining the circumstances that led to my decision to suspend their child for fighting, I found it difficult to explain why a student must receive the required three days out-of-school suspension when trying to defend himself. The packaged response I gave to a parent who questioned my decision was, "I'm sorry, but this is the policy of the school." Parents would ask, after a few choice words reflecting their displeasure, what should a student do if attacked? School officials expected students to report an attacker to a teacher or administrator and not get involved in a confrontation.

As I continually administrated the consequences for fighting, I recognized that the policy did little to curb the seemingly endless incidents of fighting among students. Fights would occur among students while en route to school in the morning, during school, and after school. I began to look more closely at the policy and discovered that it was inherently flawed. Most children in African-American communities are taught at an early age to meet aggression with aggression. In my case, I was given a general rule to go by. My father instructed me to avoid a fight if possible, but if someone should strike me, I should respond by finding a brick, hitting that person in the head, and then calling him. While this explicit response to a confrontation may not have been given to all African-Americans at an early age, the notion of retaliation in self-defense certainly was a value shared by many African-American parents.

Whether such a stance is appropriate in public schools is not the issue. Rather, its cultural underpinnings need to be understood when trying to find solutions to students' behavior and learning. When school officials construct a policy that is diametrically opposed to the norms of students, they do little to achieve the goals that the policy intended. Lomotey's (1990) work supports the notion that a deep understanding of students and their communities is paramount in helping African-American students succeed in school.

Carl

A decade ago, my colleagues and I sent letters to schools in Georgia asking them of their interest in becoming involved in a network of schools devoted to public education renewal and democratic practice. The first response resulted in 24 school teams attending initial orientation meetings and later committing themselves to membership. At the first congress meeting of our representatives from these schools, one African-American principal (Delores) turned to me and said, "I don't see many other people in this room who look like me." She had a valid point. We had 4 schools out of the 24 with predominantely African-American populations. The majority of our schools were suburban, middle class, and mostly White. Since this network was to be a reform effort to improve public education throughout the state (by assisting schools to take on leadership roles for demonstrating educational renewal practices) and since our state population was nearly one-third African-American, we had clear under-representation. The same tired excuses could be thought of as to why more African-American educators and African-American schools hadn't joined. Our university had been known for its outright segregationist stand during the period of school integration. I am White and the initial leader of this effort. Similar school reform initiatives in the United States are often seen by many African-Americans as White people's ideas to help White people.

It was easy to explain why minority educators weren't initially attracted to this work. One strategy would be to redo what we had already done—a second mailing of state-wide invitations. Instead, we asked Delores, who had brought up the matter, to discuss how we might proceed. The strategies were not dramatic, but the results have poured in over the years. As of now, more than one-third of our schools (of more than 80 members) are predominantely minority, and demonstrations of school-wide implementation of educational renewal can be observed in virtually every racial, socioeconomic, and demographic setting in the state.

So what happened? In business terms, I guess we did "niche marketing." Delores said that she and other African-American friends called colleagues at other schools who might be interested in later participation. We then set up a list of schools to follow up with mailings, phone calls, and visits. We held workshops and meetings in selected urban districts and made ourselves (both White and Black)—members of the League of Professional Schools—available to meet at district offices, principals' centers, and teacher's associations that had high percentages of minority educator participation. We asked our African-American schools to share their work and invite visits from other schools and districts. We jumped at the opportunity to be involved in the educational efforts of the Atlanta Project—the Carter Center's effort to facilitate change in urban, mainly African-American communities. We initiated formal collaborations with other colleges and universities and contracted with African-American faculty at other institutions who were highly esteemed among African-American (and general) communities to participate in our on-site facilitations, presentations, and workshops. At the same time, on our own staff we hired more minority graduate assistants, office personnel, associates, and directors.

Now, before this essay starts to appear as too much of a success story of progress, let me say that diversity is always tenuous and amenable to charges of "tokenism" (or the reverse, minority favoritism). In speaking about and acting on diversity, there always is the vulnerability of having one's intentions questioned. Leadership for diversity is not simply having more minority people as part of an organization or network; rather, it is having all members—minority or not, with their own ideas and at times contradictory perspectives, be a constitutive part of the whole. It has to do with being secure with different and at times oppositional perspectives of free thinking people with different histories. Diversity of instructional leadership personnel (whether from the ranks of administrators, teachers, staff, or parents) is the only way that we can understand our students and that students, in turn, can understand the adult world. Regardless of the specific student population in a school, whether predominately White, African-American, Asian-American, Native-American, and so forth, the imperative remains that adults who work there reflect the diversity of America. The reason is twofold.

First, how a student learns is influenced by his history of family, culture, and local community norms. Adults should be familiar with those histories in order to offer insights into how to enrich the learning process for the individual student. I disagree with the use of group classification—race, class, or gender—to determine how any particular student communicates, behaves, and learns. Students are individuals first with a complexity of histories and overlapping worlds of categorized groupings. But educators need to know those histories to fully understand their students.

Second, what students learn from other students and from other adults will enable them to participate in a much richer and truer democratic world than we currently have. When people of various cultures, races, and histories are working together on a common purpose, they realize that everyone's history belongs to everyone else. European, African, Hispanic, Asian, Native, and other histories represent the history of Americans.

Diversity is thus not solely an issue of being tolerant and fair (which the huge majority of educators, parents, and citizens agree is one of the most important goals for schools). Tolerance and fairness are the most important antecedents to equality of participation for all members of a society to analyze, argue, and resolve common issues.

Ron and Carl

Arriving at the doorsteps of many schools across the nation are school-age children who are ethnically, socially, and racially diverse. In many cases these children have in tow attitudes and beliefs that are not consistent with the institutions that seek to teach them. Educational leaders will require a level of understanding that penetrates the veneer and illuminates the underlying assumptions that guide the attitudes and behaviors of these children. To many observers, the notion of advocating for diversity in leadership positions in education is resurrecting an issue settled as a result of the Civil Rights movement. Data over the last 30 years, however, show a continuing trend of under-representation of minorities in leadership roles. We are still short of diversity as a constitutive element of education and society. Harold Hodgkinson reports that 36 percent of school-age children will be from minority backgrounds after the year 2000. Yet at the same time, "there's a lack of representation of minorities among public school faculties, and the problem is accelerating" (Elam, 1993, p. 223). This same discrepancy can be found in the number of minority teachers entering the profession and the number of minorities found among current principals, superintendents, assistant superintendents, teacher leaders, and higher education faculty.

So why is leadership for diversity not just a hiring or staffing perspective but a moral stance? We need to remember that public schools have as their primary purpose educating students for participation in full, democratic life (i.e., for the public). And that participation, although never fully realized in American democracy, is a right of all our citizens, no matter what their background. Without diversity among leaders in education, we wrongfully deny students in our nation's public schools the opportunity to benefit from knowledge, wisdom, and understanding that is embodied among people. Only through effectively educating all students can democracy flourish in this country.

American democracy has always had two different stories, one of striving toward noble aspirations of inclusion with astounding success, the other of superficial rhetoric followed by repressive practices that continue to exclude. We can argue the good story. For example, in the last 25 years, the African-American middle class has grown from 5 to 40 percent in population, and virtually every minority group of students in the United States has made dramatic gains in narrowing educational achievement gaps with White peers. But we can also argue the bad story, that America is the most economically stratified industrialized nation in the world and that many minority student groups still languish too far behind the educational and economic attainments of their White counterparts. Both stories of America are true. The American educational ideal always remains to either ignore or respond to. If we are to respond to the ideal that "all students are entitled to an education that will enable them to be free and responsible for each other," then all of us—educators and citizens in all our diversity—need to be a constitutive part of planning how to put practice in line with aspirations.

So, at the end, why is diversity of supervisory leadership a moral imperative? How else will we understand our children and each other and know how to educate all children well? What is the alternative? We can step away and hide from each other, or we can step toward each other with invitation, colleagueship, and a willingness to decide as equals what needs to be done to make educational practice one in which ". . . Democracy means everybody, including me."

Endnote

1. From conversations with my Dad, Robert L. Mells.

References

Elam, S. (1993). *The state of the nation's public schools.* Bloomington, IN: Phi Delta Kappa.

Lomotey, K. (Ed.). (1990). *Going to school: The African-American experience.* Albany, NY: State University of New York Press.

Rampersad, A. (1988). *The life of Langston Hughes: I dream a world.* Vol. 2. New York: Oxford University Press.

Postnote

Why Is Advocacy for Diversity in Appointing Supervisory Leaders a Moral Imperative?

Issues of diversity have polarized our society and tacitly shaped the way we think about and relate to one another. Some of us believe that our educational system is fundamentally based on the rhetoric of equality and justice and that in reality there are social, economic, and political conditions that contribute to and help legitimate inequalities. For these individuals, public schooling perpetuates and reinforces social class, racial, and gender stratifications in a number of insidious ways. For others still, schools in fact promote the ideals of equality, justice, and opportunity by providing a multitude of unique opportunities for personal growth and empowerment. Regardless of one's stance on this issue, statistics reflect that people of color and women, for example, have been under-represented in administrative positions in public schools. What are some social, political, economic, and cultural factors that may contribute to this under-representation and what, if anything, can and should be done about it?

Review Questions

1. In addressing our question, the authors imply that few individuals would challenge the statement that "advocacy for diversity is a moral imperative." Is this true? Who might state otherwise? What argument(s) could be generated to challenge the issue of diversity in supervision and in education in general? Construct a rationale and provide examples.

2. Critically analyze the personal statements offered by the authors. What is the essential message of each anecdote? Assess the degree to which they make their point.

3. If inclusivity is a "democratic principle," why have our institutions in society been so exclusive in regard to different racial, cultural, ethnic, and religious groups?

4. Ron Mells provides an anecdote about dealing with disciplinary problems in his capacity as assistant principal. He illustrates the cultural value conflicts that often prevent African-American students from accepting more dominant values and beliefs. Does his experience ring true for you? What point is Mells making, and how does his anecdote relate to the chapter's theme? Can you provide other examples, perhaps from your own experience, to indicate the way(s) one's cultural values might coincide or conflict with the prevailing values in a school?

5. React to the policy established at Mells' school that metes out a three-day suspension to both parties in a dispute. Is it reasonable

to expect that a student should report any attack immediately to a teacher/supervisor and not engage the attacker?

6. React to Mells' caution that we must remain sensitive to cultural norms and expectations of various ethnic groups. How might we do so?

7. How does Mells' personal experience as a school administrator help clarify or illuminate why "advocating diversity" is a vital moral imperative?

8. React to Carl Glickman's efforts in Georgia to hire "more minority graduate assistants, office personnel, associates, and directors."

9. Why does Glickman say that diversity is "not solely an issue of being tolerant and fair?" React to his rationale for supporting diversity.

10. Does your school/district promote racial and ethnic diversity among students, faculty, and administration? What steps are or should be taken to ensure representation of all groups?

For Further Research

1. Issues of diversity, especially of gender and race, were raised by Greene (1982) in relation to supervision. What recommendations does Greene make to achieve "equal access to supervisory positions?" Examine Greene's suggestions at the end of her chapter and discuss whether any of her suggestions have been taken seriously.

2. How might we improve access, recruitment, and success for prospective supervisors representative of culturally, racially, and socioeconomically diverse backgrounds?

3. A recent issue of the *Journal of Teacher Education* (volume 46, September-October 1995) addressed the issue of diversity in teacher preparation. Read selected articles from that issue, refer to many of the references cited, and explain how and why this issue may influence the way supervisors are trained, prepared, and selected.

4. Examine Nieto's (1992) premise in *Affirming Diversity* and explain the sociopolitical forces that may come to bear on the issue addressed in Glickman and Mells' chapter.

5. Advocates for diversity encourage educators to take proactive steps toward ensuring inclusion of a wide range of ethnic groups. How do advocates for diversity claim we can achieve this ideal? See Gates (1995) and Derman-Sparks (1995).

6. Does Mells' description of the role of the assistant principal as chief disciplinarian sound familiar? Compare findings of a recent survey administered in New York City (Glanz, 1994) with Mells' description. What is the role of an assistant principal? Should assistant principals play a more prominent role in instructional and curricular matters?

7. Marshall (1992) states that "Women and minorities do not attain assistant principalships as readily as white males" (p. 66). There are similar findings regarding other supervisors. Consult the following works and discuss the extent to which various minority groups have achieved equity in administrative and supervisory positions: Haven, Adkinson, and Bagley (1980), Hill and Ragland (1995), Jonas and Montenegro (1990), Lovelady-Dawson (1980), Marshall (1992), Ortiz (1982), Sagaria (1988), Strober and Tyack (1980), and Weis and Fine (1993).

8. Consult some of the periodicals below and conduct a literature review of articles that deal with issues of diversity related to hiring school personnel. Contrast their views with those of Glickman and Mells. See *Urban Education, Teaching and Teacher Education, Journal of Blacks in Higher Education, Educational Forum, Education and Urban Society, Theory into Practice*, and the *Handbook of Research on Multicultural Education*.

9. The Bylaws of the National Policy Board for Educational Administration, founded in 1988, include as one of their major purposes to recruit and place women and minorities in positions of educational leadership. Consult this document and research what has been done to further this objective of increasing minority representation in supervisory positions.

10. Examine Tyack's (1993) historical overview of diversity in America and indicate how this historical understanding supports the moral imperative discussed in this chapter.

11. Banks (1994), Cyrus (1992), Garcia (1992), Grant (1988), and Jordan (1995) suggest that racial attitudes and prejudice can be reduced with "carefully planned instructional approaches." What do you think?

12. Have you or has someone you know ever been a victim of discrimination when applying for a supervisory position? If so, how did you or the person feel? To what degree do you believe prejudice or racism influences hiring practices in school administration? How might you increase awareness and sensitivity toward diversity issues?

13. Gallegos (1995) addresses the lack of recruitment, hiring, and retention of females in university positions. Explore the lack of access women have had in education over the past 100 years. What are the prospects for the future? Similarly, Murray, Husk, and Simms (1995) indicate the lack of recruitment and selection for administration preparation programs of African Americans. The authors state that the "significant shortage of African-American teachers will impact the number of African American school administrators." Examine their research, findings, and recommendations.

References

Banks, J. A. (1994). *Multiethnic education: Theory and practice.* Boston: Allyn & Bacon.

Cyrus, V. (1992). *Race, class, and gender in the United States.* Palto Alto, CA: Mayfield.

Derman-Sparks, L. (1995). How well are we nurturing racial and ethnic diversity? In D. Levine, R. Lowe, B. Peterson, & R. Tenorio (Eds.), *Rethinking schools: An agenda for change* (pp. 17–22). New York: The New Press.

Gallegos, G. (1995). A status report of females in higher education: The unfinished agenda. *Record in Educational Leadership, 15*(1), 16–19.

Garcia, R. (1992). Countering classroom discrimination. *Theory into Practice, 23,* 105–109.

Gates, H. L, Jr. (1995). Multiculturalism: A conversation among different voices. In D. Levine, R. Lowe, B. Peterson, & R. Tenorio (Eds.), *Rethinking schools: An agenda for change* (pp. 7–8). New York: The New Press.

Gay, G. (in press). Culture and gender perspectives. In G. R. Firth & E. Pajak (Eds.), *Handbook of research on school supervision.* New York: Macmillan.

Glanz, J. (1994). Redefining the roles and responsibilities of assistant principals. *The Clearing House, 67,* 283–288.

Grant, C. A. (1988). The persistent significance of race in schooling. *Elementary School Journal, 88,* 562–569.

Greene, E. (1982). Issues of race and sex in supervision. In T. J. Sergiovanni (Ed.), *Supervision of teaching* (pp. 119–132). Alexandria, VA: Association for Supervision and Curriculum Development.

Haven, E., Adkinson, P., & Bagley, M. (1980). *Minorities in educational administration: The principalship.* Washington, DC: National Institute of Education.

Hill, M. S., & Ragland, J. C. (1995). *Women as educational leaders: Opening windows, pushing ceilings.* Thousand Oaks, CA: Sage Publications.

Jonas, E., & Montenegro, X. (1990). *Women and minorities in school administration: Facts and figures, 1989–1990.* Arlington, VA: American Association of School Administrators.

Jordan, M. L. R. (1995). Reflections on the challenges, possibilities, and perplexities of preparing preservice teachers for culturally diverse classrooms. *Journal of Teacher Education, 46,* 369–374.

Lovelady-Dawson, F. (1980). Women and minorities in the principalship: Career opportunities and problems. *NASSP Bulletin, 64,* 18–28.

Marshall, C. (1992). *The assistant principal: Leadership choices and challenges.* Newbury Park, CA: Sage Publications.

Murray, G. J., Husk, W. L., & Simms, K. (1995). A study of equal access to educational administration for African Americans. *Record in Educational Leadership, 15*(1), 92–97.

Nieto, S. (1992). *Affirming diversity: The sociopolitical context of multicultural education.* New York: Longman.

Ortiz, F. I. (1982). *Career patterns in education: Women, men, and minorities in school administration.* New York: Praeger.

Sagaria, M. (Ed.). (1988). *Empowering women: Leadership development on campus.* San Francisco: Jossey-Bass.

Strober, M., & Tyack, D. B. (1980). Why do women teach and men manage? *Signs.*

Tyack, D. B. (1993). Constructing difference. Historical reflections on schooling and social diversity. *Teachers College Record, 95,* 8–34.

Weis, L., & Fine, M. (Eds.). (1993). *Beyond silent voices: Class, race, and gender in the United States schools.* New York: State University Press of New York.

Afterword

Closing Reflections

✦ ✦ ✦ ✦

Conflict is the gadfly of thought. It stirs us to observation and
memory. It instigates invention. It shocks us out of sheep-like
passivity, and sets us at noting and contriving . . . conflict is a
"sine qua non" of reflection and ingenuity

–John Dewey

✦ ✦ ✦

Educational supervision has not had an easy time of it. Its origins,
definition, and operational forms have been a matter of tension and
debate for a considerable period of time among teachers, supervisory
practitioners, administrative officials, and theorists alike. The level of
debate has been accelerating—a condition most likely enunciated by
the stresses associated with maintaining and developing a system of
public education that is confronted by the confounding pressures of
cultural diversity, economic uncertainty, and ideological arguments
about the role of government in a democratic society. As federal officials, state governments, and local communities joust with one another
about areas of responsibility and resource allocation, the education
profession struggles to hold a steady course in providing educational
opportunities and services that exceed the bounds of hierarchy, accountability measures, and retrenchment.

Under these circumstances, educational supervision is something
of an easy target both within and without the profession. This is unfortunate, for the nature, intent, and significance of educational
supervision is maturing, conceptually and operationally, to the advantage of reconstructing educational opportunities with an understanding
of supervision that:

- Is aware of the traditions, realities, and legal structures that have
  shaped supervisory practice (Celso).
- Goes beyond "surveillance, conformity, and compliance . . . toward a liberating and emancipatory agenda" (Smyth).
- Seeks to develop "learning communities, work teams, and human
  resources" (Snyder).
- Advances a "community of supervision" where "leaders and followers influence one another" in the pursuit of "shared purposes"
  and "moral obligations," as related to the practice of supervision as
  "pedagogical leadership" (Sergiovanni).

- Is cognizant of the "moral imperative" to counter the "continuing trend of under-representation of minorities in leadership roles" (Glickman and Mells).

In this volume our colleagues explored these perspectives and a range of issues related to the status and emerging capacity of supervisory practice in education. The diversity of views presented speaks volumes about the conceptual and organizational implications that surround educational supervision. Discussion, research, and exploration of these issues and controversies will continue as the profession works to clarify further the nature and role of supervision in the overall scheme of educational leadership. These issues and the divergent views that attend them signal a level of energy and intellectual vitality. In concert they provide a context for the pursuit of ideas and the formulation of supervisory practice which supports educational process, instruction, and student learning.

We thank our colleagues for sharing their ideas, energy, and time. We know firsthand their commitment to the conversion of supervision to "pedagogical leadership"—with teachers and the students they serve.

Editors and Contributors

✦ ✦ ✦ ✦

The Editors

Jeffrey Glanz is an assistant professor in the department of instruction, curriculum, and administration at Kean College of New Jersey. His articles and reviews have appeared in several education journals, among them *Journal of School Leadership, Journal of Curriculum and Supervision, Journal of At-Risk Issues,* and *Educational Leadership.* His first book was a history of school supervision, *Bureaucracy and Professionalism: The Evolution of Public School Supervision.* He is also an editorial board member of the *Journal of Curriculum and Supervision* (ASCD) and *Educational Studies* (AESA). He is currently editor of *Focus on Education,* a journal published by the New Jersey Association for Supervision and Curriculum Development.

Richard F. Neville is professor emeritus at the University of Maryland Baltimore County (UMBC). He has served the University of Maryland system as assistant to the dean at College Park; dean of education, dean of faculty, and dean of arts and sciences at UMBC; and completed his service as acting provost of the University of Maryland Biotechnology Institute. He has published in the field of supervision, including *Instructional Supervision: A Behavior System,* co-authored with Robert J. Alfonso and Gerald R. Firth. Dr. Neville received his Ph.D. in curriculum and supervision from the University of Connecticut.

The Contributors

Robert J. Alfonso is vice president emeritus for academic affairs, East Tennessee State University. He has been dean of the College and Graduate School of Education and also associate vice president for academic affairs and dean of faculties at Kent State University. He is the author of numerous publications and papers in the field of supervision, including *Instructional Supervision: A Behavior System*, co-authored with Gerald R. Firth and Richard F. Neville. He received his Ph.D. in Educational Administration from Michigan State University.

Robert H. Anderson, former teacher, principal, and superintendent of schools, joined the faculty of Harvard University, where he became the first tenured clinically defined professor of education in that university's history. After leaving Harvard, he went to Texas Tech University, where he was dean of education. He is currently president of Pedamorphosis, Inc., a funded, not-for-profit organization and also occupies the TECO Energy Chair in Education at the University of South Florida. He is known internationally for his pioneering work in nongraded schooling, team teaching, clinical supervision, and school reorganization. He has published numerous books, chapters, and articles.

Nicholas Celso, III, is an associate professor and the coordinator of graduate programs in educational administration at Kean College of New Jersey, as well as an attorney specializing in school law and labor matters. He received his doctorate in education from Rutgers University and his law degree from Rutgers School of Law, where he served as editor of the *Law Review*. Dr. Celso also has been an elementary school teacher, director of curriculum and instruction, and assistant to the superintendent, as well as an elected board of education member.

O. L. Davis, Jr. is a professor of curriculum and instruction at The University of Texas at Austin. A former teacher and principal in Texas and Tennessee schools, his career has focused on curriculum practice (development and theory), curriculum history, and social studies education. He has edited several books and has published numerous chapters and articles. A former president of the Association for Supervision and Curriculum Development, he currently edits the *Journal of Curriculum and Supervision*.

Francis M. Duffy received his Ph.D. from the University of Pittsburgh in Curriculum and Supervision. He is a professor of administration and supervision at Gallaudet University in Washington, D.C., as well as an organization development consultant. He has also worked as a classroom teacher, executive director, and supervisor. His books include *Designing High Performance Schools* and a new work in progress, *Supervising Knowledge Work*. He has contributed a chapter, "Ideologies of Supervision," for the *Handbook of Research on School Supervision*.

Gerald R. Firth is a professor of educational leadership at The University of Georgia. He received his Ed.D. from Teachers College, Columbia University. He has served as a consultant both in the United States and abroad. He is author or co-author of several books, including *Instructional Supervision: A Behavior System,* and he has written numerous chapters and articles that have appeared in publications such as *Educational Leadership, Phi Delta Kappan, Journal of Curriculum and Supervision, Curriculum Leadership,* and many others. He is co-editor of the *Handbook of Research on School Supervision.*

Carl D. Glickman is a professor of education and the chair of the Program for School Improvement at The University of Georgia. He has been a principal of award-winning schools, the author of a leading academic text in school leadership, recipient of the Outstanding Teacher award in the College of Education, and the recipient of several national leadership awards. For the past ten years, he has been the founder and head of various university/public school collaborations that include the League of Professional Schools. These collaborations involve more than 150 elementary, middle, and secondary schools representing 45 school districts focused on school renewal through democratic governance.

Noreen B. Garman received her Ph.D. from the University of Pittsburgh with a specialty in curriculum and supervision. She is presently a professor in the Department of Administrative and Policy Studies at Pitt, where she teaches courses in supervision of instruction, curriculum studies, qualitative research, and interpretative research. She is the author of numerous articles and chapters on clinical supervision, curriculum, and qualitative research. She is presently working on a teacher development project in Bosnia.

Lee Goldsberry is an associate professor of education at the University of Southern Maine, where he has spent the past several years preparing preservice teachers, assisting experienced teachers, and contributing to local school renewal. The focus of his work has been, and is, methods of providing classroom teachers with stimulation for and assistance with the critical examination and refinement of their own teaching practices. A former elementary school teacher, he received his Ed.D. from the University of Illinois at Urbana. Among his publications is a chapter on teacher involvement in supervision for the *Handbook of Research on School Supervision.*

Stephen P. Gordon is an assistant professor in the Educational Administration Program at Southwest Texas State University. He received his doctorate in instructional supervision from The University of Georgia and is a former award winner of the "ASCD Outstanding Dissertation" on supervision. He is co-author of *Supervision of Instruction: A Developmental Approach* and author of *How to Help Beginning Teachers Succeed.* His current research interests are teacher and school empowerment. He has contributed a co-authored chapter, "Supervision and Staff Development," to the *Handbook of Research on School Supervision.*

Gary A. Griffin is a professor and head of the Department of Teaching and Teacher Education at the University of Arizona. Prior to coming to Arizona, he was professor and dean of the College of Education at the University of Illinois at Chicago. His scholarship, teaching, and service focus on teacher education, staff development, school change, and curriculum development. He has published extensively on these topics in a variety of scholarly and professional journals. He received his doctorate from the University of California at Los Angeles.

Peter P. Grimmett is a professor of education in the faculty of education at Simon Fraser University. Formerly director of the Centre for the Study of Teacher Education at the University of British Columbia, he now works in the newly established Institute for Studies in Teacher Education (INSITE) at Simon Fraser University. His publications include *Reflection in Teacher Education, Craft Knowledge and the Education of Teachers, The Transformation of Supervision, Teacher Development and the Struggle for Authenticity: Professional Growth and Restructuring in the Context of Change* (with Jon Neufeld), and *Changing Times in Teacher Education: Restructuring or Reconceptualization?* (with Marvin Wideen).

Helen M. Hazi studied under Noreen Garman and Morris Cogan at the University of Pittsburgh. She is an associate professor of education administration at West Virginia University and her current supervisory practice focuses on site visits to administrators who seek permanent certification. While her teaching specialty is instructional supervision, her research specialty is legal aspects of supervision. She has published chapters, and articles in journals such as *Educational Leadership, Phi Delta Kappan, Journal of Curriculum and Supervision*, and others. She has contributed a chapter on legal aspects of supervision to the *Handbook of Research on School Supervision*.

Ben M. Harris is currently M. K. Hage Centennial Professor Emeritus at The University of Texas at Austin. His career as an educator extends over nearly 50 years, including positions as teacher, supervisor, curriculum director, professor, and consultant. As a scholar, Harris has conducted research and taught in the fields of instructional supervision, staff development, personnel administration, and teacher evaluation. His writings have included a dozen books and hundreds of journal articles, monographs, and reports. He received his Ed.D. from the University of California at Berkeley.

Joyce E. Killian is professor of curriculum and instruction at Southern Illinois University Carbondale, where she chairs the graduate specialty area in teacher education and supervision. Her research interests include the professional growth and development of teachers and the conditions that promote that growth. She has published in *Educational Leadership, The Journal of Staff Development*, and *The Journal of Teacher Education*, among others. Her chapter on the scientific management influence on supervision appears in the *Handbook of Research on School Supervision*.

Robert J. Krajewski received his doctorate from Duke University. He is currently professor of education and director of the Upper Mississippi Cooperative Rural Center at the University of Wisconsin–LaCrosse. Blending theory and practice, he has authored more than 100 chapters and articles, guest-edited a dozen journals, and written or co-written six texts, including *Clinical Supervision,* 3rd edition. His current research interests include community assistance programs for at-risk students.

Thomas L. McGreal is a professor of educational administration at the University of Illinois at Urbana-Champaign. He has served as the state coordinator and director of research and professional development for the Illinois Alliance of Essential Schools. He specializes in the evaluation and supervision of educational personnel, research on teaching, and staff development. His publications include *Successful Teacher Evaluation* and *Personnel Administration for School Improvement.*

Ronald L. Mells, who received his Ed.D. from Peabody College of Vanderbilt University, serves as a consultant to the Iowa State Department of Education. He is responsible for several educational initiatives aimed at improving schools state-wide. These efforts focus on developing and implementing a process to identify outstanding schools and educators, improving collaborative efforts between local educational agencies and individual schools in need of school improvement, and providing technical assistance to those schools. As the education liason director to The Atlanta Project, he has successfully established collaboration between Atlanta Public Schools in the Crim Cluster and faculty members in the College of Education at The University of Georgia.

James F. Nolan, Jr. is an associate professor of leadership and teaching at Pennsylvania State University, where he received his Ph.D. in curriculum and instruction. He is the author of numerous articles in professional journals that focus on the topics of classroom management, reflective supervision, and peer coaching. He is co-author of *Classroom Management: A Professional Decision Making Approach.* He has contributed a chapter, "Supervision in Service Areas," to the *Handbook of Research on School Supervision.*

Edward Pajak received his Ph.D. from Syracuse University. He is currently a professor of educational leadership at The University of Georgia and faculty administrator for College Outreach. His books include *Approaches to Clinical Supervision: Alternatives for Improving Instruction* and *The Central Office Supervisor of Curriculum and Instruction: Setting the Stage for Success.* His articles have appeared in journals including *Journal of Staff Development, NASSP Bulletin, Educational Leadership, Curriculum, Journal of Curriculum and Supervision,* and *American Educational Research Journal,* among others. He is co-editor of the *Handbook of Research on School Supervision.*

Barbara Nelson Pavan is a professor of educational administration at Temple University. After earning her doctorate at Harvard University, she entered the principalship. She has written numerous publications on supervision, nongradedness, and gender differences in school administrative careers. Her writings have appeared in such journals as *Educational Leadership, Elementary School Journal, Kappan, Principal,* and *Urban Education.* Dr. Pavan is past president of the Council of Professors of Instructional Supervision (COPIS).

Thomas J. Sergiovanni is Lillian Radford Professor of Education and Administration and a senior fellow of the Center for Educational Leadership at Trinity University, San Antonio. Prior to joining the Trinity faculty he was professor of educational administration and supervision at the University of Illinois at Urbana–Champaign. He has broad interests in the areas of school leadership and the supervision and evaluation of teaching. Among his recent publications are *Moral Leadership: Getting to the Heart of School Improvement, Building Community in Schools,* and *Leadership for the School House: How Is It Different?*

Jean McClain Smith received her Ph.D. from The Ohio State University in organizational development and counseling. She has 34 years of experience in the public schools of Ohio, including 20 years at the Ohio State University, specializing and conducted research on student learning. She has served in various capacities within ASCD and currently is the facilitator of the Network for Instructional Supervision. She co-edits the *Instructional Supervision Network Newsletter* (ASCD).

John Smyth is Foundation Professor of Teacher Education at the Flinders University of South Australia and associate dean of research. He is also director of the Flinders Institute for the Study of Teaching. He has authored/edited eight books, the latest of which is *Critical Discourses on Teacher Development* and he has contributed a chapter, "Economic, Social, and Political Perspectives," to the *Handbook of Research on School Supervision.* He has just been awarded a three-year research grant from the Australian Research Council for a study, "Lifelong Learning Strategies for Teachers."

Karolyn J. Snyder is a professor of educational leadership and the director of the School Management Institute at the University of South Florida, Tampa. She has more than 200 publications dealing with productive schools. A recent research study of change in 28 schools has been presented and published both nationally and internationally. She is a founding board member of and on the management team for International Network for School Improvement, which involves representatives from the United States, Sweden, Russia, England, Holland, Finland, and South Africa.

Robert J. Starratt is a professor of educational administration at the Graduate School of Education at Fordham University. He holds degrees from Boston College, Harvard University, and the University of Illinois. He has published extensively and has lectured in Australia, in various Asian countries, and in Canada, as well as his native United States. His most recent books are *Transforming Educational Administration* (1996), *Building an Ethical School* (1994), *Supervision: A Redefinition* (with Thomas Sergiovanni), and *The Drama of Leadership* (1993).

Cheryl Granade Sullivan is a consultant specializing in custom educational and training services. She received her Ph.D. from Emory University. She is a visiting professor at several universities, including the University of Texas at Austin, Georgia State University, and Oglethorpe University in Atlanta. Her recent presentations and publications have focused on staff development for all teachers, instruction for the 1990s, and mentoring. She is author of *Clinical Supervision: A State of the Art Review.*

Barbara S. Thomson received her Ph.D. from The Ohio State University, where she is currently a professor in science and mathematics education. Her current research interests include the analysis of learning and teaching styles, outreach education, unified science and integrated studies curriculum development and implementation, and instructional supervision and collaboration strategies. She co-edits the *Instructional Supervision Network Newsletter* (ASCD).

Saundra J. Tracy is dean and professor of education at Butler University in Indianapolis. She earned her Ph.D. from Purdue University in educational administration. Prior to coming to Butler, she was on the faculties of Cleveland State University and Lehigh University. She has also been the director of the Greater Cleveland Administrator Assessment Center, the executive director of the Lehigh School Study Council, and the director of education for the Iacocca Institute at Lehigh. She has published numerous articles, chapters, and co-authored a book titled *Assisting and Assessing Educational Personnel.*

Duncan Waite, currently at The University of Georgia, received his doctorate from the University of Oregon, where he studied qualitative research under Harry Wolcott and conversation analysis with Jack Whalen. His research on face-to-face interactions between supervisors and teachers forms the core of his first book, *Rethinking Instructional Supervision: Notes on Its Language and Culture.* He has also published numerous articles and chapters. He continues to explore the sociocultural aspects of supervision.

Index

✦ ✦ ✦

A

Abolishment of supervision, 3–23
  argument against, 13–19
  argument for, 4–11
Accreditation, and national standards, 179
Administrative behavior, 79–80
Administrative tasks, 137
Administrators, 5, 9, 37, 79–80
  and preparation in curriculum studies, 82
Age of complexity and new work of supervisors, 299–317
  age of complexity, 301–305
    at risk populations,
      301–302
    chaos theory, 303–305
    global village, 302–303
    new marketplace requirements, 303
  developing world class professional work teams,
      306–311
    Education Quality System, 307–309
    high-performing work team standards,
      310–311
    new supervisory skills,
      312–313
    new supervisory skills,
      312–313
  new work of supervisors, 306
Ames, Everett, 323
Ames v. Bd. of Ed. (1994), 323
Argyris, Chris, 211
Artificial intelligence (AI) and expert systems, 255–256
ASCD, see Association for Supervision and Curriculum Development

Association for Supervision and Curriculum Development (ASCD) 17, 25–42
At-risk populations, 301–302

B

Black, Charles L., Jr., 149
Blaze, Jo Roberts, 114
Blumberg, Arthur, 4, 14, 81
Bobbitt, Franklin, 212
Brandt, Ron, 160
Building Community in Schools (Sergiovanni), 271
Business management practices, influence of, on educational supervision, 201–222
  argument against,
      210–217
  argument for, 202–209

C

Ceroni, Kathy, 232
Changing Curriculum, The, 27
Chaos (Gleick), 304
Chaos theory, 303–305
Classroom observation, 17–18
Cleghorn, Sharon, 329–330
Clinical supervision in public schools, 223–240
  argument against, 230–235
  argument for, 224–228
  defined, 224–225
  leadership role, 227–228
  sources of information about, 226
Coach, supervisors as, 91–112
  coaching and evaluating, 98
  coaching behaviors, 92–93
  cognitive coaching, 93–94
  fundamentals of coaching,
      92

Coach, (cont.)
  incompatibility of teacher evaluation and supervision, 101–108
  three-track model, 99
Codification of knowledge base, 190–192
Cogan, Morris, 230, 232, 234
Cognitive coaching, 93–94, 140
Collaborative teaming, 148–149
Collegial forms of supervision, 115–116, 118
  teachers, 135–154
    argument against, 144–150
    argument for, 136–142
    collaborative teaming alternative, 148–149
    collegiality defined, 144
    collegial supervision, 138–139
    fostering a collegial relationship, 140
    inappropriate for defining teacher-supervisor relationship, 145–146
    practical considerations, 146–148
    and school based management, 139
Community theory of supervision, 263–284
  how communities work, 270–271
  how organizational theories work, 270–271
  implications for leadership, 275–276
  role of supervision, 276–279
  supervision as pedagogical leadership, 279–280
  theory of community for schools, 271,–274
Competency, of teacher, 7
Complexity: Living on the Edge of Chaos (Lewin), 305

Computer, as learning center, 254–255
Computerized Observation System (COS), 252
Computer technology and the schools, 243–244
Control theory of supervision, 115–118
COPIS, *see* Council of Professors of Instructional Supervision
Costa, A., 93–94
Council of Professors of Instructional Supervision (COPIS), 17, 30, 35, 157
Counts, George S., 212
Crosby, Muriel, 32
Curriculum, 33
  definition, 33–34
  history, 35
  role/practice, 36–37
  role training, 37–38
  split with supervision reconcilable? 71–84
    argument against, 79–84
    argument for, 72–77
    field of curriculum studies, 80, 82
    history, 73–75
Curriculum field in dialogue with supervision, 216–217

D

Deming, W. Edwards, 213
Department of Supervisors and Directors of Instruction, 27, 36
Dewey, John, 49, 126, 210–211, 212, 216
Distance learning, 244–245
District expectations and standards, 176–177
Diversity in appointment of supervisory leaders, 341–354
DOSSIER program, 255
Dynamic supervision, 29

E

Educational Administration: Theory, Research, and Practice (Hoy & Miskel), 80
Educational Leadership, 27, 28, 29, 32
Education associations, and national standards, 180
Education Quality System (Synder), 300, 307–309
Effective schools, 5–6, 136
Evaluation, and supervision, 37, 44–54, 59–60
Evaluator, of teachers, 10

F

Facilitator, of staff development, 10, 15–16
Firth, Gerald, 27

G

Gall, Meredith, 230, 231, 232, 233, 234
Garmston, R., 93–94
Giroux, Henry, 287
Glatthorn, Allan, 230, 231, 233
Glickman, Carl, 124
Global village, 302–303
Goldhammer, Robert, 234, 245–247
Goldsberry, Lee, 230, 231, 232, 234
Greene, Maxine, 286–287
Gregory, Jacqueline, 232

H

Handbook of Educational Supervision (Marks, Stoops, & King-Stoops), 159
Handbook of Research on Educational Administration (Boyan), 79, 80
Hargreaves, Andrew, 235
Her Majesty's Inspectors (HMI) (England), 177
Hill, Sallie, 126

Holland, Patricia, 232
Hunter, Madeline, 94, 232

I

Inservice education, 122
Instructional design systems, 254–255
Instructional Improvement through Inquiry (III) model, 140–141
Instructional leadership, 122, 123
Instructional Supervision Network, 28

J

Journal of Curriculum and Supervision, 29–30
Joyce, B., 92–93
Jurassic Park (Crichton), 304

K

Knowledge Work Supervision (KWS) model, 201, 203–209
phase 1: preparing, 204–205
phase 2: redesign for high performance, 205–206
phase 3: achieving permanence and diffusion, 206–207
phase 4: continuous improvement of schooling, 207–208

L

Law and its effect on educational supervision, 319–340
adversarial hearings and collegiality, 323–325
promoting teacher potential and potential liability, 325–327
supervisor and labor relations disputes, 327–330
supervisor as state agent, 322–323
supervisor as survivor, 330–331

Law of Conservation of Information, 264–265
Law of Perceptual Limits, 264–265
Leadership in Administration (Selznik), 270
Leadership organizations, and national standards, 180–181
Leadership specializations, and national standards, 182–183
Lee, Robert, 325
Lee v. Sch. Dist. No. 51-4 (1992), 325–326
Leeper, Bob, 32
Lewin, Roger, 304–305
Limits of Science, The (Medawar), 264
Loose coupling concept, 214–215
Lucio, William H., 211

M

Mayo, Elton, 211
McGregor, Douglas M., 211
Medawar, Peter Brian, 264
Meier, Deborah, 278
Messenger applications and distance conferencing, 253–254
Method teaching, 73
Mezirow, Jack, 288

N

National Board for Professional Teaching Standards (NBPTS), 188
National Commission on Teacher Education and Professional Standards (NCTEPS, or TEPS), 184
National Council for Accreditation of Teacher Education (NCATE), 180,181,185,188
National Policy Board for Education Administration (NPBEA), 182,188,192,193
National Staff Development Council (NSDC), 157
National standards in preparation of supervisors, 175–200

argument against, 187–193
argument for, 176–185
Nation at Risk, A (National Commission on Excellence in Education),187,188, 212–213
Naylor, Deborah, 324
Naylor v. Bd. of Ed. (1994), 324
Newlon, Jesse, 27

O

Organization theory, 213–216, 268–270

P

Pohly, Kenneth, 277
Practitioners of instructional supervision, and national standards, 181–182
Principles of Scientific Management, The (Taylor), 211
Proactive supervision, 29
Professionalization
   of instructional supervision, and national standards, 183–184
   of supervisors, 189–190
Program specialization, 178–179
Pulley, Jerry, 124

R

Redesign management team (RMT), 205, 206, 207
Reflective practice, 94–95
Reflective supervision, 95
Reflective teaching, 95
RITE framework, for clinical teacher education, 166–169
Rosenholtz, Susan, 5
Rust, Frances 230, 231, 232

S

Saturn School (St. Paul, MN), 243
Saylor, G., 28
School based management and collegiality, 139

Schwartz, Paul, 278
Self-evaluation, 49–50, 53
Selznik, Phillip, 270
Shores, J. Harlon, 28
Short, Edmund, 30
Showers, B., 92–93
Shulman, Lee, 49
Smyth, John, 232
Society for Curriculum Study, 27, 36
Spears, Harold, 128
Staff development, and supervision, 10, 15–16, 122, 155–173
    assumptions about,164–166
    delivery systems, 158–159
    distinctive features, 166
    purposes, 156–158
Standards
    background, 187–189
    codification of knowledge base, 190–192
    defined, 187
    professionalization, 189–190
    standard-setting process, 192–193
    state, 177–178
Stepping up to the Supervisor (Haynes), 114
St. Maurice, Henry, 234
Super development, 160
Superintendent of schools, 100
Supervision
    abolishment of, 3–23
        argument against, 13–19
        argument for, 4–11
    advocating diversity in appointment of supervisory leaders, 341–354
    affect of law on, 319–340
    basic purpose, 13, 101–102, 156–158
    and benefits to supervisors, 61–62
    and benefits to teachers,43–69
    clinical, in public schools, 223–240
    community theory of, 263–284

compared with surveillance of instruction, 285–298
    -curriculum split reconcilable? 71–89
    definition, 4, 34–35
    in dialogue with curriculum field, 216–217
    dimensions of, 137–138
    distinct from administration, 216
    dynamic, 29
    history of, 35–36, 72–75, 125–128
    as influenced by business management practices, 201–222
    nature of relationship, 103–104
    necessity of, 13
    observation procedures, 104–105
    proactive, 29
    rationale, 102
    renaming the field, 113–133
    role of expertise, 105
    role/practice, 37
    role training, 38
    rooted in democratic principles, 210–211
    scope, 103
        and staff development, 155–173
        and teacher evaluation, 100–108
        and teacher's feeling of humiliation, 9
        and teacher's performance, 6
        teacher perspective, 106
        wanted by teachers, 128–129
Supervision: Perspectives & Propositions (Lucio), 211
Supervisor
    as coach, 91–112
    and collegial relationship with teachers, 135–154
    as facilitator of staff development, 10

Supervisor (cont.)
  functions of, 136–137
  and labor relations disputes,
    327–330
  learning by doing, 60–61
  national standards in prepara-
    tion of, 175–200
  and relations with teachers,
    4–5
  replaced by technology,
    241–260
  as survivor, 330–331
  as teacher evaluation, 10
  work of, in age of complex-
    ity, 299–317
*Supervisors and Teachers: A Pri-
  vate Cold War* (Blumberg),
  292
Surveillance of instruction, compared with supervision,
  285–298

T

Taylor, Frederick, 211, 212
Teacher as Stranger (Greene),
  286
Teacher evaluation, and
  incompatability with super-
    vision, 101–108
  basic purpose, 101–102
  nature of relationship,
    103–104
  observation procedures,
    104–105
  rationale, 102
  role of expertise, 105
  scope, 102–103
  teacher perspective,
    105–106
Teachers
  autonomy, 14, 16
  and benefits from super-
    vision, 43–69
  and collegial relationship
    with supervisor,
    136–154
  competency, 7

    and desire to receive
      supervision, 128–129
    and effect on student perfor-
      mance, 6
    and need for feedback,
      14–15
    and relationship with super-
      visors, 4–5
    and special relationship with
      class, 8–9
Technology, as replacement for
  role of supervisor, 241–260
  argument against, 250–257
  argument for, 242–248
  benefits and limitations of
    tool technology in super-
    vision, 250–253
  benefits of technology trans-
    formation, 248
  new roles for supervisors,
    247
  setting standards for use of
    technology in super-
    vision, 256–257
  technological replacements
    for central supervisory
    roles, 253–256
  transferring supervisory role
    to teacher, 245–247
Theory of Acceptability, 265
Theory of Institutional Leadership (Selznik), 270
Threlkeld, A. L., 27
Thurow, Lester, 302
Tonnies, Ferdinand, 272, 273
Tyler, Ralph, 48

V

Vygotsky, Lev, 118

W

Wagoner, Phylis, 326
Wagoner v. Bd. of Ed. (1994),
  326–327
Waite, Duncan, 286, 292
WISARD program, 256
Wraga, Bill, 61